THE CLERKS OF THE COUNTIES, 1360—1960

THE COUNTIES OF ENGLAND AND WALES, 1960

THE CLERKS OF THE COUNTIES
1360-1960

Compiled by

Sir EDGAR STEPHENS, C.B.E., M.A., F.S.A.

With a Foreword by

The Rt. Hon. The Viscount KILMUIR, G.C.V.O.
Lord High Chancellor of Great Britain

Published by

THE SOCIETY OF CLERKS OF THE PEACE OF COUNTIES
AND OF CLERKS OF COUNTY COUNCILS

1961

PRINTED IN GREAT BRITAIN BY
R. H. JOHNS LIMITED, NEWPORT, MON.

CONTENTS

Page

LIST OF ILLUSTRATIONS ix

FOREWORD xi

INTRODUCTION

150th Anniversary of the Society, 1960 1

Centenary Brochure of 1910 1

Publication of 1960 2

" The Clerks of the Counties, 1360—1960 " 4

Origin of the Office of Clerk of the Peace 4

Lists of the Clerks of the Counties, as appearing in Part I

(1) Generally 5

(2) Compilation of the Lists 6

(3) Method of Arrangement 6

The Society of Clerks of the Peace of Counties and of Clerks of County Councils

(1) Formation of the Society in 1810 7

(2) Subsequent Meetings of the Society 8

(3) The Members of the Society and their Officers 10

The Finances of the Society 14

The Society's Minute Books 15

Social Activities of the Society 16

150th Anniversary Dinner 17

Description of the Illustrations 18

Acknowledgments 22

PART I: THE OFFICE OF CLERK OF THE PEACE

Page

THE ORIGIN AND OFFICE OF CLERK OF THE PEACE
by H. C. JOHNSON, C.B.E., M.A. (Deputy Keeper of Public Records and Secretary of the Public Record Office)

The Clerk of the Peace before 1888

    (1) Origins   29

    (2) Appointment and Tenure of Office   30

    (3) Duties   36

    (4) Remuneration   37

    (5) Professional Qualifications and Social Background   40

The Clerk of the Peace and Clerk of the County Council after 1888   42

The Lists of Clerks of the Peace and Sources of Information   44

LISTS OF PERSONS (ARRANGED ALPHABETICALLY ACCORDING TO COUNTIES) KNOWN TO HAVE HELD THE OFFICE OF CLERK OF THE PEACE IN THE COUNTIES OF ENGLAND AND WALES FROM 1360 TO 1960 AND THE OFFICE OF CLERK OF THE COUNTY COUNCIL FROM 1889 TO 1960   51

ADDENDA   193

PART II: THE SOCIETY OF CLERKS OF THE PEACE OF COUNTIES AND OF CLERKS OF COUNTY COUNCILS

A RETROSPECT OF THE ACTIVITIES OF THE SOCIETY FROM 1810 TO 1960   197

CHAIRMEN OF THE SOCIETY, 1810–1960, AND PLACE OF MEETINGS AND OF ANNUAL DINNERS   213

VICE-CHAIRMEN, HONORARY TREASURERS AND SECRETARIES OF THE SOCIETY ...   219

THE ARMORIAL BEARINGS OF THE SOCIETY   221

THE ACTIVITIES OF THE CLERKS OF THE PEACE GOLFING SOCIETY FROM 1932 TO 1960   223

CONTENTS

APPENDICES

I: THE IMPRISONMENT OF JOHN BUNYAN IN BEDFORD GAOL, 1660–1672   237

II: DINNERS AT GREENWICH   241

III: LIST OF PERSONS PRESENT AT THE 150TH ANNIVERSARY DINNER OF THE SOCIETY   245

IV: LIST OF MEMBERS OF THE SOCIETY, 31ST DECEMBER, 1960   249

V: RULES OF THE SOCIETY, 1960   257

INDEX OF NAMES OF CLERKS OF THE COUNTIES   261

LIST OF ILLUSTRATIONS

Plate

I   Map of England and Wales, showing the sixty-two Administrative Counties and the Towns in which the County Headquarters are situate; 1960   ...   .   **Frontispiece**

Facing page

II   Sir John Wynn, Bt., Clerk of the Peace for Caernarvonshire, 1573 to 1578   4
From a print in the reference files in the National Portrait Gallery

III   Richard Graves, Clerk of the Peace for Middlesex, 1639 to 1660   6
From an engraving by George Vertue in the possession of J. H. Slatter, Esq.

IV   Roger Kenyon, Clerk of the Peace for Lancashire, 1663 to 1698   18
From a painting by an unknown artist, the property of the Rt. Hon. Lord Kenyon, in the Lancashire Record Office

V   John Robinson, Clerk of the Peace for Westmorland, 1750 to 1760   20
From an engraving by W. Bond in Appleby Moot Hall, by courtesy of the Mayor of Appleby

VI   John Marriott Davenport, Clerk of the Peace for Oxfordshire, 1831 to 1881   40

VII   Sir Richard Nicholson, Clerk of the Peace for Hertfordshire, 1865 to 1894; Middlesex, 1865 to 1909; and London, 1889 to 1913   42

VIII   The County Hall and Market Place, Abingdon, Berkshire, 1850   54
From a print in the Reading Public Library

IX   The Great Hall, Winchester, Hampshire, 1960   94

X   The Shire Hall, Warwick, 1829   172
From a painting by David Cox

XI   The County Courts, Devizes, Wiltshire, 1836   178
From a print in the possession of R. E. Sandell, Esq.

XII   The Armorial Bearings of the Society   221

XIII   Sir Hubert Thornley, Clerk of the Peace for the North Riding of Yorkshire, 1916 to 1960, by " Giles ", 1960   224

Between pages

XIV   Members at the Annual Meeting of the Golfing Society, Porthcawl, 1934   ...   ...   226—227
Photograph by courtesy of the Western Mail and Echo Limited

XV   Members at the Annual Meeting of the Golfing Society, Harlech, 1938   ...   ...   226—227
Photograph by courtesy of Messrs. J. E. Marsh & Sons, Hoylake

XVI   Members at the Annual Meeting of the Golfing Society, Woodhall Spa, 1947 ...   ...   226—227
Photograph by courtesy of the Executrix of F. Frisby, Lincoln

XVII   Members at the Annual Meeting of the Golfing Society, Hunstanton, 1959   ...   ...   226—227
Photograph by courtesy of E. E. Swain, Hunstanton

Facing page

XVIII   Sir Edgar Stephens, Clerk of the Peace for Warwickshire from 1927, by " Giles ", 1960   230

XIX   " Dinner down the River ", by Richard Doyle, 1862   242
From a print in the Guildhall Library

FOREWORD

This History has been compiled with a view to marking the 150th anniversary of the foundation of the " Society of Clerks of the Peace of Counties". It is fitting that it should be published in the year in which we are celebrating the 600th anniversary of the establishment of the office of Justice of the Peace, under the Statute of Edward III passed in the year 1361; for there is good reason to believe that this same Statute was also the occasion for the appointment of the first Clerks of the Peace.

One of the most remarkable features of our history is the development of the Keepers of the early Plantagenet times into the Justices who became responsible, not only for the administration of justice in their Counties which down to 1842 included the trial of many capital offences, but also for the whole field of local government in the Counties as it existed in those days. This situation, which existed for centuries in England and Wales, was unique. In the words of Coke:—

"It is such a form of subordinate government for the tranquillity and quiet of the Realm as no part of the Christian World hath the like".

When the spirit of reform, which became active during the 19th Century, required the setting up of new local government bodies, most of the administrative functions of the Justices were taken away from them and, in 1888, a large part of the governmental duties of the County Justices was transferred to the newly established County Councils. There were few at that time, however, who attacked the Justices on the ground that they were inefficient: the reason given for the reforms which were being introduced was that the office of Justice was out of date and that it must therefore give way to new institutions based on popular election. Maitland, writing at that time, said of the Justice:—

"As a Governor he is doomed: but there has been no accusation. He is cheap, he is pure, he is capable, but he is doomed: he is sacrificed to a theory on the altar of the spirit of the age".

At that time there were many who thought that the Justices, having been divested of their administrative functions, would lose interest in what remained and that consequently the office might become extinct. Thus Maitland went on to say:—

"The outlook is certainly gloomy. If the Justices are deprived of their governmental work, will they care to be Justices any longer? This is a momentous question; on the answer to it depends a great deal of the future history of England".

Happily this gloomy foreboding proved to be illfounded. From 1888 the Justices turned themselves wholeheartedly to their judicial functions which were steadily increased. During the last quarter of the 19th century their matrimonial jurisdiction was established, and in 1925 a large number of cases which were previously triable only by a judge and jury were brought within the jurisdiction of the Justices at Petty Sessions. At the same time there was an expansion of the judicial work of the Justices at Quarter Sessions. This process is still continuing, and at the present moment we are taking steps to carry into effect the recommendations of the Departmental Committee on the Business of Criminal Courts which will extend still further the work of the Justices at both Quarter Sessions and Petty Sessions. It is also of interest to note that recently the Justices have begun to acquire more administrative duties. The Betting and Gaming Act, 1960, and the Licensing Act, 1961, which has recently received the Royal Assent, give to the Justices functions which are strictly administrative and not judicial. It would seem therefore that Parliament is looking again to the Justices as a suitable body to exercise functions in the administrative field, which concern on the one hand the comfort and habits, and on the other the social standards of our people.

The development of the office of Justice of the Peace could not have successfully surmounted all these changes throughout its long history if the Justices had not been able to receive superbly good advice in carrying out their duties. It was the Clerks of the Peace who supplied this need. Their " six hundred years of achievement " is not a phrase but is a record of work well done.

For centuries the Clerks were the principal officers of the Justices. Lambard, in his *Eirenarcha*, gives some idea of the great variety of subjects for which the Clerks of the Peace were already responsible by the beginning of the 17th century. In addition to their Court functions, their numerous duties ranged from such matters as enrolling deeds of bargain and sale of lands to keeping registers of traders and recording presentments of absentees from Church; and of course they were responsible for executing the orders of the Justices when acting administratively in respect of such matters as the repair of highways and bridges or the control of prices and of labour. It is also interesting to note that for some two hundred years the Clerks of the Peace held office as Clerks of the Crown, and it was not until 1545 that their duties in this field were transferred to the Clerks of Assize, who date from that period.

Since 1888 the Clerks of the Peace have also become, in all but a few cases, the Clerks to the County Councils, and to-day the Clerks play an even greater part in the affairs of their Counties, and indeed in those of the country as a whole, than they did before. In 1952, when speaking at the Annual Dinner in London of " The Society of Clerks of the Peace of Counties and of Clerks of County Councils", as the Clerks' Society is now called, I pointed out that, as Home Secretary, my duties were multifarious, and that for this reason I was in a better position than most to appreciate the nature and value of the tasks falling to be performed by what could, I thought, be claimed to be the most noteworthy surviving collection of pluralists in the country. I said this with no discourtesy, but on the contrary with the greatest admiration for the ability with which the old established Clerks of the Peace had undertaken one important new function after another. Now, in addition to their duties at Quarter Sessions and with the County Councils, most Clerks also serve as Clerk to the Standing Joint Committee, the County Confirming and Licensing Authority, the Magistrates' Courts Committee, the County Combined Probation Area Committee and as Clerk to the Lieutenancy, as well as being Acting Returning Officer for Parliamentary and County Council elections, County Registration Officer and also serving on or as Secretary to numerous other local bodies. It ought not to be assumed that these are all lucrative forms of employment. Although a keen desire to serve the public without reward is a characteristic which was not always apparent among their predecessors, the Clerks of to-day cannot be criticised on these grounds. They have shown themselves to be zealous in undertaking work in the public interest without re-muneration. With few exceptions they act as Honorary Secretaries of the County Advisory Committees which assist the Lord Chancellor in fulfilling his important duty of appointing, and, where necessary, removing Justices of the Peace. In 1960 the Lord Chancellor also became responsible for the appointment of General Commissioners of Income Tax, a task which involved the setting up of an entirely new system of Advisory Committees in every County and in some Boroughs, and in each of these someone was required to undertake the secretarial work and the local administration. Here again, I found the same readiness on the part of the Clerks to undertake, without reward, a most tedious and burdensome duty.

With such a long and distinguished record behind them one would expect to find that the Clerks of the Peace had been the subject of many historical works, but this is not so. There are references, some extensive, in a number of books on the office of Justice of the Peace, and among the early ones we find some interesting passages in Fitzherbert, Lambard and Crompton, and there is a chapter on the Custos Rotulorum and Clerk of the Peace in Blackerley. More recently, a great deal of light has been thrown on the office of Clerk, as well as on that of the Justice, by the brilliant research of Miss B. H. Putnam. As far as I am aware, however, there has been no comprehensive history of the Clerks of the Peace. The Society has therefore done a great service in compiling this unique record. The chapter written by Mr. Johnson on the origin and office of the Clerk of the Peace is the first complete history of the Clerks which I have seen, and one can only regret that he has not had an opportunity to write at still greater length on this fascinating subject.

One of the outstanding features of this book is the lists of persons who have held the office of Clerk of the Peace in the Counties since 1360 and the office of Clerk of the County Councils since 1889. To have collected these names, covering the full period of six hundred years, is a tremendous achievement. They present a remarkable record of the men who, almost unobserved, have played so important a part, behind the scenes, in the government of the land. It is of great interest to know at every stage in our history what manner of men held this office and the interest of this book is that it not only gives a history in narrative form but gives a short *cursus vitae* of all the Clerks and their Deputies of whom records exist. So often history is distorted by allowing the trail to get cold and I am very glad that this has not hap-pened in the present history where even mediæval by-paths have been traced. Sir Edgar Stephens is to be congratulated on the accomplishment of what one would have thought was an almost impossible task. I have known Sir Edgar for many years and it does not surprise me to find that here, as throughout the rest of the book, we see the outcome of the most able and industrious research.

I first made the acquaintance of the Clerks' Society in 1935 when I attended, as a guest, the Annual Dinner of that year. During the intervening period my close association with the Society and many of its members has steadily increased, particularly since I became a Minister of the Crown. It is of the greatest value to any Government Department to be able to approach a body which is truly representative of experts in the whole field of local government and the administration of justice, and to receive from them ready advice and co-operation on the many subjects with which they have to deal. Indeed in modern legislation it is essential for any Minister to consider the effect on and the prospects of co-operation from Bodies representing local authorities. This means that the Clerks' advice has its effect on the Central Government. As Home Secretary I frequently had to refer to the members of the Society on such subjects as Police, Fire Brigades, Probation and Child Welfare services and many others; and since I became Lord Chancellor I have had to do the same in connection with Quarter Sessions matters; while, as I have observed, most Clerks also hold, and have held for many years, the responsible position of Secretary to my confidential Advisory Committees on Justices of the Peace.

I am glad to have this opportunity to record my appreciation of all the help which members of the Society have given, and are still giving, to the Departments for which I have been responsible, and also to express my gratitude for the assistance which they have given to me personally in carrying out my official duties.

The office of Lord Chancellor which I now hold has been associated with the office of Clerk of the Peace since the earliest times. Throughout the whole of their history the Clerks have, with few exceptions, been appointed by the Justices or by the Custos Rotulorum, but it was the Lord Chancellor who appointed the Justices and, until comparatively recent times, he appointed the Custos. After such a long association, it is appropriate that the Lord Chancellor of the day should write the Foreword to the historical record of this unique body of public servants.

KILMUIR C.

HOUSE OF LORDS,
August, 1961.

INTRODUCTION

INTRODUCTION

150th Anniversary of the Society, 1960.

Midway in time between the battles of Trafalgar and Waterloo, a meeting was arranged in London to discuss the effect of a certain Act of Parliament, passed some thirty years before, upon the holders of an ancient office dating back roughly four and a half centuries. The result of the meeting was disappointing, for there was a very small attendance and its immediate purpose, as will be seen later, was not achieved. It is, however, to this event that " The Society of Clerks of the Peace of Counties " trace their beginning, and so, under their present title, celebrate in the year 1960 their 150th anniversary. To mark the occasion the Society decided, at a meeting held on the 28th March 1956, to arrange the publication of a brochure on the lines of that issued for their centenary in 1910, but with the addition of lists containing the names of the Clerks of the Peace for the Counties of England and Wales going back as far as possible and of the Clerks of the County Councils since 1889. The amount of detail which the lists now contain has caused the projected brochure to develop into the present book.

Centenary Brochure of 1910.

The Society's centenary brochure had a dark red cover, elaborately decorated and printed in gold. Each of its thirty-seven pages of printed matter was surrounded by two borders, the inner one of black and the outer one of red. Produced for the centenary dinner on the 1st June by Sir Richard Nicholson, it was later supplemented by a second booklet, identical in style, setting out in full the thirteen speeches delivered on that occasion.

The brochure, only a few copies of which are known to have survived, consisted of a brief *Introduction;* three sections entitled *The Finances of the Society, Acts of Parliament and other matters considered by the Society* and *The Administration of the Society;* and an *Appendix* divided into three parts. The first part contained *Some interesting facts connected with past and present Clerks of the Peace,* though only eight Clerks from six Counties were mentioned. The second comprised a list of the *Names of past and present Members and dates of their joining the Society, so far as recorded in the Minutes.* In all, there were two hundred and thirteen names in this list, arranged under fifty-nine Counties and, exceptionally, the Cities of London and of Coventry, each of which supplied one member in the early years. Suffolk and Sussex were treated in the list as single Counties, no doubt because each still had a single Commission of the Peace. The Isle of Wight was not included—although it had become an administrative County in 1890 with its own Clerk—as it had no separate Commission of the Peace but was still included in that of the County of Southampton.

The final part of the *Appendix* contained a *List of Meetings and Names of Chairmen*, 1810–1910. This list gives the precise date and place of each meeting, some of which were recorded as being meetings of the " Clerks of the Peace of the Home Counties " (e.g. in 1830, 1835, 1836 and 1842) while others were of Committees appointed for specific purposes, as in 1849 and 1850; in the latter year, one of the meetings is listed as of the " Sub-Committee of the Clerks of the Peace." Altogether, there were held during that period a hundred and eighty meetings, and until 1882, with few exceptions, a new Chairman was appointed each year. From then onwards, Richard Nicholson (Hertfordshire and Middlesex, later London also), who was knighted in 1886, was re-elected annually and remained Chairman until 1910. Prior to him, it is worthy of note that John Marriott Davenport (Oxfordshire), who was a member from 1831 to 1881, first presided over a meeting of the Society in 1840, while the last occasion he did so was in June 1880. During those forty years, he had occupied the Chair on no less than twenty-nine occasions.

Publication of 1960.

It has proved convenient to arrange this book in two main Parts. The first section of Part I commences with an account of *The Origin and Office of Clerk of the Peace*, giving some indication of the type of person who held that office, particularly in the seventeenth and eighteenth centuries when considerable material becomes available. It was felt that such an account would illustrate and enliven the tabular matter which follows. The Society have been extremely fortunate in getting Mr. H. C. Johnson, C.B.E., M.A. (Oxon), Deputy Keeper of Public Records and Secretary of the Public Record Office, to contribute this for them. Mr. Johnson is well known for his valuable work in the archive world generally and, perhaps more particularly, for editing the Warwick County Records Series (Volumes I to VIII) between the years 1935 and 1953.

The second section of Part I is devoted to the *Lists of persons known to have held the Office of Clerk of the Peace in the Counties of England and Wales from* 1360 *to* 1960, *and the Office of Clerk of the County Council from* 1889 *to* 1960. So far as is known, this is the first time that an attempt has been made to bring together under one cover the names of all those who have held these offices in the Counties of England and Wales during the past six centuries. The lists as now completed contain roughly two thousand seven hundred and ninety entries. In addition, as will be seen, biographical notes, which have been supplied by individual Counties and augmented where possible from other sources, have been added about the persons whose names are included in the lists. Obviously more is known about those Clerks who have held office since 1810, but there are, nevertheless, some interesting references relating to the earlier ones. One such example is an account by Paul Cobb (Clerk of the Peace for Bedfordshire from 1660 to 1689) which was sent to Roger Kenyon (Clerk of the Peace for Lancashire from 1663 to 1698) of an appearance before Bedfordshire Quarter Sessions of John Bunyan, who " was indicted upon the Statute of Elizabeth I for being at a Conventicle." A full account of the conversation in 1661 between Cobb and Bunyan, whom the former visited in prison and tried to persuade to conform to the Church of England, will be found in Appendix I.

INTRODUCTION

Part II of the book deals with the domestic affairs of the Society, whose name was changed to " The Society of Clerks of the Peace of Counties and of Clerks of County Councils," after the passing of the Local Government (Clerks) Act, 1931. The first section of Part II contains a *Retrospect of the activities of the Society from* 1810 *to* 1960. In the early years the number of items in the Minutes was small and, in consequence, most of the recorded business has been included in the *Retrospect,* but, as the years passed and the work of the members in the Counties increased, particularly after 1888, it has been possible to refer only to some of the items. In later years, therefore, only a general indication of the business transacted at the Society's meetings can be given. Some items of importance—others of less importance—have been selected in an endeavour to outline the scope of the work of the Society and its members. For the most part, it has not been possible to do more than refer to the subjects discussed. To indicate decisions would in many cases require an explanation of some considerable length.

The second section gives a *List of the Officers of the Society from* 1810 *to* 1960, namely the Chairmen, Vice-Chairmen, Secretaries and Treasurers. Reference has already been made to the appointment, in the early days of the Society, of a different Chairman each year, until the change in practice which occurred in 1882. From that year until 1944—sixty-two years altogether—the office of Chairman changed hands only five times. Thereafter, the practice was altered again and currently the Society's Chairman is elected annually for periods not exceeding three years. The office of Honorary Secretary has been held by only nine members over the whole period of a hundred and fifty years, the record going to Acton Tindal (Buckinghamshire), who was Secretary from 1838 to 1880, after succeeding his father Thomas Tindal (Buckinghamshire), Secretary from 1822 to 1838. Still more wedded to their office have been the Honorary Treasurers, of whom there have been only eight. Here the record is held by Thomas Marriott Davenport (Oxfordshire), who was Treasurer from 1871 to 1913; he was the son of John Marriott Davenport, referred to earlier. The office of Vice-Chairman is the most recent, as its first holder was Frederic Merrifield (East and West Sussex), appointed in 1907 to assist Sir Richard Nicholson, whose rapidly failing eyesight caused him several times to tender his resignation, which the Society were unwilling to accept. This section also contains a list of the places where the Society have held their meetings—never less frequently than once a year, although on occasions the only recorded entry in the Minutes has been " There being no business to transact at this meeting, the Members present adjourned to dinner." It records too the names of the inns, taverns and hotels where the Society held, or are thought to have held, their Annual Dinners.

The third section describes *The Armorial Bearings of the Society,* granted to them by the Kings of Arms and formally handed over to the Chairman of the Society at their 150th Anniversary Dinner held at the Mansion House, London, on the 14th December 1960. The fourth and last section of Part II gives an account of *The Activities of the Clerks of the Peace Golfing Society from* 1932 *to* 1960. This branch of the parent Society was founded in 1932 for the purpose of enabling members—and particularly non-golfing members—to meet in some pleasant place far removed from the atmosphere of Westminster, on a purely social basis once a year in one or other of the Counties of England or Wales.

3

" *The Clerks of the Counties, 1360—1960.*"

The Society's publication of 1960 has thus developed into a book entitled " *The Clerks of the Counties, 1360—1960.*" This has been chosen because it is short, albeit comprehensive. Basically, the officer around whom the volume revolves is, and has been since the fourteenth century, the Clerk of the Peace. The origin and duties of his office will be dealt with later, but it would not be out of place here to mention that he is to-day, with few exceptions, also the Clerk of the County Council, Clerk of the Standing Joint Committee, Clerk of the County Confirming and Licensing Authority, County Registration Officer, Acting Returning Officer for Parliamentary Elections and Returning Officer for County Council Elections, Clerk of the Magistrates' Courts Committee, Clerk of the County Combined Probation Area Committee, Clerk to the Lieutenancy and Secretary to the Lord Chancellor's Advisory Committee, as well as, in many instances, Controller Designate for Civil Defence either for his County or for some Group within it. But this is not all; in some cases he is also Clerk of a local River Board, of a local Water Board, of a National Park Advisory Committee or Planning Board, and Clerk or Secretary of some other body of local importance. The Clerk of the Peace has also in some Counties held the office of Under Sheriff and that of Coroner as well.

It will be accepted, therefore, that the persons appointed to these offices hold responsible positions within their own Counties, and being—in effect—the principal advisers on all matters connected with the administration of justice and local government at County level, well merit the designation of *The Clerks of the Counties*. Although possessing no statutory significance, it is, nevertheless, a convenient and justifiable title for this book.

Origin of the Office of Clerk of the Peace.

On the origin and duties of the Clerk of the Peace, it is of interest to quote here two paragraphs from the Society's centenary brochure:—

" The Clerk of the Peace is described in the Authorities as an ancient common law officer, appointed to 'assist the Justices assembled in Quarter Sessions to hear and determine felonies and trespasses, under the Statute 34 Edw. 3 Cap. I., in drawing indictments, arraigning prisoners, joining issue for the Crown, entering their judgments, awarding their process and making up their records,' his tenure of office being ' so long as he shall well demean himself in his office.' He is referred to in an Act of the 37th year of King Henry VIII as an officer whom the *Custos rotulorum* ' had always appointed.' The duties above referred to were chiefly connected with the administration of justice, including the hearing of appeals authorised by many Statutes to be made to Quarter Sessions against convictions and orders of Justices, and against poor and other rates; but the Quarter Sessions had also some important administrative functions, partly by the Common law, partly by Statutes from time to time passed, including the ordering of the repair of bridges, the levying of County rates, the provision of County gaols, the control of County police, the provision of police stations and Petty Sessional Court houses, and the execution of the Acts and Orders relating to the diseases of animals; and the Clerk of the Peace acted as their officer for all these purposes.

" But no very wide-reaching changes were made by Statute in the duties of the Clerk of the Peace previously to 1888, when the Local Government Act of that year created the new administrative bodies called County Councils, and made the Clerk of the Peace their chief executive officer by the title of Clerk of the County Council."

Wm *Sharp* sc.

PLATE II

SIR JOHN WYNN, BT.

CLERK OF THE PEACE FOR CAERNARVONSHIRE

1573-1578

INTRODUCTION

Since 1910, investigations by many scholars, and notably by the late Professor Bertha Putnam, have brought to light new information, dissipating much of the obscurity that enveloped the subject for the Judges in the classic case of *Harding v. Pollock* (1829) 6 Bingham's Reports 25, who said that the origin of the office of Clerk of the Peace was " wrapped in mystery." In particular the assumption, quoted in the extract above, that the Custos Rotulorum had always appointed the Clerk of the Peace, is now discredited. It is true that he always did so after 1545, but previously he might be appointed by the Custos, or by the King by letters patent under the Great Seal, or sometimes by the Justices themselves. Additional evidence on this and other points has emerged in the course of the compilation of the lists of names contained in Part I of the present book, and has been used by Mr. Johnson in his account of the history of the office. As will be seen both there and in the lists, the office of Clerk of the Crown was in many instances also held by the Clerk of the Peace over a period of two hundred years from the fourteenth to the sixteenth centuries.

Lists of the Clerks of the Counties, as appearing in Part I.

(1) *Generally.*

Sixty-two lists, one for each administrative County in England and Wales in the year 1960, are printed in the second section of Part I. Each of the three Parts of Lincolnshire and each of the three Ridings of Yorkshire appear separately, as they have all been regarded as separate entities with their own Clerks of the Peace since the fourteenth century. It is of interest to note, however, that upon occasions the three Clerkships in Lincolnshire have been held concurrently by one person. The lists for the two Divisions of Suffolk and of Sussex are, however, only separated as from 1889. The County of Suffolk was divided in that year for administrative purposes into East and West, by the operation of the Local Government Act, 1888; the same Act provided that the Divisions of the County of Sussex (already recognised in the County of Sussex Act, 1865) should be separate administrative Counties. In both cases, in fact, the offices of Clerk remained united in one individual, in the case of East and West Sussex until 1913 and in that of East and West Suffolk until 1924. Separate Commissions of the Peace for the two Divisions of each County were granted after the passing of the Justices of the Peace Act, 1949.

The list for the County of London commences in 1889, and that for the Isle of Wight in 1890. In London, the two offices of Clerk of the Peace and Clerk of the County Council have always been held by different persons, and are listed separately; in the Isle of Wight the list is of Clerks of the County Council only until 1951, when the first appointment of a Clerk of the Peace was made. Two former members of the Society cannot be included in the lists, and it is perhaps appropriate that they should be mentioned here. The first is John Carter, Clerk of the Peace of Coventry, elected to the Society in 1810. Coventry was both a County and a City until 1842. The other is John Clarke, Clerk of the Peace of the City of London, elected in 1831, " notwithstanding the Rules of the Society."

(2) *Compilation of the Lists.*

The names of the Clerks of the Counties, together with details of their years of service and their dates of birth and death, where known, and other biographical notes, have been compiled as a result of research within the Counties themselves, the names coming primarily from the Quarter Sessions Minute and Order Books. Fundamentally, therefore, the production of the lists has been the work of the Counties, but only a few were able to supply a substantially complete list of office-holders since the end of the fourteenth century. There was, however, another source of information which was, in most cases, still untapped. By the Statute of Cambridge, enacted in 1388, it was provided that the Justices of the Peace of each County should receive four shillings a day, and their Clerk two shillings, as wages for attendance at Quarter Sessions. Payment was to be made by the Sheriff out of the fines and amercements imposed at Sessions, and an Act of 1390 provided that payment should be made by indenture. The Sheriff claimed allowance for the amount paid when he accounted at the Exchequer. The details of the payments were entered on the Pipe Rolls and so, from 1392, when the first such entry occurs, there is a long series of entries in the Rolls preserved in the Public Record Office, from which can be recovered for most Counties the names of the Clerks of the Sessions. There are gaps in the series and, although it might be expected to extend to the nineteenth century, it peters out towards the end of the seventeenth. The indentures of wages enrolled in the Pipe Rolls, however, together with the Estreats which are also preserved at the Public Record Office, are the only authority for the names of the majority of the Clerks of the Peace during the first two hundred years from 1392 onwards.

For practical purposes, it was essential that the search of the Pipe Rolls should be undertaken by one person, and the Society were able to engage the services of Miss Mabel H. Mills, an eminent record agent in London, to do this work for them. As a direct result of her researches, a further thirty-two Counties can now show a list of Clerks of the Peace extending back, more or less continuously, to the year 1400. The lists have since been checked in detail with the original sources by Mr. Johnson, and finally each was returned to its respective Clerk for approval and to enable any further particulars to be added. In all, some six hundred names were added to the lists as a result of the work of Miss Mills and Mr. Johnson.

(3) *Method of Arrangement.*

Commencing with Anglesey and concluding with the West Riding of Yorkshire, the lists, with few exceptions, are sub-divided under four headings. The first sub-division contains details of Clerks of the Peace from the earliest known date down to 1889; the second, Clerks of the Peace and of the County Council from 1889 to 1960; the third, Deputy Clerks of the Peace, so far as their names are known, prior to 1889; and the last, Deputy Clerks of the Peace and of the County Council from that year to the present. The exceptions occur where one or other of the sub-divisions is missing. This happens, for example, where no names survive of Deputy Clerks prior to 1889, perhaps because in the particular County any appointments made were *ad hoc*, and were made by the Clerk for the single Sessions in which

PLATE III

RICHARD GRAVES

CLERK OF THE PEACE FOR MIDDLESEX

1639-1660

he required the services of a Deputy. Likewise, in a few small Counties, no Deputy Clerks have been appointed since 1889.

The dates printed in the first two columns throughout the lists show the years of service of the individual Clerks. Sometimes, in earlier years, it has not proved possible to be precise, though it may be taken that references to the individual have been found in the relevant records in both years shown. The dates, therefore, may only indicate a fraction of the length of service. Where the Counties have intimated that this is so, the letter " c " (*circa*) has been used to mark the approximation. In other cases, only one date can be given. This may be because the only record which has survived in the County, or which appears in the Pipe Rolls, is of service in a single year; but it also occurs particularly in the cases of appointment, before 1545, by the King by letters patent. In such cases, the date is, of course, that borne on the letters of appointment. The biographical notes, which appear in the final column of the lists, do not contain details of *statutory* appointments, such as Clerk of the Standing Joint Committee, Clerk of the County Confirming and Licensing Authority, County Registration Officer, Acting Returning Officer for Parliamentary Elections and Returning Officer for County Council Elections, all of which are held *ex-officio* by the Clerks of the Counties, either in their capacity as Clerks of the Peace or as Clerks of the Council. These appointments are to be assumed to go with the office. Other appointments, however, are independent of the County Council or Quarter Sessions, and, where appropriate, these are specifically mentioned in the biographical notes. Such offices include those of Clerk to the Lieutenancy, Secretary of the Lord Chancellor's Advisory Committee and Clerk of the Magistrates' Courts Committee.

The lists do not show changes in office, honours awarded, or new appointments effective after the 1st January 1961. Addenda, covering the whole of England and Wales, will be inserted at the end of the lists, to show any such details which are notified in time for inclusion.

The Society of Clerks of the Peace of Counties and of Clerks of County Councils.

(1) *Formation of the Society in* 1810.

The first recorded assembly of Clerks of the Peace was held on Tuesday, the 27th March 1810, that being the day on which " a meeting was holden at the Gray's Inn Coffee House for several of the Counties in England " to give consideration to the damaging effects to Clerks of the Peace of the Parliamentary Elections Act (20 George III, cap. 17) which had been passed in 1780. Those present at this first meeting were the Clerks of the Peace for the Counties of Essex (William Bullock), who took the Chair and seems to have been the driving force behind the calling of the meeting, Salop (Joseph Loxdale), Surrey (Charles John Lawson), Sussex (William Balcombe Langridge) and certain " agents " appointed to attend on behalf of the Clerks of the Peace for Warwickshire and Worcestershire and of the Deputy Clerk of the Peace for Cheshire. The meeting was " of the opinion that the Act in question imposed very severe and nearly impracticable duties on Clerks of the Peace without any adequate compensation and under very severe and oppressive penalties[1] and that application should be made to Parliament for relief therefrom." Owing, however, to the small number of Clerks of the Peace attending the meeting, the matter was adjourned until the 15th May of that year, when it was again adjourned to the 13th November for the same reason. In November it was decided " on account of the thinness of the meeting and the little support which the proposed application to Parliament had received from the Clerks of the Peace in general, that further consideration of the subject be adjourned *sine die*."

It was nevertheless, at this meeting held on the 13th November 1810, when the two following resolutions were adopted, that the Society, as such, became formally established:—

> " *RESOLVED—That it is the Opinion of this Meeting that it would be mutually beneficial to Clerks of the Peace in the Execution of their Office by a Communication of the Practice of their respective Counties and by the Opportunity afforded of considering any Bills in their progress thro' Parliament which are likely to affect the Interest of Clerks of the Peace if a Meeting of the Clerks of the Peace were held in London once a year.*"

> " *RESOLVED—That the Clerks of the Peace now present will Assemble Annually at the Gray's Inn Coffee House in Holborn on the second Tuesday after the Morrow of All Souls'* [viz 3rd November] *being the day next after the Day on which the Estreats are required to be delivered into the Exchequer when it is Apprehended many Clerks of the Peace come to Town and that the Clerks of the Peace of every County in England and Wales be invited to join the Meeting.*"

It is evident, therefore, that as far back as 1810 some of the Clerks of the Peace realised the necessity of protecting, as a body, their own interests, and apparently it was this which resulted in the formation of the Society. It is of interest to note that their successors in office, a hundred and fifty years later, have found it desirable as Clerks of County Councils to form an Association of themselves and their Deputies for the purpose of establishing negotiating machinery for their salary scales.

(2) *Subsequent Meetings of the Society.*

For the next thirty years, meetings of the Society were held on either the second or third Tuesday in November. In 1823, it was decided that meetings should be held

---

[1]Under sections 13 and 15 of the Act, Clerks of the Peace were required to keep " duplicates " of certain assessments made thereunder by the Assessors of Land Tax; to permit the duplicates to be inspected upon demand " at all seasonable times " for a fee of one shilling " and no more;" and to make certified copies at the rate of six pence per three hundred words or figures. They were also required to attend *gratis* from 9 a.m. to 3 p.m. on each day from the issuing of a writ or precept for the Election of a Knight or Knights of the Shire until the day preceding the poll, for the purpose of permitting such inspection and making such copies. In default, the Act imposed a fine of £500, forfeiture of the Office of Clerk of the Peace, and disqualification from ever again holding the Office in any County whatsoever.

twice a year, namely, on the last Tuesday in May, " as well as on the second Tuesday after the morrow of All Souls'." In 1829, the date of the May meeting was changed from the last to the second Tuesday in the month. In March of the following year, there was minuted for the first time a meeting of a Committee of the Clerks of the Peace of the Home Counties, which had been appointed in 1814 and which was defined in 1827 as consisting of the Clerks of the Peace for Essex, Kent, Surrey, Sussex, Hertfordshire, Buckinghamshire and Cambridge-shire. In 1820, this Committee had been authorised to expend up to ten guineas in the carrying out of their functions, namely to take steps to safeguard the rights and interests of Clerks of the Peace, and (1822) to consider recent legislation in regard to fees to be taken by Clerks of the Peace. On the 7th November 1843, the dates of meetings were again changed. In future, they were to be held on the second Wednesday in May and on the second Wednesday in November. During 1844 and 1845, there were held five further meetings of the Committee of the Clerks of the Peace of the Home Counties to consider the Bill introduced into Parliament by Sir James Graham (the then Home Secretary) in the last Session of 1844 to regulate the appointment and payment of Clerks of the Peace. Similarly, in 1849, there were held four meetings of a Committee (consisting of the Clerks of the Peace for Buckinghamshire, Warwick-shire, Sussex, Hampshire, Suffolk, Bedfordshire, Berkshire and Oxfordshire) specially ap-pointed to compile a uniform table of fees for the office of Clerks of the Peace, as contemplated by the Statute 11 & 12 Victoria, cap. 43, s. 30.

This brief account of the early meetings of the Society is sufficient to illustrate their frequency and the nature of the business transacted during those early days. It is not the intention here to record the minutes of the Society or indeed its history over the past hundred and fifty years, as that is dealt with faithfully in the *Retrospect*. It is of interest, however, to note that in 1857 it was decided to abandon the November meetings of the Society " in consequence of the paucity of Members who have lately attended the half-yearly meet-ings," the Society then being on an ebb tide. Indeed from 1861 to 1902, except for a series of meetings held in 1888 and 1889 to consider the ramifications of the Local Government (England and Wales) Bill and subsequently the Act, only one—the Annual Meeting—was held each year. From the commencement of the twentieth century, the affairs and matters discussed by the Society became more extensive and less exclusively devoted to the interests of the members, although they were still carefully watched over. " In June 1897," for example, to quote the words of the centenary brochure, " it was decided to take a step which from that day has been a great advantage to the whole of the members of the Society, namely, to issue the *Periodical Circular*, which has been so ably edited by Mr. S. Thornely, Clerk of the Peace for Worcestershire, since its first issue." It contained printed notes of cases, correspondence, opinions of counsel obtained by members, and other matters of general interest to the Clerks of the Counties in their professional activities. In later years, however, the more frequent meetings of the Society, resulting in closer personal contacts between members, who were thus able to discuss together common problems relating to local government, detracted from the usefulness of the *Periodical Circular*, and it only survived its first editor by two years, publica-tion ceasing in 1933.

An Executive Committee was appointed in 1886 to deal with urgent matters between meetings, although there had been a Committee for general and financial purposes in being in 1860. In 1935 a Law Committee was also established, but it was amalgamated with the Executive Committee in the following year. The 1936 Committee was replaced in June 1947 by a Parliamentary & General Purposes Committee and a Law Committee. The former was to consist " of all members of the Society who were for the time being members of the Standing Committees of the County Councils Association, for the purpose of considering, either at the request of the Association or at the initiation of the Society itself for representation to the Association, any matter affecting local government contained in any Parliamentary Bill or Draft Order or Scheme and in relation to administrative policy generally, with power in case of urgency to take such action on behalf of the Society as they thought fit." The Law Committee was to be appointed annually and to consist of eighteen members of the Society.

It was not until October 1947 that meetings of the Society and the two new Committees finally became organised on a regular basis. Since then, at their annual meeting in March each year, a programme of meetings of the Society, its Committees, its Annual Dinner and golf fixtures has been approved for the following twelve months, so that members may now book up the dates ahead. There is no doubt that this practice has led to larger attendances and a greater interest by members in the proceedings of the Society. There are in fact now held five meetings of the Society each year, as well as four meetings each of the Parliamentary & General Purposes Committee and of the Law Committee, the former being held in the morning and the latter in the afternoon of the same day. The Society has, too, during the past fifty years played an increasingly important part in advising, when invited to do so, the County Councils Association on both administrative and legal matters. The Association, unlike the Association of Municipal Corporations, has no Law Committee, and the assistance thus given to the Association and the co-operation which exists between the two bodies is much appreciated by both parties.

(3) The Members of the Society and their Officers.

Unfortunately for purposes of record, not all Clerks of the Counties nor their Deputies since 1810 have sought election as members of the Society, the question having always been left to the individual. To-day, however, the Society are in the happy position of having every Clerk and almost every Deputy in England and Wales on their list of membership, and such lists are in future to be bound annually in the Minutes of the Society for record purposes. The particulars as to membership printed in the lists in Part I have been freshly compiled from the Minutes of the Society and, as a check over the first hundred years, comparison has been made with the list of " Past and Present Members and their dates of joining," which was published in the centenary brochure. It seems likely from the Minutes that some of the persons included in the list of 1910 would not in their own lifetimes have regarded themselves as members of any well-established Society, for their connection was very slight. To go no further than the first recorded meeting on the 27th March 1810, the Clerks of the Peace for Warwickshire (Thomas Hunt) and Worcestershire (Thomas Blayney) and the Deputy Clerk for Cheshire (Charles Potts) sent representatives on that occasion, but none of these three gentlemen appears again in the Minutes. Nevertheless, they were listed in 1910 as former members, and their names have been retained as such on the present occasion. It should be remembered, therefore, that the inclusion of a particular name in the lists as a member of the Society—especially in the early years—does not necessarily indicate an active participation in the Society's work.

The first meeting in 1810 was attended in person by the four Clerks of the Peace already mentioned on page 7. At the second meeting, they were joined by the Clerk of the Peace for Kent (John Fellows Claridge), and these five formed the nucleus of the early meetings. At the third meeting (13th November 1810) it was formally resolved that " the Clerks of the Peace of every County in England and Wales be invited to join the meeting," and in the following year that " the Clerk of the Peace of every County who may think proper to join the Meeting be considered a Member thereof but that Deputy Clerks of the Peace be admitted by Ballot and that one Black Ball do exclude." Deputies were to be proposed and seconded at one meeting, and balloted for at the next. This rule was reconsidered on the 16th November 1813, when it was provided " that two Black Balls exclude." The Society are probably exceptional in having accorded full membership to deputies almost from the outset.

The formal recording of the enrolment of Clerks of the Peace as members of the Society begins on the 16th November 1819, with the names of Richard Eales (Devon) and Robert Copeman (Norfolk). The first recorded resignation takes place on the 13th November 1821, when William Mason, late Deputy Clerk of the Peace for Essex, " having resigned his office, requested to withdraw his name from this Society, which was allowed and his name withdrawn accordingly." In 1827, the Deputy Clerk of the Peace for Worcestershire (Richard Burnaby) was proposed, apparently without his knowledge, and he subsequently wrote declining to become a member. Membership of the Society at this period was not, it seems, much sought after, especially in those Counties far from London, partly no doubt on account of the system of fines for non-attendance at meetings then imposed. At the same meeting in 1827, the Society imposed fines totalling £35 2s. 0d. upon three of their members for arrears of subscription and " absenteeship " from meetings of the Society, and two years earlier the Chairman was fined " a half dozen bottles of claret " for his absence.

In 1828, it was agreed that the Liberty of the Isle of Ely came within the description of a County in the resolutions of the Society, but that the City of Westminster did not. There may have been some embarrassment at the meeting, for the name of the Deputy Clerk of the Peace for Westminster (John Parker Gylby) appears in the list of members present, though it has been scored through, and it was resolved that he was not admissible by ballot. Eighteen months later, it was resolved that Deputy Clerks of the Peace should be nominated at one meeting, balloted for at the next, and not received as members until the following meeting. In 1829, it was resolved " That the Clerks of the Peace of the several Divisions of the County of Lincoln are to be considered as Clerks of the Peace within the meaning of the Rules of this Society." Fifty years later, there was a proposal that Clerks of the Peace of Boroughs should be admitted as members of the Society, but this was negatived. In 1891, the Rules of the Society, which had been in existence for many years, were altered so that all Clerks and Deputy Clerks should in future be proposed and seconded in writing before a meeting, at which a ballot should be held, two black balls to exclude a candidate.

This was varied in 1905, when it was decided that all members, whether Clerks or Deputies, should be elected with voting papers and that a cross should be treated as a black ball. The Rules relating to Membership are now contained in Rules 2, 3 and 4 of the Society's Rules, and were last revised in March 1948. They are set out in full in Appendix V.

Honorary membership is first mentioned in May 1837, when the Treasurer, Charles Pettitt Allen was so elected, having shortly before resigned the Deputy Clerkship, on becoming County Treasurer, for Middlesex; he continued to hold the office of Treasurer of the Society, however, until June 1871. At the meeting in November 1837, the survivor of the four founder members—Charles John Lawson (Surrey)—was also made an honorary member.

The total number of members of the Society since its formation in 1810, as mentioned in the Minutes and recorded in this volume, is four hundred and seventy-two.

Where a Clerk or Deputy has been admitted to membership, the words *Elected to Society* (with the month and year following) will be found opposite his name in the first line of the Biographical Notes in the Counties' lists. There is no need to repeat here particulars of any of the members, except perhaps to draw attention to those few who retained their membership for a period of forty-five years or more, or who held office as Clerks of the Peace for at least fifty years. They are as follows:—

Name	County	Member of the Society From To	No. of Years as Member	Held Office as Clerk of the Peace From To	No. of Years
MARKHAM, H. P.	Northamptonshire	1846–1904	58	1846–1904	58
FREER, W. J.	Leicestershire	1880–1932	52	1888–1932	44
DAVENPORT, J. M.	Oxfordshire	1831–1881	50	1831–1881	50
MARCY, W. N.	Worcestershire	1845–1894	49	1842–1894	52
FRANKLEN, SIR THOMAS	Glamorgan	1879–1928	49	1878–1928	50
THORNLEY, SIR HUBERT	Yorkshire (North Riding)	1911–1960	49	1916–1960	44
BURNABY, T. F. A.	Nottinghamshire	1845–1893	48	1858–1893	35
HOLLWAY, J. H.	Lincolnshire (Parts of Lindsey)	1830–1877	47	1829–1877	48
HODGSON, T. H.	Cumberland	1845–1891	46	1839–1891	52
HUNT, W. O.	Warwickshire	1827–1873	46	1821–1873	52
NICHOLSON, SIR RICHARD	Hertfordshire, Middlesex and London	1865–1910	45	1865–1910	45
SELBY, H. C.	Middlesex	1811–1838	27	1777–1838	61
HINCKLEY, A.	Staffordshire		—	1804–1862	58
PEMBERTON, C.	Cambridgeshire	1813–1850	37	1793–1850	57
FARR, W. D.	Hampshire		—	1809–1865	56
COLLETT, H.	Suffolk		—	1748–1802	54
EALES, R.	Devonshire	1819–1852	33	1798–1852	54
KENYON, G.	Lancashire		—	1728–1780	52
TUDOR, W.	Gloucestershire		—	1800–1852	52
PEERS, J.	Denbighshire	1844–1883	39	1833–1883	50

INTRODUCTION

Such long periods of office and of membership are not now likely to be equalled. Before 1931, the office of Clerk of the Peace had been a freehold one, and voluntary retirement from a Clerkship—the duties of which could be discharged by deputy—was not common in the nineteenth and early twentieth centuries. The Local Government Act of 1888 did not alter the tenure of the office which had remained unchanged from the time of Queen Elizabeth I, and this was affirmed by the Court of Appeal (Bankes, Atkin and Sargant, LJJ.) in 1924 in the case of *Thornely v. Leconfield*, brought by the Clerk of the Peace for West Sussex against the Lord Lieutenant of that County in his capacity as Chairman of the Standing Joint Committee, the body responsible under the Act of 1888 for appointing the Clerk. The Court of Appeal reversed the decision of the trial judge (Swift, J.) and gave the plaintiff the declaration he had asked for, namely that the tenure of the two offices of Clerk of the Peace and of the County Council was a tenure for so long as he should well demean himself. This was subsequently affirmed, on appeal, by the House of Lords (Lord Buckmaster, Lord Atkinson, Lord Sumner, Lord Wrenbury and Lord Darling). Thereupon a Royal Commission on Local Government was set up to consider, *inter alia*, the position of the Clerk of the Peace, and to this body the Society were requested to submit evidence. The work of the Royal Commission resulted in the promotion of the Local Government (Clerks) Bill, which, when enacted in 1931, provided that all Clerks appointed thereafter should hold office during good behaviour but should retire on reaching the age of sixty-five. The Act also provided that, in the future, County Councils should appoint their own Clerks and that Courts of Quarter Sessions should appoint the Clerks of the Peace, though there is machinery under which the two appointments may be held by the same person. In the great majority of cases the two offices have, in fact, remained united. The Clerks, like other officers in local government, are now eligible under the Superannuation Acts to be re-appointed, at the wish of both parties, for successive periods not exceeding twelve months each, after attaining the age of sixty-five.

The increased volume of work for which the Clerks are now responsible also has a bearing on their length of service, and hence on membership of the Society. Originally appointed by the *Custos Rotulorum* (apart from the exceptional cases, before 1545, of appointment by the King by letters patent under the Great Seal) the Clerk of the Peace was often a professional lawyer, particularly in more recent times, when the appointment was usually made from among the attorneys and solicitors in the county town. The work involved was limited in its scope and extent and, in many cases, was performed by a Deputy, appointed by the Clerk, who personally paid for his services. When the 1888 Act became law, the holder of the office of Clerk of the Peace automatically became also the Clerk of the County Council, and all subsequent appointments down to 1931 were made by the Standing Joint Committee. Nevertheless, the Clerk remained in many instances a part-time officer, a state of affairs which continued in some Counties well into the nineteen-thirties and in a few of the smaller Counties even into the nineteen-forties. But increasing legislation and the extra burdens imposed by Parliament upon County Councils as well as Quarter Sessions have made a great difference during the last twenty or thirty years. It is not without wonder, therefore, that practically all Clerks of the Counties are now only too ready to be relieved of their official responsibilities on reaching their sixty-fifth birthday. A full list of the present membership of the Society (December 1960) is printed in Appendix IV.

The Finances of the Society.

One of the earliest acts of the Society was to appoint an Honorary Treasurer. It was not originally an annual appointment, but since 1948 the Treasurer has been appointed at the Annual Meeting with the other officers. For the most part, the Treasurers have held office until retirement or death. As has already been stated, however, Charles Pettitt Allen, (the second Treasurer to hold office) continued to act though he had resigned from the Society as a subscribing member on being appointed County Treasurer of Middlesex. It is interesting to note that both C. P. Allen and his successor, Thomas Marriott Davenport, were Deputy Clerks when appointed.

The income of the Society has been derived mainly from subscriptions, fines, contributions to meet special occasions and dividends from investments. The annual sub-scription was first fixed in 1811 at £2 2s. 0d., but was soon altered to £3 3s. 0d. for the first year and £1 1s. 0d. for subsequent years. In 1905, the subscription for years after the first was increased to £2 2s. 0d. for Clerks but remained unaltered for Deputies. From time to time the subscription has since been increased and stands to-day at £6 6s. 0d. for Clerks of the Peace and/or Clerks of County Councils and £3 3s. 0d. for Deputies. In the early years a fine of 7s. 0d. (later reduced to 5s. 0d.) was levied on absentees. The practice was discontinued in 1866. The first mention of a request for a special contribution appears in the Minutes for 1845 when Clerks of the Peace, who were not members of the Society, were asked to pay £2 2s. 0d. each towards the cost of opposing a Bill then before Parliament which provided for the payment of Clerks of the Peace by salaries instead of fees. Perhaps the most interesting occasion for a special call on the members was the decision of the Society to contribute towards the costs of the litigation in 1924 and 1925 between the Clerk of the Peace for West Sussex and the Standing Joint Committee for that County, already referred to. Nearly the whole of the expenses were met by the Society, the total amount contributed being some £380.

The Society accumulated a surplus soon after their inception and the first investment (the purchase of £200 Consols) was made in 1823. The amount invested has varied down the years. In January 1933, when the value of the investments was about £440 and the cash balance stood at £487, a suggestion was made that it was unnecessary to increase the Society's funds and that a reduction in the annual subscription should be considered. This proposal did not, however, find favour. The view was preferred that it was desirable to keep a balance " sufficient to meet future contingencies." It was left to the Treasurer to invest a further sum of £300. Although the subscriptions were halved during the Second World War, expenditure fell too, and the Society's funds increased substantially. In the accounts for 1944, investments stood at £1,420. However, it has not remained the policy to maintain the Society's funds at such a high figure and by December 1958 the value of invest-ments had fallen to £490.

At first, the Treasurer's accounts do not appear to have been regularly audited.

They were submitted periodically to the Society, but no detail was included in the Minutes other than a reference to the balance. Since 1904 the Statement of Accounts has been printed in the Minutes and, from 1932 onwards, particulars of the investments have been added. From the last mentioned year, the accounts have been certified as to their accuracy by the appropriate County Treasurer. The work of the Secretary and of the Treasurer has included a considerable amount of detail and the value of the assistance they have had from members of their local staffs has been recognised by the payment of honoraria. The first reference to such a payment (not regularly repeated) appears in the Minutes for 1873. Later, payments were made yearly. In 1933, payments of £15 10s. 0d. were included in the Accounts. By 1958 the total, including payments to the staff of the Honorary Statistical Officer and of the Honorary Auditor, had risen to £105 10s. 0d. It has been the practice to bring the cost of the Annual Dinner into the general accounts of the Society. While in early years it appears that a fixed charge was made for Dinner, in the years preceding 1948 a substantial contribution to the cost of the Dinner was being made from the Society's funds. In a review of their finances in 1948, the Society decided that no part of the cost of the Dinner, except in respect of official guests, should in future be met from the funds of the Society. There have also been paid through the accounts of the Society the cost of a trophy for the Annual Meeting of the Golfing Society, the expenses of that Society's Honorary Secretary and an honorarium for clerical assistance.

The Society's Minute Books.

The signed Minutes of the Society start on the 27th March 1810, and continue to the present day. The first volume is a quarto volume now labelled in typescript on the cover *Society of Clerks of the Peace of Counties. Minute Book No. I. 27th March* 1810 *to* 10*th May* 1854. The cover is of parchment, stained green, and is secured with two clasps. The volume contains one hundred and thirty-nine leaves of laid paper with four watermarks (C. Willmott; 1814; and two distinct and separate designs) and there are marbled end papers. It is written in eight or nine different hands and, although a meeting is occasionally recorded in more than one hand, it is clear that, as a rule, the Minutes were written up after the Meetings, presumably from rough notes. Indeed it was not until the seventh meeting of the Society, held on the 15th November 1814, that a Secretary was appointed and a Minute Book ordered to be kept. It would appear, therefore, that the Minutes for the first five years were entered up in that year, and this is supported by the fact, as mentioned above, that the figures " 1814 " feature as one of the watermarks on the first few pages of the book.

The second volume of the Society's signed Minutes is a quarto volume labelled in typescript on the cover *Society of Clerks of the Peace of Counties. Minute Book No. II. 15th November* 1854 *to 8th June* 1899. The boards are covered in dark green ridged cloth, with the spine and corners renewed in dark blue leather, and there are marbled end papers. This volume contains three hundred and thirty-three leaves of light blue paper, of which the first three and last one hundred and sixty-four leaves are blank. The Minutes on the pages numbered 1 to 89 (except for eleven pages which are printed) are written by hand, and, in this part of the volume, some printed Agenda are interleaved. From p. 90 (31st May 1883) to the end, the Minutes are printed on foolscap paper; they have been cut out and then stuck down in sections on each side of the original leaves of the book, a procedure which has had a bad effect on the condition of the volume.

From the 31st May 1900 to the 24th November 1948, there are eleven Minute Books forming the continuation of the " original " (signed) series, bound in white buckram, $13\frac{1}{2}'' \times 9''$ in size, numbered 3 to 13 inclusive, which consist of plain foolscap sheets of paper, upon which have been pasted the printed Minutes, duly signed by the appropriate Chairmen. Up to and including the meeting held on the 25th June 1913, the Minutes continued to be printed on foolscap paper, but from that date to the present time they are on octavo, and until January 1922 it was the practice to paste one printed page of the Minutes on to each page of the Minute Book. Thereafter, to the end of Volume 13 (24th November 1948) the printed Minutes have been pasted in the Minute Books so as to fill the whole of the pages of the latter, the printed pages being cut where necessary. The numbering of the printed pages and of the pages in the Books, therefore, do not correspond. Furthermore, the printed indices which began in 1918, and have, since then, been circulated to members, have not been included in Minute Books 3-13; in any case, they do not cover the same periods of time.

From the 26th January 1949, the printed Minutes have been bound up after being signed by the appropriate Chairmen in separate volumes for three year periods, each including its appropriate index. The covers of these volumes are in red cloth, appropriately numbered and dated. The first of the *printed* indices to the Society's Minutes, already referred to, covers the period from the 10th January 1918 to the 28th October 1925, and from then onwards, except for the period including the Second World War, a printed index was prepared every three years covering the meetings of the Society held during that period. The index for the period including the Second World War is for the six years from the 25th January 1939 to the 24th October 1945. The first occasion on which a volume number is specifically given to the Society's Minutes, as circulated to members, is printed on the cover page of the index for the meetings of the Society held from the 23rd January 1946 to the 24th November 1948 inclusive. This is Volume 9, though the period it covers will be found in Volumes 12 and 13 in the series of the Society's official Minute Books signed by the Chairmen; from then onwards every index for each three year period bears a number in sequence. It is fairly certain, therefore, that, until a volume number was given to that index, copies of the Minutes in the hands of the members of the Society will have been bound up in volumes to which they may have given their own numbers.

Social Activities of the Society.

Undoubtedly, one of the important features of the Society to-day is its social side. In a body such as this, where the members are spread over all the Counties of England and Wales and live—in some instances—as far apart as three hundred miles, it is essential that they should be able not only to meet regularly in some convenient place to discuss common problems but also to have the opportunity of getting to know one another personally. The recognition of this fact was obviously appreciated in the earliest days of the Society, for the Minutes of the meeting held on the 15th May 1810 contain a reference that " several of the Gentlemen propose to dine together," while in 1813 it was decided that an " Annual Dinner " should be held, for which the cost was then to be 10s. 6d. per member. In 1819, it was agreed that the Society's Annual Dinner should in future be held at 6 p.m., preceding the annual meeting for business at 8 p.m. This was, however, changed to 7 p.m. in 1834, the time of the meeting being fixed for 5 p.m., and upon the understanding that no business relating to the Society should be transacted after dinner. For many years thereafter, so far as can be ascertained, the Annual Dinner regularly followed upon the holding of the annual meeting even when, as for example in the years 1856 and 1858, there was no business to transact.

Although there is no record in the Society's Minutes that the Annual Dinner has been held each year—and, if so, where—it has always been assumed that this has been so, except during the First and Second World Wars, when the Dinners were suspended from 1915 to 1918 and from 1939 to 1947 inclusive, and in the single year 1931, when it was decided not to hold a dinner in view of the then Financial Crisis. On this assumption, the 150th Anniversary Dinner at the Mansion House, London, on the 14th December 1960, was the 137th occasion that the Society's Annual Dinner had been held.

It is not proposed to comment upon the inns, taverns and hotels where the dinners have been held, as these are given at full length in the second section of Part II. Until the eighteen-eighties it was usually the custom, as has been stated, to dine where the Annual Meeting was held. Thereafter it seems generally to have been the practice to " adjourn until 6 p.m." (the meetings then being held at 12 o'clock mid-day) to some well-known tavern or hotel such as the " Trafalgar " or the " Ship " Inn at Greenwich. Dinners " down the river " at Greenwich were well-known and popular towards the end of the nineteenth century and a special note about them is contained in Appendix II.

Over the last thirty years, the social activities of the Society have been supplemented by Golf Matches (mainly against the Ministry of Health and also, on occasion, against the Town Clerks' Golfing Society and the Society of County Clerks in Scotland) and the popular Annual Meetings of the Golfing Society formed in 1932. Full details of these will be found in the fourth section of Part II.

In July 1957, the Society gave a Reception at the Middlesex Guildhall to a hundred and fifty-four American lawyers and their ladies who were in London on the occasion of the American Bar Association Convention. Many of the American guests were professionally concerned in the United States with the administration of courts and circuits, performing duties largely similar to those of Clerks of the Peace in England and Wales.

150th Anniversary Dinner.

For their 150th Anniversary Dinner, on the 14th December 1960, the Society were able, by kind permission of the Rt. Hon. the Lord Mayor of London, Sir Bernard Waley-Cohen, to meet at the Mansion House at 7.30 p.m. for 8 p.m. Besides celebrating the 150th anniversary of the formation of the Society, the Dinner commemorated the sexcentenary of the institution of the Offices of Clerk of the Peace and Clerk of the Crown and also the Grant to the Society of a Coat of Arms. A brochure, describing these events and bearing the new Arms for the first time, was specially printed and distributed to guests and members.

The Chairman of the Society (Mr. Tom C. Hayward, C.B.E.) presided at the Dinner. The guests included the Lord Mayor of London, the Lord High Chancellor, the Lord Chief Justice, the Master of the Rolls, the Minister of Housing and Local Government, thirteen of Her Majesty's Lieutenants in the Counties, nineteen Chairmen of County Councils and twenty-five Chairmen and Deputy Chairmen of Quarter Sessions. All seven of the Permanent Secretaries to the Ministries closely connected with the work of the Clerks of the Counties accepted invitations. The Society of Chairmen and Deputy Chairmen of Quarter Sessions, the Law Society and the Bar Council were represented by their respective Presidents and Secretaries, and the County Councils Association by their Chairman, Vice-Chairman and officers. Altogether there were present at the Dinner eighty-seven members and honorary members, fifty-four guests of the Society and one hundred and thirty-four guests invited by the members, a total attendance of two hundred and seventy-five. A list of all the persons present appears in Appendix III.

Grace was said by the Rt. Rev. the Lord Bishop of Chichester. The Toast of *The Lord Mayor, the Corporation of the City of London and the Sheriffs* was proposed by the Minister of Housing and Local Government (the Rt. Hon. Henry Brooke, M.P.) and responded to by the Lord Mayor. *The Society* was proposed by the Master of the Rolls (the Rt. Hon. the Lord Evershed), supported by His Grace the Duke of Norfolk, E.M., K.G., G.C.V.O., Her Majesty's Lieutenant for the County of Sussex, who handed to the Chairman the Grant of Arms to be borne by the Society. This was replied to by Sir Edgar Stephens, C.B.E., D.L. Finally, the Toast of *The Guests* was proposed by the Chairman, and the response was made by Mr. T. M. Bland, T.D., D.L., Chairman of the Executive Council of the County Councils Association. The proceedings concluded shortly before 11 p.m.

Description of the Illustrations.

(1) *Map of England and Wales*, 1960. The frontispiece shows the sixty-two Counties of England and Wales as existing in 1960. Also marked and named on the map are the towns which are the present centres of administration of the Counties, excluding London and Middlesex, which are administered from County Hall, S.E.1. and the Middlesex Guildhall, S.W.1., respectively. In order not to obscure the outlines with detail, no attempt has been made to indicate the areas of any other local government authorities.

The remainder of the illustrations fall into three categories. First there are reproductions of drawings, paintings or photographs of six former Clerks of the Peace, spanning a period of roughly four hundred years from the late sixteenth century to the early twentieth, emphasising in particular the dress of the period. Then follow four illustrations of typical County buildings of varying ages and used primarily for the administration of justice, and lastly there are some photographs showing members of the Society attending the Annual

Roger Kenyon eldest son of Roger Kenyon of Park Head mar. Alice dau. of Geo. Rigby of Peel in Com. Lan.

PLATE IV

ROGER KENYON
CLERK OF THE PEACE FOR LANCASHIRE
1663-1698

Golf Meetings between the years 1934 and 1959, as well as two contemporary drawings by "Giles" and one by Richard Doyle, dated 1862.

(2) *Sir John Wynn* (1553–1627). Facing page 4 appears John Wynn, who was Clerk of the Peace for Caernarvonshire between 1573 and 1578. He was the son of Maurice Wynn by his first wife Jane, daughter of Sir Richard Bulkeley of Beaumaris, and was the most famous member of the family of Wynn of Gwydir. He was knighted in 1606 and created Baronet in 1611. He is said to have been unscrupulous, fond of litigation, and possessed of a vile temper, but he was also a man of varied interests and a patron of education and the arts. He sought to introduce the making of "Welsh friezes" on a fairly large scale in the Conway valley, was interested in copper mines in Anglesey, and contemplated building an embankment across Treath Mawr—a project actually completed in 1811; he founded a school and almshouses at Llanrwst, petitioned for an Eisteddfod, supported his kinsmen Thomas Williems of Trefriw and Dr. John Davies of Mallwyd in their literary and scholastic work, and wrote the "History of the Gwydir Family," the manuscript copies of which were highly prized before its first printing in 1770.

(3) *Richard Graves* (1610–1669). Opposite page 6 appears Richard Graves, Clerk of the Peace and Receiver-General for Middlesex from 1639 to 1660. He was a member of a family which had been established in Cleckheaton, Yorkshire, at least from the time of King Edward IV, but his grandfather moved to London. He matriculated at Pembroke College, Cambridge in 1626, and was admitted to Lincoln's Inn in 1631. He was called to the Bar in the same year as he became Clerk of the Peace, became a Bencher in 1657, Keeper of the Black Book in 1668 and Lenten Reader in the year of his death. He acquired considerable property during the Commonwealth, including the Royal Manor of Kennington, Surrey, which was sold by order of Parliament in 1649, and the Manor of Mickleton, Gloucestershire. He was married twice and had six sons and thirteen daughters.

(4) *Roger Kenyon* (1627–1698). Facing page 18 is Roger Kenyon, who was Clerk of the Peace for Lancashire from 1663 to 1698. He was the son and heir of Roger Kenyon of Parkhead, Whalley, and married Alice, daughter and heiress of George Rigby, Clerk of the Peace between 1627 and 1644. Eight members of these two families served as Clerks of the Peace for Lancashire for a hundred and ninety-one years, without a break, from 1589 to 1780. Roger Kenyon was Clerk for thirty-five years until his death in 1698. He was Member of Parliament for Clitheroe from 1690 to 1695, and Governor of the Isle of Man from 1691 to 1692.

(5) *John Robinson* (1727–1802). The reproduction opposite page 20 is of John Robinson, Clerk of the Peace for Westmorland from 1750 to 1760. He was the eldest son of Charles Robinson, a prosperous tradesman of Appleby. Educated at Appleby Grammar School until the age of seventeen, he was then articled to Richard Wordsworth, Clerk of the Peace from 1744 to 1750, whom he succeeded in office. He was also appointed Town Clerk of Appleby in 1750 and elected Mayor in 1760. Through his connection with Sir James Lowther, afterwards Earl of Lonsdale, he was elected to Parliament for the County in 1764; later he took

sides with Lord North against Lowther over the American War, and subsequently represented Harwich in Parliament until his death. He was Secretary to the Treasury from 1770 to 1782, and Surveyor General of Woods and Forests from 1788. It is as such that he appears in the portrait which is reproduced. The paper on the table by his left hand is a " Report of 11,225,000 acorns, planted in and about Windsor Great Park " between 1790 and 1801. He is also remembered as the " Jack Robinson " of whom Sheridan said in the House of Commons, when speaking of bribery in the administration and in answer to shouts of " Name, Name! " " I could name him as soon as I could say Jack Robinson."

(6) *John Marriott Davenport* (1809–1882). Opposite page 40 is a photograph of John Marriott Davenport, who was Clerk of the Peace for Oxfordshire from 1831 to 1881, in the wig and robes of his office. He was a partner in a leading firm of solicitors in the County town, and was appointed Clerk of the Peace at the age of twenty-one. He was also, during part of his fifty-year tenure of the office, Clerk to the Lieutenancy, Under Sheriff, Secretary to the Bishop of Oxford, Deputy Diocesan Registrar and Registrar of the Court of Probate for Oxfordshire, Berkshire and Buckinghamshire. As already mentioned, he was a prominent member of the Society for fifty years, and frequently took the Chair at meetings between 1840 and 1880. The reputation which survived him was that of a model Clerk of the Peace.

(7) *Sir Richard Nicholson* (1828–1913). Facing page 42 is a photograph of Sir Richard Nicholson, the fifth son of George Nicholson solicitor of Hertford. Richard Nicholson joined the service of the New Zealand Land Company at the age of fifteen, and, while so employed, assisted in laying out the town of Wanganui; he was also the Company's surveyor for the lay-out of Dunedin (1848). Returning to England, he was admitted to the Roll of Solicitors in 1851, and became Clerk of the Peace for both Hertfordshire and Middlesex in 1865. He was very soon active in the affairs of the Society, being Chairman in 1875 and from 1882 to 1910, and Honorary Secretary from 1881 to 1910. He was knighted in 1886, and in 1889, by operation of the Act of 1888, took the further offices of Clerk of the Peace for London and Clerk of the County Councils of Hertfordshire and of Middlesex—a situation quite without parallel.

(8) *The County Hall, Abingdon.* Facing page 54 appears a print of the County Hall and Market Place, Abingdon, Berkshire. Of this Hall, the Wren Society say " No hesitation need be felt as accepting this charming little building as the design of Sir Christopher Wren." The principal craftsman employed in the stonework was Christopher Kempster of Burford, one of Wren's master masons at St. Paul's. The work was in progress from 1678 to 1683, and the total cost was £2,840. Throughout the eighteenth and early nineteenth centuries the County Hall was the meeting place of at least one meeting of Quarter Sessions each year and of one of the two sittings of the Assizes for the County. Until the mid-nineteenth century the election of Members of Parliament for the County was formally announced at the County Hall and the election of County Coroners was also held there.

(9) *The Great Hall, Winchester Castle.* Opposite page 94 is a photograph of the Assize and Sessions Court in the Great Hall, Winchester. The new court furniture has been placed

Painted by G. F. Joseph.   VIRTUTIS GLORIA MERCES   Engraved by...

JOHN   ROBINSON ESQ.R

PLATE V

JOHN ROBINSON
CLERK OF THE PEACE FOR WESTMORLAND
1750-1760

within the only surviving building of Winchester Castle, which was the focal point for County business from the thirteenth century at least; and probably—as it was a Royal residence— justice has been administered in the Great Hall since before the Norman Conquest. Among those who were there sentenced to execution were Waltheof, Earl of Huntingdon (1076), Edmund, Earl of Kent (1330), Captain John Burley (1647) and Sir Walter Raleigh (1603). The Hall, as it now stands, is substantially the work of King Henry III, and, at the west end, prominent in the photograph now reproduced, hangs the " Round Table " mentioned by John Harding in the early fifteenth century and attributed to King Arthur in Caxton's introduction to Malory's *Morte d' Arthur*.

(10) *The Shire Hall, Warwick.* Opposite page 172 is a reproduction of an old engraving dated 1829 and made from a painting by David Cox of " St. Mary's Church, County Hall and Gaol, Warwick." Records show that the site of the Shire Hall has been associated with county government at least since 1480. The present building, which is in the centre of the print, dates from 1757, and was erected to the design of Francis Hiorn of Warwick. A notable case that took place at the Assizes in the Crown Court was the trial of Abraham Thornton for the murder of Mary Ashford. Thornton, although acquitted at Warwick, was tried a second time under the procedure of appeal of murder in the King's Bench, where he claimed his right to have the issue decided by wager of battle (1817). Both appeal of murder and wager of battle were afterwards abolished as a direct result of the case. The building in the right foreground is the Old Gaol, which acquired its present façade during alterations and enlargements between the years 1779 and 1783. Later used as barracks for the Warwickshire Militia and since 1932 as offices of the County Council, the elevation to the street has changed but little over the past hundred and eighty years. On the further side of the Shire Hall, near St. Mary's Church with its tower rebuilt by Wren, is the Judges' House, built between 1814 and 1816. The portico can just be seen in the print, the Judge's coach being drawn up outside.

(11) *The County Courts, Devizes.* Facing page 178 is a print entitled " The County Courts, Devizes." These Courts were built by public subscription in 1835 to provide for the Summer Assizes (then recently transferred from Salisbury) and the Hilary meetings of the Wiltshire Quarter Sessions. They became the property of the County in 1838. The print which is reproduced was originally drawn about 1836 by Thomas Henry Wyatt, later a President of the Royal Institute of British Architects. He may also have been the architect of the building.

(12) *The Armorial Bearings of the Society.* A representation of the Society's Arms in black and white appears opposite page 221, where a full description of the Arms will be found.

(13) *and* (18) *Drawings by " Giles."* Facing pages 224 and 230 are two drawings by " Giles " of Sir Hubert Thornley and Sir Edgar Stephens, Chairmen of the Society respectively from 1947 to 1950 and from 1953 to 1956.

(14) *to* (17) *Golfing Society Groups.* Four group photographs are reproduced between pages 226 and 227 of the members attending the Golfing Society's meetings at Porthcawl (1934), Harlech (1938), Woodhall Spa (1947) and Hunstanton (1959).

(19) " *Dinner down the River* " *by Richard Doyle.* As an illustration to the note on the Society's Dinners held at Greenwich, there appears opposite page 242, a reproduction of a drawing by Richard Doyle (1824–1883) entitled " Dinner down the River." The drawing first appeared in *The Cornhill Magazine* for January 1862, and was Number " X " in a series entitled " Birds'-eye Views of Society." In view of the inclusion in this book of the two drawings by " Giles," it is of interest to note the following passage from Michael Sadleir's Introduction to " God's Englishmen " (John Bradley and Avalon Press, Ltd., 1948), which was a re-publication of forty of Doyle's drawings made in the mid-nineteenth century:—

> " Doyle's style of humorous illustration became considerably in vogue from the late 'forties onward; but he possessed a gift for portraying movement and an eye for the hazardous comedies of a milling crowd which were peculiar to himself. Thackeray, W. S. Gilbert, and a number of lesser men such as Crowquill, Concannen, MacConnell and Kenny Meadows, used the sprightly vignette for text illustration; but no one of them rivalled Doyle in presenting a multitude of tiny figures, each with an individuality and with an agility or gestures of its own. It is consoling nowadays, when enjoying the populous cartoons of the incomparable Giles, to realise that the Doyle tradition is not dead, has indeed come vigorously to life again."

Acknowledgments.

It will be realised, after a mere glance at what follows, that this is not a book that has been produced by any one person; it has been compiled only with the co-operation of many willing helpers. The first to be thanked should be the present-day Clerks of the Counties, who, with the assistance of their archivists, furnished the original draft lists. This involved in most cases an examination of Quarter Sessions Rolls and Minute, Order and Indictment Books, and also Writs to Sheriffs summoning Sessions, and Certificates on enrolled deeds, housed in the County Muniment Rooms, followed by extensive searches amongst local records and books—particularly the Victoria County Histories—to find out some facts about their predecessors in office.

Particular thanks are due to the Automobile Association for preparing the map of the Counties in England and Wales which appears as the frontispiece; also to the individuals and institutions who have made available the portraits and prints in their possession, which are here reproduced. They are mentioned by name in the *List of Illustrations.*

The Warwickshire County Council have kindly allowed the staff in my office to render considerable help in the book's production. In particular, the typing and general preparation of the matter for the printers have involved my Secretary and members of the typing staff in much extra work. The day-to-day correspondence with members of the Society affecting their own lists, the compilation of the *Retrospect,* the managerial and financial sides of the undertaking, and finally the proof-reading of the text and the preparation of the Index, have also been a heavy burden upon certain members. It would be impossible to refer to all of them individually; I will not endeavour to do so, but will be content to thank them collectively for the able assistance they have given. One name, however, that must be mentioned is that of Mr. T. J. W. Foy, M.A. (Oxon), Assistant Solicitor on my staff, who has during the past year or two undertaken much of the detail work.

To Mr. H. S. Martin, C.B.E., D.L.—lately Clerk of the County of East Sussex— I am much indebted for reading through and revising the original draft of the Retrospect, and also for writing up the story of the Dinners at Greenwich and that part of the Introduction dealing with the Finances of the Society. Thanks are also due to Mr. G. C. Lightfoot—Clerk of the County of East Suffolk—for contributing the section dealing with the Clerks of the Peace Golfing Society. His alone was the suggestion and the personal approach to " Giles," who kindly gave the two drawings in this section. All members of the Society will be thankful to Mr. H. C. Johnson for the help he has given in the final revision of the lists. Both in respect of this and also for his interesting article on the origin and office of the Clerk of the Peace, all those who are even remotely connected with local government and the constitutional history of this country are indeed grateful.

Finally, this book would not be complete without a Foreword. The Society were, therefore, most fortunate in obtaining last year from the Lord Chancellor—The Rt. Hon. Viscount Kilmuir, G.C.V.O.—a promise to write it, after he had had an opportunity of reading through the text. Having held the office of Home Secretary from October 1951 to 1954 and the office of Lord Chancellor continuously from 1954 to the present time, it would not have been possible for the members to have found anyone more appropriate, on account of their contacts with his Department while he was at the Home Office in all matters relating to Quarter Sessions, the police and the fire brigade, probation and child welfare services, to name but a few. Again during the past six years, while Lord Kilmuir has been Lord Chancellor, the members have continually been in contact with his staff at the House of Lords, whilst carrying out their functions as Clerks to the Lieutenancy and Secretaries to the Advisory Committees. Thus, in securing his assent to write the Foreword, the Society have obtained one who not merely knows about their work as Clerks of the Counties but one who knows of them personally, having attended as the guest of Sir George Etherton—the then Chairman of the Society—the Annual Dinner at Claridge's for four years consecutively from 1935 to 1938, and having been present as the Society's Chief Guest when he was Home Secretary in 1952, and again in 1954 after becoming Lord Chancellor. He was also their guest once more at the recent dinner at the Mansion House. The members, therefore, tender to him their warm thanks for his continued interest in their well-being in this year of Grace, being the year in which they have celebrated the one hundredth and fiftieth anniversary of the formation of their Society.

L. Edgar Stephens,
Honorary Treasurer of the Society.

Warwick,

31*st December,* 1960.

PART I

THE OFFICE OF CLERK OF THE PEACE

THE ORIGIN AND OFFICE OF CLERK OF THE PEACE

BY

H. C. JOHNSON, C.B.E., M.A.

THE ORIGIN AND OFFICE OF CLERK OF THE PEACE

The Clerk of the Peace before 1888.

(1) *Origins.*

It is probable that the emergence of the office which came to be known as that of the Clerk of the Peace did not long antedate its first official mention in 1380. The form of oath for Justices of the Peace entered on the Parliament Roll of that year contains instructions for the administration by the Justices of an oath to their Clerk " to conceal the counsel of the King and to perform his duties loyally."[1] Throughout the preceding century and a half of experiment in the issue of Commissions directed to local knights and gentry for the keeping of the Peace, individual members of the Commissions are known to have had Clerks in their Service, and the Statute of Labourers of 1351 refers to the Clerks of the Justices commissioned under the Statute, but there is no evidence for the existence of Clerks of the Sessions acting as officers of the Court.

It may indeed reasonably be conjectured with Sir John Vaughan, one of the Judges in the case of *Harding v. Pollock*[2] heard in the House of Lords in 1829, that the occasion of the creation of the office was the Statute of 1361 (34 Edward III, cap. 1), which transformed the Keepers of the Peace into Justices of the Peace, giving them general standing authority to hear and determine felonies and trespasses, and thereby constituting them complete judges of a court of record. Until that time there was need neither of a Custos Rotulorum nor of a Clerk of the Peace and, as Sir John believed, neither had in fact existed until then. " But," he says, " a court of record being then organised, and the Justices assembled for the first time under the Commission directed by that statute, I apprehend it would of right belong to them as incident to the administration of their justice, having records which must be in their custody, to appoint an officer, by whatever name he might be called, whether Clerk of the Crown, Clerk of the Justices, or Clerk of the Peace, to assist them in drawing their indictments, in arraigning their prisoners, in joining issues for the Crown, in entering their judgments, in awarding their process, and in making up and keeping their records." The nature of these duties, he goes on to say, may sufficiently account for the officer being sometimes called not only Clerk of the Peace, but also Clerk and Attorney for the Crown, and he cites the description in the Year Book for 1486–7 of the Clerk of the Peace at the Sessions as " Clerk of the Peace, who is Clerk and Attorney for the advantage of the King ".[3]

[1] *Rot. Parl.* III, 85.
[2] 6 Bingham's *Reports*, 25.
[3] At p. 67.

Until 1388, identification of these officials is difficult. The earliest Clerks of the Peace shown in the lists printed in this volume are so described on the authority of Miss Bertha Putnam, who in her *Yorkshire Sessions of the Peace*[1] says " the Clerk of the Peace for the East Riding is certainly Robert Bruys by 1363 and very probably for the years immediately preceding. For the North Riding he has not been identified unless, possibly by analogy with later practice, he be Thomas Gretheued, the King's attorney " so acting in a case on the roll for 1361. From 1392 up to the latter years of the seventeenth century the names of most of the Clerks of the Peace can be found in the enrolments on the Pipe Roll of the indentures made requisite by statute in 1390 for the purpose of recording the payment of wages due to the Justices and their Clerk under the Statute of Cambridge, enacted in 1388.

The title " Clerk of the Peace " does not occur in these entries on the Pipe Roll until the sixteenth century, the officer of the court being described as " Clerk of the Justices ". But there is nothing to negative the presumption that the officer so described was in fact the Clerk of the Peace. For, whether called Clerk of the Justices of the Peace or, by abbreviation, Clerk of the Peace, the same individual officer performing the same duties is clearly indicated. He is called Clerk of the Peace in patents of appointment in the fifteenth century and as early as 1412 is called Clerk of the Sessions of the Peace. In the Year Books of that year it is said that at a gaol delivery of Salisbury castle one of the Justices, Hankford, directed Horn, who was Clerk of the Sessions of the Peace, to take the name of a prisoner that had been sent thither without any sufficient proof and to cause it to be enquired of at the next sessions of the Peace.[2]

(2) *Appointment and Tenure of Office.*

It is not until 1545 that there was statutory provision for the appointment of the Clerk of the Peace by the Custos Rotulorum. The principal point at issue in the case of *Harding v. Pollock* was whether the appointment before the Act of 1545 (37 Henry VIII, cap. 1) belonged of right to the Crown or to the Custos Rotulorum of the County by virtue of his office or to any other person or persons. One of the Judges held that it belonged to the Crown; the other three were of the opinion that it belonged to the Custos. In fact it appears to have been exercised sometimes by the Justices themselves, sometimes by the Crown and sometimes, perhaps normally, by the Custos.

The language of the statute of 1545 plainly declares that the Custos Rotulorum had until recently had the nomination and appointment of the Clerk of the Peace. That this was the normal practice at the beginning of the sixteenth century is assumed in Thomas Marowe's description of the Clerk of the Peace in the lectures or reading which he gave at the Inner Temple in 1503 on the eve of his promotion to be serjeant-at-law. " The Clerk of the Peace ", he says, " is not the officer of the Court, but only the clerk of the Custos Rotulorum ".[3] There is, however, no evidence of this practice in the records. The earliest evidence

---

[1] Yorkshire Archaeological Society, Record Series, vol. 100, p. xxiv.

[2] 6 Bingham's *Reports*, 70; *cf.* Lambard, *Eirenarcha* (1614), p. 391.

[3] B. H. Putnam's *Early Treatises on the Practice of the Justice of the Peace in the Fifteenth and Sixteenth Centuries* (Oxford Studies in Social and Economic History, vol. VII, 1924) p. 363.

of the method of appointment appears to be in the wages indenture[1] of Thomas Bedford, Clerk of the Bedfordshire Justices of the Peace, in 1394. Bedford is described as the Clerk of the Justices appointed thereto by the said Justices. The common law principle, recognized in the Statute of Westminster the second, that, in the absence of regulation by the Crown, the members of a newly created court have the right to appoint the subordinate officers or clerks of the court appears to justify the assumption that in the early days of the office the Justices appointed their Clerk, though later the appointment became vested in that Justice who was specially charged with the duty of producing the requisite records at the sessions of the Court, that is, the Custos Rotulorum.

Evidence that the Clerk might be appointed by the Crown occurs as early as 1404, when John Fynchyngfeld was appointed by Royal letters patent Clerk and King's Attorney before Justices of the Peace in Essex, Hertfordshire and Suffolk.[2] It appears from the Pipe Rolls that he acted as Clerk of the Peace in Essex and Suffolk, but not in Hertfordshire. About the middle of the fifteenth century there is a group of Crown appointments which raise problems about the relationship of the Clerk to the Custos Rotulorum and to the Justices executing judicial commissions other than the Commission of the Peace. The first of these appointments, which were for life, was in 1446 when William Bysshop of Charlton was appointed Clerk of the Peace in Salop and Keeper of the records, rolls and precepts touching the keeping of the Peace and the hearing and determining of divers felonies, etc., taking the usual fees, as he had hitherto had in the office.[3]

In 1447 there was a grant in larger terms to Thomas Merton, for good service to the King and in Eton College, of the office of Clerk of the Keepers of the Peace and the Justices of Oyer and Terminer in Northamptonshire " *alias* the office of Clerk of the Crown or of the Peace ".[4] He was also appointed King's Attorney to plead, answer and sue for the King in all plaints, indictments, appeals, etc., before the Keepers and Justices and to sue, enter and enrol bills and pleas before them. He could act in person or by deputy, and in addition to the usual fees and wages he was granted a yearly payment of a hundred shillings from the farm of the Manor of Corby. In the following year Robert Repynghale, the King's Serjeant and Clerk of the Signet, for good service in the office of King's secretary and elsewhere and in Eton College and King's College, Cambridge, received a grant in similar terms, but without the yearly fee of one hundred shillings, of the like offices in all Parts of Lincolnshire.

In 1453 John West, who had been attendant in the King's service with the Coroner and Attorney in the King's Bench, was granted the office of Clerk of the Sessions of the Peace and of the Justices of Oyer and Terminer in Warwickshire, and though this office is not described as that of Clerk of the Peace and of the Crown, its duties are the same.[5] In March 1458 Henry Barbour, Under-Clerk of the Royal kitchen, was granted the office of Clerk of the Peace for Staffordshire on the surrender by William York the younger of the

[1] P.R.O. Exchequer, K.R., Accounts Various, 550/41 m. 3.
[2] *Calendar of Patent Rolls*, 1401–1405, p. 373. He later surrendered the office.
[3] *Calendar of Patent Rolls*, 1446–1452, p. 28.
[4] *Ibid*, p. 84.
[5] *Calendar of Patent Rolls*, 1452–1461, p. 77.

King's cellar of his letters patent of the preceding January, granting him the same office with the keeping of the Rolls pertaining to it, as it had been held by John Hegon[1]. Hegon is said to have held by letters patent, but his grant does not appear to have been enrolled, and evidence that any of these three grantees ever acted as Clerk of the Peace has not been found. George Scalby, a clerk of the Exchequer, had a grant in 1464 of the office of Clerk of the Crown in Yorkshire, previously held by Robert Davyson.[2] Davyson was Clerk of the Peace in the East Riding, but no grant of either office to him seems to have been enrolled.

In 1455 Parliament petitioned for, and obtained, an Act of Resumption of grants of Crown lands and revenues, in which it was declared that grants under the great seal, privy seal or Duchy of Lancaster seal of the offices of Sheriff, Escheator, Clerk of the Peace or any Bailiwick belonging to the Crown, for life or terms of years to anyone, should be void.[3] This explicit mention of the office of Clerk of the Peace in company with those of Sheriff and Escheator as offices belonging to the Crown gives grounds for expecting Crown appointments to be commonplace. The contrary appears to be the case. If grants were made under the privy seal, no evidence of them remains, as the registers have not survived. In Lancashire, where grants under the Duchy seal are to be expected, no regular appointments to the office appear to have been made before 1540. An examination of the printed calendars of patent rolls has revealed no grants of the office by letters patent between 1458 and 1506, the latter date being three years after Thomas Marowe's reading in which the Clerk of the Peace is said to be the clerk of the Custos Rotulorum.

At least eight grants of the offices of Clerk of the Peace and Clerk of the Crown in various Counties were made by letters patent in 1506, three more were made in 1507 and 1508, eight more from 1514 to 1536, eleven in 1537, six in 1538 and fourteen from 1539 to 1543, of which eight were for appointments in Wales and Chester following the Acts of 1536 and 1542 by which Wales was divided into Counties and Courts of Quarter Sessions established. Appointments by letters patent were made between 1532 and 1543 for all the Counties for which similar appointments had been made between 1506 and 1508, except for Hertfordshire. These are Cambridgeshire, Cornwall, Devon, Essex, Herefordshire, Kent, Oxfordshire, Warwickshire, Yorkshire (North Riding) and two pairs of Counties, Bedfordshire and Huntingdonshire, and Norfolk and Suffolk. Essex and Hertfordshire were paired in 1506, but it seems not unlikely that the grantee served only for Essex, and the pairing did not recur. The remaining Crown appointments for English Counties from 1532 to 1543 were for Berkshire, Gloucestershire, Hampshire, Lincolnshire (Lindsey), Somerset, Staffordshire, Surrey, Sussex, Wiltshire, Worcestershire, and three pairs of Counties, Lincolnshire (Holland and Kesteven), Northamptonshire and Leicestershire, and Nottinghamshire and Derbyshire. For Wales and Chester, following the Act of 1536, Clerks of the Peace and of the Crown were appointed between 1538 and 1542 for each of the Counties of Caernarvon, Cheshire, Denbigh, Flint and Monmouth, one for Glamorgan and South Wales, one for the Counties of Merioneth and Anglesey, one for the Counties of Pembroke, Cardigan and Carmarthen, and one for the

---

[1] *Calendar of Patent Rolls*, 1452–1461, p. 420.
[2] *Calendar of Patent Rolls*, 1461–1467, p. 342.
[3] *Rot. Parl.* V. 301.

Counties of Radnor, Brecon and Montgomery. On three occasions grants were made to two persons jointly in survivorship. The grant of the Clerkships for Devon in 1543 was made in reversion to the son of the serving Clerk, and does not appear to have taken effect until 1557. Several grants were made to persons already serving in the office of Clerk of the Peace, and a few were made for Counties where the Clerk in office, though not the grantee, appears to have continued to act. Many of the grantees are known to have been servants of the King or of Royal officials.

The phraseology of the grants quickly becomes stereotyped. Generally the appointment is to two distinct offices, one being the Clerkship of the Peace and the other the Clerkship of the Crown and of all Sessions of the Peace before the Justices of the Peace and Justices of oyer and terminer and of gaol delivery and before all Justices with a special commission of gaol delivery; and they are to be exercised in person or by deputy for the usual fees. With rare exceptions the Custos Rotulorum is directed to deliver to the grantee the records, rolls, memoranda and other writings relating to the offices and to allow him to exercise the offices as they have formerly been held. In Wales they are to be held as in England. The instruction to the Custos to deliver the records need not be taken to imply that his functions were to be taken over by the grantee, but rather that the latter was to be in no way hindered in the performance of his offices, even though he was not the clerk of the Custos and not appointed by him.

It may be that the appointment by Royal letters patent of individuals, and particularly of persons in the King's service, to hold these two offices, related and yet becoming distinct as the Justices of Assize increasingly drew to themselves the highest judicial powers of the Justices of the Peace, was designed to strengthen the administration of justice in the particular Counties for which they were appointed and to assert its control by the Crown, but it seems more likely that, regarded as offices of profit, they were treated as suitable rewards for previous service, or as enhancement of wages received for other offices, or simply as marketable commodities. As an example of this, Robert Moffett, a groom of the chamber, serving in the Navy, was in 1541 appointed by letters patent Clerk of the Peace and Clerk of the Crown for the Counties of Carmarthen, Cardigan and Pembroke for life. He sold his right and title in the office to John Ayleworth, a Receiver of the Court of Augmentations, who in turn leased it for four years at a yearly rent of £6 13s. 4d. to John Goodale, a practitioner in the Court of Requests and a Justice of the Peace of the Quorum for Carmarthenshire. Goodale occupied the office for a year and then let it to deputies whom he claimed to have trained in the work. Ayleworth had promised Goodale the first refusal if he decided to sell his interest in the office, but, anxious to make as much profit as he could out of a bargain which Moffett's state of health made precarious, he accepted, without giving Goodale a chance to exercise his option, an offer from a servant of the Duchess of Northumberland. It can only be supposed that, amid all the trafficking, the duties of the office were largely neglected.[1]

This is probably no more than an example of a common practice affecting a diversity of offices and forbidden by an Act of Parliament of 1552 (5 & 6 Edward VI, cap. 16), which included, in its prohibition of the sale of offices, the Clerkships of Courts of Record

[1] P.R.O. Court of Requests Proceedings, 6/232.

wherein justice is ministered. For the Clerkship of the Peace reform came earlier, in 1545. The preamble of the Act made in that year for the offices of Custos Rotulorum and Clerks of the Peace declared that " now of late divers and sundry persons within this Realm, being not learned nor yet mete nor able for lack of knowledge and learning to occupy the offices of Custos Rotulorum and of the Clerkship of the Peace, have of late years by labour, friendship and means " obtained life grants by the King's letters patent of Clerkships of the Peace; and that by reason of the appointment of persons insufficiently learned to exercise the office " indictments for felony and murder and other offences and misdemeanours, and the process awarded upon them, have not only been frustrate and void, sometimes by negligent engrossing, and sometimes by the embezzling or rasure of the indictments, but also sundry bargains and sales have been void for lack of sufficient enrolment, to the great hindrance of justice and to the disinheritance of some of the King's subjects". To remedy these abuses, the Act provided that for the future, saving the rights of existing holders of the office, the ancient order of appointment should be restored; the Custos Rotulorum of each County should appoint as Clerk of the Peace for his County such able person instructed in the laws of the Realm as should be able to occupy the office, holding it so long as the Custos himself held his office, either in person or by a deputy sufficiently instructed in the law and admitted by the Custos.

The rights enjoyed by the Archbishop of York and by the Bishops of Durham and Ely within the areas of their territorial jurisdiction were excepted from the operation of the Act, and they continued to appoint their own Custodes Rotulorum and Clerks of the Peace until 1836. The Palatine County of Lancaster was also excepted and the right of the Duchy to appoint the Custos and the Clerk of the Peace retained. In these exempted jurisdictions the Clerk of the Peace was not appointed by the Custos, but both Clerk and Custos were appointed by the lord of the franchise. It is tempting to argue that thus they preserved what was in fact the general practice throughout the Realm immediately before the Act of 1545, though the Judges in *Harding v. Pollock* thought otherwise. The history of the office of the Clerk of the Peace in Lancashire up to this date is obscure. A few appointments were made before 1540, but regular appointments do not begin until that year. In a suit in the Duchy Court shortly after that date, the Clerk of the Crown at Lancaster alleged that until the appointment of Randolph in 1543 the Clerkship of the Peace was never reputed an office nor granted to anyone, but was exercised by one of the clerks of the Custos Rotulorum, and that time out of mind the holders of the office of Clerk of the Crown had had the keeping of indictments and made out the process on them and received certain fees.[1] In Tudor times, the Clerk of the Peace in the Palatine County was appointed, usually for life, under letters patent sealed by the seal of the Palatinate. If required, further letters patent would ensure the reversion of the office on the death or surrender of the holder to his heirs. The Crown received substantial fees for the letters patent, and the office-holders, who could always employ a capable deputy to do the work, acquired a property which yielded them a steady annual income.[2]

[1] R. Somerville: *Lancashire Justices of the Peace:* (Historic Society of Lancashire and Cheshire, Transactions, cii) pp. 187–8.

[2] J. J. Bagley: *Kenyon v. Rigby: the Struggle for the Clerkship of the Peace in Lancashire in the Seventeenth Century:* (Historic Society of Lancashire and Cheshire, cvi) p. 35.

The Act of 1545 effectively brought to an end the close connection of the Clerkship of the Peace with that of the Crown. The duties of the latter office were henceforth performed by the Clerks of Assize, appointments of whom are said to date from this period,[1] and of whom it was said by Baron Vaughan that " it is difficult to conceive two offices bearing a stronger resemblance to each other than that of Clerk of Assize and Clerk of the Peace . . . they are the very indenture and counterpart, formed upon the same model, created by the same necessity, and discharging the same duties ".[2] A few of the grants of both offices made by letters patent before 1545 continued to be effective until their termination by surrender or the death of the holders, but all new appointments were made by the Custodes Rotulorum of the Counties. Appointments made by letters patent had been for life; in some cases, where the grant was to two persons, in survivorship, and in others in reversion. Under the Act of 1545 the appointment of the Clerk of the Peace terminated when the Custos who appointed him ceased to hold office.

A change in the terms of appointment was made by the Great Seal Act of 1689 (1 William & Mary, cap. 21) which provided that the Clerk of the Peace should be resident in the County, Division or Riding for which he served, should perform the office in person or by deputy for the usual fees, and should hold it for life so long as he should well demean himself in his office. The Justices of the Peace in Quarter Sessions were empowered, after judicial inquiry, to discharge him for misdemeanour and to appoint a successor. The order of Quarter Sessions might be quashed or confirmed by King's Bench on a *mandamus* or *certiorari*. So, Richard Baynes, Clerk of the Peace for Westmorland, was dismissed by Quarter Sessions for extortion in 1702; the order dismissing him was quashed by Queen's Bench four years later.[3] On the other hand, the dismissal of Thomas Lloyd, Clerk of the Peace for Cardiganshire, was confirmed by King's Bench in 1734.[4]

In the event of a vacancy occurring at a time when the office of Custos was also vacant, Quarter Sessions might make a temporary appointment or the Lord Chancellor (or Lord Keeper of the Great Seal) might exercise the power of the Custos, as happened in Oxfordshire in 1759. On the death of the Clerk of the Peace in that year Quarter Sessions appointed an acting Clerk, there being no Custos, from August to December. Then, the office of Custos being still vacant, the Lord Keeper appointed a Clerk of the Peace.

By the Clerks of the Peace Removal Act, 1864, a Clerk of the Peace could be removed by Quarter Sessions for misconduct otherwise than in the execution of his office. This Act was repealed by the Statute Law Revision (No. 2) Act, 1893, except as to any Clerk of the Peace appointed before the passing of the Local Government Act, 1888. This repeal did not, however, affect the principle theretofore existing, that a Clerk of the Peace is an independent officer and as such is given security of tenure. Finally, in 1931, the provisions of the Great Seal Act mentioned above were repealed by the Local Government (Clerks) Act passed in that year.

[1] H. Hall: *Repertory of British Archives* (Royal Historical Society, 1920) p. 112.
[2] 6 Bingham's *Reports*, 74.
[3] 2 Raymond's *Reports*, 1265.
[4] 2 Strange's *Reports*, 996.

(3) *Duties.*

The duties of the Clerk of the Peace in the fifteenth century have already been described in the words of Sir John Vaughan, " to assist the Justices of the Peace in drawing their indictments, in arraigning their prisoners, in joining issues for the Crown, in entering their judgments, in awarding their process, and in making up and keeping their records ". Personal attendance at Quarter Sessions was not incumbent on the Clerk. When he was appointed by the Crown, his letters patent gave him authority to act by deputy. Marowe, who calls him the clerk of the Custos Rotulorum, says he is not an officer of the Court and may appoint another to attend the Sessions on his behalf.[1] Lambard, however, denies this, insisting that the Clerk is an officer of the Court with the duty of attendance at Sessions. For, in addition to his duties as Clerk of the Court, the legislation of the sixteenth and early seventeenth century had made him responsible for recording proclamations of wages, enrolling the discharge of apprentices, keeping registers of the licences of badgers, drovers and various traders, and of persons licensed to shoot in guns, recording presentments of absentees from church and certificates of the oath of allegiance, and of certifying into the King's Bench transcripts of indictments, outlawries, attainders and convictions before the Justices of the Peace. In addition, under a statute of 1506, he enrolled deeds of bargain and sale of lands within his County, and he was, says Lambard, " in a sort incorporate by the name of his office to sue upon the statute of Hue and Cry of 27 Elizabeth ".[2]

With the Clerk also were deposited duplicate inventories of the goods, plate, jewels, vestments, bells and other ornaments of the churches, chapels, fraternities, guilds and companies in his County.[3] Once a year he had to make and engross the great Estreat of fines, amercements and forfeited recognizances which had to be approved by the Justices at their Michaelmas Sessions and sent in to the Exchequer so that the summons of the green-wax could issue for the collection by the Sheriff of the sums due. Until 1670 this schedule was usually delivered at the Exchequer by one of the Justices, but an Act of that year (22 & 23 Charles II, cap. 22) required the Clerk of the Peace to deliver the schedule to the Sheriff and to return a duplicate to the Exchequer on or before the second Monday after the morrow of All Souls' day in each year, under a penalty of £50. Failure to deliver the Estreats prevented the Sheriff from passing his account at the proper time, and might be followed by an order for the arrest of the Clerk of the Peace or his Deputy or for the payment of costs by them.

The administrative functions which the Justices of the Peace had begun to acquire before 1500 were greatly increased in the course of the following centuries. Quarter Sessions, in the words of Maitland, became " not merely a criminal court for the County, but also a governmental assembly, a board with governmental and administrative powers ".[4] For the exercise of these functions they had at their disposal for executive purposes the old machinery of the County, the Hundred and the Parish, but the whole of the office work, both in and out of Sessions, the drafting of orders and the issue of instructions, communications

---

[1] B. H. Putnam: *Early Treatises . . .*, p. 363.
[2] *Eirenarcha* (1614), pp. 393, 394.
[3] *Calendar of Patent Rolls, Edward VI*, vol. IV, p. 393; vol. V, pp. 417–418.
[4] *Constitutional History of England* (Cambridge, 1908), p. 233.

with the Privy Council and Ministers of State, fell upon the Clerk of the Peace. Until the end of the seventeenth century he was in most Counties the only officer of the Court of Quarter Sessions, and even in the eighteenth century in some Counties he was also County Treasurer. County Surveyors or Bridgemasters were appointed here and there, and occasionally other officers are to be found. But in general it may be said that at the time of the passing of the Local Government Act in 1888 the Clerk of the Peace was the principal administrative officer of his County. In addition to attending to the purely judicial duties of General and Quarter Sessions, he was the centre of the County administration as it existed before the creation of County Councils under the Act of 1888 in connection with highways, County bridges, diseases of animals, weights and measures, Coroners' districts, polling districts, reformatories, stage plays, County rate and so on.

(4) *Remuneration.*

Under the statute of Cambridge of 1388, the Clerk of the Peace received two shillings for each day he attended Quarter Sessions. This amount was payable from the fines and amercements imposed at Sessions, for which the Sheriff had to account at the Exchequer. These wages continued to be paid until the provisions of the Acts authorising their payment were repealed by an Act of 1855 (18 & 19 Victoria, cap. 126, sec. 21). Apart from this the Clerk depended upon fees for his remuneration and for the expenses of his office, which increased considerably from the end of the fifteenth century. Fees may be assumed to have been charged from the beginning. William Bysshop's letters patent as Clerk of the Peace in Salop in 1446 refer to " the usual fees as he has hitherto had in the office ". Lambard refers to certain statutory fees to which the Clerk of the Peace was entitled for enrolling bargains and sales, registering badgers and taking recognizances of persons taking rogues into their service for a year. If he took more than the statutory sum he was liable to a fine. But the amount of most fees was fixed by custom only and had no statutory limit. Abuses were perhaps to be expected and fee taking became indiscriminate, involving everyone whose business, whether of his own seeking or not, brought him to the Clerk's office, paupers only being in some cases excepted.

Complaints about the extortions of the officers of all courts of justice led to a series of commissions between 1622 and 1640 to inquire into increases of fees during the preceding half century. A few returns from Clerks of the Peace survive, which give details of the fees charged. As might be expected, no increases within the specified time are reported. Complaint was made that the Clerk of the Peace for Middlesex took three shillings or more for every ordinary recognizance; for some, double fees, and for others, ten shillings apiece. " Let him account by what warrant he receiveth so much, and how the sums are divided. Call for his books of Recognizances and you will find the number infinite, and out of divers particulars charges will be given of his great exactions. There is likewise great complaint of his exacting of fees for drawing all his indictments which are likewise very many and for which great fees are exacted. The records will show the number ".[1] The list of fees put in by the Clerk of the Peace, said to be the ancient fees theretofore received by the precedent Clerks of the Peace,

[1] P.R.O. Exchequer, King's Remembrancer, Commission on Fees, 1106.

contains a modest thirty-one items, showing the fee for a recognizance of the Peace or good behaviour as 2s. 4d., the fee for an indictment of trespass or felony at the common law, 2s.; of riot or forcible entry 3s. 4d. Even more modest is the list from the Clerk of the Peace for Cumberland. It contains but five items – for drawing an indictment, 12d.; for a recognizance taken in court, 2s. 4d.; for the release of a recognizance, 4s. 8d.; for the fees upon traverse of an indictment, 4s.; for a licence for a badger or drover and the recognizance and recording thereof in all, 2s. These fees, he says, have been taken by his predecessors time out of mind, and he has taken them only when the parties were of ability to pay them, " which seldom here happeneth, in regard of the poverty of the country ", and most of them were received in open court before the Justices.[1]

The table of fees in the *Office of the Clerk of the Peace*, printed in 1682 as a guide to practice at the Court of Quarter Sessions, comprises nearly a hundred items and shows some variations in amount from the fees detailed in the returns made fifty or sixty years earlier. A watchful eye was kept by Clerks of the Peace on all possible means of obtaining fees, and disputes arose with the clerks of individual magistrates over entitlement for fees for work done out of Sessions. In 1709 the Clerk of the Peace for Carmarthenshire brought a suit in Chancery against various Justices of the Peace about the fees due at special Sessions:[2] in 1723 the Buckinghamshire Justices took steps to prevent Clerks of Justices from depriving the Clerk of the Peace of his fees by their failure to certify to Quarter Sessions licences granted to alehouse keepers and victuallers and recognizances entered by them before Justices out of Sessions.[3]

Richard Burn remarks that while the Clerk's fees were in divers cases limited by Act of Parliament, "it seemeth to be one of the *desiderata* in the justices' law that the Clerk of the Peace his fees are not ascertained in all instances ".[4] Burn is speaking of the Court fees. These however were not the only fees the Clerk received. The Treasury records show Clerks of the Peace receiving payments of fifty pounds or thereabouts for their trouble over the Hearth Tax collection.[5] The Clerk of the Peace for Essex in 1719 claimed £6 13s. 4d. every time he sent out orders to all the high constables, and 3s. 6d. for every order made out upon the public account. In Cardiganshire in 1774 the Clerk received twenty pounds a year for the carriage of the records and statutes from one Sessions town to another, and ten guineas a year, in addition to the usual fees, for conducting all prosecutions on behalf of the County.[6]

The fees which increasingly swelled the income of the Clerk of the Peace were those derived from the execution of County business, and in the eighteenth century the office shared the prosperity that fell to the leaders of the profession of attorney. In 1754 the Clerk of the Peace for Surrey " practically sold his office for the sum of £1,600 ".[7] As County

[1] P.R.O. Exchequer, King's Remembrancer, Commission on Fees, 1105, 1113.

[2] P.R.O. *Chancery Proceedings before* 1714, Bridges, 235/22.

[3] *Buckinghamshire Calendar of Quarter Sessions Records*, V, 164.

[4] *Justice of the Peace* (3rd edition, 1756) *tit.* Clerk of the Peace. For the wide variations possible in the Court fees charged by Clerks of the Peace in 1834 see House of Commons: *Reports from Committees*, 1834, vol. xiv, pp. 319, 320.

[5] e.g. *Calendar of Treasury Books*, vol. I, pp. 604, 607, 608, 627, 629, etc.

[6] S. and B. Webb, *English Local Government: the Parish and the County* (London, 1906), p. 505, note 2.

[7] S. and B. Webb: *op. cit.* p. 503, note 4.

business increased, the itemised charges made for every transaction swelled into large sums, chargeable to the County rate. In some Counties, Quarter Sessions attempted to moderate the charges made upon the County. In Berkshire the list of fees to be taken was in 1727 referred to a committee to adjust. In 1730 the Hampshire Quarter Sessions settled a new table of fees to be taken by the Clerk of the Peace, and thirty years later the same authority ordered that the Clerk should not for the future be allowed anything out of the County rate for the making of Sessions orders for the payment of salaries or bills. In Middlesex, where the income from fees was said to amount to £2,088, and the Clerk's administration had already been subject to inquiry and censure, Quarter Sessions in 1829 declared that " in no case can they admit that he is to be paid by the County for any services performed in his capacity of Clerk of the Peace unless such payment is so directed by Act of Parliament ".[1]

Quarter Sessions had in fact little, if any, control over the Clerk's fees before 1817, when Parliament (57 George III, cap. 91) gave them power to settle a table of fees subject to confirmation by the Judges of Assize. But already a different method of remuneration was being canvassed, and in 1819 the Justices in the West Riding of Yorkshire decided to give their Clerk of the Peace a salary of £400 a year in lieu of fees. This was revoked in 1828, through doubts as to the legality of the practice.[2] The Buckinghamshire Justices recommended a similar course and appointed a committee in 1832 to settle the salary, but apparently without effect. The House of Commons Committee on County Rates in 1834 recommended that it should be within the discretion of Quarter Sessions in each County to continue payment of the Clerk of the Peace by fees, or to pay a salary in lieu of the fees and charges paid out of the county purse, leaving the Clerk in receipt of fees payable by individuals.[3] Although Parliament did not give effect to these recommendations for seventeen years, nevertheless after 1835 payment by salary was gradually substituted for payment by fees. The Clerk of the Peace for the North Riding received from Michaelmas 1837 a salary of £600 a year, in place of £20 a year for keeping the rolls and fees amounting then to about £500 a year. His successor, appointed in 1849, was paid by fees till 1859; from that date he had a salary of £889 a year without any allowance for clerks.

A return made to Parliament for the years 1841 to 1845 shows an average receipt of about £1,100 a year throughout England and Wales, ranging from about £180 a year in Anglesey to about £4,500 a year in Lancashire. Out of these sums, deputies and any other staff had to be paid.[4] In Westmorland and the North Riding the Clerk of the Peace was paid a salary, with a small variable amount in fees. In a few Counties he was paid a fixed sum by the deputy clerk, who was responsible for the duties of the office and received the fees and emoluments. In 1844, the Justices of the Peace in Somerset petitioned for legislation to empower Quarter Sessions to fix a salary to be paid to Clerks of the Peace in lieu of all fees and emoluments at that time received by them.[5] Seven years later Parliament

---

[1] S. and B. Webb, *op. cit.*, p. 505, note 3.
[2] House of Commons: *Reports from Committees*, 1834, vol. xiv, p. 146.
[3] *Ibid.*, p. 18.
[4] House of Commons: *Accounts and Papers*, 1845, vol. xxxvi, p. 265.
[5] House of Commons: *Journal*, 1844, vol. 99, p. 249.

authorised the payment of Clerks of the Peace by salary in lieu of fees, the amount to be recommended by Quarter Sessions and approved by the Secretary of State.[1] During the next few years the Home Secretary gave his approval to applications from many Counties, and by 1861 four-fifths of the Clerks of the Peace received fixed salaries of between £80 and £1,600 a year.[2] In 1894 a salary was paid in every County, and in many all fees received by the Clerk were paid into the County fund; in some Counties the staff was paid out of the County fund, in others it was partly so paid. The net emolument in Lancashire was £3,000 a year, in Durham £2,000; in other Counties it ranged between £200 and £1,730.[3]

(5) *Professional Qualifications and Social Background.*

It is probable that the early Clerks of the Peace were recruited from the attorneys and apprentices-at-law whom King Edward I in 1292 had directed his judges to provide for every County. As already mentioned, it was their duty to act as attorney for the King before the Justices, and they may be assumed to have had a legal training. Information about individuals below the highest rank in this century is haphazard, but it appears likely that the Clerk of the Peace was usually a substantial person in his County, often a landholder or a prominent officer in a large household. He belonged to the class whose executive and administrative services were the mainspring of local government and who formed the link between the Counties and the central government. Many who were Clerks of the Peace served also as Escheators, Sheriffs, Under-Sheriffs, Coroners, Town Clerks and Members of Parliament and acted on judicial and administrative commissions. Many of them were officers of the Duchy of Lancaster, Feodaries, Stewards, Bailiffs and Under-Bailiffs. Others served the Duchy of Cornwall in the like capacities. In the North Riding the succession of Clerks of the Peace included substantial tenants and officials of the Honor of Richmond.

Clerks of the Peace appointed by letters patent in reward for previous service to the King include a Clerk of the Signet, a Coroner and Attorney in the King's Bench, an under-clerk in the Royal kitchen, and a Clerk of the Wardrobe of Robes and of the King's Beds in England. Some of these, no doubt, paid little attention to the duties of the office and performed them by deputy, while retaining for themselves the greater part of the profits. Others were diligent in the office, and the most eminent of them made a valuable contribution to the sources for the history of the Justices of the Peace. Robert Repynghale, appointed for life Clerk of the Peace in Lincolnshire in 1448, had been King's serjeant and Clerk of the Signet, had given good service in the Royal foundations at Eton and Cambridge, and had received grants of the bailliage of several Honors. His family appears to have retained records of its activities in the Commission of the Peace and from them and other records he compiled a collection of precedents for Justices of the Peace, including the earliest known example of the charge to jurors.[4]

[1] 14 & 15 Victoria, cap. 55, sec. 9.

[2] House of Commons: *Accounts and Papers*, 1861, vol. 51, pp. 459–474.

[3] House of Commons: *Accounts and Papers*, 1894, vol. 71, pp. 5–13.

[4] B. H. Putnam: *Proceedings before the Justices of the Peace, Edward III to Richard III* (Ames Foundation, 1938) pp. 20–25.

PLATE VI

JOHN MARRIOTT DAVENPORT
CLERK OF THE PEACE FOR OXFORDSHIRE
1831-1881

THE ORIGIN AND OFFICE OF CLERK OF THE PEACE

The Act of 1545 required that the Clerk of the Peace should be instructed in the laws of the Realm and able to occupy the office, and it placed his appointment in the hands of the Custos Rotulorum. Often the person appointed was a friend or dependant of the Custos, such as his steward or local agent. Professionally he was likely to be a barrister or an attorney. As may be seen from the biographical notes to the lists printed below, Clerks of the Peace filled every kind of local office, and were the executive officers of all manner of public bodies, while some attained eminence in the social, political or business life of the Country. Francis Milles, who was for more than twenty years Clerk of the Peace for Hampshire, had been Sub-Warden of All Souls' College, Oxford, and secretary to Sir Francis Walsingham, Queen Elizabeth's Secretary of State. He was Clerk of the Privy Seal and Member of Parliament for Poole and Winchester.

Several Clerks of the Peace held office on various County Committees during the Commonwealth, and one, Andrew Broughton, the Clerk of the Peace for Kent, was Mayor of Maidstone and Member of Parliament for Kent and Maidstone. As Clerk of the High Court of Justice in 1649 he read the death sentence on King Charles I. At the Restoration he was proclaimed a regicide and fled the country to die in exile. George Leeman, a nineteenth century Clerk of the Peace for the East Riding of Yorkshire, who was a Deputy Lieutenant for the North Riding, Member of Parliament for York, Lord Mayor of York, and chairman of the North Eastern and the York, Newcastle and Berwick railways and of the Railway Association, is commemorated by his statue outside York station. James Preston, father and son, Clerks of the Peace successively for the North Riding from 1736 to 1787, were noted racehorse owners. The father, on the point of death after an accident at York races, begged his patron, the Lord Lieutenant, to appoint his son, a boy of sixteen, to succeed him. This he did. Twenty-five years later the son died of a fall from his horse after a race meeting.

It is clear that from the seventeenth century onwards his other interests must, for many a Clerk of the Peace, have overshadowed his duties in that office. It was a part-time office, though a lucrative one; from 1688 it was in practice a freehold office for life, with little control by the Justices of the Peace. If the Clerk of the Peace performed the office himself, he was likely to regard Quarter Sessions as one of his clients, perhaps an important one, but having a claim on only a limited part of his time. Frequently he appointed a deputy,[1] as he was authorised by statute to do, subject to the approval of the Custos Rotulorum and the Justices. The deputy, probably a solicitor or attorney practising in the County, might undertake the whole of the work. The Webbs,[2] in their study of County administration, came to the conclusion that the post of Deputy Clerk of the Peace was held almost as a hereditary possession by the principal firm of solicitors in the County town, one of the partners in which personally attended the Justices' meetings, drafted their formal resolutions and advised them in matters of law, but left all the other work to his clerks. Everything beyond the criminal business of Quarter Sessions, the orders desired by private suitors, and those absolutely required by law tended to be neglected. The Minutes of proceedings in the eighteenth century

[1] In 1834 the office was performed by deputy in thirteen counties, and partly by deputy in two others (House of Commons: *Reports from Committees*, 1834, vol. 14, p. 277).

[2] *English Local Government: the Parish and the County* (London, 1906), p. 504.

reveal, say the Webbs, the natural tendency of a solicitor's office to regard all administration as merely a matter of executing legal documents.

In the eighteenth and nineteenth centuries the office of Clerk of the Peace in some Counties remained for long periods in a single family: sometimes it passed to another member of the same firm, though of a different name. In Cumberland the Simpson family held the office from 1690 to 1768, and the Hodgsons from 1809 to 1942. In Dorset the Fooks family held it from 1826 to 1925. In Lincolnshire there are the Denshire and Brackenbury families, in Northamptonshire the Markhams, in Surrey the Lawsons, and in Lancashire the Rigby-Kenyon dynasty ran from 1589 to 1780.[1] A notion that the office might be regarded as a hereditary fee is suggested by the Will of Edmund Millicent, Clerk of the Peace for Suffolk, who died in 1623. He there requested the Custos Rotulorum to grant the office to his brother-in-law and another person in trust to pay the testator's debts and provide his children's portions, holding the office during the minority of the testator's son, to whom it was to be granted when he attained the age of twenty-one. In return, the Custos was to receive a piece of plate worth £20 out of the profits of the office each year, and his receiver, solicitor, and other servants were to have a gold ring worth £1 out of the first year's profits. Millicent's request was not granted. In other cases sons acted jointly with their fathers, and William Ring, who resigned the Clerkship of the Peace for Somerset in 1740 to be succeeded by his son, was thereupon appointed deputy to him.

In the nineteenth century the office is almost entirely in the hands of practising solicitors and attorneys. The parliamentary return of 1845 names the profession of all Clerks of the Peace, except two who have no profession. There are five barristers and a coroner; all the rest are solicitors and attorneys. The picture is much the same in 1894, when another return was made of the salaries and fees of Clerks of the Peace. One of the questions asked was whether the Clerk carried on private practice as a solicitor. Most of the replies were that he did, though some said their official duties prevented them from giving time to their private practice.

The Clerk of the Peace and Clerk of the County Council after 1888.[2]

Broadly speaking, the Local Government Act of 1888 transferred to the new County Councils the administrative functions of the Court of Quarter Sessions, as distinct from the judicial and licensing functions which were retained by the Justices of the Peace. It provided that the Clerk of the Peace should also act as Clerk of the County Council, which should be responsible for his payment. The power of appointment and removal of the Clerk was transferred from the Custos Rotulorum to the Standing Joint Committee of Quarter Sessions and the County Council, but no change was made in the tenure of the office, and he

[1] For the story of the ruinous family litigation over the clerkship in Lancashire see J. J. Bagley: *Kenyon v. Rigby* (Historic Society of Lancashire and Cheshire, cvi) pp. 35–56.

[2] Acknowledgment is made to Mr. Bernard Kenyon, Clerk of the Peace and of the County Council of the West Riding of Yorkshire, on whose memorandum submitted in 1958 to the Society's Parliamentary and General Purposes Committee this section largely draws.

PLATE VII

SIR RICHARD NICHOLSON
CLERK OF THE PEACE FOR HERTFORDSHIRE,
MIDDLESEX AND LONDON

1865-1913

was still able to act by deputy. Subject to the directions of the Custos, the Clerk of the Peace and of the County Council was to have charge of the records of the County. He remained a part-time officer, though the forces were already at work which were to necessitate the conversion of the office into a full-time appointment in the course of the next half-century.

The case of *Thornely v. Leconfield*, the work of the Royal Commission on Local Government, and the effect of the Local Government (Clerks) Act of 1931 upon the tenure of the two offices, are all mentioned in the *Introduction*.[1] The Act of 1931 was followed and in part repealed by the Local Government Act of 1933, so that the earlier Act is now restricted to provisions which relate primarily to Clerks of the Peace of Counties and to their deputies and staff. The present procedure on a vacancy occurring in the office of Clerk of the Peace is that the appointment is filled by the Court of Quarter Sessions. The office may still be linked with that of Clerk of the County Council, as by the Act of 1933 the County Council must, when appointing their Clerk, ascertain whether he would be willing to accept the office of Clerk of the Peace, and consider, in consultation with the Chairman of Quarter Sessions, his fitness for that office. Similarly, under the Act of 1931, on the office of Clerk of the Peace becoming vacant, the County Council must inform the Court of Quarter Sessions whether the person appointed to be Clerk of the County Council would be willing to accept the office of Clerk of the Peace. If he is so willing, he is deemed to have been so appointed, unless within six months of the vacancy occurring, or such further period as may be allowed by the Home Secretary, Quarter Sessions appoint some other person as Clerk of the Peace.

There are no statutory qualifications for the appointment of Clerk of the Peace or Clerk of the County Council, but the nature of the duties and the importance of the offices demand a high standard of legal qualifications and administrative experience. The Clerk of the Peace performs all duties necessary for the business of the Justices in General and Quarter Sessions, and by virtue of his office is Clerk to the Licensing Committee which exercises the functions of Quarter Sessions as confirming authority and compensation authority. The Clerk of the County Council performs his duties in accordance with the directions of the Council, and these directions may be contained in standing orders, or resolutions of the Council, or may be assumed from long continued practice approved or acquiesced in by the Council. In practice he acts as the principal administrative officer of the Council, and among his more important functions are the co-ordination of the work of the several committees of the Council, and the guidance of the Council on matters of policy.

A Clerk of the Peace of a County appointed after the passing of the Act of 1931 solely to that office, without at the same time being Clerk of the County Council, does not vacate his office on attaining the age of sixty-five years. The Act provides that, apart from voluntary resignation, the office becomes vacant on his becoming incapable through permanent ill-health, but it is otherwise subject to determination only in the event of misconduct in the execution of his office or otherwise, which the Court of Quarter Sessions considers to render him an unfit or improper person to hold the office. A Clerk of the Peace who is also Clerk of the County Council vacates both offices on resignation of one of them. He is then ineligible for reappointment as Clerk of the Peace, but may be reappointed Clerk of the County Council.

[1] *Supra*, p. 13.

If both offices are held by the same person, they terminate on his attaining the age of sixty-five years, but reappointment is possible, at the wish of both parties, for successive periods not exceeding twelve months each. A Clerk of the County Council holds office during the pleasure of the County Council, subject to the consent of the Minister of Housing and Local Government to his dismissal. If the Clerk so dismissed is also Clerk of the Peace, holding office during good behaviour, it seems probable that he will retain the Clerkship of the Peace and hold it by the same tenure as if he had been appointed to that office only.

The salary of the Clerk of the Peace is fixed by Quarter Sessions, subject to an appeal to the Home Secretary either by the County Council or by the Clerk. If he is also Clerk of the County Council, the County Council must appoint such staff as it thinks necessary to assist him in carrying out his duties as Clerk of the Peace; this staff forms part of the staff of the County Council and receives out of the County Fund such salaries as the Council may fix. If the Clerk of the Peace is not also Clerk of the County Council, it seems that the salary should include the remuneration of the staff, other than the salary of a Deputy Clerk, as no other provision appears to be made for the appointment and payment of staff in such cases. In either case, the salary is payable by the County Council out of the County fund, but all fees and costs received by the Clerk of the Peace and not expressly excluded when the salary is fixed must be paid into the County fund. The salary of the Clerk of the County Council is determined by the Council and is subject to the approval of the Minister of Housing and Local Government. It is inclusive, and all fees and costs payable to the Clerk are to be paid over to the County fund, except so far as they are expressly excluded when the salary is fixed.

The Lists of Clerks of the Peace and Sources of Information.

Generally speaking, it has only been possible to compile with certainty as to dates of appointment and relinquishment of office lists of Clerks of the Peace for the last two centuries, the period for which Quarter Sessions records survive for most Counties. During this period, these records may be expected to indicate changes in the Clerkship of the Peace as they occur. In the earlier surviving records often no mention is made of such changes, and the periods of service of particular Clerks have to be deduced from incidental evidence of their activity. It may be that the Clerks of the Peace, who were responsible for the making of the records of the Courts, did not consider their own appointments as acts of the Court to be recorded, until it became customary for a formal instrument of appointment to be made under the seal of the Custos Rotulorum, probably in the eighteenth century when such instruments had to be enrolled in the Exchequer. As late as 1696, Judges of the Common Pleas and King's Bench could consider an oral appointment made in Quarter Sessions to be valid. In the case of *Owen v. Saunders*[1] in that year, Sir John Treby, Chief Justice of the Common Pleas, held that before the Act of 1545 the Clerk of the Peace was constituted by *parol* only, and that since that time and since the Act of 1689 nomination by *parol* was possible and good in law. The same opinion was held by Lord Chief Justice Holt and the House of Lords.

[1] 1 Raymond's *Reports*, 158.

Quarter Sessions records in the custody of Clerks of the Peace exist for most Counties from the seventeenth or eighteenth century. In some few Counties they survive from the middle of the sixteenth century. For the medieval period, over fifty rolls of proceedings before the Justices of the Peace survive among the public records, and one in private hands. Mostly these rolls were specially compiled for the information of the King's Bench. References to their compilers, the Clerks of the Peace, occur very infrequently in them.

To supply deficiencies in the information obtainable from the records of Quarter Sessions, and especially to identify the Clerks of the Peace during the first three centuries of the office, recourse has been had to public records where evidence of their activity is to be found. The most important series for this purpose is the Pipe Roll, the annual roll on which is recorded the audit of the Sheriffs' accounts, extending from the twelfth century to 1832. By statutes of 1388 and 1390, the Justices of the Peace below the rank of banneret were paid wages of four shillings a day, and their Clerk two shillings, for the time of their attendance at Quarter Sessions, out of the fines and amercements arising and issuing out of the same Sessions. Payment was made by the Sheriff and indentures were made witnessing it. The Sheriff produced his indenture on his account at the Exchequer as evidence supporting his claim to an allowance of the amount paid, and the details contained in it were entered on the Pipe Roll recording the account. Ideally there should be an annual entry of this kind on the Pipe Roll for each County, except for the Palatinate Counties and Wales, whose Sheriffs did not account at the Exchequer at Westminster; and so there should be a record of the name of every Clerk of the Peace from 1390 to 1832.[1]

Fact falls far short of the ideal. No entry occurs if no Sessions were held, or if no return was made of the fines and amercements imposed, or if wages were not paid. For Cumberland and Westmorland there are no wages entries before the sixteenth century, and for Northumberland none before the late seventeenth. Often the return of fines and amercements was delayed and the Pipe Roll entry covers several years. During the fifteenth and sixteenth centuries there are many gaps in the record of the payment of wages, and towards the end of the seventeenth century the names of the Clerks of the Peace cease to be given. Precise indication of the date or even the Sessions when a new Clerk was appointed is infrequently given, and in the seventeenth and eighteenth centuries the Exchequer clerks often described the working Deputy Clerk of the Peace as Clerk of the Peace, an error common in all sources of this period, whether they are records of Quarter Sessions or of the Exchequer. A few of the Pipe Rolls between 1450 and 1690 have not been examined for the purpose of compiling the lists, which may to that extent be defective. To save time, alternate rolls during that period were omitted in the preliminary work, and not all the omissions have been made good.

To supplement the Pipe Rolls, use has been made of documents subsidiary to the Sheriff's accounts. These are the Indentures recording the payment of wages to Justices of the Peace and their Clerks, and the Estreats of fines and amercements at Quarter Sessions.

---

[1] The Pipe Roll was discontinued on the abolition of the Office of Lord Treasurer's Remembrancer in 1833. The audit of the Sheriffs' accounts then devolved upon the Commissioners of Audit, whose books do not record the statements of the wages paid to the Justices and Clerks of the Peace, though payment continued to be made until 1855, when the clauses of the Statutes of 1388 and 1390 which authorised it were repealed.

The Indentures are to be found among the Sheriffs' administrative accounts in the class of Exchequer, King's Remembrancer, Accounts Various. Comparatively few have survived. The Estreats of fines and amercements are the lists of financial penalties payable into the Exchequer as a result of the activities of the Court and extracted, or estreated, from the record thereof. The Estreats vary in form: but often they contain the names of the Justices and the name of the Clerk of the Peace present at each Sessions in the year. In such cases they indicate the Sessions at which a change in the holder of the Clerkship was made. The Exchequer, King's Remembrancer, class of Estreats runs from the thirteenth century to the nineteenth, but is far from complete. A few Estreat Rolls, properly belonging to this class, are to be found in the class of Exchequer, King's Remembrancer, Sheriffs' Accounts; others in that of Exchequer, King's Remembrancer, Accounts Various; and others in that of Exchequer, Lord Treasurer's Remembrancer, Rolls of Estreats. The last named class should, strictly speaking, consist of the duplicates delivered into the Exchequer under the Act of 1670.

The Estreats from 1670 are usually signed by the Clerk of the Peace or his deputy: the latter sometimes describes himself as Clerk of the Peace. From the same date, draft Estreats are to be found occasionally among the records of Quarter Sessions in the custody of Clerks of the Peace. The delivery of the Estreats at the Exchequer was recorded on rolls, supplementary to the Memoranda Rolls, which are to be found among the Miscellaneous Rolls of the Lord Treasurer's Remembrancer. The entries on these rolls, which run from 1507 to 1603 and from 1683 to 1719, with a few rolls of later date, usually give the period they cover and the name of the person who delivered them at the Exchequer. From 1670, as has been said above, this is the Clerk of the Peace or his deputy, but sometimes it is an agent: and again the deputy is sometimes described as Clerk of the Peace.

In 1717 the Court of Exchequer made a general order that Clerks of the Peace, *inter alios*, should enter their appointments in the Lord Treasurer's Remembrancer's Office on a roll kept by the Filacer, who was to make a list from it for the Barons of the Exchequer, so that they might know who were the proper persons to deliver Estreats before them. As a result of this order, two rolls of entries of appointments of Clerks of the Peace and their deputies, 1720 to 1830, were made. They are to be found in the Exchequer, Lord Treasurer's Remembrancer, class of Miscellaneous Rolls. They are continued in a register in the Exchequer, King's Remembrancer, class of Miscellaneous Books, series II. The entries give the substance of the instruments of appointment, including the date and period of tenure. Not all appointments appear to have been enrolled or registered. Appointments were also in some cases enrolled on the Lord Treasurer's Remembrancer's Memoranda Roll until the abolition of that office in 1833, and afterwards on the King's Remembrancer's Memoranda Roll.

The lists of Clerks of the Peace for Durham and Lancashire have been compiled from the Palatinate and Duchy records respectively.

The Sheriffs of the Welsh Counties and of Cheshire did not account at the Exchequer at Westminster, and the audit of their accounts is not recorded on the Pipe Roll. Instead they accounted, under the Act of 1542, before the King's Auditors, who were to make due allowance to the Sheriff for the money he paid in wages to the Justices and the Clerk of the Peace. The documents brought by the Sheriff to his account included a claim for the money paid to the Justices and their Clerk, but their names are not given. They also included certified copies of the Estreats of fines, etc. at Quarter Sessions, the originals of which were delivered to the appropriate local Welsh Exchequer. These sometimes give the name of the Clerk of the Peace as attending Sessions and are sometimes certified by him or his deputy. This series forms the Exchequer, Land Revenue, class of Sheriffs' Accounts for Wales and Cheshire, and extends from the middle of the sixteenth century to the nineteenth. It has many gaps and for some Counties has contributed very few names to the lists.

In the fifteenth and early sixteenth centuries, some Clerks of the Peace, as has already been stated, were appointed by Royal letters patent. These grants of office are enrolled on the Patent Rolls of the Chancery, and references to them are to be found in the printed *Calendars of Patent Rolls* and *Letters and Papers, Foreign and Domestic, Henry VIII*. Some search has also been made in the Chancery class of Warrants for the Great Seal, and in the Signet Office Docquet Book for 1534 preserved among the Miscellaneous Books of the Duchy of Lancaster.

Other classes of public records which have yielded information about Clerks of the Peace are those of Chancery Proceedings, Star Chamber Proceedings and Court of Requests Proceedings. The State Papers Domestic contain many returns made by Clerks of the Peace to the Privy Council, particularly during the sixteenth and seventeenth centuries, and some names have been forthcoming from this source. Volume 104 of the State Papers Domestic, Elizabeth, contains a report of the allotments of Justices of the Peace within their several divisions in the divers Shires, giving the names of resident Justices and of Coroners and Clerks of the Peace. This volume has provided an almost complete list of Clerks of the Peace, and of some of their Deputies, for a date at which most other sources fail. The records of the Commissions on Fees, 1622 to 1640, contain a few returns by Clerks of the Peace, some of which give the names of the Clerks for a particular County for the preceding half century. Most of these records are in the Exchequer, King's Remembrancer, class, Commission on Fees; others are in the same department's class of Miscellaneous Books, series II, and others in the State Papers Domestic, Charles I, while some are in the British Museum, Additional Manuscripts, and others in the Tanner Manuscripts in the Bodleian Library. Besides these manuscript sources, use has been made of the *Calendars of Manuscripts* issued by the Historical Manuscripts Commission, the printed *Reports of Cases* and the *Parliamentary Papers*. Other sources of information on particular Clerks of the Peace are mentioned in the biographical notes below.

LISTS OF PERSONS
KNOWN TO HAVE HELD THE OFFICE OF
CLERK OF THE PEACE IN THE COUNTIES OF ENGLAND AND WALES
FROM 1360 TO 1960
AND THE OFFICE OF CLERK OF THE COUNTY COUNCIL
FROM 1889 TO 1960

E

ANGLESEY

From	To	Surname	Forenames	Birth	Death	Biographical Notes

CLERKS OF THE PEACE from 1542

From	To	Surname	Forenames	Birth	Death	Biographical Notes
1542		REYNOLDS	John			*Alias* John ap Rhydderch. Also Clerk of the Peace for Merioneth and Clerk of the Crown in both Counties, appointed by letters patent, 24th January, 33 Henry VIII; Yeoman of the Guard. Co-defendant, with the Clerk of the Peace for Caernarvonshire, in suit brought by the inhabitants of the respective Counties, complaining of "demands for excessive fees and excessively frequent appearances from persons bound over to the Peace" (see Lewis, *An Inventory of the Early Chancery Proceedings concerning Wales*, p. 17).
1573	1575	BUCKLEY	John			
1582	1587	HOLLAND	Edward			
1589	1592	BULKLEY	George			
1593	1604	GRYFFITH	William			
1605	1635	BOULTON	Richard			
1641	1654	HUGHES	William			
1671	1672	MICHAELL	Richard			
1674	1684	ROBERTS	Owen			
1725		LEWIS	Richard			
1768	1788	LEWIS	Ambrose			Of Beaumaris; Attorney.
1788	1799	POOLE	Richard	1736	1799	Of Beaumaris; Attorney.
1799	1809	GRINDLEY	Samuel		c.1810	
1810	1840	POOLE	William Price	1779	1841	
1841	1860	OWEN	Owen	1797	1866	Of Beaumaris; Attorney (admitted 1820).
1861	1874	OWEN	Richard	1837	1875	Of Beaumaris; Attorney (admitted 1860).
1875	1889	GRIFFITH	John Lloyd	1839	1902	*Elected to Society, June* 1880. Solicitor (admitted 1865). M.A. (Cantab). Clerk to the Justices, Holyhead and Valley division; Clerk of the Holyhead U.D.C; Chairman of the Board of Guardians.

CLERKS OF THE PEACE AND OF THE COUNTY COUNCIL from 1889

From	To	Surname	Forenames	Birth	Death	Biographical Notes
1889	1901	GRIFFITH	John Lloyd	1839	1902	See above.
1902	1912	ROBERTS	John Rice	1837	1920	Solicitor (admitted 1864). M.A. Justice of the Peace; Deputy Lieutenant. Town Clerk of Beaumaris; Clerk to the Borough Justices.
1912	1939	JONES	Walter Owen	1881	1939	*Elected to Society, May* 1912. Solicitor (first class honours; Clement's Inn and Daniel Reardon prizes; Scott Scholarship) (admitted 1904). B.A. (Wales). M.B.E., 1918. Clerk to the Lieutenancy.
1940		JONES	William	1896		*Elected to Society, March* 1941. Solicitor (admitted 1920). O.B.E., 1946. Secretary to the Advisory Committee; Clerk of the Magistrates' Courts Committee; Part-time Member of Local Government Commission for Wales, 1959; Member of General Optical Council, 1959. Second Lieutenant, Manchester Regiment and Royal Air Force, 1914–18 War.

DEPUTY CLERKS OF THE PEACE AND OF THE COUNTY COUNCIL from 1889

From	To	Surname	Forenames	Birth	Death	Biographical Notes
1912	1949	EVANS	Thomas Roberts	1860	1949	*Deputy Clerk of the Peace only.* Solicitor (admitted 1887). Clerk of the Holyhead U.D.C.
1948		DAVIES	Idris	1916		*Elected to Society, January* 1949. *Deputy Clerk of the County Council, 1948; Deputy Clerk of the Peace, 1949; Acting Clerk, 1959.* Solicitor (admitted 1946). LL.B. (London). Flight Lieutenant, Royal Air Force, 1939–45 War.

BEDFORDSHIRE

From	To	Surname	Forenames	Birth	Death	Biographical Notes

CLERKS OF THE PEACE from 1390

From	To	Surname	Forenames	Birth	Death	Biographical Notes
1390	1422	BEDFORD	Thomas			Feodary of the Duchy of Lancaster in Bedfordshire and Buckinghamshire, 1400 (see Somerville, *Duchy of Lancaster*, I, p. 591); Member of Parliament for Bedford, 1386, 1393–94, 1397, 1402, 1413. Also Clerk of the Peace for Buckinghamshire, 1390–97.
1423	1426	ABBOT	John			
1426	1438	STRATTON	Thomas			
1438	1443	LUTY	Thomas			Almost certainly Thomas Lucy, whose family held Manors of Carlton and Wilden, c.1400.
1450	1453	TOPPYNG	Henry			
1461	1466	HOLME	John			
1480	1502	SPENCER	Robert			Probably, with his joint successors, member of family holding Manor of Rowlands (Parish of Cople).
1506	1530	SPENCER / SPENCER	John / Thomas			Brothers: appointed jointly in survivorship for Bedfordshire and Huntingdonshire by letters patent, 28th November, 22 Henry VII. John appointed Town Clerk of Bedford on 20th June, 1514.
1537		JEKES	John			Appointed by Letters patent, 16th May, 29 Henry VIII.
1538	1545	MORGAN	David			
1551	1575	ADAMS	William			
1578	1615	PAYNE	William		1624	Attorney of the Court of Common Pleas; Town Clerk of Bedford; held Manors of Hinwick and Podington.
1619	1627	AUDLEY	Thomas			Attorney of the King's Bench and of the Bedford Court of Pleas; owned property in Houghton Conquest and neighbourhood.
1631	1637	HORNE	Thomas			
1639		FARRER	Thomas			
1645		MORDANT	John			
1651	1658	CHRISTIE	Thomas	1622	1697	Attorney of the Bedford Court of Pleas; acted for Bedford Corporation in legal matters, 1650–60; Member of Parliament for Bedford, 1685–87, 1689, 1690–95. The forename John appears in the Pipe Rolls, 1653–56, probably in error for Thomas.
1660	1689	COBB	Paul	1633	1699	Of family owning Manor in Parish of Sharnbrook; Attorney of the Bedford Court of Pleas; elected Mayor of Bedford, 1683; named as Mayor in new Charter of the Borough, 11th July, 1684; visited John Bunyan in Bedford Gaol, 3rd April, 1661. Bunyan's account of their conversation, as set out in his *Grace Abounding to the Chief of Sinners*, 1666, is printed as Appendix I, below.
1689	1696	PENINGTON	James			
1697	1710	FIRBY	John	c.1622	c.1714	
1711	1714	HOOPER	Edmund Giles			Michael Dymoke, Deputy Clerk of the Peace, is described in the Estreats, probably incorrectly, as Clerk of the Peace, 1711, 1713 and 1714.
1714	1716	PEPIATT	John			
1721	1731	REDDALL	Ambrose	1671	1731	
1731	1744	MALLETT	Gabriel			
1745	1755	GOLDSMITH	William		1755	Family held Manors of Chalton and Streatley.
1756	1759	HORTON	Henry		1759	
1759	1775	MARSH	John			
1775	1798	PALMER	Jeremy Fish	1739	1798	Registrar of Archdeaconry of Bedford, 1775–78; his family held property at Ickwell.
1798	1847	PEARSE	Theed, the elder	c.1764	1847	*Elected to Society, May* 1825. Attorney. Town Clerk of Bedford. His nephew, subsequently Mr. Justice Hawkins (Baron Brampton), articled to him, c.1836.
1847	1857	PEARSE	Theed, the younger	1793	1857	*Elected to Society, November* 1843. Son of Theed Pearse, the elder; Attorney. Town Clerk of Bedford.
1857	1889	PEARSE	Theed William	1819	1890	*Elected to Society, November* 1857. Son of Theed Pearse, the younger; Attorney (admitted 1843). Town Clerk of Bedford; Clerk to the Justices, Bedford division, and to the Bedford Borough Justices.

BEDFORDSHIRE (*Continued*)

From	To	Surname	Forenames	Birth	Death	Biographical Notes

CLERKS OF THE PEACE AND OF THE COUNTY COUNCIL from 1889

From	To	Surname	Forenames	Birth	Death	Biographical Notes
1889	1890	PEARSE	Theed William	1819	1890	See above.
1890	1891	BUTTERWORTH	Alexander Kaye	1854	1946	*Elected to Society, June* 1890. Solicitor (admitted 1884). LL.B. (London). In 1891, joined the service of the Great Northern Railway Company, afterwards becoming its General Manager; knighted, 1914.
1891	1925	MARKS	William Woodfine	1855	1925	*Elected to Society, June* 1891. Solicitor (admitted 1878). Clerk to the Lieutenancy; Honorary legal adviser to the Bedford County Hospital, the Bedfordshire Nursing Association and the Bedfordshire Territorial Association; Honorary Secretary and co-Founder of the Bedfordshire Cricket Club. Previously senior prosecuting solicitor to the Liverpool Corporation; commended by the Home Secretary for his work in connection with the prosecutions arising out of the Fenian riots; also responsible for the prosecution of Mrs. Maybrick, convicted of murdering her husband with arsenic taken from flypapers, a *cause célèbre* believed to be the first capital charge in England arising out of arsenical poisoning, 1889. Gave evidence before the Royal Commission on County Boroughs, 1923.
1925	1951	GRAHAM	Joseph Bramwell	1885	1951	*Elected to Society, June* 1915. Solicitor (admitted 1913). C.B.E., 1945; Deputy Lieutenant. Clerk to the Lieutenancy; Under Sheriff; Clerk to the Bedfordshire and Northamptonshire Joint Board for the Mentally Defective; Honorary Legal Adviser to the Bedford County Hospital and to the Bedfordshire Territorial Association. Previously Deputy Clerk of the Peace and of the County Council.
1951		BREWIS	George Oldfield	1909		*Elected to Society, May* 1939. Solicitor (admitted 1931). Secretary to the Advisory Committee; some time Clerk to the Magistrates' Courts Committee. Previously Deputy Clerk of the Peace and of the County Council of Gloucestershire and Deputy Clerk of the County Council of Nottinghamshire. Major, Royal Artillery, 1939–45 War.

DEPUTY CLERKS OF THE PEACE prior to 1889

From	To	Surname	Forenames	Birth	Death	Biographical Notes
1712		DYMOKE	Michael			See note to Edmund Giles Hooper, Clerk of the Peace, 1711–14, above.
1715		WEALE	William			
1717	1718	HOWAN	Thomas			

DEPUTY CLERKS OF THE PEACE AND OF THE COUNTY COUNCIL from 1889

From	To	Surname	Forenames	Birth	Death	Biographical Notes
1915	1925	GRAHAM	Joseph Bramwell	1885	1951	Subsequently Clerk of the Peace and of the County Council, see above.
1930	1941	NEW	Leslie Penry	1895		*Elected to Society, May* 1930. Solicitor (admitted 1920). Subsequently Clerk of the Peace and of the County Council of Cornwall, *q.v.*
1942	1945	POOLE	John Rea	1915		*Elected to Society, July* 1942. Solicitor (admitted 1938). M.A. (Cantab). Previously assistant solicitor, Dorset County Council; subsequently emigrated to Australia and qualified as Barrister-at-law.
1946	1951	STEVENS	Frederick Brewerton	1913		*Elected to Society, January* 1946. Solicitor (admitted 1938). LL.B. (London). Under Sheriff; Clerk to Rating Appeals Tribunal. Wing Commander, Royal Air Force, 1939–45 War. Went into private practice, 1951.
1951	1960	LINES	David Hugo	1920		*Elected to Society, July* 1951. Solicitor (admitted 1948). B.A. (Oxon). Clerk to the Lieutenancy; some time Clerk of Rating Valuation Panel. Previously assistant solicitor, Bedfordshire County Council. Lieutenant, R.N.V.R., 1939–45 War. Resigned to enter private practice in 1961.
1959		BACKHOUSE	Horace John	1922		*Elected to Society, December* 1960. *Deputy Clerk of the Peace,* 1959; *Deputy Clerk of the County Council,* 1961. Solicitor (admitted 1949). Previously assistant solicitor, Bedfordshire County Council. Squadron Leader, R.A.F., 1939–45 War; D.F.C.

BERKSHIRE

From	To	Surname	Forenames	Birth	Death	Biographical Notes
CLERKS OF THE PEACE from 1392						
1392	1395	HUSCARLE	Brian			Probably also Coroner for Berkshire.
1419	1441	BOTELER	William			
1442	1445	WODEHILL	John			
1449	1466	POMEROY	John			
1466	1472	POMEROY	William			
1472	1496	VINCENT	Thomas			
1499	1507	HUNSDON	Peter			
1515	1518	BOND	William			
1519	1520	CASTELL	Edmund			
1520	1523	ANDREWS	Richard			Also Clerk of the Peace for Oxfordshire, 1512–16, 1521.
1523	1541	EDMUNDS	William			Also Clerk of the Peace for Oxfordshire, 1528; Mayor of Reading, 1540 and 1550; Member of Parliament for Reading, 1522–23.
1542		BOTHE	Christopher			Appointed Clerk of the Peace and of the Crown by letters patent, 18th January, 33 Henry VIII; the King's footman.
1542	1543	GAYRE	Robert			
1544	1583	NOKE	Thomas			Probably attorney of Wokingham.
1585	1589	NEWBURY	Henry			
1590	1592	HAMOND	Francis			Probably of Wokingham.
1593	1617	WELLINGTON	George			Of Wokingham. Appointed Town Clerk of Wokingham for life by Charter of Incorporation, 1612.
1619	1621	HICKS	Fabian			
1623	1641	HERON	James		1663	Born at Elyng Green, Oxfordshire. Town Clerk and Clerk of the Peace of Abingdon, 1628–63; Governor, Christ's Hospital, Abingdon, 1645–63, and Treasurer, 1647, 1653, 1657–61.
1648	1657	WARCUPP	Robert			
1661	1664	HERCY	John			Probably of Cruchfield House, Bray. Under-Steward of Windsor, 1638–51; Recorder of Wokingham, 1662–69.
1688	1691	GROVE	William			Previously Deputy Clerk of the Peace.
1691	1697	STEVENS	Henry			
1697	1718	STEVENS	Thomas			
1719	1733	GRAPE	James			Possibly of Wokingham. Treasurer of Militia, 1715; Clerk, Windsor Borough Court of Record, c.1730.
1733	1738	GRAPE	Richard			
1738	1741	TYRRELL	Avery		1741	Of New Windsor; Attorney.

PLATE VIII

The County Hall and Market Place
Abingdon, Berkshire

1850

From	To	Surname	Forenames	Birth	Death	Biographical Notes
1742	1759	BROOKLAND	William		1759	Of New Windsor; Attorney. Treasurer of Berkshire, 1742–59; Recorder of Windsor, 1750–59; Common Clerk of Windsor, 1743–59; Under Sheriff, 1739–40 and 1741–42; Clerk to General Meeting of the Lieutenancy.
1759	1781	TYRRELL	William		1781	Of Inner Temple and New Windsor. Under Sheriff, 1755–56; Assistant Recorder, Windsor, 1759; Town Clerk, Windsor, 1759–74, 1780; Clerk to General Meeting of the Lieutenancy; Clerk to Committee to enlarge powers of Thames Navigation Commissioners, 1770.
1781	1790	PIGGOTT	Francis		1790	Of Pelling Place, Old Windsor.
1790	1811	HILL	Joseph		1811	Of Wargrave.
1811	1840	BUDD	William	1759	1840	*Elected to Society, November 1824.* Of Newbury; Attorney. Friend and correspondent of William Cobbett, who dedicated his book "*The Woodlands*" (London, 1825) to him in the terms set out at the foot of this list. Summarily dismissed from office after expressing in Court his opinion of Quarter Sessions generally and various members in particular; reinstated after apologising by affidavit. Previously Deputy Clerk of the Peace.
1840	1877	MORLAND	George Bowes	1808	1878	*Elected to Society, November 1840.* Of Abingdon; Attorney (admitted 1829). Governor, Christ's Hospital, Abingdon, 1833–78; Clerk to the Governors, 1842–65.
1877	1889	MORLAND	John Thornhill	1838	1923	*Elected to Society, June 1879.* Of Abingdon; eldest son of George Bowes Morland; Harrow School and Trinity College, Cambridge; M.A. Solicitor (admitted 1863). Justice of the Peace, 1878–1923. Clerk to the Governors of Christ's Hospital, Abingdon from 1865; Councillor, Abingdon Borough Council, 1866–83; Alderman, 1883–1923; six times Mayor between 1874 and 1902. Coxed Cambridge University Boat, 1859 and 1860. Previously Deputy Clerk of the Peace.

CLERKS OF THE PEACE AND OF THE COUNTY COUNCIL from 1889

From	To	Surname	Forenames	Birth	Death	Biographical Notes
1889	1923	MORLAND	John Thornhill	1838	1923	See above. Also Clerk to the Lieutenancy from 1893; Honorary Freeman of Abingdon, 1922.
1923	1951	NEOBARD	Harold John Cooke	1886		*Elected to Society, May 1922.* Of Reading; Solicitor (admitted 1912). O.B.E., 1919. Justice of the Peace; Deputy Lieutenant. Clerk to the Lieutenancy; Secretary to the Advisory Committee; Clerk to the Berkshire and Reading Fire Authority from 1947. Previously Deputy Clerk of the Peace and of the County Council. Captain, 7th Battalion Royal Berkshire Regiment, 1914–18 War; Chevalier, Legion of Honour.
1951		DAVIES	Ellis Roger	1905		*Elected to Society, October 1936.* Solicitor (admitted 1929). Clerk to the Lieutenancy; Secretary to the Advisory Committee; Clerk of the Magistrates' Courts Committee; Clerk to the Berkshire and Reading Fire Authority. Previously assistant solicitor, Swansea County Borough and Manchester City Councils, and Deputy Clerk of the Peace and of the County Council of Berkshire.

From	To	Surname	Forenames	Birth	Death	Biographical Notes

DEPUTY CLERKS OF THE PEACE prior to 1889

From	To	Surname	Forenames	Birth	Death	Biographical Notes
1667	1675	CHAMPION	George			
1676	1688	GROVE	William			Subsequently Clerk of the Peace, see above.
1777		BROOKLAND	George			Of New Windsor.
1781	1790	PAYN	James		1822	Of Maidenhead; Attorney. Also County Treasurer, 1779–1822; Recorder of Maidenhead, 1800–22; Clerk to General Meeting of the Lieutenancy; Clerk to General Meeting, Reading and Hatfield Turnpike Trust, from 1786; Clerk to Inclosure Commissioners, Braywick, 1786.
1790	1811	BUDD	William	1759	1840	Subsequently Clerk of the Peace, see above.
1877		MORLAND	John Thornhill	1838	1923	Subsequently Clerk of the Peace, see above.

DEPUTY CLERKS OF THE PEACE AND OF THE COUNTY COUNCIL from 1889

From	To	Surname	Forenames	Birth	Death	Biographical Notes
1891	1907	MORLAND	Francis John	1867	1907	*Elected to Society, June* 1891. Third son of John Thornhill Morland; Solicitor (admitted 1890).
1910	1917	THORNE	Harold Underhill Hatton		1917	*Elected to Society, June* 1911. Solicitor (admitted 1904). Lieutenant-Colonel, Royal Berkshire Regiment and Royal Scots, 1914–18 War; killed in action.
1917	1921	CHAMBERS	Charles Graham		1921	*Elected to Society, January* 1918. Solicitor (admitted 1896). B.A. (Oxon). Acting Deputy, 1914–17.
1922	1923	NEOBARD	Harold John Cooke	1886		Subsequently Clerk of the Peace and of the County Council, see above.
1923	1926	JOHNSON	Arthur Ainslie	1889	1933	*Elected to Society, December* 1923. Solicitor (admitted 1912). Subsequently Clerk of the Peace and of the County Council of Salop, *q.v.*
1927	1932	KELLY	John Bradshaw	1889		*Elected to Society, October* 1927. Solicitor (admitted 1922). Subsequently Clerk of the Peace and of the County Council of Huntingdonshire, *q.v.*
1933	1935	JAMES	Charles Bartleet	1904		*Elected to Society, July* 1933. Solicitor (admitted 1928). Previously assistant solicitor, Worcestershire County Council.
1935	1951	DAVIES	Ellis Roger	1905		Subsequently Clerk of the Peace and of the County Council, see above.
1951		BOYNTON	John Keyworth	1918		*Elected to Society, March* 1951. Solicitor (Cliffords Inn and Mellersh prizes) (admitted 1939). LL.B. (London). Previously assistant solicitor, Derbyshire County Council. Captain, Royal Armoured Corps, 1939–45 War; M.C.

Dedication of The Woodlands, *referred to in the note on William Budd, Clerk of the Peace 1811–1840, supra:*

Kensington, 1st December, 1825.

My dear Sir,

> *The following work, which relates to a subject that has, in all the various situations of life, even from my boyish days, engaged my attention and been to me a source of delight, I dedicate to you, in order that my children may, when they can no longer hear it from their father's lips, have, what I hope may be, a lasting record of an expression of that great respect and affection that I bear you, on account of your numerous excellent qualities; and particularly on account of your constant exertions in behalf of that now-suffering class, without whose labour there can be no trees to shade, no houses to lodge, no clothes to cover, and no corn to feed us. Those exertions, so judicious, so unwearied and so free from all ostentation, are the subject of admiration with all who have the happiness to know you; but, I trust with no one in a higher degree than with*

Your faithful Friend,

And most obedient Servant,

WILLIAM COBBETT.

BRECONSHIRE

From	To	Surname	Forenames	Birth	Death	Biographical Notes
		CLERKS OF THE PEACE from 1542				
1542	1545	THOMAS	William			Appointed Clerk of the Peace and of the Crown for Breconshire, Montgomeryshire and Radnorshire by letters patent, 21st January, 33 Henry VIII.
1545		CLERC	William			Appointed Clerk of the Peace and of the Crown for the same three Counties by letters under the Signet, 21st May, 37 Henry VIII, the offices being in the King's hand by reason of felonies committed by William Thomas, who had fled the realm; the appointment to take effect from the preceding Lady Day and to be confirmed by letters patent after Thomas had been convicted by due course of law. Clerc is called "our well beloved servant" and was possibly the clerk in the privy seal office who was the King's private secretary. If so, he probably held these offices only until Thomas obtained a pardon.
c.1573		WINTER	John			
1662	1673	LLOYD	John			
1677	1679	WILLIAMS	W. M.			
1681	1686	POWELL	William			
1687	1688	HARCOURT	Godfrey			
1690	1692	WILLIAMS	William			
1701		HIGGONS				
1768	1810	WILKINS	John			Appears as Deputy Clerk of the Peace and Deputy Prothonotary from 1761.
1812	1846	POWELL	John		1846	In the period 1768–1846 the Clerk of the Peace signed the Estreats by surname only. "Powell" appears 1812–27 and 1839–46 and was probably the same individual in both periods.
1846	1873	WILLIAMS	Edward		1873	
1873	1883	THOMAS	David		1883	
1883	1889	THOMAS	Henry Edgar		1909	*Elected to Society, May* 1884. Solicitor (admitted 1873).

CLERKS OF THE PEACE AND OF THE COUNTY COUNCIL from 1889

From	To	Surname	Forenames	Birth	Death	Biographical Notes
1889	1909	THOMAS	Henry Edgar		1909	See above.
1909	1926	HARRIES	Henry Frederick William		1926	*Elected to Society, May* 1909. Solicitor (admitted 1886). B.A.
1926	1946	JOLLY	Albert			*Elected to Society, June* 1926. Solicitor (admitted 1907).
1946		WELLS	Charles Martin Sidney	1908		*Elected to Society, January* 1945. Solicitor (admitted 1932). M.A. (Cantab); L.M.T.P.I. Clerk to the Lieutenancy; Secretary to the Advisory Committee; Clerk of the Magistrates' Courts Committee, and of the Breconshire and Radnorshire Joint Fire Brigade Committee. Previously Deputy Clerk of the Peace and of the County Council of Lincolnshire (Parts of Kesteven).

BUCKINGHAMSHIRE

From	To	Surname	Forenames	Birth	Death	Biographical Notes
		CLERKS OF THE PEACE from 1390				
1390	1397	BEDFORD	Thomas			Feodary of the Duchy of Lancaster in Buckinghamshire and Bedfordshire, 1400 (see Somerville, *Duchy of Lancaster*, I, p. 591); Member of Parliament for Bedford, 1386, 1393–94, 1397, 1402, 1413. Also Clerk of the Peace for Bedfordshire, 1390–1422.
1391		REYNER	John			Probably as deputy for Thomas Bedford.
1422	1427	COLLES	William			
1431	1445	LOUGHTON (LANGTON)	John			Party to a fine concerning lands at Great and Little Kimble, Stone, Hartwell, etc., 1438 (see Lipscomb, *History and Antiquities of the County of Buckingham*).
1448	1456	PYGOT	Richard			Probably identical with the Richard Pygot whose career is given in Somerville, *op. cit.*, p. 473.
1460	1461	MARTYN	John			One John Martyn, senior, of Whitchurch, party to a fine, 1469, and served as one of the two representatives in Parliament for Chepping Wycombe, 1441 and 1446 (see Lipscomb, *op. cit.*).
1508		CROSSE	George			
1526	1528	EDE	John			One John Ede resident at Weston Turville, 1528 (see *V.C.H.*).
1536		ELMYS (ELMES)	John			John Elmes was Lord of Overbury Manor, Great Missenden, c.1540 (see *V.C.H.*).
1541	1547	LYON	John			The rectory and advowson of Halton granted to John Lyon and Alice, his wife, 1547 (see Lipscomb, *op. cit.*).
1551		HORNYOLD	Anthony			
1555	1559	SEYMOUR	John			
1561	1569	CLERKE	Henry			
1575	1583	HATLEY	Richard			
1584	1593	REYNOLDS	Timothy			
1597	1602	ALLEN	Robert			
1603	1613	STYLE	John			Brass to John Style, d.1613, in Little Missenden church.
1615	1616	MOORE	Thomas			One Thomas Moore bailiff of Buckingham, 1629 (see Lipscomb, *op. cit.*).
1617	1627	HATCHE	John		?1635	One John Hatch owned the "Red Lion" at Fenny Stratford, and land in Wavendon (see *V.C.H.*).
1629		COCKES	John			
1631	1652	PERKINS	Christopher			
1647		WALBANCK	John			In Quarter Sessions records for Easter, 1647, "John Walbanck, the Clerk of the Peace, was fined 100 marks for not attending the Court with the Records of the Court, and for neglect of duty". Christopher Perkins, described as Deputy Clerk of the Peace, was also fined 40 marks on the same occasion.
1653	1658	DAWSON	Thomas			
1664	1677	WELLS	Henry			
1678	1681	WEEDON	Thomas			Of Wedon Hill, Amersham.
1681	1686	WEEDON	Cavendish			Of Wedon Hill; grandson of Sir Henry Croke, of Chequers. Justice of the Peace, 1686–87.
1686		GILMORE	William			Of Amersham.
1686	1688	NEALE	Francis		1726	Of Ivinghoe. Dismissed from Clerkship when Thomas Wharton became *Custos Rotulorum*.
1689	1702	SMITH	Thomas			Appointed in place of Francis Neale by Thomas Wharton and retained Clerkship until Wharton's influence waned with accession of Queen Anne.
1702	1726	NEALE	Francis		1726	Re-appointed when William, Lord Cheyne and Viscount Newhaven (Wharton's antagonist) became *Custos Rotulorum*. Also County Treasurer.

BUCKINGHAMSHIRE (*Continued*)

From	To	Surname	Forenames	Birth	Death	Biographical Notes
1726		WELLES	Samuel			Several persons bearing this name were attorneys at Chepping Wycombe.
1727	1764	HAYTON	William	?1709	1764	Of Ivinghoe; grandson of Francis Neale. Also County Treasurer.
1764	1787	MINSHULL	William	1732	1807	Of Aylesbury. Also County Treasurer. Receiver General of Land Tax; Clerk to Wendover-Buckingham Turnpike Trust; Clerk to Inclosure Commissioners of Hartwell and Stone, 1776–77.
1787	1813	CHAPLIN	Acton		1815	Of Aylesbury. Deputy Lieutenant, 1815. Also County Treasurer. Joint Clerk of Grand Junction Canal Company and of the Commissioners, 1793–1805.
1813	1838	TINDAL	Thomas	1783	1850	*Elected to Society, November* 1813. *Honorary Secretary,* 1822–38. Of Aylesbury; brother of Sir Nicholas Conyngham Tindal, Chief Justice of the Common Pleas; Attorney. Also County Treasurer until 1850; Under Sheriff. His son, Acton Tindal (see below) served as his deputy from the year 1834.
1838	1880	TINDAL	Acton	1811	1880	*Elected to Society, May* 1834. *Honorary Secretary,* 1838–80. Of Aylesbury; son of Thomas Tindal and grandson of Acton Chaplin; Attorney (admitted 1834). Under Sheriff; Lord of the Manor of Aylesbury, 1849; Clerk to the Justices, Aylesbury division; Clerk of the Aylesbury Guardians, 1835–38; Registrar of the Archdeaconry of Buckinghamshire.
1880	1888	BAYNES	Edward Robert	1816	1898	*Elected to Society, June* 1881. Of Aylesbury; descended from Thomas Wogan, one of the Regicides; Solicitor (admitted 1838). Clerk to the Lieutenancy; Clerk to the Justices, Brill division; Clerk to the Commissioners of Taxes for the Three Hundreds of Ashendon, and Clerk to the Committee of Visitors to the County Lunatic Asylum.
1888	1889	CROUCH	William	1855	1928	*Elected to Society, November* 1888. Of Aylesbury; Solicitor (admitted 1877).

CLERKS OF THE PEACE AND OF THE COUNTY COUNCIL from 1889

From	To	Surname	Forenames	Birth	Death	Biographical Notes
1889	1924	CROUCH	William	1855	1928	See above. Also Secretary to the Advisory Committee.
1924	1955	CROUCH	Guy Robert	1890	1956	*Elected to Society, June* 1919. Of Aylesbury; younger son of William Crouch; Solicitor (admitted 1912). LL.B. Deputy Lieutenant. Clerk to the Lieutenancy from 1946; Secretary to the Advisory Committee; Clerk of the Magistrates' Courts Committee. Previously Deputy Clerk of the Peace and of the County Council. Major, Oxfordshire and Buckinghamshire Light Infantry, 1914–18 War; commanded Buckinghamshire Battalion, 1922–26; Brevet Colonel 1926; Honorary Colonel (jointly with H.R.H. the Duchess of Kent), 645 L.A.A. Regiment, R.A., 1951–55; M.C., T.D.
1955		MILLARD	Richard Edward	1914		*Elected to Society, October* 1945. Solicitor (admitted 1936). LL.B. Clerk to the Lieutenancy; Secretary to the Advisory Committee; Clerk of the Magistrates' Courts Committee. Previously Deputy Clerk of the Peace and of the County Council.

DEPUTY CLERKS OF THE PEACE AND OF THE COUNTY COUNCIL from 1889

From	To	Surname	Forenames	Birth	Death	Biographical Notes
1913	1916	CROUCH	Lionel William	1886	1916	*Elected to Society, June* 1913. Of Aylesbury; elder son of William Crouch; Solicitor (admitted 1909). Captain, Oxfordshire and Buckinghamshire Light Infantry, 1914–18 War; killed in action.
1916	1924	CROUCH	Guy Robert	1890	1956	Subsequently Clerk of the Peace and of the County Council, see above.
1924	1945	FOLEY	Henry Arthur	1896		*Elected to Society, April* 1924. Solicitor (admitted 1923). Captain, Somerset Light Infantry, 1914–18 War; M.C. Went into private practice, 1945.
1945	1955	MILLARD	Richard Edward	1914		Subsequently Clerk of the Peace and of the County Council, see above.
1955		HAMILTON	Richard Neville Dalton	1913		*Elected to Society, January* 1955. Solicitor (admitted 1936). LL.B. Major, Royal Army Ordnance Corps, 1939–45 War.

CAERNARVONSHIRE

From	To	Surname	Forenames	Birth	Death	Biographical Notes
CLERKS OF THE PEACE from 1541						
1541	1549	GRUFFYDD *alias* VAUGHAN	John			*Alias* John ap Robert. Appointed Clerk of the Peace and of the Crown by letters patent, 6th July, 33 Henry VIII; described as "of London"; Clerk of Faculties in Chancery. Co-defendant, with Clerk of the Peace for Anglesey and Merioneth, in suit brought by the inhabitants of the respective Counties, complaining of "demands for excessive fees and excessively frequent appearances from persons bound over to the Peace" (see Lewis, *An Inventory of the Early Chancery Proceedings concerning Wales*, p. 17).
1552	1572	WYNN	Owen		1590	Son of John Wyn ap Meredydd of Gwydir, the *Custos Rotulorum.*
1573	1578	WYNN	John	1553	1627	Son of Maurice Wyn of Gwydir, the *Custos Rotulorum;* All Souls College, Oxford, and Furnival's Inn, Inner Temple. Knighted, 1606; created Baronet, 1611. Member of Parliament for County, 1586–87; High Sheriff of Caernarvonshire, 1587–88 and 1603; of Merioneth, 1588–89 and 1600–01; of Denbighshire, 1606–07; Member of the Council in the Marches, 1608; *Custos Rotulorum* of the County, 1618. See plate II.
1580	1587	SPICER	William			Second son of William Spicer of Caernarvon.
	1604	JONES	Morris		1604	Of Llanbeblig; son of natural daughter of John Wyn ap Meredydd of Gwydir (see notes to Owen Wynn, above); married into Craflwyn family of Beddgelert. Baron of Exchequer of North Wales; Steward to Bishop of Bangor. Elegy composed by Hugh Machno at his death (see N.L.W. Brogyntyn MS. 3, p. 167).
1606	1646	JONES	Richard			Younger brother of Morris Jones, see above.
1646	1659	HUGHES	Ellis			Described in 1639–40 as servant of Richard Jones, his predecessor.
1660		SPICER	William			Son of William Spicer, deputy constable of Caernarvon Castle· great-great-nephew of William Spicer, Clerk of the Peace, 1580–87; Major in Royalist army; "friend and old fellow-prisoner" of Sir Richard Grosvenor. Appointed by Sir Owen Wynn, *Custos Rotulorum,* who shortly afterwards died; not re-appointed by Sir Richard Wynn, the succeeding *Custos Rotulorum.*
1660	1670	WILLIAMS	John			Had his "chamber" at Conway and his house "neere Pont-y-Go", Denbighshire.
1671	1674	TRYGARN	Morris			Son of Robert Trygarn of Trygarn, and of Bryncroes; Attorney.
1676	1687	JONES	Edward			Had his "chamber" at Caernarvon.
1698	1703	MAURICE	John			
1703	1704	WILLIAMS	Gruffydd			
1705		PARRY	John			
1705	1708	GLYNNE	Thomas			
1709	1752	ELLIS	Henry	c.1675	1752	Son of Thomas Ellis of Llandegwning and Porthdinllaen; uncle of the Rev. John Ellis, Archdeacon of Merioneth; Solicitor. Under Sheriff, 1703.
1752	1764	PARRY	Vincent	1721	1767	Great-grandson of Geoffrey Parry of Rhydolion, an officer in Cromwell's army and a Puritan preacher; brother of Love Parry of Madryn.
1764	1768	LEWIS	John			Of Plas yn Rhiw, Llyn; son of Thomas Lewis, County Coroner.
1769	1792	HOWARD	Richard	1744	1792	Son of Robert Howard, Collector of H.M. Customs at Conway; Attorney. Constable of Caernarvon Castle.

From	To	Surname	Forenames	Birth	Death	Biographical Notes
1792	1815	HUGHES	John			
1815	1823	POOLE	Owen Anthony		1823	Of Caernarvon; son of Richard Poole of Cae Nest and of Beaumaris, Clerk of the Peace for Merioneth, 1783–99; Solicitor.
1823	1858	POOLE	Richard Anthony	1797	1863	*Elected to Society, April* 1845. Of Cae Nest, Merioneth, and Twthill, Caernarvonshire; nephew of Owen Anthony Poole; Solicitor. Also County Treasurer. Subsequently Justice of the Peace and Deputy Lieutenant.
1858	1878	POOLE	William Thearsby	1825	1893	Son of Richard Anthony Poole; Solicitor (admitted 1847). Subsequently Justice of the Peace and Deputy Lieutenant.
1878	1881	BARBER	Henry			Of Bangor; Solicitor (admitted 1841). Clerk to the Lieutenancy. Part author of *A History of Friars School, Bangor*.
1881	1889	BODVEL-ROBERTS	John Hugh	1837	1904	*Elected to Society, June* 1886. Solicitor (admitted 1860). Coroner. Assumed the name Bodvel, his wife being descended from the Bodvels of Bodfel, Llyn.

CLERKS OF THE PEACE AND OF THE COUNTY COUNCIL from 1889

From	To	Surname	Forenames	Birth	Death	Biographical Notes
1889	1903	BODVEL-ROBERTS	John Hugh	1837	1904	See above.
1903	1932	BODVEL-ROBERTS	Arthur John			*Clerk of the Peace only.* Son of John Hugh Bodvel-Roberts; Solicitor (admitted 1894). Clerk to the Lieutenancy.
1903	1917	ROBERTS	Sir John (Thomas)	1861	1917	*Clerk of the County Council only.* Solicitor (admitted 1884). Mayor of Caernarvon, 1909–11; knighted on occasion of Investiture of the Prince of Wales at Caernarvon, 1911.
1917	1922	MORRIS	John Jones		1922	*Elected to Society, March* 1918. *Clerk of the County Council only.* Of Portmadoc; Solicitor (admitted 1880). Member of Caernarvonshire County Council, 1895–1917.
1922	1945	JONES	David Griffith	1877		*Elected to Society, December* 1923. *Clerk of the County Council,* 1922; *Clerk of the Peace,* 1932. Solicitor (admitted 1908). Clerk to the Lieutenancy, 1932–33; Clerk to the Gwyrfai R.D.C., 1914–22; Member of Caernarvonshire County Council, 1910–22; Member of the Welsh Gorsedd of Bards; Chairman of the Properties Board of the Presbyterian Church of Wales; founder-member and treasurer of the Caernarvonshire Historical Society.
1945	1956	JONES	Gwilym Thomas	1908	1956	*Elected to Society, July* 1942. Solicitor (admitted 1937). M.A. (Wales). F.S.A. Clerk to the Lieutenancy; Secretary to the Advisory Committee; Clerk of the Magistrates' Courts Committee and of the Gwynedd Police Authority; Legal Adviser to the Gwynedd River Board; Secretary of the North Wales Combined Probation Area Committee; Deputy Clerk of the Snowdonia National Park Joint Advisory Committee. Vice-Chairman of the Council of the National Eisteddfod of Wales; Member of the Welsh Gorsedd of Bards; founder-member and honorary secretary of the Caernarvonshire Historical Society.

CAERNARVONSHIRE *(Continued)*

From	To	Surname	Forenames	Birth	Death	Biographical Notes
1956		OWEN-JONES	John Eryl	1912		*Elected to Society, April* 1946. Solicitor (admitted 1938). M.A. (Cantab); LL.B. (Wales). Clerk to the Lieutenancy; Secretary to the Advisory Committee; Clerk of the Magistrates' Courts Committee and of the Gwynedd Police Authority; Secretary of the North Wales Combined Probation Area Committee; Deputy Clerk of the Snowdonia National Park Joint Advisory Committee; Member of the Welsh Gorsedd of Bards; honorary secretary of the Caernarvonshire Historical Society. Previously assistant solicitor, Chester City Council, and Deputy Clerk of the Peace and of the County Council of Caernarvonshire. Squadron Leader, R.A.F. (Judge Advocate General's Department), 1939–45 War.

DEPUTY CLERKS OF THE PEACE prior to 1889

From	To	Surname	Forenames	Birth	Death	Biographical Notes
1546	1570	SMYTHE	John			Of Caernarvon.
1571	1575	JONES	Morris		1604	Subsequently Clerk of the Peace, see above; and see Flenley, *Calendar of the Register of the Council in the Marches of Wales*, p. 135.
1669	1670	VAUGHAN	John			
1815		WILLIAMS	William (?)			
1819	1820	PRICE	John			
1840		POWELL	Edward Griffith		1880	Of Coed Mawr; Attorney. Justice of the Peace; Deputy Lieutenant; High Sheriff, 1875.
1845		MILLINGTON	John			

DEPUTY CLERKS OF THE PEACE AND OF THE COUNTY COUNCIL from 1889

From	To	Surname	Forenames	Birth	Death	Biographical Notes
1894	1903	BODVEL-ROBERTS	Arthur John			*Deputy Clerk of the Peace only.* Subsequently Clerk of the Peace, see above.
1903	1917	ROBERTS	Sir John (Thomas)	1861	1917	*Deputy Clerk of the Peace only.* Simultaneously Clerk of the County Council, see above.
1917	1922	MORRIS	John Jones		1922	*Deputy Clerk of the Peace only.* Simultaneously Clerk of the County Council, see above.
1922	1932	JONES	David Griffith	1877		*Deputy Clerk of the Peace only.* Simultaneously Clerk of the County Council, and subsequently Clerk of the Peace and of the County Council, see above.
1932	1940	JONES	William	1896		*Elected to Society, March* 1941. Solicitor (admitted 1920). Subsequently Clerk of the Peace and of the County Council of Anglesey, *q.v.*
1942	1945	JONES	Gwilym Thomas	1908	1956	Subsequently Clerk of the Peace and of the County Council, see above.
1946	1956	OWEN-JONES	John Eryl	1912		Subsequently Clerk of the Peace and of the County Council, see above.
1956		HOPKINS	Garth			*Elected to Society, March* 1957. Solicitor (admitted 1947). Previously Deputy Clerk of the Cwmamman U.D.C., and assistant solicitor, Caernarvonshire County Council.

CAMBRIDGESHIRE

From	To	Surname	Forenames	Birth	Death	Biographical Notes
CLERKS OF THE PEACE from 1390						
1390	1392	BURGOYNE	John			
1392	1397	CANNE	Robert			
1397	1410	ALEYN	William			
1414	1428	TAILLARD	Walter			Steward for Duchy of Lancaster of Sutton and Potton (see Somerville, *Duchy of Lancaster*, I, p. 593).
1430	1443	PARYS	Richard			
1445	1485	BATTISFORD	John			
1486	1503	HUGHSON	Nicholas			
1506	1516	HILDERSHAM	Thomas			Appointed jointly in survivorship by letters patent, 28th November, 22 Henry VII.
1506		HUGHSON	William			
1517	1520	BURGEYNER	Thomas			
1521	1524	PYNE	John			
1528	1530	BREVENS	Baldwin			
1532		CHAPMAN	John			
1538		MYLSENT	John			Appointed Clerk of the Peace and of the Crown by letters patent, 18th March, 29 Henry VIII.
1538	1546	PYCHARD	Edward			
1550	1559	PECK	Robert			
1561	1563	WILCOK	Henry			
1567	1569	PECK	Robert			
c.1575		MILLICENT	Thomas			
1577	1599	COSYN	William			
1601	1619	FOLKES	Simon			
1621	1625	BECK	Roger			In the seventeenth century, the Sheriff accounted for payment to the Clerks of the Peace for both Cambridgeshire and Huntingdonshire without distinguishing them. Some Clerks may have acted for both Counties, and some may be wrongly ascribed in the lists.
1633		BECK	Roger (? George)			
1637	1641	BECK	George			
1651	1658	PERRY	James			
1662	1681	KING	Samuel			

CAMBRIDGESHIRE (*Continued*)

From	To	Surname	Forenames	Birth	Death	Biographical Notes
1691	1694	BALDWYN	Ralph			
1694	1711	SEYLIARD	Thomas			
1712	1740	LUCK	Thomas		c.1740	
1740	1756	YORK	Thomas			
1756	1764	MOORE	Thomas			
1764	1793	DAY	James			Previously Deputy Clerk of the Peace.
1793	1850	PEMBERTON	Christopher	c.1767	1850	*Elected to Society, November* 1813. Attorney, practised in Cambridge for more than 60 years. Buried at Newton, Cambridgeshire.
1850	1872	EVANS	Hugh Robert			*Elected to Society, May* 1850. Attorney (admitted 1827). Clerk to the Ely Justices; Deputy Registrar of the Diocese of Ely.
1872	1889	WORTHAM	Hale		1899	*Elected to Society, June* 1872. Solicitor (admitted 1844). Clerk to the Justices, Arrington and Melbourne divisions.

CLERKS OF THE PEACE AND OF THE COUNTY COUNCIL from 1889

From	To	Surname	Forenames	Birth	Death	Biographical Notes
1889	1899	WORTHAM	Hale		1899	See above.
1899	1912	GINN	Samuel Reuben	1852	1934	*Elected to Society, May* 1900. Solicitor (admitted 1873). Clerk to the Lieutenancy. Mayor of Cambridge, 1897–98.
1912	1945	TABRUM	Ashley	1879	1952	*Elected to Society, October* 1912. Magdalene College, Cambridge; Solicitor (Clement's Inn and Daniel Reardon prizes) (admitted 1903). O.B.E., 1920. Clerk to the Lieutenancy; Secretary to the Advisory Committee.
1945		PHYTHIAN	Charles	1905		*Elected to Society, June* 1945. Liverpool College; Solicitor (admitted 1930). Clerk to the Lieutenancy; Secretary to the Advisory Committee; Clerk of the Magistrates' Courts Committee. Captain, K.O.Y.L.I., 1939–45 War.

DEPUTY CLERKS OF THE PEACE prior to 1889

From	To	Surname	Forenames	Birth	Death	Biographical Notes
c.1575		PECK	Robert			
1693	c.1712	BUXTON	John			
1712		GOODALL	James			
1713	1722	STUTEVILLE	Thomas			
1722	1739	GOODALL	James			
1739	1740	WHITE	Andrew			
1758	1764	DAY	James			Subsequently Clerk of the Peace, see above.
1789		RANDALL	Edward			

DEPUTY CLERKS OF THE PEACE AND OF THE COUNTY COUNCIL from 1889

From	To	Surname	Forenames	Birth	Death	Biographical Notes
1929	1940	STRINGER	Philip Austin Selborne	1895		*Elected to Society, March* 1929. Solicitor (admitted 1922). Subsequently Clerk of the Peace and of the County Council of Wiltshire, *q.v.*
1946		HANN	William Liddell	1910		*Elected to Society, July* 1946. Solicitor (honours) (admitted 1932).

CARDIGANSHIRE

From	To	Surname	Forenames	Birth	Death	Biographical Notes
CLERKS OF THE PEACE from 1541						
1541		MOFFET	Robert			Appointed Clerk of the Peace and of the Crown for Cardiganshire, Carmarthenshire and Pembrokeshire by letters patent, 9th December, 33 Henry VIII; Groom of the Chamber.
c.1573			Thomas ap Harrie			Coroner.
c.1700	c.1709	LEWIS	David			
1734	1743	LLOYD	Thomas		1743	Dismissal by Quarter Sessions confirmed by King's Bench, Mich. 8 George II (2 Strange's Reports 996). Apparently reinstated.
1743	1746	MORGAN	John			
1747	1770	LLOYD	James	1721	1800	Of Ffosybleiddied; Barrister-at-law.
1770	1772	LLOYD	Jeremiah			
1772	1814	LLOYD	Herbert		1814	Attorney.
1814	1844	BENYON	John			Attorney.
1844	1888	ROBERTS	Frederick Rowland	1818	1888	Attorney (admitted 1839). Clerk to the Lieutenancy.

CLERKS OF THE PEACE AND OF THE COUNTY COUNCIL from 1889

From	To	Surname	Forenames	Birth	Death	Biographical Notes
1889	1906	FRYER	Henry Charles		1906	*Elected to Society, June 1894.* Wadham College, Oxford; B.A. Barrister-at-law. Deputy Lieutenant.
1907	1921	ROBERTS	Frederick Richard	1859	1921	*Elected to Society, March 1918.* Solicitor (admitted 1883). Clerk to the Lieutenancy. Previously Deputy Clerk of the Peace and of the County Council.
1921	1949	EVANS	Ivor	1881		*Elected to Society, May 1921.* Solicitor (admitted 1908). M.A. (Oxon). Clerk to the Lieutenancy; Clerk to the Commissioners of Taxes; Under Sheriff. Captain, Royal Artillery, 1914–18 War.
1949		CARSON	James Eric Rutherford	1915		*Elected to Society, November 1949.* University of Wales and St. John's College, Cambridge. LL.B. (Wales). Solicitor (admitted 1944). L.M.T.P.I. Clerk to the South Cardiganshire Water Board and to the Magistrates' Courts Committee.

DEPUTY CLERKS OF THE PEACE AND OF THE COUNTY COUNCIL from 1889

From	To	Surname	Forenames	Birth	Death	Biographical Notes
1889	1906	ROBERTS	Frederick Richard	1859	1921	Subsequently Clerk of the Peace and of the County Council, see above.
1907	1933	EVANS	Evan	1850	1933	Solicitor (admitted 1878).
1954	1955	GRIFFITHS	David Wynmor Lewis	1924		Solicitor (admitted 1950). LL.B. (Wales).
1958		JONES	David Alun Rhagfyr	1921		*Elected to Society, December 1958.* Solicitor (admitted 1951). LL.B. (Wales).

CARMARTHENSHIRE

From	To	Surname	Forenames	Birth	Death	Biographical Notes
		CLERKS OF THE PEACE from 1541				
1541		MOFFET	Robert			Appointed Clerk of the Peace and of the Crown for Carmarthenshire, Cardiganshire and Pembrokeshire by letters patent, 9th December, 33 Henry VIII; Groom of the Chamber.
c.1550		POWELL	John			Son of Thomas Powell of Llanwrda; great-grandfather of Sir John Powell, knight, 1633–96, puisne Judge of the King's Bench; great-great-grandfather of Sir Thomas Powell, baronet, 1664–1720, Attorney General of Carmarthen Circuit and Member of Parliament for Carmarthen, 1710–15.
c.1573		WILLIAMS	Thomas			
	c.1660	JONES	Richard			
1660	c.1682	LLOYD	John			
c.1682	c.1689	EVANS	John			Previously Deputy to John Lloyd, his predecessor.
c.1689	c.1700	LEWIS	Benjamin			
c.1700	c.1711	DAVIES	Morgan			Of Llangaing.
?1745		DAVIES	Richard			
1748	c.1755	PRICE	James			Of Cilgwyn, Parish of Myddfai; Attorney.
	1773	DAVIES	Evan	1724	1773	
c.1792	1799	LLWYD	Richard Jones	1756	1799	Of Pantglas; Barrister-at-law.
1799	1833	MORGAN	Charles	1757	1833	Solicitor. Registrar of the Diocese of St. David's.
1833	1844	JONES	Edward	1779	1844	Solicitor. Justice of the Peace for Breconshire; four times Mayor of Llandovery.
1844	1886	BISHOP	Charles	1799	1886	Of Dolgarreg, near Llandovery; Solicitor (admitted 1824). Father of Judge Bishop, Judge of County Court Circuits No. 28 (1886–91) and No. 31 (1891–1910).
1886	1889	JONES	Thomas	1826	1901	*Elected to Society, May* 1888. Son of Edward Jones, see above; Solicitor (admitted 1852). Clerk to the Lieutenancy; County Treasurer; Registrar and High Bailiff of Llandovery County Court; Clerk to the Guardians and to the County Roads Board. Seven times Mayor of Llandovery.
		CLERKS OF THE PEACE AND OF THE COUNTY COUNCIL from 1889				
1889	1901	JONES	Thomas	1826	1901	See above.
1901	1931	NICHOLAS	John William	1862	1931	*Elected to Society, May* 1903. Son of Thomas Nicholas of Pentre Parr, Llandilo; Solicitor (admitted 1886). Clerk to the Lieutenancy; Secretary to the Advisory Committee; Coroner. First Chairman of Llandilo U.D.C. Author of two novels.
1931	1952	JOHNS	Daniel	1884	1952	*Elected to Society, June* 1931. Son of John Johns of Parceithyn, Llanstephan; Barrister-at-law, Middle Temple (called 1922). M.Sc. (Wales). O.B.E., 1946. Clerk to the Lieutenancy; Secretary to the Advisory Committee; Clerk of Carmarthenshire and Cardiganshire Joint Fire Brigade Committee. Some time member of Carmarthen Borough Council; Organising Secretary of County Branch of National Farmers' Union, to 1923.
1952		THOMAS	Wynne Simpson	1912		*Elected to Society, November* 1952. Son of Edgar Thomas, M.B.E., of Llwynhendy, near Llanelly; Solicitor (admitted 1936). Clerk to the Lieutenancy; Secretary to the Advisory Committee; Clerk of the Magistrates' Courts Committee; of the Carmarthenshire and Cardiganshire Joint Fire Brigade Committee and of the Carmarthenshire and Cardiganshire Police Authority. Previously assistant solicitor, Llanelly Borough and Carmarthenshire County Councils. Major, Royal Artillery, 1939–45 War; Despatches.
		DEPUTY CLERKS OF THE PEACE AND OF THE COUNTY COUNCIL from 1889				
1942	1948	MILLS-OWEN	Richard Hugh	1910		*Elected to Society, July* 1942. Solicitor (first class honours: Cliffords Inn prize) (admitted 1932). Subsequently in Colonial Legal Service, Kenya; later Judge of Supreme Court, Hong Kong.
1956		PEREGRINE	Gwilym Rhys			*Elected to Society, July* 1956. Solicitor (admitted 1949). Captain, General List, 1939–45 War.

CHESHIRE

From	To	Surname	Forenames	Birth	Death	Biographical Notes
CLERKS OF THE PEACE from 1538						
1538		FLETEWODE	John			Appointed by letters patent, 27th December, 30 Henry VIII.
1571	1582	BANESTER	John			
c.1582	1583	BRAMLEY				
1583	1604	WERDEN	Richard			
1604	1614	WHITBY	Robert			
1614	1626	MAYNWARINGE	Peter			Previously Deputy Clerk of the Peace.
1627	1650	MOLAND	John			
c.1650	1659	HOUGHTON	William			
1660	1680	COBBE	William			
1684	1691	ASHETON	Samuel			
1692	1713	JACKSON	William			Previously Deputy Clerk of the Peace.
1717	1734	TAGG	Thomas			Previously Deputy Clerk of the Peace.
1761	1781	WIDDENS	William			
1782	1817	STEPHENS	John			
1818	1845	POTTS	Henry	1777	1848	*Elected to Society, March* 1845. Probably son of Charles Potts, Deputy Clerk of the Peace; Solicitor.
1846	1860	JOHNSON	George			
1861	1889	POTTS	Charles William	1815	1890	*Elected to Society, April* 1874. Son of Henry Potts, see above; Solicitor (admitted 1837). Previously Deputy Clerk of the Peace.

CLERKS OF THE PEACE AND OF THE COUNTY COUNCIL from 1889

From	To	Surname	Forenames	Birth	Death	Biographical Notes
1889	1890	POTTS	Charles William	1815	1890	See above.
1890	1931	POTTS	Reginald	1856	1931	*Elected to Society, June* 1890. Son of Charles William Potts; Solicitor (admitted 1878). Clerk to the Lieutenancy, 1919–31.
1932	1952	SCRIMGEOUR	Geoffrey Cameron	1887	1959	*Elected to Society, December* 1926. Son of the Rev. R. C. Scrimgeour of Sibton, Suffolk; Rugby School and Caius College, Cambridge; B.A. Solicitor (admitted 1912). Hon. LL.M. (Liverpool); O.B.E., 1948; Deputy Lieutenant, 1952. Clerk to the Lieutenancy; Clerk to Cheshire Police Authority; to Visitors under Lunacy Acts; to Cheshire Rivers Board; to Cheshire Rivers Catchment Board; to North-East Cheshire Rivers Catchment Board; to Rivers Birket and Fender Catchment Board. Previously Deputy Clerk of the Peace and of the County Council. Major, Royal Artillery, 1914–18 War; D.S.O., M.C. and bar; Despatches.

CHESHIRE (*Continued*)

From	To	Surname	Forenames	Birth	Death	Biographical Notes
1952	1959	CARSWELL	Hugh	1892		*Elected to Society, December 1935.* Son of William Carswell of Capesthorne, Cheshire; Oundle School; Solicitor (admitted 1919). Hon. LL.M. (Liverpool). Clerk to the Lieutenancy; to Cheshire Police Authority; to Visitors under Lunacy Acts; to Cheshire Rivers Board; Clerk of the Magistrates' Courts Committee. Previously Deputy Clerk of the Peace and of the County Council. Captain, Cheshire Regiment, 1914–18 War.
1959		HETHER-INGTON	Arthur Carleton	1916		*Elected to Society, July 1946.* Son of A.S. Hetherington of Silloth, Cumberland; St. Bees School; Solicitor (admitted 1938). Clerk to the Lieutenancy; to Cheshire Police Authority; to Visitors under Lunacy Acts; Clerk of the Magistrates' Courts Committee. Previously Deputy Clerk of the Peace and of the County Councils of Cumberland and of Cheshire. Lieutenant Colonel, Royal Artillery, 1939–45 War; M.B.E. (Mil.).

DEPUTY CLERKS OF THE PEACE prior to 1889

From	To	Surname	Forenames	Birth	Death	Biographical Notes
	1614	MAYNWARINGE	Peter			Subsequently Clerk of the Peace, see above.
c.1649	c.1672	MILTON	Humphrey			
c.1681	c.1684	LARGE	John			
c.1691	1692	JACKSON	William			Subsequently Clerk of the Peace, see above.
c.1714	1716	TAGG	Thomas			Subsequently Clerk of the Peace, see above.
c.1735	c.1760	LOWE	George			Always addressed as Clerk of the Peace, but signed documents as deputy. No record of another person as Clerk in this period.
c.1782	c.1810	POTTS	Charles			*Represented at first meeting of Society, March 1810.*
1841	1861	POTTS	Charles William			Subsequently Clerk of the Peace, see above.
1861	1889	ROBERTS	Thomas			*Elected to Society, June 1862.* Solicitor (admitted 1852).

DEPUTY CLERKS OF THE PEACE AND OF THE COUNTY COUNCIL from 1889

From	To	Surname	Forenames	Birth	Death	Biographical Notes
1889	1904	ROBERTS	Thomas			See above.
1904	1926	POTTS	Hubert		1931	Solicitor (admitted 1886).
1926	1932	SCRIMGEOUR	Geoffrey Cameron	1887	1959	Subsequently Clerk of the Peace and of the County Council, see above.
1933	1935	BRUTTON	Charles Phipps	1899		*Elected to Society, November 1932.* Solicitor (admitted 1926). Subsequently Clerk of the Peace and of the County Council of Dorset, *q.v.*
1936	1952	CARSWELL	Hugh	1892		Subsequently Clerk of the Peace and of the County Council, see above.
1952	1959	HETHER-INGTON	Arthur Carleton	1916		Subsequently Clerk of the Peace and of the County Council, see above.
1959		BOURNE	John Hugh Neville	1916		*Elected to Society, June 1959.* Solicitor (admitted 1941). Previously Assistant Clerk to Surrey County Council.

CORNWALL

From	To	Surname	Forenames	Birth	Death	Biographical Notes
		CLERKS OF THE PEACE from 1391				
1391	1410	KNIGHT	Henry			
1416	1418	POLREDEN	Paschoe			
1418	1419	TREWYK	John			
1419	1434	CAY	John			
1446	1462	UPTON	Elias			
1462	1466	CLAY	Robert			
1466		KYMPE	John			
1466	1467	CLAY	Robert			
1468	1470	WOLVEDON	Robert			
1484	1502	GAYER	John			
1507	1532	GAYER	Reynold			Appointed Clerk of the Peace and of the Crown for life by letters patent, 4th February, 22 Henry VII; confirmed, 8th May, 6 Henry VIII.
1518	1536	COKKE	Thomas			Appears to have acted as Clerk of the Peace, but was probably Deputy.
1532	1536	NANFAN	William			Appointed successor to Reynold Gayer by letters patent, 4th July, 24 Henry VIII.
1536	1551	GODOLPHIN (GODOLGHAN)	John			Appointed successor to William Nanfan by letters patent, 10th March, 27 Henry VIII.
1551	1552	GODOLPHIN (GODOLPAN)	William			
1554	1567	ROSCARROCK (RESTORRAK)	John			
1568	1589	GODOLPHIN	William			
1590	1605	EDGCOMBE	Peter			
1605	1627	DUNRICHE	Edmund			
1630	1632	SPRYE	John			
1632	1639	SPRYE	George			
1646	1652	TREGASLE (TREGATTLE)	John			
1653	1658	TREISE	John			
1658	1659	EDWARDS	Pasco			

CORNWALL (*Continued*)

From	To	Surname	Forenames	Birth	Death	Biographical Notes
1661	1669	PEARSE	Robert			
1669	1670	HORWELL	Thomas			
1670	1682	PEARSE	Robert			
1685	1709	HORWELL	Thomas			Referred to in *R. v. Lloyd* (see notes to Thomas Lloyd, Clerk of the Peace for Cardiganshire, 1734–43) as having been dismissed by Quarter Sessions under 1 William and Mary, c. 21. Horwell's case taken to the King's Bench, but he died before judgment given.
1713	1718	HERLE	Nicholas			
1728	1738	DOWN	Thomas		1738	
1739	1742	LYNE	Philip		1742	Of Liskeard; possibly identical with Philip Lyne, Town Clerk of Bossiney in 1733 (see Vivian, *Visitations of Cornwall*, p. 594).
1743	1769	LYNE	John			Son of Philip Lyne; of Liskeard; possibly identical with John Lyne, Deputy Town Clerk of Bossiney in 1733 and Town Clerk, 1763–81 (see Vivian, *op. cit.*); Vice-Treasurer of Gaol and Marshalsea money, 1743; Vice-Treasurer of the County, 1744–69.
1769	1793	HEXT	Samuel	1733	1800	Born at St. Austell; married, 1757, Margery, daughter of John Taylder of Helland (Mabe). Vice-Treasurer of the County.
1794	1822	HEXT	Thomas	1762	1822	Son of Samuel Hext.
1822	1840	COODE	Edward, the elder	1766	1845	Of St. Austell; married, 1790, Dorothy, daughter of Thomas Robins; Attorney. Also County Treasurer. Previously Deputy Clerk of the Peace.
1840	1865	COODE	Edward, the younger	1792	1865	Son of Edward Coode, the elder; married, 1820, Mary, daughter of P. Clements of Trevarner; Attorney. Also County Treasurer, 1845–62.
1865	1889	STOKES	Henry Sewell	1808	1895	*Elected to Society, June 1866.* Eldest son of Henry Stokes, proctor and notary of Gibraltar; married, 1834, Louisa Rachel Evans; Solicitor (admitted 1832); practised as advocate in Stannaries Court. Also County Treasurer. Mayor of Truro, 1856; Town Clerk of Truro, 1859. Wrote several volumes of poetry, 1830–84; Publisher of *The Cornish Guardian and Western Chronicle*, 1833–35.

CLERKS OF THE PEACE AND OF THE COUNTY COUNCIL from 1889

From	To	Surname	Forenames	Birth	Death	Biographical Notes
1889	1895	STOKES	Henry Sewell	1808	1895	See above.
1895	1898	COODE	William		1898	*Elected to Society, June 1896.* Solicitor (admitted 1861).
1898	1921	COWLARD	Christopher Lethbridge			*Elected to Society, March 1918.* Solicitor (admitted 1869).

From	To	Surname	Forenames	Birth	Death	Biographical Notes
1921	1930	PLATTS	Walter Leslie	1885	1958	*Elected to Society, June* 1921. Solicitor (admitted 1908). Secretary to the Advisory Committee. Subsequently Clerk of the Peace and of the County Council of Kent, *q.v.*
1930	1941	SHEERS	Thomas Angrave Homer	1881	1941	*Elected to Society, June* 1924. Of Truro; Solicitor (admitted 1902). Secretary to the Advisory Committee. Previously Deputy Clerk of the Peace and of the County Council.
1941	1946	NEW	Leslie Penry	1895		*Elected to Society, May* 1930. Solicitor (admitted 1920). Secretary to the Advisory Committee. Previously Deputy Clerk of the Peace and of the County Council of Bedfordshire. Captain, 5th Battalion, Bedfordshire Regiment, 1914–18 War.
1946		VERGER	Edward Thomas	1909		*Elected to Society, March* 1942. Solicitor (admitted 1933). Secretary to the Advisory Committee; Clerk of the Magistrates' Courts Committee. Previously Deputy Clerk of the Peace and of the County Council.

DEPUTY CLERKS OF THE PEACE prior to 1889

From	To	Surname	Forenames	Birth	Death	Biographical Notes
c.1575		BEAUCHAMP				
1578		FLEMING	Nicholas			
1590		WARMINGTON	Sampson			
	1605	BEAUCHAMP	William			
1705		PHILLIPS	John			
1710		BOOTH	Philip			
1711	1712	WALSH (WELSH)	Philip			
1794	1822	COODE	Edward, the elder	1766	1845	Subsequently Clerk of the Peace, see above.
c.1840	c.1865	CHILSON	William			

DEPUTY CLERKS OF THE PEACE AND OF THE COUNTY COUNCIL from 1889

From	To	Surname	Forenames	Birth	Death	Biographical Notes
1924	1930	SHEERS	Thomas Angrave Homer	1881	1941	Subsequently Clerk of the Peace and of the County Council, see above.
1941	1946	VERGER	Edward Thomas	1909		Subsequently Clerk of the Peace and of the County Council, see above.
1946		DORÉ	Clifford William dos Santos	1909		*Elected to Society, March* 1947. Solicitor (admitted 1932).

CUMBERLAND

From	To	Surname	Forenames	Birth	Death	Biographical Notes
CLERKS OF THE PEACE from c.1573						
c.1573		MIDLETON	John			
1578	1585	RAILTON	Anthony			
1586	1587	MIDDLETON	Christopher			
1588	1619	PEIRSON (PEARSON)	Richard			
1624	1625	SLEDDALL	Thomas			
1626	1635	CURWEN (CURWYN)	Anthony			
1661	1690	BENSON	William		c.1690	Acted occasionally as County Treasurer.
1690	1711	SIMPSON	Lancelot	1643	1711	Of Allerthwaite, near Penrith (see Dugdale, *Visitation of Cumberland*); Attorney. Under Sheriff, 1673; Seneschal of the Manors of Inglewood Forest; his Will, dated 1711, preserved in the local Registry.
1711	1728	SIMPSON	Hugh		c.1728	Eldest son of Lancelot Simpson; Solicitor. Muster Master of Cumberland Militia; County Treasurer, 1702; appeared before the Justices in 1691 and fined for "riotously entering the house of Thomas Stamper at Rash in Bolton and for taking of his custody one Robert Feare a prisoner upon a commission of rebellion."
1728	1768	SIMPSON	Thomas	1706	1768	Second son of Hugh Simpson; Attorney (admitted 1730). Muster Master and Treasurer of Cumberland Militia. For the correspondence of Hugh and Thomas Simpson during the Jacobite risings of 1715 and 1745, see *Cumberland Record Series*, I.
1768	1809	BAYNES later GARFORTH	John	1723	1809	Solicitor, in practice in London, where he usually resided; took additional name of Garforth on succeeding to his uncle's estates in Yorkshire; Agent for Sir James Lowther, later Earl of Lonsdale; Alderman, Carlisle City Council; Member of Parliament for Haslemere, Surrey, later for Cockermouth, 1789–1802, both boroughs controlled by Sir James Lowther; from 1792 at latest exercised his office by deputy.
1809	1839	HODGSON	William	1773	1850	Attorney (admitted 1795). Five times Mayor of Carlisle; also Town Clerk. For his early career in London, see Robson, *The Attorney in Eighteenth Century England*, chapter 9.
1839	1889	HODGSON	Thomas Houghton	1813	1892	*Elected to Society, May* 1845. Eldest son of William Hodgson; Solicitor (admitted 1834).

CLERKS OF THE PEACE AND OF THE COUNTY COUNCIL from 1889

From	To	Surname	Forenames	Birth	Death	Biographical Notes
1889	1891	HODGSON	Thomas Houghton	1813	1892	See above.
1891	1910	HODGSON	Charles Bernard	1824	1910	Fifth son of William Hodgson; Solicitor (admitted 1846). Clerk to the Justices, Cumberland Ward and Longtown divisions. Previously Deputy Clerk of the Peace and of the County Council.
1910	1927	HODGSON	Charles Courtenay	1860	1927	*Elected to Society, May* 1904. Nephew of Charles Bernard Hodgson; Solicitor (admitted 1888). B.A. (Dunelm). O.B.E., 1918; Hon. M.A. (Oxon). Previously Deputy Clerk of the Peace and of the County Council; Secretary to the Education Committee from 1902.

From	To	Surname	Forenames	Birth	Death	Biographical Notes
1927	1942	HODGSON	Charles William Allan	1869	1942	*Elected to Society,* May 1928. Son of Charles Bernard Hodgson; Solicitor (admitted 1895). Clerk to the Justices, Cumberland Ward and Longtown divisions; Chairman of Cumberland Infirmary Committee. Clerk of Committees, 1910–27.
1942	1946	WHEATLEY	George Andrew	1908		*Elected to Society,* March 1939. Solicitor (admitted 1932). M.A., B.C.L. (Oxon). Clerk to the Lieutenancy; Secretary to the Advisory Committee. Previously Deputy Clerk of the Peace and of the County Council; subsequently Clerk of the Peace and of the County Council of Hampshire, *q.v.*
1946		SWIFT	George Norman Cyrus	1906		*Elected to Society,* April 1940. Solicitor (admitted 1930). Clerk to the Lieutenancy; Secretary to the Advisory Committee; Clerk of the Magistrates' Courts Committee. L.M.T.P.I. Previously Deputy Clerk of the Peace and of the County Council of Hertfordshire.

DEPUTY CLERKS OF THE PEACE prior to 1889

From	To	Surname	Forenames	Birth	Death	Biographical Notes
1757		COOKE	Ralph			Of Penrith.
1779		BARNES	Philip			Of Carlisle.
1782		BARNES	John			Of Carlisle.
1792	1809	HODGSON	Joseph		1809	Of Carlisle; brother of William Hodgson, Clerk of the Peace, 1809–39.
1848	1889	HODGSON	Charles Bernard	1824	1910	Subsequently Clerk of the Peace and of the County Council, see above.

DEPUTY CLERKS OF THE PEACE AND OF THE COUNTY COUNCIL from 1889

From	To	Surname	Forenames	Birth	Death	Biographical Notes
1889	1891	HODGSON	Charles Bernard	1824	1910	See above.
1892	1910	HODGSON	Charles Courtenay	1860	1927	Subsequently Clerk of the Peace and of the County Council, see above.
1935	1940	HOWE	Bertram Charles	1871	1940	*Deputy Clerk of the Peace only.* Solicitor (admitted 1896). M.A. (Cantab).
1939	1942	WHEATLEY	George Andrew	1908		*Deputy Clerk of the County Council, 1939; Deputy Clerk of the Peace, 1941.* Subsequently Clerk of the Peace and of the County Council, see above.
1942	1945	BAINES	Leslie Henry	1909		*Elected to Society,* December 1942. Solicitor (admitted 1934). M.A. (Oxon). Subsequently Clerk of the Peace and of the County Council of the Isle of Wight, *q.v.*
1946	1952	HETHER-INGTON	Arthur Carleton	1916		*Elected to Society,* July 1946. Solicitor (admitted 1938). Subsequently Deputy Clerk, later Clerk of the Peace and of the County Council of Cheshire, *q.v.*
1952		GRAHAM	Robert Lawrence	1910		*Elected to Society,* November 1952. Solicitor (admitted 1950). B.A. (Com.) (Manchester).

DENBIGHSHIRE

From	To	Surname	Forenames	Birth	Death	Biographical Notes
		CLERKS OF THE PEACE from 1540				
1540		MADOK	Robert			Appointed Clerk of the Peace and of the Crown by letters patent, 16th December, 32 Henry VIII.
c.1573		CHALLENOR	John			Also Clerk of the Peace of the Borough of Denbigh.
1622	1623	THELWALL				
1626	1635	HATFEILD	William			
1651	1660	KYFFIN	Watkin			Possibly of Glascoed; Sheriff, 1662; also Sheriff of Montgomeryshire.
1660		PRITCHARD	Thomas			Steward of the Manor of Chirkland; compiled a precedent book now among the Chirk Castle MSS. in the National Library of Wales.
1691	1703	EVANS	J.			
1719	1740	LLOYD	Thomas			
1741	1750	LLOYD	Richard		1750	
1750	1766	HOSIER	John		1766	
1766		HUMPHREYS	John			Attorney.
	1803	GARTSIDE	Danvers		1803	
1803	1833	JONES	John		1833	Appears as Deputy Clerk of the Peace, 1801–02.
1833	1883	PEERS	Joseph			*Elected to Society, May 1844.* Attorney (admitted 1824). Clerk to the Justices.
1883	1889	ADAMS	Llewelyn		1899	*Elected to Society, May 1884.* Solicitor (admitted 1845). Clerk to the Lieutenancy; Clerk to the Justices.

From	To	Surname	Forenames	Birth	Death	Biographical Notes
		CLERKS OF THE PEACE AND OF THE COUNTY COUNCIL from 1889				
1889	1899	ADAMS	Llewelyn		1899	See above.
1899	1926	EVANS	William Robert	1848	1931	*Elected to Society, June 1905.* Solicitor (admitted 1897). LL.B. (London). Justice of the Peace. Subsequently Deputy Clerk of the Peace and of the County Council. Grandfather of Dr. Charles Evans, member of Everest Expedition under Sir John Hunt, 1953.
1926	1930	PARRY	Edward	1871	1930	*Elected to Society, October 1926.* Previously Town Clerk, Denbigh, and Deputy Clerk of the Peace and of the County Council.
1930	1949	JONES	Sir William	1888		*Elected to Society, October 1930.* Solicitor (admitted 1922). C.B.E., 1941; knighted, 1949. Regional Fuel Controller for Wales, 1942–45; Member of Royal Commission on Capital Punishment, 1949; Deputy Chairman of Quarter Sessions, 1953. Previously Deputy Clerk of the Peace and of the County Council.
1949		BUFTON	William Evan	1906		*Elected to Society, May 1939.* Solicitor (admitted 1932). LL.B. (Wales). Previously Clerk of the Peace and of the County Council of Pembrokeshire.

From	To	Surname	Forenames	Birth	Death	Biographical Notes
		DEPUTY CLERKS OF THE PEACE AND OF THE COUNTY COUNCIL from 1889				
1899	1918	ROBERTS	John		1918	
1919	1926	PARRY	Edward	1871	1930	Subsequently Clerk of the Peace and of the County Council, see above.
1926	1927	EVANS	William Robert	1848	1931	Previously Clerk of the Peace and of the County Council, see above. Consultative Solicitor to the County from 1926 until his death.
1927	1930	JONES	William	1888		Subsequently Clerk of the Peace and of the County Council, see above.
1930	1931	EVANS	William Robert	1848	1931	*Deputy Clerk of the Peace only.* See above.
1930	1947	ROBERTS	William	1897		*Deputy Clerk of the County Council only.* Private, King's Own Royal Lancaster and Suffolk Regiments, 1914–18 War; Lieutenant Colonel, 1939–45 War.
1948		ROWLANDS	William John	1897		*Elected to Society, December 1942.* Solicitor (admitted 1932). Previously Deputy Clerk of the Peace and of the County Council of Merioneth. Private, Royal Welch Fusiliers, 1914–18 War.

DERBYSHIRE

From	To	Surname	Forenames	Birth	Death	Biographical Notes
CLERKS OF THE PEACE from 1391						
1391	1396	de STANTON	Thomas			
1416	1419	BROUN	Richard			
1420	1421	HORNYNG-GLOWE	Henry			
1425	1434	WAREN	John			
1441	1450	de la POLE	Henry			
1464	1516	HUNT	Thomas			
1510		HUNT	John			Possibly as Deputy.
1518		HUNT	John			
1537		EYNSWORTH	Henry			
1537		PRESTON	Thomas			Appointed Clerk of the Peace and of the Crown in Derbyshire and Nottinghamshire by letters patent, 4th July, 29 Henry VIII.
1539	1544	BOUNE	Edward			Also Clerk of the Peace for Nottinghamshire, 1538–46.
1550	1563	WATSON	John			John in County records; James on Pipe Roll.
1564	1578	COOKE (COKE)	Richard			
1583	1609	BAXTER	John			
1611	1613	ALPORT	Richard			
1619		DEANE	William			
1622	1625	OSBORNE	John			
1629	1645	LEVINGE	Thomas			Coroner for Borough of Derby, 1627–31.
1646	1649	JACKSON	Thomas			Thomas in County records; John on Pipe Roll.
1649	1653	CHARNELLS	Thomas			
1654	1659	SCLATER	John			
1661	1665	ALLESTRY	Roger			
1666	1672	ASHE	Thomas			
1674	1676	ROLLESTON	John			Previously Deputy Clerk of the Peace.
1682	1699	ADDERLEY	John		1699	
1699	1708	ADDERLEY	Charles		1719	Son of John Adderley; became financially embarrassed and absconded from Derby, 1708. Previously Deputy Clerk of the Peace.
1708	1709	BAGNOLD	John			Common Clerk, Coroner and Clerk of the Peace for the Borough of Derby, 1682–1708.
1710	1760	HAYNE	Joseph		1760	Acted regularly by Deputy.
1760	1773	HEATHCOTE	Godfrey	1701	1773	An eminent attorney.
1774	1823	MAYNARD	Anthony Lax		1825	Up to Epiphany Sessions 1793 he signed as Anthony Lax but after that date as Anthony Lax Maynard. His mother, after the death of her husband, took the name and arms of her great-grandfather, John Maynard of Kirk Levington in Yorkshire.
1823	1830	LOCKETT	William Jeffrey			Clerk to the Lieutenancy; Justice of the Peace, 1833. Previously Deputy Clerk of the Peace.

DERBYSHIRE (*Continued*)

From	To	Surname	Forenames	Birth	Death	Biographical Notes
1830	1849	CHARGE	John		1849	Major in the Scarsdale Regiment, Derbyshire Militia, commissioned 24th September 1808.
1849	1880	BARBER	John		1880	*Elected to Society, May* 1854. Attorney (admitted 1821). Clerk to the Lieutenancy.
1880	1889	BUSBY	Charles Stanhope Burke			*Elected to Society, June* 1881. Solicitor (admitted 1838). Coroner for the Scarsdale Hundred, 1845–80; First President of the Derby Law Society, 1886–88.

CLERKS OF THE PEACE AND OF THE COUNTY COUNCIL from 1889

From	To	Surname	Forenames	Birth	Death	Biographical Notes
1889	1894	BUSBY	Charles Stanhope Burke			See above.
1894	1930	HUGHES-HALLETT	Norton Joseph	1850	1938	*Elected to Society, June* 1890. Solicitor (admitted 1876). O.B.E., 1920; Deputy Lieutenant. Secretary to the Advisory Committee; President of the Derby Law Society, 1897. Previously Deputy Clerk of the Peace and of the County Council.
1930	1950	SKINNER	Horace Wilfrid	1884	1955	*Elected to Society, November* 1924. Solicitor (admitted 1906). LL.B. (London). C.B.E., 1941. Justice of the Peace, 1951. Clerk to the Lieutenancy; Secretary to the Advisory Committee. Previously Deputy Clerk of the Peace and of the County Council.
1950		GILMAN	Denis George	1904		*Elected to Society, October* 1947. Solicitor (admitted 1927). Clerk to the Lieutenancy; Secretary to the Advisory Committee; Clerk of the Magistrates' Courts Committee; Clerk of the Peak Park Planning Board. President of the Derby Law Society, 1957. Previously Deputy Town Clerk and Deputy Clerk of the Peace, Derby County Borough, assistant solicitor, Derbyshire County Council, and Deputy Clerk of the Peace and of the County Council.

DEPUTY CLERKS OF THE PEACE prior to 1889

From	To	Surname	Forenames	Birth	Death	Biographical Notes
1660	1665	ROLLESTON	John			Subsequently Clerk of the Peace, see above.
	1699	ADDERLEY	Charles		1719	Subsequently Clerk of the Peace, see above.
1718		WRIGHT	John			With Hugh Bateman, below, regularly appointed Deputy by Joseph Hayne, Clerk of the Peace 1710–60.
1730		BATEMAN	Hugh			
1795	1823	LOCKETT	William Jeffrey			Subsequently Clerk of the Peace, see above.

DEPUTY CLERKS OF THE PEACE AND OF THE COUNTY COUNCIL from 1889

From	To	Surname	Forenames	Birth	Death	Biographical Notes
1889	1894	HUGHES-HALLETT	Norton Joseph	1850	1938	Subsequently Clerk of the Peace and of the County Council, see above.
1924	1930	SKINNER	Horace Wilfrid	1884	1955	Subsequently Clerk of the Peace and of the County Council, see above.
1947	1950	GILMAN	Denis George	1904		Subsequently Clerk of the Peace and of the County Council, see above.
1951	1960	WOTHERSPOON	Robert Andrew	1912		*Elected to Society, July* 1951. Solicitor (admitted 1937). Subsequently Clerk of the Peace and of the County Council of Yorkshire (North Riding), *q.v.*
1960		CROSSLEY	Harry	1918		*Elected to Society, June* 1960. Solicitor (admitted 1947). Previously assistant solicitor, Kettering Borough and Derbyshire County Councils. Major, Royal Artillery, 1939–45 War.

DEVON

From	To	Surname	Forenames	Birth	Death	Biographical Notes

From	To	Surname	Forenames	Birth	Death	Biographical Notes
1391	1393	RAYMOND	Thomas			
1394	1398	LAKE	John			
1400	1420	STOKE	Thomas			
1423	1446	FOULHILL	Thomas			
1447	1454	KIRTON	John			
1456	1480	VIELL	Richard			
1481	1502	PROUSE	Nicholas			
1503	1506	HERT	John			
1506	1525	HALS	William			Appointed Clerk of the Peace, Clerk of the Crown, Justice of Oyer and Terminer and Justice of Gaol Delivery by letters patent, 5th November, 22 Henry VII.
1525	1556	SOUTHCOTE	John			Appointed to the said offices by letters patent, 17th November, 19 Henry VIII, on surrender of patent by Hals; also appears in Pipe Rolls as Clerk of the Peace at Michaelmas 1525.
1557	1589	SOUTHCOTE	George			Son of John Southcote; granted reversion of the offices by letters patent, 1st March, 34 Henry VIII.
1590	1591	COMYN	William			
1592	1596	COTTELL	Mark			Appointed Deputy by his successor, 1596; Justice of the Peace c.1604–17. A working Clerk.
1596	1606	VAGHAN	Hugh			Servant and officer of Earl of Bedford, by whom appointed.
1609	1612	BERRY	Bartholomew			Justice of the Peace, c.1627–33.
1612	1641	VAGHAN	Charles			
1641	1645	SHAPCOTT	Thomas	1617		Son of Thomas Shapcott of Exeter; matriculated at Exeter College, Oxford, 1633. Barrister-at-law, Inner Temple (called 1641). Royalist sympathiser. See Foster, *Judges and Barristers*.
1646		VAGHAN	Charles			A Parliamentarian, appointed by the Commons in 1642, but unable to act until his party captured Exeter.
1649	1653	ROWE	Nicholas			
1653	1658	RADDON	Edward			
1658	1659	FITZWILLIAM	Henry			County Treasurer, 1665. Previously Deputy Clerk of the Peace.
1660	1670	NORTHCOTE	John			Second son of Sir John Northcott of Newton St. Cyres; Pensioner, Emmanuel College, Cambridge, 1647. Justice of the Peace, 1688–95.
1670	1694	VAUGHAN	Hugh		1694	Of Ottery; matriculated at Christ Church, Oxford, 1658; B.A. c.1662. Barrister-at-law, Inner Temple (called 1668). See Foster, *Judges and Barristers*.
1695	1723/4	MARTYN	William, the elder			
1723/4	1727/8	FORTESCUE	Joseph			

DEVON (*Continued*)

From	To	Surname	Forenames	Birth	Death	Biographical Notes
1727/8	1759	INCLEDON	Robert			
1759		SPRY	William			
1761	1764	SPRY	William			Re-admitted.
1764	1775	TURNER	Richard			Of Tavistock.
1775	1776	HELLIAR	John			
1776	1785	BASTARD	Edmund			
1785	1798	KELLY	Redmund			
1798	1852	EALES	Richard		1852	*Elected to Society, November* 1819. Previously Deputy Clerk of the Peace.
1852	1857	PRING	Thomas	1793		*Elected to Society, April* 1853. Pensioner, Jesus College, Cambridge, 1817.
1857		KENNAWAY	Mark			
1857	1878	FORD	Henry			Pensioner, Trinity College, Cambridge, 1839; M.A. Solicitor (admitted 1845).
1878	1889	MICHELMORE	Henry			*Elected to Society, June* 1879. Solicitor (admitted 1861). Clerk to the Lieutenancy.

CLERKS OF THE PEACE AND OF THE COUNTY COUNCIL from 1889

From	To	Surname	Forenames	Birth	Death	Biographical Notes
1889	1912	MICHELMORE	Henry			See above.
1912	1915	BAILEY	Frank		1919	*Elected to Society, May* 1912. Previously Deputy Clerk of the Peace and of the County Council.
1915	1937	MILLER	Brian Stothert	1871	1951	*Elected to Society, June* 1916. Solicitor (admitted 1894). Previously Deputy Clerk of the Peace and of the County Council.
1937	1947	WITHYCOMBE	Arthur John	1881		*Elected to Society, June* 1923. Barrister-at-law, Gray's Inn (called 1910). Previously Deputy Clerk of the Peace and of the County Council.
1947	1952	DAVIS	Herbert Amphlett	1887		*Elected to Society, January* 1937. Solicitor (admitted 1913). Secretary to the Advisory Committees; Clerk of the Magistrates' Courts Committee; Clerk of the Devon River Board, 1950. Previously Deputy Clerk of the Peace and of the County Council. Lieutenant, R.N.V.R., 1914–18 War.
1952		GODSALL	Harold Graham	1909		*Elected to Society, October* 1947. Exhibitioner, St. Catharine's College, Cambridge; M.A. Solicitor (admitted 1935). Clerk to the Lieutenancy from 1954; Secretary to the Advisory Committees; Clerk of the Magistrates' Courts Committee; Clerk of the Devon River Board. Previously Deputy Clerk of the Peace and of the County Council.

DEVON (*Continued*)

From	To	Surname	Forenames	Birth	Death	Biographical Notes

DEPUTY CLERKS OF THE PEACE prior to 1889

From	To	Surname	Forenames	Birth	Death	Biographical Notes
1596		COTTELL	Mark			Previously Clerk of the Peace, see above.
1646	1649	INGLETT	Giles			Appears to have performed all the duties of Clerk of the Peace while Deputy.
1654	1658	FITZWILLIAM	Henry			Subsequently Clerk of the Peace, see above.
1712	1722	MARTIN	William, the younger			
1726		FORTESCUE	John			Attorney. A break in his service occurred c.1727–28 at commencement of Robert Incledon's Clerkship.
1728/9	1731	FORTESCUE	John			Re-appointed.
1761	c.1764	GULLETT	Christopher			Originally appointed by William Spry on his readmission as Clerk the Peace, 1761. Spry's successor, Richard Turner, was probably a working Clerk with no Deputy. Gullett was re-appointed Deputy by John Helliar, Clerk of the Peace, in 1775, and by Edmund Bastard in 1776 or 1777.
1775	1782	GULLETT	Christopher			Re-appointed.
1784	1798	EALES	Richard		1852	Subsequently Clerk of the Peace, see above.
1818	1828	MORTIMER	Samuel			
1831	1856	DRAKE	Thomas Edward			Attorney.

DEPUTY CLERKS OF THE PEACE AND OF THE COUNTY COUNCIL from 1889

From	To	Surname	Forenames	Birth	Death	Biographical Notes
1889	1906	MICHELMORE	Henry William			
1906	1912	BAILEY	Frank		1919	Subsequently Clerk of the Peace and of the County Council, see above.
1912	1915	MILLER	Brian Stothert		1951	Subsequently Clerk of the Peace and of the County Council, see above.
1915	1919	MEABY	Kenneth George Tweedale	1883		*Elected to Society, June* 1916. Solicitor (admitted 1907). Subsequently Clerk of the Peace and of the County Council of Nottinghamshire, *q.v.*
1920	1937	WITHYCOMBE	Arthur John			Also County Accountant. Subsequently Clerk of the Peace and of the County Council, see above.
1937	1947	DAVIS	Herbert Amphlett			Subsequently Clerk of the Peace and of the County Council, see above.
1947	1952	GODSALL	Harold Graham			Subsequently Clerk of the Peace and of the County Council, see above.
1952		LUCAS	Charles Vivian	1914		*Elected to Society, May* 1952. Solicitor (admitted 1939). LL.B. (London). Major, Royal Artillery, 1939–45 War.

DORSET

From	To	Surname	Forenames	Birth	Death	Biographical Notes
CLERKS OF THE PEACE from 1390						
1390		de VEEL	Robert			
1395	1411	HORDERE	John			
1417	1447	BARET	John			
1486	1487	PAYN	Robert			
1499	1507	MOLEYNS	Thomas			
1523	1524	DEVELYN	John			
1549		GRONE	Robert			
1551	1572	VALLYS	Richard			
c.1575	1577	HYLLYARD	John			
1587	1597	SHERLEY	William			
1603	1623	ALEXANDER	Philip			
1625	1627	SYMES	John			
1629	1637	SMITH	William			
1641	1648	DERBY	William			Town Clerk of Dorchester, 1629–38 and 1639–49; Mayor, 1638.
1649	1650	LEWEN	Robert			
1655	1658	SCOVILE	Richard			Town Clerk of Dorchester, 1638–39 and 1649–56.
1662	1680	RANDALL	John			
1680	1703	ATWELL	Edward			
1703	1726	COWARD	Thomas		1726	
1726	1727	COMBE	Bryan			Previously Deputy Clerk of the Peace.
1727	1754	TEMPLEMAN	William		1754	
1754	1792	WALLIS	John		1792	
1792	1826	BURNET	William		1828	*Elected to Society, November* 1810. Attorney.
1826	1839	FOOKS	Thomas			Attorney. Governor of Sherborne School, 1805. For members of this family, see E. C. Ffooks, *The Family of Ffooks of Sherborne.*
1839	1840	FOOKS	John			Son of Thomas Fooks; Attorney. Resigned Clerkship on marriage.
1840	1872	FFOOKS	William			*Elected to Society, May* 1847. Son of Thomas Fooks, younger brother of John; adopted double "F" in spelling of surname; Solicitor (admitted 1837). Governor of Sherborne School, 1840; Steward, 1845.
1872	1888	FFOOKS	Thomas			*Elected to Society, June* 1872. Son of Thomas Fooks, younger brother of John and William; Solicitor (admitted 1840). Justice of the Peace. Under Sheriff, 1860, 1864, 1869. Governor of Sherborne School. Previously Deputy Clerk of the Peace.
1888	1889	FFOOKS	Edward Archdall	1859	1932	*Elected to Society, May* 1888. Nephew of Thomas Ffooks; Solicitor (admitted 1882). Clerk to the Lieutenancy; Under Sheriff, 1888–1929. Previously Deputy Clerk of the Peace.

From	To	Surname	Forenames	Birth	Death	Biographical Notes

CLERKS OF THE PEACE AND OF THE COUNTY COUNCIL from 1889

From	To	Surname	Forenames	Birth	Death	Biographical Notes
1889	1925	FFOOKS	Edward Archdall	1859	1932	See above. Also Secretary to the Advisory Committee; President of the Dorset Law Society, 1917–23.
1925	1935	TORR	John Leslie	1867	1947	*Elected to Society, January* 1925. Solicitor (admitted 1908). Clerk to the Lieutenancy; Secretary to the Advisory Committee. Previously Deputy Clerk of the Peace and of the County Council.
1935		BRUTTON	Charles Phipps	1899		*Elected to Society, November* 1932; *Vice-Chairman*, 1958–60. Solicitor (admitted 1926). O.B.E., 1946; C.B.E., 1954. Clerk to the Lieutenancy; Secretary to the Advisory Committee; Clerk of the Magistrates' Courts Committee. Previously Deputy Clerk of the Peace and of the County Council of Cheshire. Captain, Grenadier Guards, 1914–18 War.

DEPUTY CLERKS OF THE PEACE prior to 1889

From	To	Surname	Forenames	Birth	Death	Biographical Notes
1715	1726	COMBE	Bryan			Subsequently Clerk of the Peace, see above.
1727		STICKLAND	Nathaniel			
1749	1750	SMITH	Robert			
1750		LAMBERT	A.			
1761		WAY	John			
1792		BOSWELL	Edward			Solicitor. Clerk to the Lieutenancy; Treasurer for the Western Division of Dorset, 1808. Author of *The Civil Division of the County of Dorset*, 1795, and of *The Ecclesiastical Division of the Diocese of Bristol, c.1826.*
1820		FOX	Thomas			
1871	1872	FFOOKS	Thomas			Subsequently Clerk of the Peace, see above.
1886	1888	FFOOKS	Edward Archdall	1859	1932	Subsequently Clerk of the Peace, see above.

DEPUTY CLERKS OF THE PEACE AND OF THE COUNTY COUNCIL from 1889

From	To	Surname	Forenames	Birth	Death	Biographical Notes
1908	1925	TORR	John Leslie	1867	1947	Subsequently Clerk of the Peace and of the County Council, see above.
1925	1927	KELLY	John Bradshaw	1889		*Elected to Society, October* 1927. Solicitor (admitted 1922). Subsequently Clerk of the Peace and of the County Council of Huntingdonshire, *q.v.*
1927	1949	ROE	Bertram Charles	1888	1954	*Elected to Society, March* 1930. Solicitor (admitted 1926).
1949		TEMPLEMAN	Arthur Cowley	1902		*Elected to Society, May* 1949. Solicitor (admitted 1925).

DURHAM

From	To	Surname	Forenames	Birth	Death	Biographical Notes
		CLERKS OF THE PEACE from c.1416				
c.1416	c.1419	THORNBURGH	William			
1438	c.1457	RAKETT	Richard			
c.1472	c.1509	RAKETT	John			
c.1513	c.1514	FAIRFAX	Thomas			
c.1523	c.1530	BENTLEY	John			
c.1540	c.1561	MENNELL	Robert			Serjeant-at-law.
		TAYLFAR	John			Served after Mennell and before Layton; dates uncertain.
c.1567	c.1577	LAYTON	Thomas			Clerk of the Justices in Eyre, of Assize and Gaol Delivery; Clerk of the Peace of Durham and Sadberge; Clerk of the Chancery and Attorney General of the County Palatine of Durham.
c.1584		TAILBOYS	Robert			
1589	1610	WILTON	Edmund		1610	Joint appointment from 1591. Scot resigned on death of Wilton, 1610.
1591	1610	SCOT	Richard			
1610	1613	BARNES	John		1613	Son of Bishop Richard Barnes.
1613	1634	MARTIN	George			
1634	c.1655	RICHARDSON	John			
c.1647	c.1660	FARRER	John			
1656		GILPIN	James			
c.1660	c.1679	RICHARDSON	John			
1679	c.1699	CROSBY	Thomas			
c.1708	1720	STONEHEWER	Richard			
1720	1725	STONEHEWER	Thomas			Son of Richard Stonehewer.
1725		DUNCUM	William			
c.1735	1749	YOUNG	William			
1749	1779	WYNDHAM	Wadham			
1779		EGERTON	John William			
c.1784	c.1800	PEARSON	George			Previously Deputy Clerk of the Peace.
c.1800	1838	PRICE	Barrington			Described in Order Books as Clerk of the Peace and Solicitor for the County.
1839	1865	WHARTON	Gerald Blisson			
1865	1879	PHILIPSON	Ralph Park			Attorney (admitted 1819). Justice of the Peace, Newcastle-upon-Tyne.
1880	1889	SIMEY	Ralph	1834	1911	*Elected to Society, June* 1880. Solicitor (admitted 1855).

DURHAM (*Continued*)

From	To	Surname	Forenames	Birth	Death	Biographical Notes

CLERKS OF THE PEACE AND OF THE COUNTY COUNCIL from 1889

From	To	Surname	Forenames	Birth	Death	Biographical Notes
1889	1911	SIMEY	Ralph	1834	1911	See above.
1911	1937	JEVONS	Harold	1869	1937	*Elected to Society, November* 1911. Solicitor (admitted 1893). Deputy Lieutenant. Secretary to the Advisory Committee; Clerk to the Visiting Committee of Durham County Mental Hospital; Solicitor to Durham Water Board. Previously Deputy Town Clerk, Swansea, and Town Clerk, Wigan.
1937		HOPE	James Kenneth	1896		*Elected to Society, October* 1927. Solicitor (admitted 1922). C.B.E., 1946; Hon. M.A. (Dunelm); Deputy Lieutenant. Secretary to the Advisory Committee; Clerk of the Magistrates' Courts Committee; Recorder of City of Durham. Previously assistant solicitor, Bedfordshire County Council, and Deputy Clerk of the Peace and of the County Council of Durham. Lieutenant, 1st Battalion, Bedfordshire Regiment, 1914–18 War.

DEPUTY CLERKS OF THE PEACE prior to 1889

From	To	Surname	Forenames	Birth	Death	Biographical Notes
1735	1763	MANN	John			Appointed Treasurer in 1748 and held office until resignation in 1760.
1763	c.1777	HOPPER	William			
c.1777	c.1784	PEARSON	George			Subsequently Clerk of the Peace, see above.
c.1825	1838	DUNN	John			
1839	1852	SCRUTON	Walter		1852	
1852	c.1864	TIPLADY	John			
c.1873		WATSON	John			

DEPUTY CLERKS OF THE PEACE AND OF THE COUNTY COUNCIL from 1889

From	To	Surname	Forenames	Birth	Death	Biographical Notes
1893	1905	SIMEY	George Iliffe		1927	*Elected to Society, June* 1893. Solicitor (admitted 1892). Subsequently Clerk of the Peace and of the County Council of Somerset, *q.v.*
1905	1911	WHEATLEY	Robert Albert	1873	1954	*Elected to Society, May* 1908. Solicitor (admitted 1897). M.A., B.C.L. (Oxon). Subsequently Clerk of the Peace and of the County Council of Pembrokeshire, *q.v.*
1919	1921	MEABY	Kenneth George Tweedale	1883		*Elected to Society, June* 1916. Solicitor (admitted 1907). Subsequently Clerk of the Peace and of the County Council of Nottinghamshire, *q.v.*
1921	1927	KING	Harold	1887	1960	*Elected to Society, October* 1921. Solicitor (admitted 1912). Subsequently Clerk of the Peace and of the County Council of Somerset, *q.v.*
1927	1937	HOPE	James Kenneth	1896		Subsequently Clerk of the Peace and of the County Council, see above.
1937	1942	SCURFIELD	William Russell	1908		*Elected to Society, January* 1938. Solicitor (admitted 1930). LL.B. (London). Subsequently Clerk of the Peace and of the County Council of Worcestershire, *q.v.*
1942	1949	UNDERWOOD	Henry Louis	1909		*Elected to Society, June* 1945. Solicitor (admitted 1934). M.A. (Cantab). Subsequently Clerk of the Peace and of the County Council of Pembrokeshire, *q.v.*
1945	1960	UPTON	Harry	1895		*Elected to Society, June* 1945. *Second Deputy Clerk of the Peace and of the County Council, 1945; Deputy, 1949.* Solicitor (admitted 1940). Lieutenant, Gloucestershire Regiment, attached Royal Air Force, 1914–18 War.
1950		GOODWIN	Laurence Eric	1911		*Elected to Society, January* 1950. *Second Deputy Clerk of the Peace and of the County Council, 1950; Deputy, 1960.* Solicitor (admitted 1939). M.A. (Oxon). Previously assistant solicitor, Durham County Council. Lance Sergeant, Welch Regiment and Intelligence Corps, 1939–45 War.
1960		LOMAS	James			*Elected to Society, July* 1960. *Second Deputy Clerk of the Peace and of the County Council.* Solicitor (admitted 1948). LL.B.

ESSEX

From	To	Surname	Forenames	Birth	Death	Biographical Notes
CLERKS	**OF THE PEACE**	from 1392				
1392	1398	WILLINGHALE	Thomas			
1404	1433	FYNCHYNG-FELD	John			Appointed Clerk and King's Attorney before Justices of the Peace in Essex, Hertfordshire and Suffolk by letters patent, 11th March, 5 Henry IV; Feodary of the Duchy of Lancaster for Essex, Hertfordshire and Kent, 1399–1401 (see Somerville, *Duchy of Lancaster*, I, p. 609).
1412		STAMPE	Thomas			Probably Deputy for John Fynchyngfeld.
1434	1437	STOWRE	Adam			
1438	1468	DRAKES	Thomas			
1468	1477	PLUMMER	Robert			Later Justice of the Peace and Commissioner for various purposes; possibly Sheriff of the County, 1494.
1478	1482	FITZWILLIAM	Thomas			
1482	1505	PARKER	Robert			
1506	c.1509	DAVYSON	Robert			Appointed Clerk of the Peace, of the Crown, of the Sessions of the Peace, and of Oyer and Terminer by letters patent, 31st July, 21 Henry VII; also in Hertfordshire.
1506	1516	PARKER	John			Possibly also Justice of the Peace, 1506.
1516	1522	BARNABY	John			
1523	1524	CRAWFORD	Lionel			
1524	1526	CRAFFORD (CRAYFORD)	Guy			Later Justice of the Peace; possibly Guy Crafford who was admitted to Lincoln's Inn, 1514, subsequently Bencher.
1527	1533	CAMPION	Edward			
1534	1538	LYNDSELL (LYNDESEYE)	Richard		1538	Appointed Clerk of the Peace and of the Crown by letters patent, 4th July, 29 Henry VIII; but already serving in 1534.
1538	1545	BRADBURY	William			Appointed to the same offices by letters patent, 25th June, 30 Henry VIII, but payments to him recorded from 1536, possibly as Deputy.
1545	1547	WELBORE	Michael			
1550	1563	CARROWE	John	c.1514	1564	Steward of the Royal Liberty of Havering-atte-Bower from 1554. Probably a Devonshire Carew, admitted New College, Oxford, 1530, and withdrew to Lincoln's Inn, 1531. Closely connected with Sir William Petre, Secretary of State; his Will, proved 1564, mentions wife, sons Edward and John, daughters, and a brother Edward; he bequeathed the "books appertaining to my office" to Sir William Petre.
1563	1566	RUTTER	William			
1566	1572	WHITE	George			
1572	1576	RAMME (RAME)	Francis			
1577	1600	BROWNE	Richard			Addressed at Leicester House, London, while Earl of Leicester was *Custos Rotulorum* (1581–88).
1603		BROWNE	Richard			
1603	1606	LEEKE	Gifford			
1604	1608	WALLINGER	John			Apparently jointly with Gifford Leeke, 1604–06. See also list of Deputy Clerks, 1604–07.
1608		DAVIES	William			
1609	1610	WRIGHT	John			

ESSEX (*Continued*)

From	To	Surname	Forenames	Birth	Death	Biographical Notes
1611	1622	ELDRED	Edward			Of Stebbing; Clerk of Indictments, 1601. Previously Deputy Clerk of the Peace.
1624	1628	MORE	Marmaduke			
1629	1637	DOWE	Richard			
1638	1640	WINGFIELD	Robert			
1640	1641	ROWDEN	Francis			
1641	1648	PULLEY	Richard			
1649	1660	GOULDES-BURGH	Thomas		c.1661	Owned property in the Ongar area (see *V.C.H.* IV, p. 161, and *Cal. Committee for Compounding with Delinquents*, 2643).
1660	1680	KEMPSON	Anthony			
1680	1686	ASHPOOLE	Thomas		1687	Of Braintree, where a son, John, of him and his wife Mary, was baptised on 2nd December, 1684. Previously Deputy Clerk of the Peace. Buried as "aturney Clerk of ye Sesyons" (see Braintree Parish Registers).
1687	1688	MATTOCK	Charles			
1688		WOODCOCK	Roger			Possibly Deputy Clerk only.
1689	1722	REYNOLDS	Samuel			Of Colchester; Attorney, Lord of the Manor of Peldon.
1722	1735	REYNOLDS	Charles			
1735	1754	AYLMER	Brabazon		1754	Of Mowden Hall, Ulting. Admitted, Inner Temple, 1716; Bencher, 1750.
1754	1759	JOHNSON	Edward			His appointment, together with that of his successor, enrolled in the Exchequer.
1759		KEITH	Giles			Of Chich St. Osyth.
	1770	BROOKE	George			County Solicitor, 1741.
1770	1785	ENNEW	Samuel			Of Colchester; Attorney. Steward of the Manor of Shenfield. Previously Deputy Clerk of the Peace.
1785	1822	BULLOCK	William	1750	1822	*Founder member of Society, March* 1810. Son of the Rev. Richard Bullock, D.D., Prebendary of Westminster and a chaplain to King George II; married Charlotte, daughter of Collin Hossack of Colchester, M.D.; three daughters, of whom one married Robert Gibson, father of William Gibson, Clerk of the Peace, 1847–60; lived at Shelley House, near Ongar, and left charity for the Parish of Shelley worth £10 a year; described by a County historian as "a person of rare excellence."
1822	1847	PARKER	Charles George	1780	1847	*Elected to Society, November* 1822. Youngest son of John Oxley Parker, solicitor, of Chelmsford; married Isabella, daughter of James Houson, barrister-at-law, of Lincoln's Inn; succeeded his father as Deputy Registrar for the Archdeaconries of Essex, Colchester and Middlesex, 1826; previously Coroner; the historian of the family believes he died worth "not far short of half a million sterling."
1847	1860	GIBSON	William	1798	1860	Grandson of William Bullock, Clerk of the Peace, 1785–1822; of Rainsford Lodge, Chelmsford; Solicitor. Previously Deputy Clerk of the Peace.
1860	1889	GIBSON	Henry	1831	1904	*Elected to Society, June* 1866. Son of William Gibson; Brentwood School and Cheltenham College; of Ongar; Solicitor (admitted 1852). Married Ellen Elizabeth, daughter of George Nottidge of Bocking, 1856; two sons and three unmarried daughters. Previously Deputy Clerk of the Peace.

ESSEX (*Continued*)

From	To	Surname	Forenames	Birth	Death	Biographical Notes

CLERKS OF THE PEACE AND OF THE COUNTY COUNCIL from 1889

From	To	Surname	Forenames	Birth	Death	Biographical Notes
1889	1904	GIBSON	Henry	1831	1904	See above.
1904	1909	GIBSON	Herbert William	1863	1935	*Elected to Society, June 1897.* Son of Henry Gibson; Solicitor (admitted 1884). Clerk to the Kent and Essex Sea Fisheries Committee, 1890–1935. Previously Deputy Clerk of the Peace and of the County Council.
1909	1934	GOOLD	John Heyden	1868	1937	*Elected to Society, June 1910.* Solicitor (admitted 1890).
1934	1941	HOLCROFT	Edward Stanley	1884		*Elected to Society, November 1933.* Solicitor (admitted 1907). Previously assistant solicitor, Wolverhampton County Borough and Berkshire County Councils, and Deputy Clerk of the Peace and of the County Councils of Oxfordshire and Essex. Captain, 1914–18 War.
1941	1950	NEGUS	Raymond Ewings	1883	1950	*Elected to Society, October 1934.* *Clerk of the Peace only.* Barrister-at-law, Inner Temple (called 1909). M.A. (Oxon). Attorney General, St. Lucia (B.W.I.) 1919–20. Associate, Eastern Circuit. Previously Deputy Clerk of the Peace. Lieutenant Colonel, Army List, 1914–18 War; D.S.O.
1941	1954	LIGHTBURN	John Edward	1891		*Elected to Society, July 1932.* *Clerk of the County Council only.* Solicitor (admitted 1914). Previously Deputy Clerk of the Peace and of the County Council of Kent.
1950		PIPER	Walter John	1910		*Elected to Society, July 1952.* *Clerk of the Peace only.* Solicitor (admitted 1950). Clerk of the Magistrates' Courts Committee. Previously Deputy Clerk of the Peace. Captain, R.A.S.C., 1939–45 War; Despatches.
1954		BERRIDGE	Christian Gerard Timperley	1904		*Elected to Society, November 1934.* *Clerk of the County Council only.* Solicitor (admitted 1927). Previously joint Deputy Clerk of the County Council.

DEPUTY CLERKS OF THE PEACE prior to 1889

From	To	Surname	Forenames	Birth	Death	Biographical Notes
1590	1604	MACHYN	Robert			Sometimes referred to as Clerk of the Peace; the forename also appears as Roger in the Pipe Roll for 1602.
c.1601	1611	ELDRED	Edward			Subsequently Clerk of the Peace, see above.
1604	1606	KELYNGE	John			Kelynge, Enyver and Davyes (see below) appear to have acted jointly with John Wallinger, Clerk of the Peace, but were possibly his deputies.
1606	1607	ENYVER	Thomas			
1607		DAVYES	William			
1624	1626	MANN	John			
1628	1629	FREEMAN	Thomas			
1632	1659	COLE	John			
1660		HERRIS	William			County Solicitor.
c.1672	1680	ASHPOOLE	Thomas		1687	Subsequently Clerk of the Peace, see above.

ESSEX (*Continued*)

From	To	Surname	Forenames	Birth	Death	Biographical Notes
1688		MATTOCK	Charles			Possibly the Charles Mattock who was admitted to Lincoln's Inn 1691, described as son of Charles Mattock of the City of London, deceased. The father may have been Clerk of the Peace, 1687–88, see above.
1689		WARDE	Anthony			
1694	1710	MATTOCK	Charles			
c.1704	1706	WOODCOCK	Roger			
c.1711	1735	WITHAM	Nathaniel			County Solicitor.
1735	1759	BROOKE	George			Of Halstead.
1759	1769	ENNEW	Samuel			Subsequently Clerk of the Peace, see above.
1786	c.1817	CAWKWELL	Thomas	1755	1818	Described on his tomb in Chelmsford Cathedral Yard as "resident Clerk in the Clerk of the Peace Office."
1817	1821	MASON	William			*Elected to Society, November* 1818.
1821		GIBSON	William	1798	1860	Subsequently Clerk of the Peace, see above.
1856	1860	GIBSON	Henry	1831	1904	Subsequently Clerk of the Peace, see above.

DEPUTY CLERKS OF THE PEACE AND OF THE COUNTY COUNCIL from 1889

From	To	Surname	Forenames	Birth	Death	Biographical Notes
1896	1904	GIBSON	Herbert William	1863	1935	Subsequently Clerk of the Peace and of the County Council, see above.
1905	1919	BARLOW	George Frederick			Previously Chief Clerk in the office of Clerk of the Peace.
1919	1928	CARTER	Charles Harold	1886	1946	*Elected to Society, October* 1920. Solicitor (admitted 1914). Subsequently Clerk of the Peace and of the County Council of Northumberland, *q.v.* Author of a *Handbook on the Local Government Act*, 1888, published 1924.
1928	1934	HOLCROFT	Edward Stanley	1884		Subsequently Clerk of the Peace and of the County Council, see above.
1934	1941	NEGUS	Raymond Ewings	1883	1950	*Deputy Clerk of the Peace only.* Subsequently Clerk of the Peace, see above.
1934	1954	BERRIDGE	Christian Gerard Timperley	1904		*Joint Deputy Clerk of the County Council only.* Subsequently Clerk of the County Council, see above.
1934		LEWIS	Lawrence George Lisle	1907		*Elected to Society, November* 1934. *Joint Deputy Clerk of the County Council, 1934; first Deputy Clerk of the County Council, 1954.* Solicitor (Daniel Reardon, John Mackrell and Edmund Thomas Child prizes) (admitted 1929). M.B.E., 1942.
1941	1950	CLAY	Frederick William	1884	1956	*Deputy Clerk of the Peace only.*
1950	1950	PIPER	Walter John	1910		*Deputy Clerk of the Peace only.* Subsequently Clerk of the Peace, see above.
1951		GRUNDY	Francis Estlin Christopher	1916		*Deputy Clerk of the Peace only.* Barrister-at-law, Middle Temple (called 1939). LL.B., (London). Captain, R.A.S.C., (Sudan Defence Force), 1939–45 War.
1954		MILLS	John Spencer	1917		*Elected to Society, November* 1954. *Second Deputy Clerk of the County Council only.* Solicitor (admitted 1940). LL.B. (Manchester). Captain, Royal Artillery, 1939–45 War; M.C.

FLINTSHIRE

From	To	Surname	Forenames	Birth	Death	Biographical Notes

CLERKS OF THE PEACE from 1542

From	To	Surname	Forenames	Birth	Death	Biographical Notes
1542	1575	DUTTEN	Thomas			Of Sherborne, Gloucestershire, and the Inner Temple; appointed Clerk of the Peace and of the Crown by letters patent, 5th March, 33 Henry VIII.
c.1582	1584	JONES	Oliver			Previously Deputy Clerk of the Peace.
c.1664		LEWIS	Henry			
1720	1733	WILLIAMS	Thomas			
1733	1746	CRACHLEY	Thomas			Of Deiniol's Ash, Hawarden.
1747	1765	THELWALL	Edward			
1765	1792	WYNNE	William, the elder			Previously Deputy Clerk of the Peace.
1792	1820	WYNNE	William, the younger			Solicitor. Also County Treasurer.
1820	1844	ROBERTS	Hugh			
1844	1888	ROBERTS	Arthur Troughton			*Elected to Society, February 1859.*
1888	1889	KELLY	Thomas Thelwall		1901	*Elected to Society, June 1886.* Solicitor (admitted 1861). Clerk to the Lieutenancy; Under Sheriff; joint Clerk to the Justices, Mold, Hope, Hawarden and Northop divisions. Previously Deputy Clerk of the Peace.

CLERKS OF THE PEACE AND OF THE COUNTY COUNCIL from 1889

From	To	Surname	Forenames	Birth	Death	Biographical Notes
1889	1901	KELLY	Thomas Thelwall		1901	See above.
1901	1911	BROMLEY	Richard			*Elected to Society, May 1902.* Solicitor (admitted 1888). Previously Coroner.
1911	1932	TILBY	Henry Albert	1867	1947	*Elected to Society, May 1912.* O.B.E., 1920.
1932	1944	DAVIES	John Harvey	1884		*Elected to Society, November 1932.* C.B.E., 1939. Previously Deputy Clerk of the Peace and of the County Council.
1945		JONES	William Hugh	1901		*Elected to Society, January 1945.* Solicitor (honours) (admitted 1932). Clerk to the Lieutenancy; Secretary to the Advisory Committee; Clerk of the Magistrates' Courts Committee. Previously Deputy Clerk of the Peace and of the County Council.

DEPUTY CLERKS OF THE PEACE prior to 1889

From	To	Surname	Forenames	Birth	Death	Biographical Notes
c.1573	1575	JONES	Oliver			Subsequently Clerk of the Peace, see above.
1733	1747	LLOYD	William			
1755		OWEN				
1764	1765	WYNNE	William, the elder			Subsequently Clerk of the Peace, see above.
1885	1888	KELLY	Thomas Thelwall		1901	Subsequently Clerk of the Peace, see above.

DEPUTY CLERKS OF THE PEACE AND OF THE COUNTY COUNCIL from 1889

From	To	Surname	Forenames	Birth	Death	Biographical Notes
1901	1919	OLLIVE	Thomas Holt			
1919	1932	DAVIES	John Harvey	1884		Subsequently Clerk of the Peace and of the County Council, see above.
1932	1935	WILLIAMS	Idwal	1896	1935	Solicitor (admitted 1920).
1936	1943	DACEY	William Leslie	1908		Solicitor (admitted 1931). LL.B. (London). Subsequently Deputy Secretary, later Secretary, of the County Councils Association.
1944	1945	JONES	William Hugh	1901		Subsequently Clerk of the Peace and of the County Council, see above.
1948		REES	Thomas Morgan Haydn	1915		*Elected to Society, March 1948.* Solicitor (admitted 1946). B.Q.M.S., Royal Artillery, 1939–45 War.

GLAMORGAN

From	To	Surname	Forenames	Birth	Death	Biographical Notes
CLERKS OF THE PEACE from 1539						
1539	c.1546	CARNE	Roger			Of Nash Manor and Cowbridge; "My Lord Chancellor's Servant" appointed Clerk of the Peace and of the Crown in Glamorgan and South Wales by letters patent, 6th July, 31 Henry VIII.
c.1554	1578	MEYRCKE	Rice		1587	Landed gentleman of Cottrell St. Nicholas'; genealogist and historian; author of *A Booke of Glamorganshire Antiquities*, 1578, published by Sir Thomas Phillips, 1825.
c.1590		WILLIAMS	Thomas			
c.1612		THOMAS	Edmund			
1621		THOMAS	William			
1650		MORGAN	William			
c.1684	1699	THOMAS	William		1704	Also County Treasurer. Town Clerk of Cardiff, 1690–1704. In 1721, Jane, widow and executrix of Thomas Edwards of Ogmore, and surviving executrix under Will (1701) of William Thomas, was ordered to deliver up the County rolls and records.
1719	1727	JENKINS	Edward			
1727	1729	RICHARDS	Michael	1672	1729	Married Mary, daughter of Roger Powell of Energlyn. Also County Treasurer. Town Clerk of Cardiff, 1714–29.
1730	1763	PHILLIPS	John		1763	Vice Chamberlain of Glamorgan, 1733.
1763	1794	EDWARDS	Thomas	1716	1794	Of Llandaff; Steward of Cardiff Lordship, 1759–71.
1795	1797	HOLLIER	Henry			Town Clerk of Cardiff, 1786–89; Clerk of the General Meeting, 1802; Receiver General of the County, 1813; Collector of Customs. Alderman and Bailiff of Cardiff; Steward to the Marquess of Bute.
1798	1815	WOOD	John, the elder	1755	1817	Of Cardiff; Attorney. Justice of the Peace. Also County Treasurer, 1785–1802; Town Clerk of Cardiff, 1789–1804; Clerk of the Glamorganshire Canal Company and the Cardiff Turnpike Trust; Under Sheriff, 1787, 1789, 1791, 1795, 1797, 1800, 1806; partner in banking business of "The Cardiff Bank" (Wood, Evans & Co.)
1815	1846	WOOD	John, the younger	1783	1846	Son of John Wood, the elder; of Cardiff and of Cwm, Carmarthenshire; Attorney. Deputy Lieutenant. Also County Treasurer, 1802–15. Town Clerk of Cardiff, 1804–15; Clerk to Swansea Turnpike and Wych Tree Bridge Trusts, 1832; Under Sheriff, 1797–98, 1801–02, 1804, 1807, 1814; banker; declared bankrupt, 1823.
1846	1878	DALTON	Thomas	1798	1878	Of Cardiff; Attorney (admitted 1819). Clerk to the Lieutenancy; Commissioner in bankruptcy of John Wood the younger, and solicitor to his assignees. A noted pedestrian, habitually walked from Cardiff to Swansea when Sessions held there. Previously Deputy Clerk of the Peace.
1878	1889	FRANKLEN	Thomas Mansel	1840	1928	*Elected to Society, June* 1879. Of St. Hilary, Cowbridge; nephew of Christopher Rice Mansel Talbot, the Lord Lieutenant. Barrister-at-law, Lincoln's Inn (called 1865). LL.D. Clerk to the Lieutenancy, 1884–?1889.
CLERKS OF THE PEACE AND OF THE COUNTY COUNCIL from 1889						
1889	1928	FRANKLEN	Sir Thomas (Mansel)	1840	1928	See above. Knighted, 1921.
1929	1943	ROWLAND	Henry David	1875	1958	*Elected to Society, January* 1929. Barrister-at-law, Middle Temple (called 1915). C.B.E., 1949. Secretary to the Advisory Committee. Clerk to the South Wales War Zone Court, 1939–45 War.

GLAMORGAN (*Continued*)

From	To	Surname	Forenames	Birth	Death	Biographical Notes
1943	1953	PARRY	David James	1888		*Elected to Society, March* 1935. University College of Wales, Aberystwyth, and Trinity College, Cambridge; M.A., B.Sc. Solicitor (admitted 1921). C.B.E., 1951. Justice of the Peace. Secretary to the Advisory Committee; Clerk of the Magistrates' Courts Committee. Previously Deputy Clerk of the Peace and of the County Council. Lieutenant, Royal Flying Corps, 1914–18 War.
1953		JOHN	Richard	1904		*Elected to Society, May* 1952. Solicitor (admitted 1938). Secretary to the Advisory Committee; Clerk of the Magistrates' Courts Committee. Special Constable, Glamorgan County Constabulary, 1939–52; Long Service Medal and Bar. Previously Deputy Clerk of the Peace and of the County Council.

DEPUTY CLERKS OF THE PEACE prior to 1889

From	To	Surname	Forenames	Birth	Death	Biographical Notes
1722		MORGAN	Watkin	1692	1738	County Clerk, 1717, 1724, 1726; Sub-steward of Manors of Llandough and St. Mary Church for Thomas Lord Mansel, 1726–29; probably the Watkin Morgan who was Steward to the Cardiff Lordship, Mayor of Cardiff and Constable of Cardiff Castle, 1737; buried at Llandough-juxta-Cowbridge.
1737	1747	POWELL	Richard			Of Llandow; County Clerk 1731, 1741; Under Sheriff, 1729, 1737, 1740, 1745.
1749	1756	MORGAN	Thomas			Of Coed-y-gores, Llanedeyrn. County Clerk, 1722; probably the Thomas Morgan who was Mayor of Cardiff and Constable of Cardiff Castle, 1738.
1756	1763	B	H.			
1771	1781	THOMAS	Thomas		1786	Attorney; Town Clerk of Cardiff, 1766–86; Under Sheriff, 1774, 1776, 1780, 1781, 1784.
1795	1797	VAUGHAN	William	1769	1829	Originally from Clâs, Swansea; became Squire of Llanelay, Llanharan. Barrister-at-law. Under Sheriff, 1796, 1798, 1803, 1812; Marshal and Registrar of the Great Sessions for Glamorgan, Breconshire and Radnorshire.
1829	1846	DALTON	Thomas	1798	1878	Subsequently Clerk of the Peace, see above.
1847	1866	COKE	Henry Simmonds			
1850		MORGAN	Isaac			
1866	1878	DALTON	Thomas Masters			Of Cardiff and Coedriglan; nephew of Thomas Dalton, Clerk of the Peace, 1846–78. Solicitor (admitted 1854). Under Sheriff, 1859–61.
1880	1883	SPENCER	Richard Evans	1834	1901	Solicitor (admitted 1859). Under Sheriff, 1871. Justice of the Peace for Cardiff Borough.
1883	1884	DAWSON	G. F.			
1888	1889	STEPHEN	Harry Lushington			Barrister-at-law, Inner Temple (called 1885).

DEPUTY CLERKS OF THE PEACE AND OF THE COUNTY COUNCIL from 1889

From	To	Surname	Forenames	Birth	Death	Biographical Notes
1889	1890	STEPHEN	Harry Lushington			See above.
1890	1928	ALLEN	William Edward Romilly	1862	1943	*Elected to Society, May* 1918. Solicitor (admitted 1890). Justice of the Peace for Pembrokeshire.
1929	1935	JENKINS	William Gough	1870	1944	*Elected to Society, March* 1929. Solicitor (admitted 1914). Justice of the Peace for Glamorgan.
1935	1943	PARRY	David James	1888		Subsequently Clerk of the Peace and of the County Council, see above.
1943	1952	WALTER	Arthur Clifford	1907	1952	*Elected to Society, October* 1943. Solicitor (admitted 1936).
1952	1953	JOHN	Richard	1904		Subsequently Clerk of the Peace and of the County Council, see above.
1953		WALTERS	Tom Vivian	1916		*Elected to Society, November* 1953. Solicitor (admitted 1940).

GLOUCESTERSHIRE

From	To	Surname	Forenames	Birth	Death	Biographical Notes
		CLERKS OF THE PEACE from 1392				
1392	1399	LECCHE	Henry			
1401	1405	HASELTON	John			
1406	1412	BRUYSE	William			
	1417	BROUNE	John			
1417	1450	BRUGGE	Thomas			
1452	1460	BODYNG	John			
1461	c.1465	PAYNE	Thomas			
1477	1484	HANCHICH	Thomas			Possibly Thomas Hanchich of St. Paul's, Bedford, whose Will proved in Prerogative Court of Canterbury, 1509.
1489	1495	ADMERS (ADMAS)	William			
1498	1511	PLOMER	John			
1516	1530	STRAUNGE	John			
1535	1537	STRAUNGE	Antony			
1537		PARRY	Thomas			Appointed Clerk of the Peace and of the Crown by letters patent, 18th June, 29 Henry VIII.
1540	1541	SHOTTESSORE	William			Possibly a variant of the surname Shottesford or Shotsford which occurs in Gloucestershire in this period.
1544	1546	WERELL	Henry			
1555	1557	PARKAR	Thomas			
1558	1579	GEORGE	Christopher	c.1527	1598	In his Will mentions "my Chamber in the Middle Temple."
1580	1587	STRATFORD	William			
1588	1601	ALSTON	Thomas			Possibly Thomas Alston of Apperley in Deerhurst, gentleman, whose Will proved at Gloucester, 1620.
1602	1603	CAMBE	Arthur			
1604	1607	ROBERTS	Nicholas			
1608	1637	RAYMOND	George			Probably George Raymond of Thornbury (see *Heralds' Visitation* 1682–83) who died 1642 aged 68.
1638	1641	DOWESWELL	George			
1647	1658	PURY	Thomas, the younger	1619	1693	Prominent with his father, Thomas Pury, the elder, in the defence of Gloucester against the Royalists, 1643 ("Captain of Horse and Foot"); Clerk of the Petty Bag, 1643–61; Member of Parliament for Monmouth, 1646–53; for Gloucester, 1656–68.
1661	1663	HAMPSON	Henry			
1664	1678	MORSE	Robert		1678	
1678	1689	HYETT	Benjamin	1651	1711	Attorney. Previously Deputy Clerk of the Peace. Ancestor of the Hyett family, of Painswick House, Gloucestershire.
1689	1723	STEPHENS	Thomas			Town Clerk of Gloucester and Diocesan Registrar; probably member of well-known County and legal family.
c.1724	1741	JAMES	William	c.1695	1741 or 1742	Deputy Constable of St. Briavel's Castle, 1727; his family were Forest of Dean gentry.
1742	c.1781	YOUNG	Robert			

GLOUCESTERSHIRE (*Continued*)

From	To	Surname	Forenames	Birth	Death	Biographical Notes
c.1781	1800	AUSTIN	Anthony	c.1746	1800	Of well-known clothier family, of Wotton-under-Edge; Justice of the Peace. From 1781 to 1873 the duties of the office were carried out by the Deputy Clerks, see list below.
1800	1852	TUDOR	William			Born William Cole; brother of Mary Cole, the butcher's daughter who eventually married the fifth Earl of Berkeley—she too used the surname Tudor before her marriage. A prominent witness in the Berkeley peerage claim (1810–11) which depended upon an alleged earlier marriage between his sister and the fifth Earl.
1853	1855	ELLIS	William Joyner		1855	Coroner; Clerk to the Lieutenancy.
1855	1872	BERKELEY	Henry Augustus Fitzhardinge			Probably the third (b.1789) of the four sons of the fifth Earl of Berkeley and Mary Cole, regarded as illegitimate after the decision in the Berkeley peerage claim; or possibly son of the same.
1873	1877	RIDDIFORD	George		1877	*Elected to Society, November 1856.* Of Dursley; Solicitor. Clerk to the Lieutenancy. Previously Deputy Clerk of the Peace.
1878	1889	GUISE	Francis Edward	1820	1893	Barrister-at-law, Lincoln's Inn (called 1846). Clerk to the Lieutenancy; Recorder of Hereford.

CLERKS OF THE PEACE AND OF THE COUNTY COUNCIL from 1889

From	To	Surname	Forenames	Birth	Death	Biographical Notes
1889	1893	GUISE	Francis Edward	1820	1893	See above.
1893	1933	GARDOM	Edward Theodore	1849	1933	*Elected to Society, June 1893.* Solicitor (admitted 1874). O.B.E., 1918. Clerk to the Lieutenancy. Previously Deputy Clerk of the Peace and of the County Council.
1933	1943	MOON	Richard Lovering	1903		*Elected to Society, May 1927.* Son of Walter Moon, Town Clerk of Liverpool; Solicitor (admitted 1926). Clerk to the Lieutenancy. Previously Deputy Clerk of the Peace and of the County Council of Warwickshire.
1943		DAVIS	Guy Heath	1904		*Elected to Society, March 1935.* Solicitor (admitted 1929). Clerk to the Lieutenancy; Secretary to the Advisory Committee; Clerk of the Magistrates' Courts Committee. Previously Deputy Clerk of the Peace and of the County Council of East Suffolk.

DEPUTY CLERKS OF THE PEACE prior to 1889

From	To	Surname	Forenames	Birth	Death	Biographical Notes
c.1672	1673	DORNEY	Philip			Son of John Dorney, Town Clerk of Gloucester.
1673	1678	HYETT	Benjamin	1651	1711	Subsequently Clerk of the Peace, see above.
c.1781	c.1790	WHITHORNE	Conway			
c.1796	c.1800	PERRY	Thomas			Of Wotton-under-Edge; Solicitor.
1801	1852	BLOXSOME	Edward D.		1852	*Elected to Society, November 1814.* Clerk to the Lieutenancy.
1853	1873	RIDDIFORD	George		1877	Subsequently Clerk of the Peace, see above.

DEPUTY CLERKS OF THE PEACE AND OF THE COUNTY COUNCIL from 1889

From	To	Surname	Forenames	Birth	Death	Biographical Notes
1892	1893	GARDOM	Edward Theodore	1849	1933	Subsequently Clerk of the Peace and of the County Council, see above.
1933	1939	GOODCHILD	Frank Ernest			Solicitor (admitted 1902).
1939	1947	BREWIS	George Oldfield	1909		*Elected to Society, May 1939.* Solicitor (admitted 1931). Subsequently Clerk of the Peace and of the County Council of Bedfordshire, *q.v.*
1947		ROGERS	Donald George	1915		*Elected to Society, June 1947.* Solicitor (admitted 1938). LL.B. (London).

HAMPSHIRE

From	To	Surname	Forenames	Birth	Death	Biographical Notes
CLERKS OF THE PEACE from 1393						
1393	1399	DENE	John			One John Dene of Kyngesle appointed, with others, Commissioner to inquire into goods of late King at Worldham, 1378; Writ of Supersedeas extant in case brought by John Dene and others, 1400; received payment of 3s. 4d. from Chamberlains of Winchester, 1398.
1400	1416	EMORY	Thomas			One Thomas Emory Mainprisor of Sir John Lisle, 1402; Under Sheriff, 1409–10, receiving payment of 3s. 4d. from Hordarian of St. Swithun's, for serving writs for non-payment of tithe; Counsel in litigation against Abbot of Beaulieu, 1411; sued for King before Justices of the Peace and Justices of Oyer and Terminer, 1412/3; legal adviser to City of Winchester, receiving 6s.8d. from the Chamberlains of the City, 1416; Commissioner to inquire into absconding of bondmen of Manor of Appuldercombe, 1399; into lands of God's House, Southampton, 1401/2; into lands of Priory of St. Denys and of Hospital of St. Mary Magdalene, Southampton, 1408/9; into counterfeiters, 1417; Justice of the Peace, 1419.
1417	1424	WALLOP	Richard			Possibly son of Richard Wallop, active as Knight of the Shire 1391–1431; Scholar of Winchester, 1405; proceeded to New College, Oxford 1414–15. Verderer in Forest of Buckholt, but ousted from office, 1435, as he had no lands within the forest boundaries; Plaintiff in action of debt against William Stanter of Hyndon, Wiltshire, 1444; Witness to Charter conveying lands in Berkshire, 1449; present with Justices of Assize on occasion of presentation of petition by Bishop of Winchester's tenants of Alverstoke, 1463.
1424	1441	CATEVAN	John			One John Catevan was scholar of Merton College, Oxford 1388–1402, as Founder's kin. Possibly Mainprisor in case of excommunication, 1413; Manor of Bradefeld quit-claimed by John Elerton of Kegworth, Leicestershire, to John Catevan and others, probably as trustees, 1427; acted for City of Winchester in litigation in London, 1432; Under Sheriff, 1434–35.
1442	1463	TALTON	Thomas			
1464	1471	WASKHAM	Robert			Possibly Chancery Clerk, 1441–57; Attorney to give seisin of land at West Meon, 1443; Commissioner of Array in Hundreds of Bishops Sutton, Bountesborough, East Meon and Finchdean, 1457.
1472	1479	STONEHAM	Robert			Possibly enfeoffed in Manor of Ashby-de-la-Zouch by James, Earl of Wiltshire, 1458.
1480	1493	CLERK	Richard			Possibly son of Richard Clerk, Mayor of the Staple of Wool at Exeter, 1491; specially admitted to Lincoln's Inn, 1466; Escheator, 1471–72, and Treasurer, 1514–15, of Lincoln's Inn. Commissioner to impress for making bows in City of London, 1489; and to inquire into alienations without licence, and into wards concealed, in Surrey, 1508.
1495	1504	CUFFOLD	William		1504	Probably William Cuffold or Cufaud of Cufaud in Sherborne St. John, and of Winchester; had lands in Basingstoke, Basilden, Woodgreen (Berkshire) and Sherfield-on-Loddon; Lord of the Manor of Cufaud; paid fine of 40s. 0d. to be excused office of Bailiff in Winchester, 1499; his son William was Rector of Droxford, Fellow and Vice-Warden of New College, Oxford, 1501–25.
1504	1524	LEE	John			One John Lee of Shalden a minor under Reginald Sandes and Robert Norton, trustees, 1485–86; admitted, Lincoln's Inn, 1488/9.
1524	1530	COKE	Thomas			One Thomas Coke was scholar of Hincksey Hall, Oxford, 1501–04. Clerk to the City of Winchester, 1512–23; Collector of Subsidy, Winchester, 1523–24; Member of Parliament for Winchester, 1529.
1530	1539	BARLEY (BURLEY)	Richard			Family lived at Ewhurst and Oakley before 1516; one Barley admitted, Middle Temple, 1510; one Richard Burley, Butler of of Lincoln's Inn, 1513–14; one Barley "berebrewer", Lincoln's Inn, 1515–16.

93

From	To	Surname	Forenames	Birth	Death	Biographical Notes
1541	c.1575	HENSLOWE	Ralph		1577	Eldest son of Thomas Henslowe, yeoman, farmer of the manor of West Boarhunt belonging to Southwick Priory; married (1) Clare, daughter of William Pound, (2) Katherine, daughter of Geoffrey Poole of Lordington, Sussex; connected by marriage with descendants of William Cuffold, Clerk of the Peace, 1495–1504. Appointed Clerk of the Crown for Hampshire by letters patent, 8th December, 33 Henry VIII; Member of Parliament for Portsmouth, 1555; Receiver General of lands of Earl of Southampton, 1570–71. Purchased Manor of West Boarhunt from Thomas, Lord Wriothesley, 1545; freeholder of lands in Hound, Bursledon and Botley; leaseholder of Manor of Hayling and lands in Stower, Wiltshire; also of lands in Iwerne Minster, Dorset, in right of his wife Katherine; listed as Catholic recusant, 1572; Will, 1577; tomb in West Boarhunt church.
1581	1606	MILLES	Francis			Of God's House and Bitterne Manor, Southampton; perhaps built Pear Tree House, Southampton; M.A. (Oxon) 1562; Fellow and Sub-Warden of All Souls College; admitted Gray's Inn, 1589; Secretary to Sir Francis Walsingham, 1574–75; Clerk of the Privy Seal; Burgess of Southampton, 1582; Member of Parliament for Poole, 1585–86; Commissioner for assessment and levy of subsidy, 1599; member of the Spanish Company, under Charter of 1605. (See Southampton Record Society, *Assembly Books of Southampton*, IV, pp. xxxiv *et seq.*)
1613	1638	SEARLE	Gilbert		1638	Son and heir of Roger Searle of North Warnborough; admitted, Middle Temple, 1595. Described as "of Odiham", 1611; owner of house called Wingoddes in Up Nately; Justice of the Peace, 1619; received on mortgage from the Earl of Southampton the manor houses of East and West Stratton, 1631; Will proved, 1639 (see P. C. C. Wills 1 Harvey); buried in Winchester Cathedral.
1646	1653	LONG	George			Possibly of Beckington, Somerset; purchaser of Manor of Preston Candover, 1636; adherent of Parliament, compensated for devastation of lands during Civil War, 1645; father of George Long, admitted Lincoln's Inn, 1652; uncle of Lislebone Long, Recorder of London and acting Speaker of the House of Commons; Will proved, 1657 (see P. C. C. Wills 22 Ruthven).
1654		HARRIS	Richard			Possibly son of Nathaniel Harris, D.C.L., Rector of Bletchingley, Surrey, and Canon of Hereford; nephew of John Harris, D.D., Warden of Winchester College, 1630–58; Scholar of Winchester College, 1631; of New College, Oxford; M.A., M.D.; Fellow, 1638. Registrar and Scribe of the Acts for the Archdeaconry of Surrey, 1663.
1655	1659	CHAMPION	John			Mayor of Winchester, 1651–52 and 1658–59; Solicitor to the City; Joint Town Clerk, 1655; Auditor of the Twenty-Four, 1648–49 and 1653–54; Alderman; Sequestrator of Committee for Compounding for Hampshire, 1649–54; Commissioner in Hampshire, with others, for raising assessment of £60,000 by the month, 1657; excluded from City Corporation by House of Lords, and required to surrender keys of the Coffer, 1660. Tenant of land in High Street and of site of St. Paul's Church, Winchester; also of tenement in Whitchurch Manor belonging to Winchester Cathedral, 1661; stated in 1668 to be still accountable for sums received in 1649–53 from sequestered estates.
1662	1669	STANESBY	Richard	1602	1674	Eldest son of Robert Stanesby of Micheldever; matriculated, Oriel College, Oxford, 1617; B.A., 1619. Lessee from Earl of Southampton of house and land in Micheldever, 1649; Major, Hampshire Militia, 1660; Muster Master, 1664; Will proved, 1674, in Archdeaconry Court at Winchester.
1670	1674	BERDOE	John		1675	Will of John Berdoe of St. Clement Danes, Middlesex, proved by Anne his relict, 1675.
1674	1703	COBB	Thomas		c.1703	Probably son of Richard Cobb of Winchester; father of Charles Cobb, Archbishop of Dublin, 1743–65. Freeman of Winchester and called to the Bench, 1676; Receiver General of Taxes in Hampshire and the Isle of Wight, 1691–99; petitioned for place of Auditor to Winchester Cathedral, 1665, of Receiver General of the Post Office, 1689, and for lease of the King's lands near Winchester, 1690–92; Treasury proceedings against him for not having passed accounts, 1700–02, carried on after his death against his sureties, including the Duke of Bolton.

THE GREAT HALL, WINCHESTER, HAMPSHIRE

1960

From	To	Surname	Forenames	Birth	Death	Biographical Notes
1703	1724	COWARD	Thomas	c.1665	1726	Second son of Thomas Coward of Winchester; Scholar, Winchester College, 1675, and St. Alban Hall, Oxford (B.A., 1681); Barrister-at-law, Middle Temple (called 1688). Freeman of Winchester; Recorder, 1691–1719, 1720–26; Mayor, 1719–20; Burgess of Portsmouth, 1703; Recorder, 1703–26; Justice of the Peace, 1724–26; Steward of Duke of Bolton's Manor of Putham, 1706; buried in St. Laurence's Church, Winchester.
1724	1749	BLAKE	John			Possibly son of John Blake, Mayor of Winchester, 1703–04 and 1714–15. Freeman and called to the Bench, Winchester, 1721.
1748/9	1758	KEENE	Morgan	1694	1758	Son and heir of Morgan Keene of Wincanton, Somerset; of the Close, New Sarum, Wiltshire; admitted, Lincoln's Inn, 1711. Steward to Charles, Duke of Bolton, 1754–56; father of Grace, wife of the Rev. Charles Tarrant, Dean of Carlisle and Peterborough; Will proved, 1758 (see P.C.C. Wills 16 Hutton); buried in Salisbury Cathedral (memorial inscriptions).
1758	1765	CUDDON	Thomas		1775	Son of Ebenezer Cuddon of Shaddingfield Hall, Suffolk; pensioner, Trinity Hall, Cambridge 1745; Barrister-at-law, Middle Temple (called 1755). Freeman of Winchester and called to the Bench, 1757; Recorder of Basingstoke, 1761–66; Justice of the Peace, 1766; Master in Chancery; owned property in Imber and Eddington, Wiltshire.
1765	1767	DUTHY	John		1784	Deputy Steward, 1755, and Deputy Clerk, 1758, of Bishopric of Winton; Clerk to the General Meetings of Militia, 1767–70; Clerk and Treasurer of the Winchester-Bagshot turnpike road to 1773; Justice of the Peace, 1775–83; Receiver General of Land Tax for Hampshire to 1784. His son, John Duthy, was probably author of *"Sketches of Hampshire"*, 1839.
1767	1790	DURNFORD	George	1720	1790	Son of the Rev. Thomas Durnford, Rector of Rockbourne and Whitsbury, and of Susan, great niece of Edward Stillingfleet, Bishop of Worcester. Also County Treasurer, 1754–67. Freeman of Winchester, 1756; Coroner, 1758; six times Mayor of Winchester between 1759 and 1790; Clerk to the Lieutenancy, 1772–77; Under Sheriff, 1779–80; Collector of post horse duties, 1779; Commissioner of Itchen Navigation, 1786; Head Distributor of Stamps for Western Division of Hampshire for "more than 40 years" to 1788; Proctor General to the Bishop of Winchester; memorial inscription in St. Thomas' Church, Winchester.
1790	1807	GAUNTLETT	Peter	1748	1807	Son of John Gauntlett, merchant, Alderman of Winchester; Scholar, Winchester College, 1760, and New College, Oxford, 1766; married Elizabeth, daughter of William and Ann Yalden of Winchester, 1773. Wine merchant; Steward of St. John's House, Winchester, 1774; member of the Hampshire Club, established for the "support of public liberty" under presidency of Duke of Bolton, 1776–93; pressed for parliamentary reform, and opposed election of Henry Flood as Member of Parliament, 1783; Will and codicil proved, 1807 (see P.C.C. Wills 33 Lushington); memorial inscription in St. Thomas' Church, Winchester.
1807	1809	MATHEW	Thomas Limbrey Sclater	c.1741	1809	Son of Richard Sclater, Alderman of City of London, and of Magdalen, daughter and heiress of John Limbrey of Tangier Park and Hoddington House, Hampshire; took name of Mathew by Royal Sign Manual, 1802. Member of the Hampshire Club, 1776; buried at Upton Gray.
1809	1865	FARR	William Dale	1772	1865	Only son of William Farr, M.D., physician to the Royal Hospital, Plymouth; Exeter School and St. John's College, Cambridge; LL.B. 1797; Barrister-at-law, Lincoln's Inn (called 1797). Married Elizabeth Anne, daughter of James Lukin of Teddington, Middlesex, and Littlehampton, Sussex, 1806; owned property in the Isle of Wight; died at Iford and buried at Christchurch Priory.
1865	1889	EARLE	Thomas Hughes	1833	1891	*Elected to Society, June 1866.* Third son of Henry Earle, solicitor, Clerk to the Lieutenancy and Alderman of Andover; Eton College and King's College, Cambridge; 29th Wrangler, 1857; M.A., 1860; Fellow 1857–75; Barrister-at-law, Lincoln's Inn (called 1858). Married Isabel, daughter of William Francis of Blackheath. Captain, 1st Battalion, Hampshire Rifle Volunteers, to 1875; inherited Enham Place, Knight's Enham, and owned Manor of Wield.

From	To	Surname	Forenames	Birth	Death	Biographical Notes

CLERKS OF THE PEACE AND OF THE COUNTY COUNCIL from 1889

From	To	Surname	Forenames	Birth	Death	Biographical Notes
1889	1891	EARLE	Thomas Hughes	1833	1891	See above.
1891	1894	WEBB	George Arthur	1837	1900	*Elected to Society, June 1891.* Of Winchester, later of Shawford; Crier, 1860–61, and Clerk, 1862–86, of the Sheriff's County Court; Chief Clerk in Office of Clerk of the Peace, 1867–81; Clerk to Visitors of Lunatic Asylum, 1865–81; Honorary Secretary, Winchester Conservative Association; Auditor, Hampshire Friendly Society and Winchester Savings Bank; first Secretary of Winchester Cricket Club. Previously and subsequently Deputy Clerk of the Peace and of the County Council.
1895	1923	BARBER	Henry	1857	1923	*Elected to Society, May 1895.* Son of John Barber, of Nottingham; Solicitor (admitted 1879). LL.B. (London). Justice of the Peace. Clerk to the Lieutenancy from 1900; Governor, from 1899, and Treasurer, from 1904, of Winchester School for Girls. Previously assistant solicitor, Liverpool County Borough Council, Deputy Registrar of Liverpool Court of Passage, and Town Clerk of Huddersfield.
1924	1946	BARBER	Frederic Viccars	c.1876	1956	*Elected to Society, June 1901.* Nephew of Henry Barber; Solicitor (admitted 1898). LL.B. (London). Clerk to the Lieutenancy. Assistant Secretary, Military Appeal Tribunal, 1914–18. Alderman, Hampshire County Council, 1946–56. Previously Deputy Clerk of the Peace and of the County Council.
1946		WHEATLEY	George Andrew	1908		*Elected to Society, March 1939.* Son of Robert Albert Wheatley, Clerk of the Peace and of the County Council of Pembrokeshire, 1912–39; Rugby School and Exeter College, Oxford; M.A., B.C.L. Solicitor (admitted 1932). C.B.E., 1960. Clerk to the Lieutenancy. Previously assistant solicitor, Pembrokeshire, East Suffolk, and Yorkshire (North Riding) County Councils, and Deputy Clerk, later Clerk, of the Peace and of the County Council of Cumberland.

DEPUTY CLERKS OF THE PEACE prior to 1889

From	To	Surname	Forenames	Birth	Death	Biographical Notes
1564	1568	LAWRENCE	Thomas			
1573	1576	LAWRENCE	William		1583	Four times Mayor of Winchester between 1548 and 1573; Member of Parliament for Winchester, 1557–58; acted for City in securing custody of the Castle, 1559; had lease of the Hermit's Tower, the City Ditch and Bewmonds (the Castle Green); owned Danemark meadow and field outside Westgate; Will proved, 1583 (see P.C.C. Wills 13 Rowe).
1588	1589	HARDY	Richard			Born at Sydling, Dorset; cousin of Francis Milles, Clerk of the Peace 1581–1606; specially admitted to Lincoln's Inn, 1590. Burgess of Southampton, signing Proclamation of King James I, 1603; took conveyance, with others, of West Shamlord in Whippingham. Will proved, 1607 (see P.C.C. Wills 33 Huddlestone).
1603		HARDY	Robert			
1606		HYDE	Roger			Married Joan Baker, in right of whom he held Manor of Upper Eldon, King's Somborne, c.1602–41; Town Clerk, Romsey, 1616; Justice of the Peace, 1631–41.
1607		FAWKENER	Anthony			
1633	1649	AYLWYN	John		1654	Of Basingstoke; Attorney to Court of Record, Basingstoke, 1624; Burgess, 1631; Bailiff, 1631, 1639–40; Town Clerk, 1639; Clerk and Justice of the Peace, Basingstoke, 1641; Alderman, 1641; Mayor, 1642, 1649; Deputy Recorder of Basingstoke, 1647; Warden of the Chapel of the Holy Ghost, Basingstoke, 1634–36; Will proved, 1654 (see P.C.C. Wills 197 Alchin).

From	To	Surname	Forenames	Birth	Death	Biographical Notes
1672	1690	IMBER	Matthew			Probably son of John Imber, M.A. (Oxon), usher at Winchester College, who later kept a school at St. John's Hospital Chapel, and became Vicar of Christchurch. Coroner, c.1678; Notary Public and Proctor of the Consistory Court, 1704; published "*The Case, or an Abstract of the Customs of the Manor of Merdon in the Parish Hursley*", 1707.
1675	1692	BROWNE	Matthew			Apparently jointly with Matthew Imber; of Winchester.
1691	1709	GOOD	Richard		1713	Of Winchester; Auditor of the Commonalty, Winchester, 1673; of the Twenty-Four, 1692–95; Mayor, 1699; Under Sheriff; acted as Solicitor for County in Exchequer, 1692.
1695	1715	GOOD	Arthur			Son of Richard Good.
1715	1721	CLARKE	Henry			Possibly connected with Clarke family of Hyde Abbey and Avington. Town Clerk of Winchester, 1704–29.
1717	c.1758	IMBER	Thomas		1761	Of Winchester; Attorney. Steward of the Society of Natives in Winchester, 1723; Treasurer and Receiver of the County, 1741–54; Registrar of Archdeaconry of Winchester, 1725–61; Proctor of Consistory Court; mural tablet in St. Thomas' Church, Winchester.
1763		PRIOR	William	c.1707	1764	Of Winchester; Alderman; Coroner, 1752–64; owned the Three Tunns Inn; Will proved in Archdeaconry Court, 1764; mural tablet in St. Laurence's Church, Winchester.
1764		HOLLOWAY	Richard		1798	Of Winchester; Attorney. Deputy Registrar of Archdeaconry of Winchester, 1796; Proctor of Consistory Court.
1765	1773	KNOTT	Charles		1800	Son of Thomas and Mary Knott of Hursley; Attorney. Deputy Registrar of Archdeaconry of Winchester and Proctor of Consistory Court, 1773; Master Extraordinary of Court of Chancery, 1774; Steward of Vernhams Dean Manor, 1776–79, and of Allington Manor, 1777; Treasurer to County Hospital; later acting Clerk of the Peace, 1788. Buried at Hursley.
1766		PEYTON	Higgons			Barrister-at-law. Clerk of the Peace and Town Clerk of Basingstoke, 1763–69; Filacer for Kent, Surrey and Sussex, 1783.
1772	1773	FLEETWOOD	John		1789	Of St. Mary Calendar, Winchester; married Martha Mullens, of Hambledon. Attorney. Coroner, 1774–89; Clerk to the Justices, Alton division, 1787; Proctor of the Consistory Court.
1773	1788	RAVEN	James		1788	Of Winchester; Attorney. Clerk to Commissioners of Winchester Pavement, 1773–88.
1788	1790	HOLLIS	George	c.1762		Of Winchester; married (1) Jane Parry of Michelmersh, 1792; (2) Sophronia Clark of St. Bartholomew Hyde, Winchester, 1802; Attorney. Also County Treasurer, 1799–1823. Freeman of Winchester, 1781, later Chamberlain; Clerk and Treasurer of Oxdown Gate, Popham-Winchester Turnpike Road, 1791; Under Sheriff, 1795–1823; Deputy for Replevins, Winchester, 1824–30; Proprietor of Itchen Navigation, c.1809–37; author of works relating to County and its administration.
1790	1798	CORBIN	Robert Reeks		1798	Of Winchester; married Elizabeth Earle of Winchester, 1798; Attorney. Coroner, 1791–98; Clerk to Itchen Navigation Commissioners, 1795; Will proved, 1798 (see P.C.C. Wills 640 Walpole).
1798	1808	KERBY	Peter			Attorney. Clerk to Commissioners of Appeal under Income Tax, 1799–1800; to Commissioners of New Alresford Inclosure, 1807; Captain, Infantry Battalion, 1807; Burgess of New Alresford, 1809–13.
1808	1858	WOODHAM	Thomas			*Elected to Society, May 1845.* Attorney. Freeman of Winchester. Clerk to the Lieutenancy, 1817, re-appointed 1852; Clerk to the Justices, Winton division; Clerk to Visitors of Private Lunatic Asylums, 1835–57; Deputy for Replevins, Winchester, 1838–39; Under Sheriff, 1858; Secretary of Committee for Relief of Sufferers by Fire, Chilbolton, 1811; Deputy Steward, 1824, later Steward, 1853, of Manor of Twyford; Proctor of the Consistory Court; purchased Manor of Farley Chamberlayne.

From	To	Surname	Forenames	Birth	Death	Biographical Notes
1858	1864	WOODHAM	Thomas Burnett			*Elected to Society, May 1859.* Grandson of Thomas Woodham. Under Sheriff, 1858–95; Clerk to Visitors of Lunatic Asylums, 1859–64; Clerk to the Justices, Winton division, 1859–1911.
1859	1878	ELDRIDGE	James			*Clerk of the Peace for election purposes in Isle of Wight.* Of Newport, Isle of Wight; Solicitor (admitted 1832). Town Clerk, Newport.
1888	1889	WEBB	George Arthur	1837	1900	Subsequently Clerk of the Peace and of the County Council, see above.

DEPUTY CLERKS OF THE PEACE AND OF THE COUNTY COUNCIL from 1889

From	To	Surname	Forenames	Birth	Death	Biographical Notes
1889	1891	WEBB	George Arthur	1837	1900	See above.
1894		GOOLD	John			
1895	1900	WEBB	George Arthur	1837	1900	Re-appointed Deputy after serving as Clerk in recognition of his long service to the County.
1900	1924	BARBER	Frederic Viccars	c.1876	1956	Subsequently Clerk of the Peace and of the County Council, see above.
1924	1955	HICKSON	Cuthbert Gollan	1893		*Elected to Society, June 1924.* Solicitor (admitted 1920). LL.B. (Manchester).
1946	1951	BAINES	Leslie Henry	1909		*Elected to Society, December 1942.* *Joint Deputy Clerk of the Peace only.* Solicitor (admitted 1934). M.A. (Oxon). Deputy Clerk of the Peace for Hampshire while Clerk of the County Council of the Isle of Wight (*q.v.*), prior to establishment of Isle of Wight Quarter Sessions in 1951.
1955	1957	LANE	Walter Ernest	1920		*Elected to Society, January 1955.* *Deputy Clerk of the Peace and First Deputy Clerk of the County Council.* Solicitor (admitted 1948). M.A. (Cantab). Subsequently Clerk of the Peace and of the County Council of Lincolnshire (Parts of Lindsey), *q.v.*
1955	1960	BAINS	Malcolm Arnold	1921		*Elected to Society, January 1955.* *Second Deputy Clerk of the County Council, 1955; Deputy Clerk of the Peace and First Deputy Clerk of the County Council, 1957.* Solicitor (admitted 1945). LL.B. (Dunelm). Subsequently Deputy Clerk of the County Council of Kent, *q.v.*
1957		MARTIN	John Hawksley	1922		*Elected to Society, March 1957.* *Second Deputy Clerk of the County Council, 1957; Deputy Clerk of the Peace and First Deputy Clerk of the County Council, 1960.* Son of Hubert Sinclair Martin, Clerk of the Peace and of the County Council of East Sussex, 1939–59; Solicitor (admitted 1950). B.A. (Cantab). Previously assistant solicitor, Worcestershire and Warwickshire County Councils. Lieutenant, R.N.V.R., 1939–45 War.
1960		SMYTH	Arthur Hugh Manistre	1918		*Elected to Society, June 1960.* *Second Deputy Clerk of the County Council only.* Solicitor (John Mackrell prize) (admitted 1949). M.A. (Oxon). Previously Deputy Town Clerk, Wolverhampton. Major, D.C.L.I., 1939–45 War.

HEREFORDSHIRE

From	To	Surname	Forenames	Birth	Death	Biographical Notes
CLERKS OF THE PEACE from 1396						
1396	1426	HARPER	William			
1426	1458	WELYNGTON	John			
1464	1467	WELYNGTON	Thomas			
1470	1480	WELYNGTON	John			
1482	1486	BREYNTON	George			
1498	1501	GOODMAN	John			
1504	1505	WARNCOMBE	Richard			
1507	1514	CLAYTON	William			Appointed Clerk of the Peace and of the Crown by letters patent, 18th April, 22 Henry VII.
1516	1525	WARNCOMBE	Richard			
1525	1528	HAVERD	Thomas			
1530	1531	HACKYLUETT	John			
1531	1537	BAKER	John			
1537	c.1575	LYGON	Roger			Appointed Clerk of the Peace and of the Crown by letters patent, 21st June, 29 Henry VIII.
1541	1548	WARNCOMBE	John			Warncombe, and also Hawt, Baughan and John Clerk (see below) were presumably deputies to Lygon, who was still in office c.1575.
1549		HAWT	James			
1550	1553	BAUGHAN	Roger			
1554	1573	CLERK	John			
1574	1615	CLERK(E)	Thomas			Deputy to Roger Lygon until the latter's death.
1615	1617	SCUDAMORE	William			
1618	1621	PAYNE	Toby			
1625	1630	HALL	Richard			
1631	1633	SEITBORNE	Richard			
1647	1649	MARSTON	Richard			
1649	1652	PHILPOTT	Nicholas			
1653	1658	SYDALL	James			
1660	1670	PHILPOTT	Nicholas			
1671	1688	TRAUNTER (TRANTER)	Simon			
1688	1709	WILLIAMS	Paul			
1710	1752	WILLIAMS	Thomas			Appointed John Weare of Hereford as Deputy, 1740.

HEREFORDSHIRE (*Continued*)

From	To	Surname	Forenames	Birth	Death	Biographical Notes
1752	1797	FALLOWES	Benjamin			"The younger"; of Leominster; possibly bailiff of Leominster, 1762 and 1776; re-appointed John Weare as Deputy, 1752.
1797	1804	KINNERSLEY	James			
1804	1817	FALLOWES	Benjamin			
1817	1836	BIRD	Thomas			Antiquarian; his collection sold, 1837, at Drybridge House, Hereford.
1836	1882	CLEAVE	John		1882	*Elected to Society, February* 1849. Attorney (admitted 1813).
1882	1889	SYMONDS	James Frederick	1820	1911	*Elected to Society, June* 1882. Solicitor (admitted 1841). Justice of the Peace. Clerk to the Lieutenancy; Alderman, Hereford City Council.

CLERKS OF THE PEACE AND OF THE COUNTY COUNCIL from 1889

From	To	Surname	Forenames	Birth	Death	Biographical Notes
1889	1904	SYMONDS	James Frederick	1820	1911	See above.
1904	1924	SYMONDS	John Reginald	1850	1924	*Elected to Society, May* 1900. Solicitor (admitted 1872). Clerk to the Lieutenancy; Secretary to the Advisory Committee; Under Sheriff. Alderman, Hereford City Council. Previously Deputy Clerk of the Peace and of the County Council.
1924	1937	MAPLES	Edward William	1872	1951	*Elected to Society, January* 1925. Cambridge and London Universities and Trinity College, Dublin; M.A. (Cantab), LL.D. (Dublin). Barrister-at-law, Gray's Inn (called 1909). O.B.E., 1918. Justice of the Peace; Deputy Lieutenant; Honorary Freeman of City of Hereford. Clerk to the Lieutenancy; Secretary to the Advisory Committee. Previously County Director of Education. Subsequently Alderman, Herefordshire County Council, 1937–51; Chairman, Herefordshire Quarter Sessions, 1946–48; Vice Chairman of Executive Council of County Councils Association, 1941; President of Association, 1945–50.
1937		HANSEN	Richard Claussen	1905		*Elected to Society, October* 1932. Solicitor (admitted 1929). Clerk to the Lieutenancy; Secretary to the Advisory Committee; Clerk of the Magistrates' Courts Committee. Previously assistant solicitor, Grimsby County Borough and Herefordshire County Councils, and Deputy Clerk of the Peace and of the County Council.

DEPUTY CLERKS OF THE PEACE AND OF THE COUNTY COUNCIL from 1889

From	To	Surname	Forenames	Birth	Death	Biographical Notes
1889	1904	SYMONDS	John Reginald	1850	1924	Subsequently Clerk of the Peace and of the County Council, see above.
1919	1920	NELSON	Richard Albany			Of Hereford; Solicitor (admitted 1907). B.A., LL.B. (Cantab).
1920		SYMONDS-TAYLER	Richard Herbert	1867	1949	Of Hereford; Solicitor (admitted 1894). B.A. Justice of the Peace. Mayor of Hereford, 1926–27.
1932	1937	HANSEN	Richard Claussen	1905		Subsequently Clerk of the Peace and of the County Council, see above.
1941		CANT	Francis Denis Victor	1909		*Elected to Society, March* 1942. Solicitor (admitted 1931). Previously assistant solicitor, Dudley County Borough Council and assistant Town Clerk, Hereford.

HERTFORDSHIRE

From	To	Surname	Forenames	Birth	Death	Biographical Notes
		CLERKS OF THE PEACE from 1391				
1391	1392	GERNOUN	Adam			
1392	1393	MORDON	Robert			
1401	1429	WARYNER	Henry			
1404		FYNCHYNG-FELD	John			Appointed Clerk and King's Attorney before Justices of the Peace in Hertfordshire, Essex and Suffolk by letters patent, 11th March, 5 Henry IV. Appears to have acted in Essex and Suffolk only, *q.v.*
1429	1467	HORNE	John			Manor of Chamberlains (Parish of Reed) came into his possession; he presented to the Church, 1477, but "must have died soon after" as his son-in-law presented in 1479 (see *V.C.H.* III, p.251); as great-grandson of Eleanor de Buckland, petitioned for restoration to his family under Settlement of 1313 of Manor of Buckland, 1468; Manor of Horne, held of Manor of Buckland, came into possession of his son-in-law; Advowson of Buckland in his possession, 1478 (see *V.C.H.* IV, pp. 44–5, 48).
1472	1482	BELE	John		1516	Brass to John Bele, d. 1516, and to his two wives with two children, in Radwell Church (see *V.C.H.* III, p. 247).
1483	1501	INGRAM	Thomas		1501	Was party to deed relating to land in Parish of Sandon, 1492 (see Chauncey, *Historical Antiquities of Hertfordshire*, I, p. 161). Described as "of Stortford" in his Will proved 1501 (see P.C.C. Wills 16 Moone).
1501	1508	SOPER	Thomas			
1506		DAVYSON	Robert			Appointed Clerk of the Peace and of the Crown by letters patent, 31st July, 21 Henry VII; also in Essex.
1508	1535	HAYWORTH	John			Manor of Mackerye End (Parish of Wheathampstead) conveyed to John Willey alias Heyworth, 1465, whose son John settled his lands upon his adopted daughter Margaret Hoo, 1558; Brass to John Heyworth and Elizabeth his wife (four sons, five daughters), 1520, and tablet to John Heyworth (?his son) d. 1558 and his wife Margaret (two sons, one daughter), both in Wheathampstead Church (see *V.C.H.* II, pp. 300, 310–1).
1535	1536	CAVENDISSHE	William			"Cromwell's servant, 1534" (see *V.C.H.* IV, p. 410); Manor of Birchall (Parish of Hertingfordbury) conveyed to William and Margaret his wife, 1539 (see *V.C.H.* III, p. 466); Manor of Northaw granted by King Henry VIII to same parties, 1539–40; Manor of Childwick (Parish of St. Michael's) granted to Sir William and Margaret his wife, 1540 (see *V.C.H.* II, pp. 358–9, 398).
1536	1559	HANCHETT	Thomas	c.1516	1574	Manor of Berwick (Parish of Barkway) sold to "Thomas Hanchett of Albury", 1553 (see *V.C.H.* IV, p. 32). See also East Herts. Arch. Soc. Transactions, XI, pp. 38–40. The forename appears as Richard in the Pipe Roll for 1551–2; possibly an error for Thomas.
1560	1565	BRYCKETT	Robert			Manor of Westwick (Parish of St. Michael's) conveyed to him and John Byll as Trustees by Ralph Rowlatt, 1557 (see *V.C.H.* II, p. 394); Brass in Barley Church, 1563 (?) (see *V.C.H.* IV, p. 41); described as "of Barley, gent." in his Will proved 1566 (see P.C.C. Wills 19 Crymes).
1567	1570	HAMOND	William		1570	Manor of Garnons (Parish of Great Munden) conveyed to William Hamond and others, 1526; another William Hamond holding it, 1586 (see *V.C.H.* III, p. 127); described as "of Great Munden" in his Will, proved 1570 (see P.C.C. Wills 38 Lyon).
1570	1603	BROCKETT	William		1611	Purchased Camfield estate (Parish of Essendon) from Sir Edward Denny, 1601; died seised of it (see *V.C.H.* III, p. 459).
1605	1613	ALEYN	Thomas			
1614	1616	SNELLINGE	John			

HERTFORDSHIRE (*Continued*)

From	To	Surname	Forenames	Birth	Death	Biographical Notes
1617	1620	ROWLEY	John			Manor of Rushden sold to John and William Rowley, 1604 (see *V.C.H.* III, p. 266); Brass to Anna, wife of John Rowley, 1613, and inscription to Anna his second wife, 1650, both in Barkway Church (see *V.C.H.* IV, p. 35).
1620		DOUTHWAITE	W.			
1621	1657	HIDE	Edward		1657	Manor of Barwick (Parish of Standon) conveyed to him by William Newce in payment of debts, 1648 (see *V.C.H.* III, p. 359); described as "of Great Hadham, senior, gent." in his Will, proved 1657 (see P.C.C. Wills 248 Ruthen); buried Much Hadham, 1657.
1657	1660	WILLYMOTT	James		1662	Manor of Kelshall sold to him, 1628; held until his death when it passed to his son James, Sheriff of County in 1683 (see *V.C.H.* III, p. 241).
1660	1673	BURGES	Thomas			
1673	1686	CHAUNCEY	John		1692	Lived in Hertford; brother of Sir Henry Chauncey; buried at Cheshunt, 1692 (see Clutterbuck, *History of Hertfordshire*, II, p. 402). *Note:* described as Deputy Clerk of the Peace in Pipe Roll for 1673–74.
1687	1689	RICHARDS	Thomas			
1689	1720	TOLLER	Bostock, the elder	1666	1724	Buried at St. Andrews, Hertford; Rebecca, his wife, died 1718, aged 50.
1720	1761	TOLLER	Bostock, the younger	1692	1761	Buried at All Saints, Hertford; Ann, his wife, died 1768, aged 75.
1761	1768	THOROWGOOD	Henry			
1768	1780	NICHOLLS	Thomas			
1780	1813	ROOKE	Benjamin, the elder		1813	Previously Deputy Clerk of the Peace.
1813	1825	ROOKE	Benjamin, the younger			
1825	1851	STORY	John Samuel			*Elected to Society, May 1825.* Writ to "Keeper of our Peace" and Justices to admit him as Clerk, which they had refused to do when he first appeared, 1825 (see Sessions Records II, p. 295).
1851	1865	BOSWORTH	Thomas Holmes			*Elected to Society, February 1859.* Attorney. Previously of Westerham, Kent.
1865	1889	NICHOLSON	Sir Richard	1828	1913	*Elected to Society, June 1865.* *Honorary Secretary, 1881–1910; Chairman, 1882–1910.* Fifth son of George Nicholson of Hertford, Solicitor, Clerk to the Lieutenancy of Middlesex, 1843–53; Solicitor (admitted 1851). F.S.A., 1858; knighted 1886. Appointed Clerk of the Peace for Hertfordshire and Middlesex, 1865, and concurrently held those two clerkships, together with that for London from 1889, until 1894. Clerk to the Lieutenancy from 1869. Chairman of Law Fire Insurance Co. Ltd. and director of Law Life Assurance Co. Ltd. In early life, trained as surveyor and went to New Zealand, assisting to lay out towns of Wanganui and Dunedin; returned to England and as solicitor successfully prosecuted claim of Lord Shrewsbury and Talbot to the Earldom of Shrewsbury, 1857–59; contested parliamentary election at Hastings, 1876; played important part in passing Local Government Act, 1888. Left over £350,000; buried in Westminster Cemetery, Hanwell. See Plate VII.

102

From	To	Surname	Forenames	Birth	Death	Biographical Notes

CLERKS OF THE PEACE AND OF THE COUNTY COUNCIL from 1889

From	To	Surname	Forenames	Birth	Death	Biographical Notes
1889	1894	NICHOLSON	Sir Richard	1828	1913	See above.
1894	1930	LONGMORE	Sir Charles (Elton)	1855	1930	*Elected to Society, June 1894.* *Honorary Secretary, 1911–25; Vice-Chairman 1910–14; Chairman, 1914–25.* Eldest son of Matthew Skinner Longmore of Hertford; Haileybury; Solicitor (admitted 1879). C.B. (civil), 1911; K.C.B. (civil), 1913. Clerk to the Lieutenancy; Member of Court of Lieutenancy, City of London. Member of Council of Law Society; of Disciplinary Committee; President, 1914–15; Member of Home Office Committee on Criminal Appeal Act, and of Departmental Committee on Swine Fever, 1911. Commissioned in the Hertfordshire Regiment; commanded 1st Battalion, 1900–13, and 2nd Battalion, 1914–16; Honorary Colonel, 1914; Lieutenant-Colonel, Territorial Forces Reserve; Chairman, Hertfordshire Territorial Forces Association; V.D., T.D.
1930	1948	LONGMORE	Philip Elton	1884	1954	*Elected to Society, January 1929.* Son of Sir Charles Longmore; Rugby School and Exeter College, Oxford; M.A. Solicitor (admitted 1911). C.B.E., 1941. Justice of the Peace and Deputy Lieutenant, 1948. Clerk to the Lieutenancy; Secretary to the Advisory Committee. Previously Clerk to Hertford Board of Guardians, 1912–30; of Hertford R.D.C. 1912–28; of Welwyn R.D.C. 1912–24; of Hatfield R.D.C. 1921–28, and Deputy Clerk of the Peace and of the County Council. Major, Hertfordshire Regiment, 1914–18 War; D.A.A.G. 2nd Army, 1916; D.A.A.G., G.H.Q., Italy, 1917; Despatches (twice).
1948		MOON	Arthur Neville	1908		*Elected to Society, April 1946.* Son of Walter Moon, Town Clerk of Liverpool; Blundell's School; Solicitor (admitted 1932). Deputy Lieutenant, 1959. Clerk to the Lieutenancy, Secretary to the Advisory Committee, Clerk of the Magistrates' Courts Committee. Previously Deputy Clerk of the Peace and of the County Council. Major, Royal Artillery, 1939–45 War.

DEPUTY CLERKS OF THE PEACE prior to 1889

From	To	Surname	Forenames	Birth	Death	Biographical Notes
1768	1780	ROOKE	Benjamin, the elder		1813	Subsequently Clerk of the Peace, see above.
1825	1842	MEDLAND	William			
1851	1870	DORANT	James Annesley			*Elected to Society, February 1859.* Joint appointment from 1867 with William Mathew Armstrong, see below, of St. Albans; Attorney (admitted 1813).
1867	1870	ARMSTRONG	William Mathew			Of Hertford; Attorney (admitted 1835).
1870	1874	BEAL	Edward William	1847	1936	*Elected to Society, June 1877.* Solicitor (admitted 1870). M.A. (London). Clerk to the Justices, St. Albans division; Clerk to the Visiting Justices, Harpenden and Much Hadham asylums. Deputy Clerk of the Peace for Middlesex, 1874–83.
1874	1875	GILL	Alfred			
1876	1889	DUMVILLE	Peter Williamson			Solicitor (admitted 1862).

HERTFORDSHIRE (*Continued*)

From	To	Surname	Forenames	Birth	Death	Biographical Notes

DEPUTY CLERKS OF THE PEACE AND OF THE COUNTY COUNCIL from 1889

From	To	Surname	Forenames	Birth	Death	Biographical Notes
1889	1894	DUMVILLE	Peter Williamson			See above. Subsequently County Treasurer.
1897	1900	SWORDER	Thomas Joseph			Solicitor (admitted 1868). Clerk of the Hertford and Welwyn R.D.Cs.
1901	1929	LONGMORE	Philip Raynsford			*Elected to Society, June* 1910. Solicitor (admitted 1897). M.A., O.B.E., 1920.
1929	1930	LONGMORE	Philip Elton	1884	1954	Subsequently Clerk of the Peace and of the County Council, see above.
1930	1940	LONGMORE	Philip Raynsford			See above.
1940	1946	SWIFT	George Norman Cyrus	1906		*Elected to Society, April* 1940. Solicitor (admitted 1930). Subsequently Clerk of the Peace and of the County Council of Cumberland, *q.v.*
1946	1948	MOON	Arthur Neville	1908		Subsequently Clerk of the Peace and of the County Council, see above.
1948	1956	BOYCE	Frederick Peter	1915		*Elected to Society, November* 1948. Solicitor (Clement's Inn prize) (admitted 1939). Subsequently Clerk of the Peace and of the County Council of Norfolk, *q.v.*
1956		MANSON	John Neville	1918		*Elected to Society, October* 1956. Solicitor (admitted 1949). B.A. (Oxon). Major, Royal Artillery, 1939–45 War.

HERTFORDSHIRE — LIBERTY OF ST. ALBANS

CLERKS OF THE PEACE from c.1575

From	To	Surname	Forenames	Birth	Death	Biographical Notes
c.1575		WESTE	William			
1683		RICHARDS	Thomas			
1691	1705	TOMBES	John			
1735	1764	MARIOTT	John			
1764	1785	HALL	John			Attorney of the Court of Common Pleas.
1786	1805	COWPER	John			
1805	1819	PALMER	John			
1820	1851	STORY	John Samuel			Also Clerk of the Peace for Hertfordshire, see above.
1851	1865	BOSWORTH	Thomas Holmes			Also Clerk of the Peace for Hertfordshire, see above.
1865	1878	NICHOLSON	Richard	1828	1913	Also Clerk of the Peace for Hertfordshire, see above.

DEPUTY CLERKS OF THE PEACE from 1851

From	To	Surname	Forenames	Birth	Death	Biographical Notes
1851	1865	DORANT	James Annesley			Also Deputy Clerk of the Peace for Hertfordshire, see above.
1877	1878	DUMVILLE	Peter Williamson			Also Deputy Clerk of the Peace for Hertfordshire, see above.

HUNTINGDONSHIRE

From	To	Surname	Forenames	Birth	Death	Biographical Notes
		CLERKS OF THE PEACE from 1390				
1390	1392	MULLISWORTH	William			
1392	1411	CANNE	Robert			
1411	1415	MULLISWORTH	William			
1416	1421	SPENSER	William			
1422	1427	COUPHULL	John			
1427	1449	CASTELL	William			
1452	1454	EST	Richard			
1466	1469	CHEKER	John			
1475	1503	ARNOLD	Robert			
1506	1530	SPENCER	John			Brothers: appointed jointly in survivorship for Huntingdonshire and Bedfordshire by letters patent, 28th November, 22 Henry VII.
		SPENCER	Thomas			
1538	1557	SLADE	Richard			Appointed Clerk of the Peace and of the Crown by letters patent, 5th February, 29 Henry VIII.
1567		SYBLEY	William			
1575	1581	EDWARDS	George			
1585	1595	WENTWORTH	Matthew			
1599		LOK	Eliazer			
1601	1603	FOLKES	Simon			
1609	1625	BARNES	John			In the seventeenth century, the Sheriff accounted for payment to the Clerks of the Peace for both Huntingdonshire and Cambridgeshire without distinguishing them. Some Clerks may have acted for both Counties, and some may be wrongly ascribed in the lists.
1651	1652	JENKINSON	John			
1653	1656	PERCIVAL	William			
1662	1709	CLARKE	Robert			
1711	c.1718	CLARKE	John			
1734	1768	THONG	Thomas			
1769	1779	OVERALL	Francis			
1779	1784	JOHNSON	Adrian			
1784	1796	STEPHENSON	William		1796	
1797	1799	JOHNSON	Samuel		1799	Of St. Ives.
1799	1834	SHERARD	Robert		1835	*Elected to Society, November* 1815. Of Oundle, Northamptonshire; Attorney.

HUNTINGDONSHIRE (*Continued*)

From	To	Surname	Forenames	Birth	Death	Biographical Notes
1835	1838	DAY	Neville	1802	1839	*Elected to Society, November* 1835. Of St. Neots; Attorney.
1839	1860	GREENE	Benjamin Aislabie	1805	1860	*Elected to Society, May* 1841. Of St. Ives; Attorney.
1860	1889	MAULE	Edward	c.1820	1900	Solicitor (admitted 1847). Clerk to the Lieutenancy; Town Clerk of Huntingdon; Clerk to the Justices, Leightonstone division.

CLERKS OF THE PEACE AND OF THE COUNTY COUNCIL from 1889

From	To	Surname	Forenames	Birth	Death	Biographical Notes
1889	1898	MAULE	Edward	c.1820	1900	See above.
1898	1932	MAULE	John Percy	1854	1932	*Elected to Society, November* 1888. Solicitor (admitted 1881). Previously Deputy Clerk of the Peace and of the County Council.
1932	1954	KELLY	John Bradshaw	1889		*Elected to Society, October* 1927. Solicitor (admitted 1922). Clerk to the Lieutenancy; Secretary to the Advisory Committee; Clerk of the Magistrates' Courts Committee. Previously assistant solicitor, Cumberland County Council; assistant Town Clerk, Hastings; assistant solicitor, Dorset County Council; Deputy Clerk of the Peace and of the County Councils of Dorset and of Berkshire. Lieutenant, Durham Light Infantry, 1914–18 War.
1954		AYLWARD	Anthony Case	1916		*Elected to Society, March* 1947. Solicitor (admitted 1938). Clerk to the Lieutenancy; Secretary to the Advisory Committee; Clerk of the Magistrates' Courts Committee. Previously Deputy Clerk of the Peace and of the County Council of Lincolnshire (Parts of Kesteven). Major, Wiltshire Regiment and South Waziristan Scouts, 1939–45 War.

DEPUTY CLERKS OF THE PEACE prior to 1889

From	To	Surname	Forenames	Birth	Death	Biographical Notes
1710		ASKHAM	Dingley			
1797		HARRIS	Joseph			
1799		MARGETTS	William			
1801		SHERARD	Caryer		1823	
1888	1889	MAULE	John Percy	1854	1932	Subsequently Clerk of the Peace and of the County Council, see above.

DEPUTY CLERKS OF THE PEACE AND OF THE COUNTY COUNCIL from 1889

From	To	Surname	Forenames	Birth	Death	Biographical Notes
1889	1898	MAULE	John Percy	1854	1932	See above.
1898	1921	MAULE	Montague George	1852	1921	Solicitor (admitted 1881). Town Clerk, Huntingdon; Coroner.
1921	1936	BICKERS	Herbert Edwin	1869	1955	*Elected to Society, November* 1932.
1952	1956	WALDEN	Harry George	1903		*Elected to Society, January* 1953. Solicitor (admitted 1935). LL.B. (London). Went into private practice, 1956.
1956		LAVERACK	John Anthony Smith	1921		*Elected to Society, December* 1956. Solicitor (admitted 1948).

ISLE OF ELY

From	To	Surname	Forenames	Birth	Death	Biographical Notes
CLERKS OF THE PEACE from 1748						
1748		AUBREY	Samuel			Clerk of the Crown; Clerk of the Assize; Prothonotary; Chirographer and Under-secretary (Palatinate offices).
1801	1826	BELLAMY	James		1826	
1826	1852	JACKSON	Hugh			*Elected to Society, November 1829.*
1852	1867	METCALFE	Charles			*Elected to Society, May 1852.* Solicitor (admitted 1818). Registrar, Wisbech County Court.
1867	1889	METCALFE	Frederick Morehouse		1893	*Elected to Society, June 1868.* Solicitor (admitted 1852).
CLERKS OF THE PEACE AND OF THE COUNTY COUNCIL from 1889						
1889	1893	METCALFE	Frederick Morehouse		1893	See above.
1894	1907	JACKSON	Edward Hugh		1907	*Elected to Society, June 1894.* Solicitor (admitted 1850).
1907	1935	COPEMAN	Charles Edward Fraser	1867	1949	*Elected to Society, April 1907.* Solicitor (admitted 1895). B.A. (Cantab). C.M.G., 1917. Justice of the Peace. Secretary to the Advisory Committee; Clerk to the Commissioners of Taxes. Town Clerk, Wisbech, 1904–20. Colonel, Cambridgeshire Regiment; T.D.
1935		THURLOW	Richard Francis Gardom	1905		*Elected to Society, November 1932.* Grandson of Edward Theodore Gardom, Clerk of the Peace and of the County Council of Gloucestershire, 1893–1933; Solicitor (admitted 1928). Secretary to the Advisory Committee; Clerk of the Magistrates' Courts Committee. Previously Deputy Clerk of the Peace and of the County Council.
DEPUTY CLERKS OF THE PEACE prior to 1889						
1763		COCKERAM	Isaac			
1778		BELLAMY	James			
1801	1826	GIRDLESTONE	Steed			Of Wisbech St. Peter's.
DEPUTY CLERKS OF THE PEACE AND OF THE COUNTY COUNCIL from 1889						
1893		RYALL	Frederick			
1920	1922	OLLARD	John William Arthur	1893		*Deputy Clerk of the Peace only.* Solicitor (admitted 1919).
1922	1926	PETTEFAR	George	1888		*Deputy Clerk of the Peace only.* Solicitor (admitted 1922).
1931	1935	THURLOW	Richard Francis Gardom	1905		Subsequently Clerk of the Peace and of the County Council, see above.
1950		ROOK	David James	1920		*Elected to Society, January 1950.* Solicitor (admitted 1947). LL.B., L.A.M.T.P.I.

ISLE OF WIGHT

From	To	Surname	Forenames	Birth	Death	Biographical Notes
		CLERKS OF THE COUNTY COUNCIL from 1890				
1890	1892	ESTCOURT	Arthur Sotheron	1853	1892	Solicitor (admitted 1879). LL.B. (Cantab). Previously Town Clerk, Newport, I.O.W., and Guardian of the Poor for Newport.
1892	1896	FARDELL	John Wilson	1839	1896	Solicitor (admitted 1861). Clerk to the County and Ryde Justices. Previously Town Clerk, Ryde, and Clerk to the Sandown Local Board.
1896	1904	WOOLDRIDGE	William Henry	1842	1907	Solicitor (admitted 1863). Clerk to the Newport Borough Justices. Previously Clerk to the Sandown U.D.C.
1904	1937	DUFTON	John	1871		Public Assistance Officer. Previously Assistant Clerk, Pudsey U.D.C. and Clerk, Tong U.D.C. and Ventnor U.D.C.
1938	1945	WHITE	Percival Edward	1902		*Elected to Society, April* 1934. Solicitor (admitted 1926). LL.B. (London). Clerk of the Isle of Wight Rivers Catchment Board; Public Assistance Officer. Subsequently Clerk of the Peace and of the County Council of Montgomeryshire, *q.v.*
1946		BAINES	Leslie Henry	1909		*Elected to Society, December* 1942. Solicitor (admitted 1934). M.A. (Oxon). Clerk to the Lieutenancy in relation to Isle of Wight matters; Secretary to the Advisory Committee; Clerk of the Isle of Wight River Board and of the Isle of Wight Water Board; Deputy Clerk of the Peace for Hampshire until 1951; Public Assistance Officer until 1948. Previously assistant solicitor, Hertfordshire and Yorkshire (North Riding) County Councils and Deputy Clerk of the Peace and of the County Council of Cumberland.

CLERK OF THE PEACE AND OF THE COUNTY COUNCIL from 1951

From	To	Surname	Forenames	Birth	Death	Biographical Notes
1951		BAINES	Leslie Henry	1909		See above.

KENT

From	To	Surname	Forenames	Birth	Death	Biographical Notes
		CLERKS OF THE PEACE from 1395				
1395	1420	CROWE	Thomas			
1420	1446	HORE	John			
1446	1452	ROGER	John			Of Headcorn; frequently Under Sheriff. He or his son was Under Treasurer of England.
1453	1481	BRENT	Roger			Keeper of Sandwich castle; Justice of the Peace from 1481. Probably identical with Roger Brent of Canterbury, whose Will and testament were dated 4th and 24th February, 1486/7, in Consistory Court of Canterbury (ref. P.R.C. 32/3 f. 138).
c.1482	1493	SHELDWYCH (SHELDWYTH)	Nicholas			Probably Nicholas Sheldwich or Sheldwych, whose Will was proved 1st September 1494 in Archdeaconry Court of Canterbury (ref. P.R.C. 17/6 f. 69).
1495	1497	FYNEUX	William			Possibly William Fyneux the elder, late of Hougham, whose Will was dated 18th November 1532 in Consistory Court of Canterbury (ref. P.R.C. 32/15 f. 237).
1499	1503	TYLLY	John			
1505	1506	MOTTON	Thomas			
1506	1526	LUCAS	John			Appointed Clerk of the Peace and of the Crown by letters patent, 29th October, 22 Henry VII.
1526	1533	LOVEKYN	Arthur			
1533	1534	BARROWE	John			
1534	1536	CAUNTON	Nicholas			
1536	1540	BARROWE	John			
1542	1568	CAUNTON	Nicholas			Appointed Clerk of the Peace and of the Crown by letters patent 3rd March, 33 Henry VIII.
1570	1575	CHEYNEY	Robert			
1576	1584	HYDE	Ralph			
1587	1591	LAWLEY	George			
1593	1594	MASCALL	Thomas			
c.1595	c.1611	WEBBE	John			
1613	1616	HOOPER	John			
1617	1624	NYN	John			May have remained in office longer, with deputies acting; presented at Maidstone for non-repair of highways, 1629.
1624	1627	ROMNEY	John			Of Maidstone.
1627	1629	PADDY	Samuel			Of Maidstone.
1629	c.1633	SEAGARS	Francis			
c.1635	c.1638	FOWLER	John			
1640	1660	BROUGHTON	Andrew		1687	Freeman, 1630, and Mayor, 1648 and 1660, of Maidstone; as Clerk of the High Court of Justice, 1649, read death sentence on King Charles I; Member of Parliament for Kent, 1653 (the "Little Parliament"); Clerk of Court which tried John Lilburne the Leveller 1653; Member of Parliament for Maidstone, 1658. Deposed from Mayoralty, mentioned in proclamation for arrest of regicides, and fled to Continent, 1660; died at Geneva aged 84.
1660	1670	DERING	Christopher			
1670	1672	HEAD	Henry			Possibly of St. Nicholas', Rochester and descended from family resident at Rainham.
1673	c.1680	TWISDEN	Francis			Possibly son of Sir Thomas Twisden of Bradbourne.
1681	1687	SAUNDERS	Robert			Acted in Sessions business from 1678. Possibly identical with Robert Saunders, Town Clerk of Maidstone prior to 1688, and Mayor, 1681 and 1688. Removed from office after Michaelmas Sessions 1687, presumably on grounds of being an anti-Catholic Whig; re-appointed 1689.

KENT (*Continued*)

From	To	Surname	Forenames	Birth	Death	Biographical Notes
1688	1688/9	KENNETT	John			A pro-Catholic; was ordered to hand over records of the office in his custody, 15th July 1689.
1689	1690	OWEN	Philip		1700	Appointment challenged by Robert Saunders. Common Pleas found for Owen; decision reversed in King's Bench, 1690. On writ of error brought in Parliament in Hilary Vacation 1699/1700, original judgment of Common Pleas affirmed, but Owen died three or four days later.
1690	1702	SAUNDERS	Robert			Re-appointed; see above.
1702	1753	FULLER	David		1753	Attorney. Also County Treasurer, 1706–17. Bought Chillingdon Manor, Maidstone, 1746.
1753	1773	AUSTEN	Francis			Of Sevenoaks; Attorney. Under Sheriff, 1735; Agent to Duke of Dorset, the *Custos Rotulorum*, 1733–34.
1773	1808	AUSTEN	Francis Motley		1815	Son of Francis Austen; of Wilmington.
1808	1822	CLARIDGE	John Fellows		1822	*Elected to Society, May* 1810. *Honorary Secretary,* 1814–22. Previously Deputy Clerk of the Peace.
	1855	DARELL	Philip John	1817	1855	Second son of Edward Darell of Calehill, Kent; probably acted through deputies; died at Algiers.
1855	1865	WILDES	Henry Atkinson			*Elected to Society, November* 1834. Attorney (admitted 1816). Clerk to the Lieutenancy; Under Sheriff, 1856. Declared bankrupt 1863; removed from office, May 1865, for misdemeaning himself by refusing to make an order for payment of bill of Frederick Scudamore, solicitor of Maidstone, who acted as Clerk in suit which Wildes brought against Quarter Sessions for non-payment of his salary. Unsuccessfully questioned validity of his dismissal in the Queen's Bench; thereafter unsuccessfully sued his successor for money had and received, and later unsuccessfully sought *Quo warranto* against him. Previously Deputy Clerk of the Peace.
1865	1889	RUSSELL	Francis			*Elected to Society, June* 1865. Barrister-at-law, Inner Temple (called 1841). Recorder of Tenterden.

CLERKS OF THE PEACE AND OF THE COUNTY COUNCIL from 1889

From	To	Surname	Forenames	Birth	Death	Biographical Notes
1889	1891	RUSSELL	Francis			See above.
1891	1929	PROSSER	Walter Byron	1849	1933	*Elected to Society, June* 1892. Barrister-at-law, Inner Temple (called 1875). O.B.E., 1918.
1929	1953	PLATTS	Walter Leslie	1885	1958	*Elected to Society, June* 1921. *Vice-Chairman,* 1947–50; *Chairman,* 1950–52. Solicitor (admitted 1908). Clerk to the Lieutenancy and to the Dartford Tunnel Committee. F.S.A.; L.M.T.P.I. Senior Vice President, Town Planning Institute; Chairman, Executive Council, National Association of Parish Councils. Previously Deputy Town Clerk, Kingston-upon-Hull, and Clerk of the Peace and of the County Council of Cornwall. R.N.V.R., 1914–18 War.
1954	1960	BISHOP	Gerald	1894		*Elected to Society, March* 1941. Solicitor (admitted 1920). Clerk to the Lieutenancy; Secretary to the Advisory Committee, Clerk of the Dartford Tunnel Committee, of the Kent Joint Advisory Water Committee, and of the Kent and Essex Sea Fisheries Committee. Previously assistant solicitor, Yorkshire (West Riding) County Council and Deputy Clerk of the County Council of Kent. Captain, Northamptonshire Regiment, 1914–18 War.
1960		HECKELS	Geoffrey Thomas	1904		*Elected to Society, January* 1954. Solicitor (admitted 1928). Clerk to the Lieutenancy; Secretary to the Advisory Committee; Clerk of the East and West Kent Magistrates' Courts Committees, of the Dartford Tunnel Committee, of the Kent Joint Advisory Water Committee, and of the Kent and Essex Sea Fisheries Committee. Previously assistant Town Clerk, Cambridge, assistant solicitor, Nottingham City Council, and Deputy Clerk of the Peace and of the County Council of Kent. Major, Rifle Brigade, 1939–45 War.

From	To	Surname	Forenames	Birth	Death	Biographical Notes

DEPUTY CLERKS OF THE PEACE prior to 1889

From	To	Surname	Forenames	Birth	Death	Biographical Notes
1562	1575	FRANKLYN	John			Possibly John Franklyn or Frankelen whose Will was proved 3rd September 1576 in Consistory Court of Canterbury (ref. P.R.C. 32/32 f. 206).
1654		GODDIN	John			
1749		WILLARD	Thomas			Of Maidstone.
1753	1761	EASTCHURCH	Samuel			Of Maidstone.
1763		WILLARD	Thomas			
1764	1765	WEEKLY	John			
1774		COAST	William Stacey			
1776		PARKER	Robert			
1791	1793	NICHOLSON	Thomas			
1791		CLARIDGE	John Fellows		1822	Subsequently Clerk of the Peace, see above.
1794		NICHOLSON	Thomas			
1822	1832	SCUDAMORE	William			*Elected to Society, November* 1823. Attorney. Clerk to the Lieutenancy. Also County Treasurer.
1832	1855	WILDES	Henry Atkinson			Under Sheriff, 1834–35. Subsequently Clerk of the Peace, see above.
1885		SCUDAMORE	Frederick		1888	Of Maidstone; Solicitor (admitted 1840). Under Sheriff, 1861, 1863–67, 1869–70, 1873–88.

DEPUTY CLERKS OF THE PEACE AND OF THE COUNTY COUNCIL from 1889

From	To	Surname	Forenames	Birth	Death	Biographical Notes
1931	1941	LIGHTBURN	John Edward	1891		*Elected to Society, July* 1932. Solicitor (admitted 1914). Subsequently Clerk of the County Council of Essex, *q.v.*
1941	1948	LANCASTER	Roy Cavander	1896		*Deputy Clerk of the Peace only.* Barrister-at-law, Gray's Inn (called 1924). Captain, The Buffs, 1914–18 War.
1941	1954	BISHOP	Gerald	1894		*Deputy Clerk of the County Council only.* Subsequently Clerk of the Peace and of the County Council, see above.
1948	1957	SCOTT	Jack David	1915		*Elected to Society, November* 1948. *Deputy Clerk of the Peace only.* Solicitor (admitted 1938). LL.B. Clerk of the East and West Kent Magistrates' Courts Committees. Major, Royal Artillery, 1939–45 War.
1954	1960	HECKELS	Geoffrey Thomas	1904		*Deputy Clerk of the County Council,* 1954; *Deputy Clerk of the Peace,* 1957. Subsequently Clerk of the Peace and of the County Council, see above.
1957		OLDHAM	John Hugh			*Elected to Society, May* 1957. *Second Deputy Clerk of the Peace,* 1957; *Deputy Clerk of the Peace,* 1960. Solicitor (admitted 1937). M.A. (Cantab); D.P.A. (London). Previously assistant solicitor, Middlesex, East Suffolk and Warwickshire County Councils. Major, Middlesex Regiment, 1939–45 War; T.D.
1960		BAINS	Malcolm Arnold	1921		*Elected to Society, January* 1955. *Deputy Clerk of the County Council only.* Solicitor (admitted 1945). LL.B. (Dunelm). Previously assistant solicitor, Taunton Borough, Sunderland County Borough and Nottinghamshire County Councils, and Deputy Clerk of the Peace and of the County Council of Hampshire. Flying Officer, Royal Air Force, 1939–45 War.

LANCASHIRE

From	To	Surname	Forenames	Birth	Death	Biographical Notes
CLERKS OF THE PEACE from 1440						
1440	1447	GARDINER	John			Possibly the John Gardiner who was benefactor of the Royal Grammar School, Lancaster.
1447		CLIFTON	William			Possibly the father of William Clifton of Kidsnape, who died in 1517 leaving three daughters, one of whom, Anne, married Bartholomew Hesketh, see below.
1539	1540	HESKETH	Bartholomew		c.1543	Grandson of Thomas Hesketh of Rufford (d.1463) by William his sixth son, founder of a chantry at Rufford; Justice of the Peace, 1516–17; *Custos Rotulorum*, 1535.
1540	1543	CUDWORTH	Ralph	1506	1558	Son and heir of John Cudworth of Werneth in Oldham.
1543	1576	RANDOLPH	Bernard			
1576	1589	LATHAM	Ralph			Married Etheldred, daughter of Peter Cutts of Arkesden in Essex; possibly one of the Lathoms of Parbold; (there were also Lathoms at Mossborough in Rainford); held Clerkship for life, but surrendered in 1589.
1589	1612	RIGBY	Roger			Second son of Alexander Rigby of Burgh and brother of Edward Rigby, Clerk of the Crown.
1612	1621	RIGBY	Alexander, the elder		1621	Son of John Rigby of Wigan (d.1594) and cousin of Roger Rigby; Attorney, Gray's Inn. Clerk to Sir Gilbert Gerard, Master of the Rolls. Previously Deputy Clerk of the Peace.
1621	1627	RIGBY	Alexander, the younger	1594	1650	Eldest son of Alexander Rigby, the elder; of Middleton, near Preston; held Clerkship in trust. Colonel in Parliamentary Army; besieger of Lathom House, and Commander of Parliamentary forces in Lancashire. Member of Parliament for Wigan, 1640–50; Baron of the Exchequer, 1649–50.
1627	1644	RIGBY	George	1602	1644	Brother of Alexander Rigby, the younger; Attorney.
1644	1648	RIGBY	Alexander, the younger	1594	1650	Re-appointed: see above.
1648	1663	RIGBY	Joseph	1600	1671	Brother of George and Alexander Rigby; Attorney. Major in Parliamentary Army. (*Note:*—Charles Worsley was *de jure* but not *de facto* Clerk of the Peace from 22nd February to 24th June, 1654).
1663	1698	KENYON	Roger	1627	1698	Son and heir of Roger Kenyon of Parkhead, Whalley; married Alice, daughter and heiress of George Rigby. Member of Parliament for Clitheroe, 1690–95; Governor of the Isle of Man, 1691–92. See Plate IV.
1698	1728	KENYON	George, the elder	1666	1728	Third son and heir of Roger Kenyon; Barrister-at-law. Vice Chancellor of County Palatine of Lancaster, 1706; Member of Parliament for Wigan, 1713–15. Great uncle of the first Lord Kenyon, Attorney General, later Master of the Rolls and Chief Justice of the King's Bench.
1728	1780	KENYON	George, the younger	1702	1780	Second son and heir of George Kenyon the elder; Barrister-at-law, Middle Temple (called 1726). M.A. (Cantab). Fellow of St. John's College, Cambridge.
1780	1796	STEPHENS	Humphrey		1796	Granted reversion of patent of Clerkship of the Peace in 1771 for his own life and the lives of the Hon. John Charles Villiers and his brother the Hon. George Villiers.
1796	1825	STEPHENS	Edward			
1825	1838	CLARENDON	John Charles Villiers, 3rd Earl	1757	1838	Barrister-at-law, Lincoln's Inn (called 1779). M.A., LL.D. (Cantab). Privy Councillor, 1787. King's Counsel in Duchy of Lancaster, 1782–86; Surveyor of Woods, northern part of Duchy, 1786–1826; Member of Parliament for Old Sarum 1784–90, Dartmouth 1790–1802, Wick 1802–05, and Queenborough 1807–12 and 1820–24; Comptroller of Royal Household, 1787–90; Chief Justice in Eyre North of Trent, 1790–1838; Prothonotary of County of Lancaster, 1804–1838; Envoy to Portugal, 1807–10.

From	To	Surname	Forenames	Birth	Death	Biographical Notes
1825	1827	VILLIERS	Hon. George	1766	1827	Held office jointly with third Earl of Clarendon, his uncle. Clerk of Council and Keeper of Duchy of Lancaster records, c.1792–1827.
1838	1879	HARPER	Robert John		1879	Duchy of Lancaster Receiver of South Parts, 1802; Axebearer at Needwood, 1826.
1879	1889	HULTON	Frederick Campbell	1841	1899	*Elected to Society, April* 1874. Grandson of Edward Gorst, joint Deputy Clerk of the Peace, 1800–23; Solicitor (admitted 1863). Registrar of Preston County Court, c. 1880–99; Clerk to the Visiting Justices of the Asylum of Whittingham, 1872–89. Previously Deputy Clerk of the Peace.

CLERKS OF THE PEACE AND OF THE COUNTY COUNCIL from 1889

From	To	Surname	Forenames	Birth	Death	Biographical Notes
1889	1899	HULTON	Frederick Campbell	1841	1899	See above.
1899	1922	CLARE	Sir Harcourt (Everard)	1854	1922	*Elected to Society, May* 1900. Solicitor (admitted 1875). Knighted, 1916. Clerk of Lancashire Asylums Board, of Lancashire Insurance Committee, of Mersey and Irwell Joint Committee and of Ribble Joint Committee. Previously Town Clerk of Liverpool.
1922	1944	ETHERTON	Sir George (Hammond)	1878	1949	*Elected to Society, July* 1922. *Vice Chairman,* 1933–35; *Chairman,* 1935–44. Solicitor (admitted 1902). O.B.E., 1919; knighted, 1927; Deputy Lieutenant; Order of St. Anne of Russia. Clerk to the Lieutenancy and Secretary to the Advisory Committee, 1929–47; Clerk of Lancashire Rivers Board, 1922–44, and of Lancashire Mental Hospitals Board. Member of Railways Assessment Authority, 1930–47; of Board of Trustees, Preston and District Savings Bank, 1923–44; of Governing Body of Rossall School; Visiting Fellow of Nuffield College, Oxford, 1939. Previously Deputy Town Clerk of Woolwich and Portsmouth, and Town Clerk of Portsmouth and Liverpool; subsequently member of War Damage Commission, 1944–48, and of Requisitioned Land and War Works Commission, Central Land Board, 1947–48.
1944	1960	ADCOCK	Sir Robert (Henry)	1899		*Elected to Society, January* 1945. *Vice Chairman,* 1950–52; *Chairman,* 1952–53. Solicitor (admitted 1923). C.B.E., 1941; knighted, 1950; Deputy Lieutenant. Clerk to the Lieutenancy and Secretary to the Advisory Committee from 1948; Clerk to the Magistrates' Courts Committee. Previously assistant solicitor, Manchester County Borough and Nottinghamshire County Councils, and Deputy Town Clerk and Town Clerk, Manchester.
1960		McCALL	Charles Patrick Home	1910		*Elected to Society, March* 1949. Solicitor (admitted 1936). Clerk to the Lieutenancy; Secretary to the Advisory Committee; Clerk of the Magistrates' Courts Committee. Previously assistant solicitor, Dorset and Hampshire County Councils, and Deputy Clerk of the Peace and of the County Council. Lieutenant Colonel, Royal Artillery and R.A.O.C., 1939–45 War; M.B.E. (Mil.); T.D.

DEPUTY CLERKS OF THE PEACE prior to 1889

From	To	Surname	Forenames	Birth	Death	Biographical Notes
1547	1572	KENYON	William		1572	Of Manchester; Baron of the Exchequer at Lancaster, 1547–58; Deputy Escheator and Farmer of the Shrievalty, 1555–56. By Will left his interest in the office of Clerk of the Peace, which he held by deputation from Bernard Randolph, to his brothers Thomas and Michael Kenyon.
c.1573		RIGBY	Alexander			
c.1573		ANDERTON	James			Clerk of Common Pleas at Lancaster.
1605	1612	RIGBY	Alexander		1621	The first known deputation was in 1605 but it is probable that since Roger Rigby was not a lawyer he appointed his cousin Alexander, when he purchased the letters patent for his office in 1589. Subsequently Clerk of the Peace, see above.
1612	1616	IRELAND	William			Of Holborn.
1616	1628	MAWDESLEY	Robert			Of Wigan; brother-in-law of George Rigby, Clerk of the Peace, 1627–44. Town Clerk of Wigan.

LANCASHIRE (*Continued*)

From	To	Surname	Forenames	Birth	Death	Biographical Notes
1628	1647	TOMPSON	Alexander			Of Langtree; yeoman; cousin of George Rigby.
1628		MORTE	Thomas		1674	Of Little Hulton.
1672		ROWE	Henry			Of Wigan.
1698		EDGE	Richard	c.1641	c.1705	Of Middle Hulton.
1698		KENYON	Thomas			Of Manchester.
1779	1800	TAYLOR	James			
1800	1825	GORST	John, the elder	1765	1825	Of Preston; Solicitor.
1800	1823	GORST	Edward	1765	1823	*Represented at second meeting of Society, May* 1810. Held office jointly with his brother, John Gorst the elder; of Preston; Solicitor.
1825	1857	GORST	Edward Chaddock		1857	Son of Edward Gorst; Attorney.
1825	1837	BIRCHALL	Thomas, the elder	1777	1837	Of Ribbleton Hall; Attorney.
1838	1857	GORST	John, the younger		1861–5	Son of John Gorst the elder; Attorney.
1838	1879	BIRCHALL	Thomas, the younger			Son of Thomas Birchall the elder; Solicitor (admitted 1832).
1858	c.1890	WILSON	Thomas		c.1890	Of Cooper Hill, Walton-le-Dale; Solicitor (admitted 1842).
1869	1879	HULTON	Frederick Campbell	1841	1899	Subsequently Clerk of the Peace, see above.
1879	1889	SADLER	Samuel Campbell Hulton			*Elected to Society, June* 1898. Nephew of Frederick Campbell Hulton; Solicitor (admitted 1863).

DEPUTY CLERKS OF THE PEACE AND OF THE COUNTY COUNCIL from 1889

From	To	Surname	Forenames	Birth	Death	Biographical Notes
1889	1904	SADLER	Samuel Campbell Hulton			See above.
1891	1925	MUSPRATT	John Petty	1857	1945	*Elected to Society, June* 1898. *Second Deputy Clerk of the Peace and of the County Council,* 1891; *Deputy,* 1904. Solicitor (admitted 1881). B.A.
1926	1945	CLEAVER	Harold Willoughby	1879	1950	*Elected to Society, May* 1926. Solicitor (admitted 1901).
1937	1950	JOLLIFFE	Archibald Henry	1895		*Elected to Society, January* 1937. *Second Deputy Clerk of the Peace and of the County Council,* 1937; *Deputy,* 1945. Solicitor (admitted 1919). O.B.E., 1945. Subsequently Clerk to the Mersey River Board. Lieutenant Colonel, Cheshire Regiment, 1939–45 War; M.C.
1946	1948	McCOMB	James Ellis			*Elected to Society, October* 1946. *Second Deputy Clerk of the Peace only.* Solicitor (admitted 1932). Subsequently General Manager, Hatfield Development Corporation. Group Captain, Royal Air Force, 1939–45 War; D.F.C.
1949	1960	McCALL	Charles Patrick Home	1910		*Second Deputy Clerk of the Peace and of the County Council,* 1949; *Deputy* 1951. Subsequently Clerk of the Peace and of the County Council, see above.
1951		INMAN	Peter Donald	1916		*Elected to Society, March* 1951. *Second Deputy Clerk of the Peace and of the County Council,* 1951; *Deputy* 1960. Solicitor (admitted 1946). LL.B. (Leeds). Major, K.O.Y.L.I., 1939–45 War; T.D.
1960		OWEN	Robert Penrhyn			*Elected to Society, March* 1960. *Second Deputy Clerk of the Peace and of the County Council.* Solicitor (admitted 1947). Previously assistant solicitor, Lancashire County Council. Captain, Royal Welch Fusiliers, 1939–45 War.

LEICESTERSHIRE

From	To	Surname	Forenames	Birth	Death	Biographical Notes
		CLERKS OF THE PEACE from 1393				
1393	1405	FAULKES	John			
1406	c.1439	HALLE	William			
1444	1446	WYMONDES-WOLD	John			Deputy Steward of Honor of Leicester, 1443 (see Somerville, *Duchy of Lancaster*, I, p. 563).
1446	1456	PALMER	John			
1475	1490	REYNOLD	Richard			
1498	1499	REYNOLD	William			
1501		FYLDYNG	Peter			
1516	1517	FOULER	John			Bailiff and Town Clerk of Leicester, 1518 (see Somerville, *op. cit.*, p. 571).
1517	1524	BRABAZON	William			
1525	1527	WALDRAM	Thomas			
1537		JOSKYN	James			Appointed Clerk of the Peace and of the Crown for Leicestershire and Northamptonshire by letters patent, 26th June, 29 Henry VIII. Also Clerk of the Wardrobe of Robes and of the King's Beds in England.
1545		CHARNOK	William			
1555	1556	GRENEWODE	James		1558/9	Buried at Belgrave, Leicester.
1569		EDON				
1572	1585	COTTON	Thomas			
1589	1593	BENT	William			Later escheator and feodary.
1599		OLIVER	Richard			
1601	1615	NEEDHAM	Edward			
1617	1621	CUTLER	Henry			
1623	1625	GERARD	Thomas			
1629	1633	NEWTON	Joseph			
1635	1641	NEWTON	John			
1648		CHAMPANTIE	John			
1650	1654	DYSON	Ralph			
1655	1658	MAJOR	John			
1662	1666	RAYSON	George			
1667	1675	GREEN	Theophilus			
1676	1681	PALMER	Edward			
c.1684		JACQUES	Warner			
1688	c.1742	WATTS	John			Clerk and Treasurer to the Lieutenancy, 1715.
1743	1747/8	CARTER	Thomas	c.1683	1747/8	Buried at St. Mary de Castro, Leicester.
1748	1756	PECK	Thomas	c.1719	1756	Buried at Enderby.
1756	1784	PARKE	Reuben	1717	1784	Clerk to the Lieutenancy, c. 1765. Buried at Melton Mowbray.
1784	1785	FOSTER	Jonathan, the elder		1785	Clerk to the Lieutenancy, April 1785. Buried at Aylestone Leicester.
1785	1815	FOSTER	Jonathan, the younger			
1815	1841	FREER	Thomas	1766	1841	Attorney. Previously Deputy Clerk of the Peace. Buried at Blaby.
1842	1873	FREER	William	1801	1873	*Elected to Society, November* 1849. Cousin of Thomas Freer; Attorney (admitted 1822). Under Sheriff, 1858. Buried at Houghton-on-the-Hill.

From	To	Surname	Forenames	Birth	Death	Biographical Notes
1873	1888	REEVE	William Napier	1811	1888	*Elected to Society, June 1867.* Solicitor (admitted 1834). Clerk to the Lieutenancy; Under Treasurer. Had practised at Braintree, Essex, before appointment as Deputy Clerk of the Peace. Buried at Bocking, Essex.
1888	1889	FREER	William Jesse	1853	1932	*Elected to Society, June 1880.* *Vice Chairman and Honorary Treasurer, 1914–32.* Grandson of William Freer, Clerk of the Peace 1842–73; Solicitor (admitted 1875). V.D., F.S.A. Clerk to the Lieutenancy; Under Sheriff, 1882; Deputy Constable at Leicester Castle, 1884; Under Treasurer, 1887. Previously Deputy Clerk of the Peace.

CLERKS OF THE PEACE AND OF THE COUNTY COUNCIL from 1889

From	To	Surname	Forenames	Birth	Death	Biographical Notes
1889	1932	FREER	William Jesse	1853	1932	See above. Also Deputy Lieutenant, 1911; Secretary to the Advisory Committee. Buried at Houghton-on-the-Hill.
1932	1946	RUMSEY	Lucas Eustace	1879		*Elected to Society, May 1922.* Solicitor (admitted 1902). Previously Deputy Clerk of the Peace and of the County Council.
1946		CHATTERTON	John Arthur	1905		*Elected to Society, March 1934.* Solicitor (admitted 1929). Secretary to the Advisory Committee; Clerk of the Magistrates' Courts Committee. Previously assistant solicitor, Lincolnshire (Parts of Lindsey) County Council, and Deputy Clerk of the Peace and of the County Council of Oxfordshire.

DEPUTY CLERKS OF THE PEACE prior to 1889

From	To	Surname	Forenames	Birth	Death	Biographical Notes
c.1575		BENT	William			
1686		BROWN	William			
1687		WADLAND	Thomas			
1800	1815	FREER	Thomas	1766	1841	Subsequently Clerk of the Peace, see above.
1845		COOKE	James			
1867	1873	REEVE	William Napier	1811	1888	Subsequently Clerk of the Peace, see above.
1880	1888	FREER	William Jesse	1853	1932	Subsequently Clerk of the Peace, see above.
1888	1889	ROWLATT	George	1850	1922	*Elected to Society, June 1889.* Born at Weston-by-Welland, Northamptonshire; Solicitor (admitted 1871). Under Sheriff, 1884–1922.

DEPUTY CLERKS OF THE PEACE AND OF THE COUNTY COUNCIL from 1889

From	To	Surname	Forenames	Birth	Death	Biographical Notes
1889	1922	ROWLATT	George			See above.
1922	1932	RUMSEY	Lucas Eustace	1879		Subsequently Clerk of the Peace and of the County Council, see above.
1932	1946	FREER	Charles Edward Jesse	1901		*Elected to Society, July 1932.* *Deputy Clerk of the Peace only.* Nephew of William Jesse Freer, Clerk of the Peace 1888–1932; born Winckley; took the name of Freer, 1922; Solicitor (admitted 1924). Deputy Lieutenant. Clerk to the Lieutenancy; Secretary to the Advisory Committee; Under Sheriff, 1932. Subsequently Deputy Chairman of Quarter Sessions, 1946; Chairman, 1949. Lieutenant Colonel, Royal Artillery, 1939–45 War; Deputy Judge Advocate-General in Iceland, 1941–42, and at S.H.A.E.F., 1943–44.
1939		KNIGHT	Clifford	1906		*Elected to Society, October 1946.* *Deputy Clerk of the County Council, 1939; Deputy Clerk of the Peace, 1948.* Solicitor (admitted 1928). Previously assistant solicitor, Cornwall and Leicestershire County Councils.
1946	1948	FOWLER	Edward George Bennett	1873	1956	*Deputy Clerk of the Peace only.* Solicitor (admitted 1894). Coroner, City of Leicester.
1960		LANG	Gordon Robert			*Elected to Society, December 1960.* *Second Deputy Clerk of the Peace only.* Solicitor (admitted 1948). M.B.E.

LINCOLNSHIRE, PARTS OF HOLLAND

From	To	Surname	Forenames	Birth	Death	Biographical Notes
CLERKS OF THE PEACE from 1395						
1395	c.1406	SYKELPRUYS	Reginald			The name occurs as witness to grant of land at Pinchbeck, 1335, and as party to deed there, 1438.
c.1406	1413	STEVENSON	William			
1417	1427	MAYNE	Robert			
1427	1456	HEREBENE (HARDBENE)	John			
1448		REPYNGHALE	Robert			Appointed by letters patent Clerk of the Keepers of the Peace and of Justices of Oyer and Terminer *alias* Clerk of the Crown and of the Peace and to the office of King's Attorney before the Justices of the Peace in all Parts of Lincolnshire, 1st April, 26 Henry VI. The evidence of the Pipe Rolls is that he acted in Kesteven and Lindsey.
1482	1502	COK	Richard			
1503	1513	PALMER	Thomas			
1523	1533	OGLE	Richard			Of Pinchbeck; Justice of the Peace, 1547.
1535	1539	BURTON	John			
1541	1542	BURTON	Thomas			
1543	1571	IRBY	Leonard		1571	Appointed by letters patent Clerk of the Peace and of the Crown in Holland and Kesteven; possibly Deputy Steward of Long Sutton for Duchy of Lancaster, 1561. Member of Parliament for Boston, 1554–57 and 1563–71.
1571	1584	ELWOOD	John			Also Clerk of the Peace for Kesteven.
1585	1589	WELBYE	Humfrey			Also Clerk of the Peace for Kesteven. Related by marriage to Leonard Irby, above.
1589	1597	ROBINSON	Matthew			Also Clerk of the Peace for Kesteven.
1607	1633	ROSSETER	Christopher			Also Clerk of the Peace for Kesteven; and for Lindsey, 1630–33.
1633	c.1637	RICHARDSON	Robert			Clerk of the Peace for all Parts of Lincolnshire.
1646		WALCOTT	Humfrey			Clerk of the Peace for all Parts of Lincolnshire.
1646	1647	CORRY	Thomas			Also Clerk of the Peace for Kesteven.
1649	1668	RUSHWORTH	Charles			Also Clerk of the Peace for Kesteven.
1669		THORNTON	Christopher (?John)			Clerk of the Peace for all Parts of Lincolnshire.
1670	1672	DEATH	Welcome			Also Clerk of the Peace for Kesteven.
1673	1683	SMITH	Nathaniel			Also Clerk of the Peace for Kesteven; subsequently for Lindsey, 1683–85.
1683	1707	ABBOTT	Thomas			Also Clerk of the Peace for Kesteven. Mayor of Boston, 1682, 1696, 1701; Judge of Admiralty of Port of Boston, 1701.
1708	1744	ABBOTT	Samuel			Clerk of Sewers; Mayor of Boston, 1715, 1727; Judge of Admiralty of Port of Boston and Deputy Recorder of Boston, 1730.
1744	1748	WEST	James			Of Boston.
1748	1758	DENSHIRE	Langton		1758	Treasurer of South Division of Kesteven, 1743.

LINCOLNSHIRE, PARTS OF HOLLAND (*Continued*)

From	To	Surname	Forenames	Birth	Death	Biographical Notes
1758	1782	DENSHIRE	George		1782	Brother of Langton Denshire; of Stamford and of Thetford. Also Clerk of the Peace for Kesteven, 1741–82.
1783	1811	THIRKILL	Francis, the elder		1811	Solicitor. Town Clerk of Boston, 1783. Previously Deputy Clerk of the Peace.
1812	1839	THIRKILL	Francis, the younger	1786	1839	*Elected to Society, May* 1830. Son of Francis Thirkill the elder; Solicitor. Mayor of Boston, 1826, 1832.
1839	1864	CARTER	John Richard		1864	*Elected to Society, March* 1850. Solicitor.
1864	1866	ATTER	James		1866	*Elected to Society, June* 1866. Attorney (admitted 1839). Town Clerk of Stamford; Under Sheriff, Rutland; Coroner.
1866	1889	WHITE	Francis Thirkill		1899	*Elected to Society, June* 1868. Solicitor (admitted 1835). Mayor of Boston, 1853.

CLERKS OF THE PEACE AND OF THE COUNTY COUNCIL from 1889

From	To	Surname	Forenames	Birth	Death	Biographical Notes
1889	1899	WHITE	Francis Thirkill		1899	See above.
1899	1912	JOHNSON	Henry Chaderton		1912	*Elected to Society, May* 1902. Solicitor (admitted 1888).
1912	1920	GANE	William Henry		1920	*Elected to Society, May* 1912. Solicitor (admitted 1882). Secretary to the Advisory Committee; Clerk to the Boston Borough Justices.
1920	1954	MARRIS	Harold Colquhoun	1883		*Elected to Society, January* 1920. Trinity Hall, Cambridge; Solicitor (admitted 1906). O.B.E., 1942. Secretary to the Advisory Committee; Clerk of the Magistrates' Courts Committee. Captain, 4th Battalion, Lincolnshire Regiment, 1914–18 War.
1954		WALTER	Hugh Albert Harold	1905		*Elected to Society, December* 1942. Solicitor (admitted 1929). M.A., LL.B. (Cantab). Secretary to the Advisory Committee; Clerk of the Magistrates' Courts Committee. Previously assistant solicitor, Yorkshire (North Riding) and Derbyshire County Councils, and Deputy Clerk of the Peace and of the County Council.

DEPUTY CLERKS OF THE PEACE prior to 1889

From	To	Surname	Forenames	Birth	Death	Biographical Notes
1680		RUSHWORTH				
1748	1769	JACKSON	Samuel			
1769	1771	THIRKILL	Francis, the elder		1811	Subsequently Clerk of the Peace, see above.
1857	1860	MILLINGTON	John Boyfield			
1860	1866	STANILAND	M.			
1866		ATTER	Frederick			

DEPUTY CLERKS OF THE PEACE AND OF THE COUNTY COUNCIL from 1889

From	To	Surname	Forenames	Birth	Death	Biographical Notes
1942	1954	WALTER	Hugh Albert Harold	1905		Subsequently Clerk of the Peace and of the County Council, see above.
1954		ROBERTS	Eric John	1917		*Elected to Society, May* 1954. Solicitor (admitted 1947). LL.B. (London); L.M.T.P.I. Previously assistant solicitor, Northamptonshire and Salop County Councils. Private, R.A.P.C., 1939–45 War; invalided 1942.

LINCOLNSHIRE, PARTS OF KESTEVEN

From	To	Surname	Forenames	Birth	Death	Biographical Notes
		CLERKS OF THE PEACE from 1391				
1391	1428	BLUET	John			
		de la MARE	Brian			Served for an undetermined period between 1400 and 1408.
1428	1446	CHEVERCOURT	John			
1448	1455	REPYNGHALE	Robert			Appointed by letters patent Clerk of the Keepers of the Peace and of Justices of Oyer and Terminer *alias* Clerk of the Crown and of the Peace and to the office of King's Attorney before the Justices of the Peace in all Parts of Lincolnshire, 1st April, 26 Henry VI; Clerk of the Signet and King's Secretary, 1443–52; Author of volume of precedents (Harl. MS. 773) using examples employed in Kesteven.
1494	1495	STONYWELL	Nicholas			
1509		BOUGHTON	Henry			
1510	1533	IRBY	Anthony		1552	
1535		THARROLD	William			
1543	1571	IRBY	Leonard		1571	Appointed by letters patent Clerk of the Peace and of the Crown in Kesteven and Holland; possibly Deputy Steward of Long Sutton for Duchy of Lancaster, 1561.
1571	1584	ELWOOD	John			Also Clerk of the Peace for Holland.
1585	1589	WELBYE	Humfrey			Also Clerk of the Peace for Holland. Related by marriage to Leonard Irby, above.
1590	1597	ROBINSON	Matthew			Also Clerk of the Peace for Holland.
1607	1633	ROSSETER	Christopher			Also Clerk of the Peace for Holland; and for Lindsey, 1630–33.
1633	c.1637	RICHARDSON	Robert			Clerk of the Peace for all Parts of Lincolnshire.
1646		WALCOTT	Humfrey			Clerk of the Peace for all Parts of Lincolnshire.
1646	1647	CORRY	Thomas			Also Clerk of the Peace for Holland.
1649	1668	RUSHWORTH	Charles			Also Clerk of the Peace for Holland.
1669		THORNTON	Christopher (?John)			Clerk of the Peace for all Parts of Lincolnshire.
1670	1672	DEATH	Welcome			Also Clerk of the Peace for Holland.
1673	1683	SMITH	Nathaniel			Also Clerk of the Peace for Holland; subsequently for Lindsey, 1683–85.
1683	1707	ABBOTT	Thomas			Also Clerk of the Peace for Holland.
1708	1727	BLACKWELL	Joshua			Admitted, Clement's Inn, 1685; Principal, c. 1714–22. Clerk to the Lieutenancy; Treasurer for stocks, gaol and marshalsea.
1727	1741	DENSHIRE	George, the elder		1743/4	Of Stamford. Admitted, Clement's Inn, 1702. Mayor of Stamford, 1709, 1722; Lord of the Manor of Thurlby-by-Bourne.
1741	1782	DENSHIRE	George, the younger	1705/6	1782	Son of George Denshire, the elder; of Stamford; Treasurer for South Division of Kesteven, 1733–43. Also Clerk of the Peace for Holland, 1758–82.
1783	1798	BANKES	Robert Langton	1747	1823	Of New Sleaford. Previously Deputy Clerk of the Peace.
1798	1823	CHEALES	Benjamin	1758	1823	Son of the Rev. William Cheales, rector of Thorpe by Newark; of Sleaford; Solicitor (admitted 1779). Clerk of the General Meetings of the Lieutenancy, c.1809–17; Treasurer for South Division of Kesteven, 1787–1823; for North Division, 1794–1823. Previously Deputy Clerk of the Peace.
1824	c.1842	FORBES	William			*Elected to Society, May 1830.* Of Sleaford; Attorney. Clerk to the Lieutenancy; Clerk of Gaol Sessions; Treasurer for North and South Divisions of Kesteven.

From	To	Surname	Forenames	Birth	Death	Biographical Notes
1842	1866	MOORE	Maurice Peter		1865	*Elected to Society, May* 1849. Of Sleaford; Attorney (admitted 1831). Also County Treasurer, 1842–43; Clerk of Court of Requests; monument in Sleaford Parish Church.
1866	1867	WILES	George			Of Horbling and Donington in Holland; Attorney (admitted 1828). Clerk to the Commissioners of Taxes; to the Black Sluice Commissioners.
1867	1889	PHILLIPS	Joseph			*Elected to Society, June* 1867. Of Stamford; Solicitor (admitted 1846).

CLERKS OF THE PEACE AND OF THE COUNTY COUNCIL from 1889

From	To	Surname	Forenames	Birth	Death	Biographical Notes
1889	1902	PHILLIPS	Joseph			See above.
1902	1919	HOLDICH	Thomas Hinman			*Elected to Society, May* 1903. Solicitor (admitted 1878). Secretary to the Advisory Committee.
1919	1931	PIPER	Arthur Drury	1872	1931	*Elected to Society, October* 1919. Solicitor (admitted 1898). Secretary to the Advisory Committee.
1931	1941	PHIPPS	Walter Thomas	1882	1954	*Elected to Society, November* 1929. Barrister-at-law, Middle Temple (called 1922). M.A., B.Sc. (Cantab). Secretary to the Advisory Committee; Chief Education Officer. Previously Deputy Clerk of the Peace and of the County Council. Served in 1914–18 War.
1941	1944	BANWELL	George Harold	1900		*Elected to Society, October* 1941. Solicitor (admitted 1922). Secretary to the Advisory Committee; Clerk of the Lincolnshire Archives Committee. Previously Town Clerk, Lincoln; subsequently Secretary of The Association of Municipal Corporations; knighted 1955.
1944		BLOW	Joseph Edward	1907		*Elected to Society, April* 1934. Solicitor (admitted 1930). Secretary to the Advisory Committee; Clerk of the Magistrates' Courts Committee; Clerk of the Lincolnshire County Committee and of the Lincolnshire Archives Committee. Previously Deputy Clerk of the Peace and of the County Council.

DEPUTY CLERKS OF THE PEACE prior to 1889

From	To	Surname	Forenames	Birth	Death	Biographical Notes
1754	1758	COOKE	John			Of Stamford.
1764	1774	BANKES	Robert	1724	1803	Son-in-law of George Denshire, Clerk of the Peace, 1727–41.
1780	1782	BANKES	Robert Langton	1747	1823	Subsequently Clerk of the Peace, see above.
1786	1798	CHEALES	Benjamin	1758	1823	Subsequently Clerk of the Peace, see above.
1866		PEAKE	Henry			Of Sleaford; Solicitor (admitted 1846). Clerk to the Justices, Sleaford division.

DEPUTY CLERKS OF THE PEACE AND OF THE COUNTY COUNCIL from 1889

From	To	Surname	Forenames	Birth	Death	Biographical Notes
1927	1931	PHIPPS	Walter Thomas	1882	1954	Subsequently Clerk of the Peace and of the County Council, see above.
1934	1944	BLOW	Joseph Edward	1907		Subsequently Clerk of the Peace and of the County Council, see above.
1944	1946	WELLS	Charles Martin Sidney	1908		*Elected to Society, January* 1945. Solicitor (admitted 1932). M.A. (Cantab), L.M.T.P.I. Subsequently Clerk of the Peace and of the County Council of Breconshire, *q.v.*
1946	1954	AYLWARD	Anthony Case	1916		*Elected to Society, March* 1947. Solicitor (admitted 1938). Subsequently Clerk of the Peace and of the County Council of Huntingdonshire, *q.v.*
1954		PEARSON	Reginald Arthur	1919		*Elected to Society, May* 1954. Solicitor (admitted 1943).

LINCOLNSHIRE, PARTS OF LINDSEY

From	To	Surname	Forenames	Birth	Death	Biographical Notes
CLERKS OF THE PEACE from 1391						
1391	1397	KELE	Robert			
1409	1410	KYME	John			
1411	1449	DUFFIELD	Richard			
1448		REPYNGHALE	Robert			Appointed by letters patent Clerk of the Keepers of the Peace and of Justices of Oyer and Terminer *alias* Clerk of the Crown and Clerk of the Peace and to the office of King's Attorney before the Justices of the Peace in all Parts of Lincolnshire, 1st April, 26 Henry VI; Clerk of the Signet and King's Secretary, 1443–52. Duffield, Hecham and Wall may have been his Deputies, as he appears to have acted principally in Kesteven.
1451	1453	HECHAM	Henry			
1453	1482	WALL	William			
1483	1491	PEPPYR	Thomas			
1494	1516	TASKER	Nicholas			
1516	1521	TREGOLD	Robert			
1538	1545	SKELTON	William			Appointed Clerk of the Crown and Clerk of the Peace by letters patent, 8th February, 29 Henry VIII.
1563	1597	THEWE	John			
1599	1607	SOMERSCALES	Robert			
1608	1609	KENT	Robert			
1616	1630	SMITH	Robert			
1630	1633	ROSSETER	Christopher			Also Clerk of the Peace for Holland and Kesteven, 1607–33.
1633	c.1637	RICHARDSON	Robert			Clerk of the Peace for all Parts of Lincolnshire.
1646		WALCOTT	Humfrey			Clerk of the Peace for all Parts of Lincolnshire.
1646	1647	PEACHELL(?)	Thomas			
1648	1656	DOWSE	Thomas			
1662	1679	THORNTON	John (? Christopher)			Apparently Clerk of the Peace for all Parts of Lincolnshire in 1669. the forename appears as Christopher in the Pipe Roll for that year;
1682	1683	QUADRING	Robert			
1683	1685	SMITH	Nathaniel			Clerk of the Peace for Holland and Kesteven, 1673–83.
1685	c.1717	DAVENPORT	George			
1717	c.1731	EDISON	Nathaniel			Previously Deputy Clerk of the Peace.
1731	1746	SAPSFORD	Henry			
1746	1771	BRACKENBURY	Thomas		1771	Of Spilsby. Also County Treasurer; Clerk to the Alford and Spilsby Commissioners of Sewers.
1771	1787	CHAPMAN	Robert		1787	Of Spilsby. Also County Treasurer. Previously Deputy Clerk of the Peace.
1787	1809	BRACKENBURY	Joseph, the elder		1811	Nephew of Thomas Brackenbury; of Spilsby; Clerk to Alford and Spilsby Commissioners of Sewers.
1809	1829	BRACKENBURY	Joseph, the younger			Son of Joseph Brackenbury, the elder; of Spilsby; Attorney.
1829	1877	HOLLWAY	John Hardwick		1877	*Elected to Society, May* 1830. Of Hundleby, near Spilsby; Solicitor.
1877	1889	BURTON	John Francis			*Elected to Society, June* 1869. Of Lincoln; Solicitor (admitted 1849). Previously Deputy Clerk of the Peace.

LINCOLNSHIRE, PARTS OF LINDSEY (*Continued*)

From	To	Surname	Forenames	Birth	Death	Biographical Notes

CLERKS OF THE PEACE AND OF THE COUNTY COUNCIL from 1889

From	To	Surname	Forenames	Birth	Death	Biographical Notes
1889	1891	BURTON	John Francis			See above.
1891	1919	SCORER	Charles			*Elected to Society, June* 1891. Solicitor (admitted 1868). Secretary to the Advisory Committee. Previously Deputy Clerk of the Peace and of the County Council.
1919	1947	SCORER	Eric West	1882		*Elected to Society, June* 1916. Son of Charles Scorer; Solicitor (admitted 1906). O.B.E., 1941. Secretary to the Advisory Committee; Clerk of the Lincolnshire Police Committee; Coroner. Previously Deputy Clerk of the Peace and of the County Council.
1947	1957	COPLAND	Herbert	1891		*Elected to Society, April* 1934. Solicitor (admitted 1932). O.B.E., 1946. Secretary to the Advisory Committee; Clerk of the Magistrates' Courts Committee; Clerk of the Lincolnshire Police Committee. Honorary Secretary, Lindsey Blind Society; Secretary, Lincolnshire Probation Area Committee, and Mid-Eastern Regional Council for County Council Roadmen. Previously Deputy Clerk of the Peace and of the County Council.
1957		LANE	Walter Ernest	1920		*Elected to Society, January* 1955. Solicitor (admitted 1948). M.A. (Cantab). Secretary to the Advisory Committee; Clerk of the Magistrates' Courts Committee; of the Lincolnshire Police Committee and the Lincolnshire Police Accounts Committee. Secretary, Lincolnshire Probation Area Committee; Honorary Secretary, Lindsey Blind Society, and Lindsey Society for Welfare of Handicapped Persons; Secretary Mid-Eastern Regional Council for County Council Roadmen. Previously Deputy Clerk of the Peace and of the County Council of Hampshire. Flight Lieutenant, Royal Air Force, 1939–45 War.

DEPUTY CLERKS OF THE PEACE prior to 1889

From	To	Surname	Forenames	Birth	Death	Biographical Notes
1709	1710	BENNETT	William			
1711		HARVEY	William			
1712		LONG	Charles			
1713	1717	EDISON	Nathaniel			Subsequently Clerk of the Peace, see above.
1717		SYMONS	William			
1718		HEALD	George			
1719		STEVENS	Edward			
1750	1765	CHAPMAN	Robert		1787	Of Spilsby. Subsequently Clerk of the Peace, see above.
1809		BABINGTON	Edward			Of Spilsby.
1829		COLLINSON	John			Of Doncaster.
1869	1877	BURTON	John Francis			Subsequently Clerk of the Peace, see above.

DEPUTY CLERKS OF THE PEACE AND OF THE COUNTY COUNCIL from 1889

From	To	Surname	Forenames	Birth	Death	Biographical Notes
1891	1891	SCORER	Charles			Subsequently Clerk of the Peace and of the County Council, see above.
1916	1919	SCORER	Eric West	1882		Subsequently Clerk of the Peace and of the County Council, see above.
1934	1947	COPLAND	Herbert	1891		Secretary, East Lindsey and East Lincolnshire Joint Planning Committees, 1938–47. Subsequently Clerk of the Peace and of the County Council, see above.
1947		PEPLER	George Richard Summerland	1912		*Elected to Society, October* 1947. Solicitor (admitted 1938). M.A. (Cantab). Major, Royal Artillery, 1939–45 War.

LONDON

From	To	Surname	Forenames	Birth	Death	Biographical Notes

CLERKS OF THE PEACE from 1889

From	To	Surname	Forenames	Birth	Death	Biographical Notes
1889	1913	NICHOLSON	Sir Richard	1828	1913	*Elected to Society, June 1865.* *Honorary Secretary, 1881–1910; Chairman, 1882–1910.* Fifth son of George Nicholson of Hertford, solicitor, Clerk to the Lieutenancy of Middlesex, 1843–53; Solicitor (admitted 1851). F.S.A., 1858; knighted, 1886. Became, by virtue of his office as Clerk of the Peace for Middlesex and by operation of the Local Government Act, 1888, sec. 118(8), first Clerk of the Peace for the County of London, and concurrently held those two Clerkships and that of Hertfordshire, *q.v.*, until 1894; thereafter Clerk of the Peace for London and Clerk of the Peace and of the County Council of Middlesex. Clerk to the Lieutenancy. See Plate VII.
1889	1904	*WYATT*	*Sir Richard (Henry)*	1823	1904	*Deemed by virtue of his office as Clerk of the Peace for Surrey (q.v.) and by operation of the Local Government Act 1888, sec. 118(10) to be Clerk of the Peace for the County of London for the purposes of Quarter Sessions held at Newington.*
1913	1938	DIX	John	1864	1938	*Elected to Society, June 1913.*
1938	1940	ENSOR	Alick Charles Davidson	1907		*Elected to Society, October 1935.* Solicitor (admitted 1928). Previously assistant solicitor, Surrey County Council; prosecuting solicitor, Newcastle County Borough Council; assistant solicitor to Metropolitan Police and chief lecturer on criminal law, Metropolitan Police College, and Deputy Clerk of the Peace for Middlesex.
1941		BURGESS	Clarkson Leo	1902		*Elected to Society, July 1941.* Barrister-at-law, Middle Temple (called 1927). B.A. (Cantab). C.B.E., 1951.

DEPUTY CLERKS OF THE PEACE from 1889

From	To	Surname	Forenames	Birth	Death	Biographical Notes
1948	1957	SWIFT	Alfred	1898	1957	*Elected to Society, January 1948.* Captain, 1914–18 War.
1957		SAYERS	Warwick Waghorn	1912		*Elected to Society, December 1957.* Solicitor (admitted 1937). Major, Royal Sussex Regiment, 1939–45 War.

CLERKS OF THE COUNTY COUNCIL from 1889

From	To	Surname	Forenames	Birth	Death	Biographical Notes
1889	1896	de la HOOKE	Harry	1839	1906	Entered Metropolitan Board of Works, 1865; Assistant Clerk, 1889.
1896	1900	STEWART	Charles John	1851	1932	Barrister-at-law, Inner Temple (called 1883). K.B.E., 1918. Previously Senior Official Receiver in Companies Liquidation; subsequently Public Trustee.
1900	1915	GOMME	Sir (George) Laurence	1853	1916	Entered Metropolitan Board of Works, 1873. Knighted, 1911. F.S.A.; F.S.S. Justice of the Peace; Secretary to the Lieutenancy. Fellow of the Anthropological Institute; President of Folk Lore Society. Previously Statistical Officer, London County Council.
1915	1925	BIRD	Sir James	1863	1925	Entered Metropolitan Board of Works, 1877. Knighted, 1918. Justice of the Peace. Clerk to the Lieutenancy. Previously Deputy Clerk of the County Council.
1925	1933	COX	Sir Montagu (Hounsel)	1873	1936	Entered service of Council, 1892. Barrister-at-law, Lee Prizewinner of Gray's Inn (called 1902). LL.B. (London). Knighted, 1933. Justice of the Peace. Clerk to the Lieutenancy and Honorary Clerk to the Advisory Committee. Previously Deputy Clerk of the County Council.
1933	1939	GATER	Sir George (Henry)	1886		*Elected to Society, January 1934.* M.A. (Oxon). Knighted, 1936; K.C.B., 1941; G.C.M.G., 1944. Justice of the Peace. Clerk to the Lieutenancy and Honorary Clerk to the Advisory Committee. Previously Assistant Director of Education, Nottinghamshire; Director of Education, Lancashire; Education Officer, London County Council. Subsequently Permanent Under Secretary for the Colonies, 1939–47, seconded successively as Joint Secretary, Ministry of Home Security, as Secretary, Ministry of Supply and as Secretary, Ministry of Home Security; Chairman, School Broadcasting Council, 1948; Warden of Winchester College, 1951; Member, B.B.C. General Advisory Committee, 1952. Brigadier General, 1914–18 War; D.S.O., 1916; C.M.G., 1918; Commander, Legion of Honour; Croix de Guerre.

From	To	Surname	Forenames	Birth	Death	Biographical Notes
1939	1946	SALMON	Sir Eric (Cecil Heygate)	1896	1946	*Elected to Society, April* 1940. Hon. M.A. (Oxon). Knighted, 1943. Justice of the Peace; Deputy Lieutenant. Clerk to the Lieutenancy and Honorary Clerk to the Advisory Committee. Previously with the Ministry of Health, and Deputy Clerk of the County Council. Captain, Royal West Kent Regiment, 1914–18 War; M.C.
1946	1947	OLIVER	Laurence Herbert	1881		Entered service of the Council, 1900. C.B.E., 1946. Justice of the Peace, 1945. Previously Deputy Clerk of the County Council; subsequently Member of Public Works Loans Board. Second Lieutenant, R.A.S.C., 1914–18 War.
1947	1956	ROBERTS	Sir (James Reginald) Howard	1891		*Elected to Society, June* 1947. Solicitor (admitted 1913). C.B.E., 1946; knighted, 1949. Justice of the Peace; Deputy Lieutenant. Officer of Legion of Honour and of Order of Orange-Nassau; Chevalier of Order of Dannebrog, of Royal Order of North Star, of Order of Star of Ethiopia and of Portuguese Military Order of Christ. Clerk to the Lieutenancy and Honorary Clerk to the Advisory Committee. Previously assistant solicitor, Sheffield, Stoke-on-Trent and Liverpool County Borough Councils; Deputy Town Clerk, Liverpool; Town Clerk, Kingston-upon-Hull; Solicitor, London County Council. Subsequently Vice President, R.I.P.A.; President, R.O.S.P.A.; President, Town Planning Institute; Member of Surrey County Council; of Court of Governors, Administrative Staff College, and of South Eastern Gas Board. Lieutenant, Duke of Lancaster's Own Yeomanry, 1914–18 War; London Region Transport Officer, Civil Defence, 1939–45 War.
1956		HART	Sir William (Ogden)	1903		*Elected to Society, December* 1955. Barrister-at-law, Lincoln's Inn (called 1928). M.A., B.C.L. (Oxon). C.M.G., 1946; knighted, 1961. Justice of the Peace. Clerk to the Lieutenancy and Honorary Clerk to the Advisory Committee. Previously Fellow, Tutor and Bursar of Wadham College, Oxford, 1926–47; Oxford University Lecturer in Law, 1933–39 and 1946–47; Lecturer in Local Government Law, Law Society's School of Law, 1937–39; University Member of Oxford City Council, 1932–41 and 1946–47; General Manager, Hemel Hempstead Development Corporation, 1947–56, and Member of Hertfordshire Education Committee, 1952–56. Head of British Merchant Shipping Mission, Washington, and United Kingdom Member of United Maritime Executive Board, 1939–45 War.

DEPUTY CLERKS OF THE COUNTY COUNCIL from 1889

From	To	Surname	Forenames	Birth	Death	Biographical Notes
1889	1891	SPENCER	Alfred	1840	1915	Subsequently Chief Officer, Public Control Department.
1895	1905	BLAXLAND	William Athelston	1845	1926	Solicitor (admitted 1867).
1905	1915	BIRD	James	1863	1925	Subsequently Clerk of the County Council, see above.
1915	1925	COX	Montagu Hounsel	1873	1936	Subsequently Clerk of the County Council, see above.
1925	1933	WADDINGTON	Walter Hargreaves	1870	1957	Entered service of the Council, 1889; previously Clerk of the Public Health, Rivers and Highways Committees and Assistant Clerk of the Council.
1934	1939	SALMON	Eric Cecil Heygate	1896	1946	Subsequently Clerk of the County Council, see above.
1939	1946	OLIVER	Laurence Herbert	1881		Subsequently Clerk of the County Council, see above.
1947		RANDALL	Terence George	1904		*Elected to Society, November* 1950. Entered service of the Council, 1921. B.A. (London). O.B.E., 1946; C.B.E., 1959. Previously Clerk of the Air Raid Precautions Committee and Assistant Clerk of the Council.

MERIONETH

From	To	Surname	Forenames	Birth	Death	Biographical Notes
		CLERKS OF THE PEACE from 1542				
1542		REYNOLDS	John			*Alias* John ap Rhydderch. Also Clerk of the Peace for Anglesey and Clerk of the Crown in both Counties, appointed by letters patent, 24th January, 33 Henry VIII; Yeoman of the Guard. Co-defendant, with Clerk of the Peace for Caernarvonshire, in suit brought by the inhabitants of the respective Counties, complaining of "demands for excessive fees and excessively frequent appearances from persons bound over to the Peace" (see Lewis, *An Inventory of the Early Chancery Proceedings concerning Wales*, p. 17).
1546			Hugh ap Meredith Wyn			
c.1565	1575	JONES	Edward			
c.1586	1594	EDWARDS	Robert			Of Llwyndu, Llanaber; son of Edward Edwards and Elin, daughter of the house of Taltreuddyn; his son married into the powerful Corsygedol family.
1623		LLOYD	Thomas			Possibly of Hendre'r Mur.
1634		EVANS	David			
1635		ELLIS	David			
c.1657		VAUGHAN	Tudor			Of Caerynwch; member of family of solicitors a number of whom acted as deputy sheriffs in the seventeenth century.
1676		ROBERTS	William			
1699	1730	LLOYD	Robert			
1733	1751	OWEN	Edward			Of Garthyngharad; possibly the Edward Owen who was Clerk of the Crown, North Wales circuit, 1725; descendant of Lewis Owen, Vice-Chamberlain and Baron of the Exchequer of North Wales, Member of Parliament for Merioneth, 1547–52, who was murdered by Red Bandits of Mawddwy, 1555.
1751	1783	GARNONS	John	1704	1783	Described as "Of Rhiwgoch" in right of his wife Jane; son of Richard Garnons of Nantlle and Catherine Anwyl of Cae Dafydd; Solicitor. Deputy Prothonotary and Deputy Clerk of the Crown, North Wales circuit. Portrait of his eldest son John Vaughan Garnons, a County Justice, hangs in Grand Jury Room at Caernarvon.
1751	1759	GARNONS	Griffith		1759	Of Rhiwgoch; youngest son of John Garnons, with whom he was jointly and severally appointed; Under Sheriff.
1783	1799	POOLE	Richard	1736	1799	Of Caenest and of Beaumaris; son of the Rev. Anthony Poole, Rector of Mallwyd; father of Owen Anthony Poole, Clerk of the Peace for Caernarvonshire, 1815–23; Attorney. Justice of the Peace.
1799	1817	ANWYL	Edward			Of Brynadda. Previously Deputy Clerk of the Peace.
1817		GRIFFITH	Griffith			Appointed "for the present time". Previously Deputy Clerk of the Peace.
1817	1826	WILLIAMS	Humphrey		1826	
1826		WILLIAMS	John Jones			Appointed "pro hac vice".
1826	1831	ANWYL	David			Of Bronwylfa, near Bala; Solicitor.
1831	1842	WILLIAMS	John Jones			Of Dolgelley.
1842	1859	WILLIAMS	David	1799	1869	*Elected to Society, March 1845.* Of Bron Eryri; Solicitor at Portmadoc. Deputy Lieutenant of Merioneth and Caernarvonshire; Sheriff of Merioneth, 1861–62, and of Caernarvonshire, 1862–63; Member of Parliament for Merioneth, 1868. Father of Sir Arthur (Osmond) Williams, Member of Parliament for Merioneth, 1900–10, and constable of Harlech castle.
1859	1881	BREESE	Edward	1835	1881	*Elected to Society, June 1878.* Nephew of David Williams; Solicitor (admitted 1857). Antiquarian; published *Kalendars of Gwynedd*, 1873. David Lloyd George, later Earl of Dwyfor, began his career in Breese's office at Portmadoc.
1881	1889	JONES	Robert		1906	*Elected to Society, June 1882.* Solicitor (admitted 1868). Clerk to the Lieutenancy.

From	To	Surname	Forenames	Birth	Death	Biographical Notes

CLERKS OF THE PEACE AND OF THE COUNTY COUNCIL from 1889

From	To	Surname	Forenames	Birth	Death	Biographical Notes
1889	1906	JONES	Robert		1906	See above.
1906		CASSON	Randal		1914	Temporary appointment from 27th November to 17th December only. Solicitor (admitted 1874). Uncle of Sir Lewis Casson, the actor. Previously and subsequently Deputy Clerk of the Peace and of the County Council.
1907	1920	BREESE	David	1870	1923	*Elected to Society, May* 1907. Son of Edward Breese, Clerk of the Peace 1859–81; Solicitor (admitted 1894).
1921	1954	OWEN	Hugh John	1880		*Elected to Society, November* 1920. Solicitor (admitted 1903). Deputy Lieutenant. Clerk to the Lieutenancy; Secretary to the Advisory Committee; Clerk of the Magistrates' Courts Committee; of the Snowdonia Park Joint Advisory Committee; of the War Zone Courts, Wales (North Section) 1940–45; Chairman, Merioneth Historical and Records Society. Author of several books on Merioneth. Captain, R.A.O.C., 1914–18 War; Chairman, Idris Flight, Air Training Corps, 1939–45 War.
1954		JONES-WILLIAMS	Dafydd Wyn	1916		*Elected to Society, November* 1948. Solicitor (admitted 1939). LL.B. (Wales). Deputy Lieutenant. Clerk to the Lieutenancy; Secretary to the Advisory Committee; Clerk of the Magistrates' Courts Committee and of the Snowdonia Park Joint Advisory Committee. Previously Deputy Clerk of the Peace and of the County Council. Captain, 10th Royal Hussars, 1939–45 War; later Lieutenant Colonel, commanding 446 (Royal Welch) Airborne L.A.A. Regiment, R.A.; M.C., T.D.

DEPUTY CLERKS OF THE PEACE prior to 1889

From	To	Surname	Forenames	Birth	Death	Biographical Notes
1549		MEREDYTH	Hugh			Attorney.
1733	1766	ANWYL	William			Of Llandecwyn, later of Brynadda; Attorney.
1767	1783	EVANS	William			Of Rhiwgoch.
1767	1799	ANWYL	Edward			Jointly with William Evans until 1783; subsequently Clerk of the Peace, see above.
1800		GRIFFITH	Griffith			Subsequently Clerk of the Peace, see above.
1848		JONES	John Humphreys			Appointed by David Williams, Clerk of the Peace, for one month only from 16th October.

DEPUTY CLERKS OF THE PEACE AND OF THE COUNTY COUNCIL from 1889

From	To	Surname	Forenames	Birth	Death	Biographical Notes
	1906	CASSON	Randal		1914	Subsequently Clerk of the Peace and of the County Council, see above.
1907	1914	CASSON	Randal		1914	Re-appointed after temporary service as Clerk.
1914	1920	STOKES	Adrian		1948	Solicitor (admitted 1896).
1921	1936	JONES	Rowland Guthrie	1873	1936	*Deputy Clerk of the Peace only.* Solicitor (admitted 1896). Coroner; Under Sheriff.
1936	1936	WHITLEY	Raymond Archer	1908		*Elected to Society, April* 1946. Solicitor (admitted 1934). B.A. (Oxon). Subsequently Deputy Clerk of the Peace and of the County Council of Yorkshire (East Riding), *q.v.*
1936	1948	ROWLANDS	William John	1897		*Elected to Society, December* 1942. Solicitor (admitted 1932). Subsequently Deputy Clerk of the Peace and of the County Council of Denbighshire, *q.v.*
1948	1954	JONES-WILLIAMS	Dafydd Wyn	1916		Subsequently Clerk of the Peace and of the County Council, see above.
1954		LLOYD-JONES	Evan John	1918		*Elected to Society, May* 1954. Solicitor (admitted 1949). LL.B. (Wales). County Secretary, Forces Help Society. Lieutenant, R.A.S.C., 1939–45 War.

MIDDLESEX

From	To	Surname	Forenames	Birth	Death	Biographical Notes
CLERKS OF THE PEACE from 1424						
1424	1433	HYNSTOKE	Thomas			
1433	1434	GODYNGE	William			
1436	1439	GOREWAY	Thomas			
1440	1448	LUYT	Thomas			
1505	1529	ROBERTS	Thomas			
1530	1532	STAVERTON	Richard			
1535	1536	HALES	John			
1537	1538	WELBECK	John			
1541		GREVYLE	John			
1542		ROBERTS	Mathew			
1549	1552	RANDOLPH	Bernard		?1583	Possibly born at Ticehurst, Sussex; Barrister-at-law, Inner Temple (Bencher, 1566); Common Serjeant of the City of London. By Will (1582), bequeathed £200 to Fishmongers' Company on condition, *inter alia*, that Company paid £4 per annum to a divinity student at Cambridge.
1552	1553	HOGESON	Robert			
1553	1558	WATSON	John			
1559	1593	CLERK	Henry			
1593	1607	FERMOR	Henry			
1608	1611	CARTWRIGHT	Richard			
1612	1619	LONGE	George	1580	1655	Of Clerkenwell; Barrister-at-law, Lincoln's Inn (admitted 1620); Clerk of the Pleas of the Exchequer, 1619. Justice of the Peace. Buried in St. James' Church, Clerkenwell.
1619	1623	LAMBE	William			Appointed by Sir Thomas Edmondes.
1624	1626	HOOKER	John			
1626	1627	SANBY				
1627	1639	WALKER	Christopher		c.1654	Possibly Barrister-at-law, Lincoln's Inn (called 1642, Bencher 1652); Steward of the Leete of Manor of St. John of Jerusalem, 1641. In 1647 "Mr. Walker" on instruction of the Justices joined with then Clerk of the Peace in drawing bill in Chancery concerning site, etc., of Hicks Hall, New Prison and house of correction.
1639	1660	GRAVES	Richard	1610	1669	Barrister-at-law, Lincoln's Inn (called 1639, Bencher 1657, keeper of the Black Book, 1668, and Lenten Reader 1669). Ordered by the Justices to attend Committee of Parliament to offer reasons against petition of City of Westminster to incorporate and sever their administration from County of Middlesex, April 1650. See Plate III.
1660	1672	SHELTON	Edward		1672	Barrister-at-law, Inner Temple (called 1651); buried in Inner Temple Church.
1673	1683	ADDERLEY	William			Possibly of East Burnham, Buckinghamshire; Barrister-at-law, Lincoln's Inn (called 1670). Petitioned the Justices for permission to have his office at Hicks Hall to avoid the hiring charges for rooms over Cursitors' Office, June 1676; four years after resigning office, was ordered to pay £20 owed by him to County.
1683	1689	SMITH	John			Possibly identical with John Smith, Clerk of the Peace for Westminster, 1692–1709.
1689		SCAWEN	Edward			
1689	1692	HARCOURT	Simon		1724	Second son of Vere Harcourt, Archdeacon of Nottingham, of Plumtree, Nottinghamshire; grandson of Sir Robert Harcourt and Frances Vere; cousin of Simon Harcourt, Viscount, Lord Chancellor in 1713. Barrister-at-law, Middle Temple (called 1683, Bencher 1706); Master of the Crown Office; see also below.

From	To	Surname	Forenames	Birth	Death	Biographical Notes
1692	1693	FOX	John		1697	Lawyer on household staff of Russell family, c. 1658; Receiver General of Bedford Estates, 1682; Nominee of Earl of Bedford, Lord Lieutenant and *Custos Rotulorum* from 1691; reputed on his death to be " of incredible wealth."
1693	1724	HARCOURT	Simon		1724	See above; opposed nomination of John Fox, claiming entitlement to the office during good behaviour by virtue of 1 William and Mary c. 21, s. 5; re-admitted after procuring Writ of *Mandamus*, 1693; erected presses in Grand Jury Room at Hicks Hall for keeping Sessions records, 1696–97.
1724	1746	WALTER	Peter		1746	Possibly Deputy Steward of Honor and Manor of Hampton Court, 1712–46; one Peter Walter rendered accounts for Middlesex and Buckinghamshire estates of Lord Paget, 1689–1702. Died at Stalbridge, Dorsetshire " a very noted money Scrivener " reputedly worth £300,000, mostly left to his grandson Peter Walter, Member of Parliament for Shaftesbury; his character drawn by Pope in " *Poetical Epistles.*"
1746	1770	WALLER	James		1773	Possibly Barrister-at-law, Lincoln's Inn (admitted 1721). Clerk to the Lieutenant, 1731–35; Clerk to the Deputy Lieutenants; Clerk of the High Court of Chancery; removed from office of Clerk of the Peace, 1770, on grounds of negligence in drawing bills of indictment resulting in miscarriages of justice; of failing to attend Sessions or to appoint proper deputies; of failing to take proper care of records, some having been left for twelve years at Maidenhead, Berkshire, in hands of executor of a deceased deputy; and for taking unlawful fees. Waller denied all charges, claiming always to have exercised office by deputies whom he appointed at yearly salaries; obtained Writ of *Certiorari*, heard at Westminster Hall, 1772, when Court of King's Bench refused to reverse Order of the Justices.
1770	1777	BUTLER	Thomas		1777	Appointed by Duke of Northumberland; Steward, Manor of Isleworth Syon, c. 1767–68.
1777	1838	SELBY	Henry Collingwood	1748	1839	*Elected to Society, November* 1811. Married Frances Wilkie at Dorrington near Wooler, 1769; Barrister-at-law, Gray's Inn (called 1777, Bencher 1797). Appointed Clerk of the Peace by Duke of Northumberland; Steward, Manor of Isleworth Syon; Commissioner on Duke's estates until 1796; residence in the north at Swansfield House, Alnwick, Northumberland; trustee of Brentford Turnpike Trust from 1785; took part in Middlesex Tontine for raising money to build house of correction, 1790; supporter of William Mainwaring, Member of Parliament for Middlesex, 1784–1804; claimed, from 1777, to vote for the Knights of the Shire in respect of his freehold office for life as Clerk of the Peace, and in respect of his seat in Court and of office premises provided by the Justices; claim objected to, 1804, and objection upheld by Committee of House of Commons; died aged 91.
1838	1865	ELLIS	Charles Arthur Hill Heaton	1789	1865	Son of John Thomas Ellis, High Sheriff of Hertfordshire, 1784, Member of Parliament; family originally from Flintshire; married Louisa, daughter of Sir Josias Stacey, fourth Baronet; Barrister-at-law (called 1821). Appointed Clerk of the Peace by Duke of Portland. Father of Charles John Heaton Ellis, 9th Lancers and 6th Dragoon Guards, who died before Delhi, 1857; grandfather of Admiral Edward H. F. Heaton Ellis, A.D.C. to King George V.
1865	1889	NICHOLSON	Sir Richard	1828	1913	*Elected to Society, June* 1865. *Honorary Secretary, 1881–1910; Chairman, 1882–1910.* Fifth son of George Nicholson of Hertford, solicitor, Clerk to the Lieutenancy of Middlesex, 1843–53; Solicitor (admitted 1851). F.S.A., 1858; knighted 1886. Appointed Clerk of the Peace for Middlesex and for Hertfordshire, *q.v.*, 1865, and held those two Clerkships, together with that of London from 1889, until 1894; thereafter Clerk of the Peace and of the County Council of Middlesex and Clerk of the Peace for London. Clerk to the Lieutenancy from 1854; Clerk to the Visiting Justices of County prisons from 1879. See Plate VII.

MIDDLESEX (*Continued*)

From	To	Surname	Forenames	Birth	Death	Biographical Notes

CLERKS OF THE PEACE AND OF THE COUNTY COUNCIL from 1889

1889 1909 NICHOLSON Sir Richard 1828 1913 See above.

1909 1918 AUSTIN Walter George c.1848 1921

Elected to Society, June 1891.
Clerk to the Lieutenancy; Secretary to the Advisory Committee. Previously Deputy Clerk of the Peace and of the County Council.

1919 1935 HART Sir Ernest (Sidney Walter) 1870 1957

Elected to Society, February 1918.
Chairman and Honorary Secretary, 1925–35.
Nephew of Walter George Austin. M.B.E., 1918; knighted 1935. Justice of the Peace for Middlesex, 1935–36; subsequently for Surrey. Clerk to the Lieutenancy; Secretary to the Advisory Committee; Joint Honorary Secretary, Middlesex Appeals Tribunal, 1916–18; Honorary Secretary, Society of Chairmen and Deputy Chairmen of Quarter Sessions, 1919–35; of North and of West Middlesex Joint Town Planning Committees, 1926–35 and 1922–35 respectively; of Middlesex and Northern Home Counties Joint Vagrancy Committee, 1934–35; Member, Home Office London Probation Committee, 1922–36; of Advisory Committee on Probation and After-Care, 1932–36; Chairman, Records Preservation Section of British Records Association, 1935–38; of Horley Army Cadets Local Committee, 1942–49. Previously Deputy Clerk of the Peace and of the County Council.

1935 1954 RADCLIFFE Sir Clifford (Walter) 1888

Elected to Society, June 1919.
Son of Joseph Radcliffe, Professor of Civil Sanitary Engineering in Faculty of Science and Technology of the University of Manchester; Manchester Grammar School and St. John's College, Cambridge; M.A. Solicitor (admitted 1916). Deputy Lieutenant, 1940; C.B.E., 1942; knighted, 1953. Clerk to the Lieutenancy; Secretary to the Advisory Committee; Clerk of the Magistrates' Courts Committee; Honorary Secretary of Society of Chairmen and Deputy Chairmen of Quarter Sessions; Honorary Solicitor to Middlesex King Edward VII Memorial Fund and Middlesex Association for the Blind; Honorary Secretary of Standing Consultative Committees of London and Northolt Airports; Clerk of Middlesex and Surrey Thames Bridges Joint Committee; Member of Middlesex Cadet Committee, 1942–47; of North Thames Gas Board, 1955–58. Previously assistant Town Clerk, Sunderland; assistant solicitor, Tynemouth County Borough and Fulham Borough Councils; County Solicitor, and Deputy Clerk of the Peace and of the County Council of Middlesex.

1955 1959 GRAVES Arthur Glendower 1893

Elected to Society, May 1955.
Clerk of the Peace only.
Taunton School; Solicitor (admitted 1920). Deputy Lieutenant, 1955. Clerk to the Lieutenancy; Secretary to the Advisory Committee; Honorary Secretary, Society of Chairmen and Deputy Chairmen of Quarter Sessions. Previously Deputy Clerk of the Peace and of the County Council. Second Lieutenant, Somerset Light Infantry, seconded Lieutenant, Royal Flying Corps, 1914–18 War.

1955 GOODACRE Kenneth 1910

Elected to Society, January 1955.
Clerk of the County Council, 1955; Clerk of the Peace, 1959.
Doncaster Grammar School. Solicitor (admitted 1934). Deputy Lieutenant, 1960. Clerk to the Lieutenancy; Secretary to the Advisory Committee; Clerk of the Magistrates' Courts Committee; Honorary Secretary of Society of Chairmen and Deputy Chairmen of Quarter Sessions; Honorary Solicitor to Middlesex King Edward VII Memorial Fund and Middlesex Association for the Blind; Honorary Secretary of Standing Consultative Committee of London Airport; Clerk of Middlesex and Surrey Thames Bridges Joint Committee; Representative on Council of National Library for the Blind; Member of Home Office Advisory Council on Child Care and Central Training Council in Child Care. Previously assistant solicitor, Doncaster and Barrow-in-Furness County Borough Councils; Deputy Town Clerk, Blackburn; Town Clerk and Under Bailiff, Leicester. Lieutenant Colonel, East Lancashire Regiment, 1939–45 War; T.D.

From	To	Surname	Forenames	Birth	Death	Biographical Notes
		DEPUTY CLERKS OF THE PEACE prior to 1889				
1652	c.1662	LEWIS				
c.1689		WARD	Anthony			Possibly Anthony Ward, Attorney for Earl of Montagu, October 1696.
c.1691	c.1704	REYNOLDS	John			
c.1707	1724	HARDISTY	Robert	c.1656		Attorney of Court of Queen's Bench; appeared for inhabitants of Ossulstone Hundred, 1690–1707; Chapel Warden of Stratford-le-Bow; possibly Clerk to the Lieutenancy, c. 1714.
1724	1727	WALLER	John			Clerk to the Lieutenancy, c. 1724–30; Treasurer of Trophy Money, c. 1726–30.
1728	1753	WILKINSON	Thomas			Formerly assistant to Robert Hardisty, Deputy Clerk of the Peace, c. 1707–24, his kinsman; Justices allowed him " a pint of wine each day " during Sessions, the cost " to be defrayed out of colt money"; Receiver of rents of County estates, 1728–40; Clerk to Committee for paving the Haymarket, 1730.
1753	1757	HELY	John		c.1758	Certain Sessions records were left " twelve years " in custody of his executor (see note to James Waller, Clerk of the Peace, 1746–70).
1757	1759	TYRRELL	William			Of the Inner Temple.
1759	1769	JEFFERSON	James		1772	County Treasurer, 1765–72; Receiver of County rents.
1770		REES	David			Attorney, Court of Common Pleas; Solicitor to High Court of Chancery; appointed by James Waller, Clerk of the Peace, to succeed James Jefferson " having of a sudden quitted the said office " (according to Waller); but appointment apparently not accepted by Justices.
1770	1772	JEFFERSON	James		1772	Re-appointed by Thomas Butler, Clerk of the Peace, 1770–77.
1773	1784	EYLES	Charles		1785	Solicitor. Deputy Steward of Manor of Isleworth Syon; Acting County Treasurer, 1785.
1785	1826	STIRLING	Thomas	c.1745	1839	*Elected to Society, November 1813.* Solicitor. Deputy Steward of Manor of Isleworth Syon; Attorney and Solicitor for the County; Coroner, Western District, 1816–39; Clerk to the Visiting Justices and Committees, to 1839. In 1858 his son, a barrister, unsuccessfully claimed compensation for Stirling's services to the County over 47 years, alleging he had only received £1,100, an annual average of £23 10s. 0d.
1826	1829	ALLEN	Emanuel		1829	Solicitor. Vestry Clerk of St. Anne, Soho, c. 1801–20; in his obituary in the " Gentleman's Magazine " the annual perquisites and emoluments received by him as Clerk (sic) of the Peace were estimated at £4,000.
1830	1836	ALLEN	Charles Pettitt	1794	1871	*Elected to Society, November 1830.* *Honorary Treasurer, 1835–71.* Son of Emanuel Allen; Solicitor. County Treasurer, 1836–71; County Solicitor from 1826; Clerk to Visiting Justices of Westminster House of Correction; Vestry Clerk of St. Anne, Soho; Clerk to Paving Commissioners, and to Commissioners of Land and Assessed Taxes, same parish.

From	To	Surname	Forenames	Birth	Death	Biographical Notes
1836	1838	UNWIN	Joseph			Solicitor. Clerk to Commissioners for Redemption and Sale of Land Tax, Middlesex, 1813.
1838	1845	EDMONDES	Henry			*Elected to Society, May* 1841. Of the Middle Temple.
1845	1861	MAUDE	Arthur Grey			*Elected to Society, November* 1846. Solicitor.
1858	1859	ALLEN	Charles			" Jointly and severally " with Arthur Grey Maude; Solicitor.
1861	1864	BALDWIN	George Dimsdale			*Elected to Society, June* 1862.
1864	1874	FRANCIS	William			
1874	1883	BEAL	Edward William	1847	1936	*Elected to Society, June* 1877. Solicitor (admitted 1870). M.A. (London). Clerk to the Justices for Tower, Finsbury and Paddington divisions; Clerk of the London Standing Joint Committee and of the Court of General Assessment Sessions, later the County of London Quarter Sessions in Assessment Appeals. Deputy Clerk of the Peace for Hertfordshire, 1870–74.
1883	1889	THRELFALL	Charles		1899	*Elected to Society, June* 1885. Solicitor (admitted 1875).

DEPUTY CLERKS OF THE PEACE AND OF THE COUNTY COUNCIL from 1889

From	To	Surname	Forenames	Birth	Death	Biographical Notes
1889	1890	BUCK	Henry London			*Elected to Society, June* 1891. *Deputy Clerk of the Peace only.* Barrister-at-law, Middle Temple (called 1873).
1889	1909	AUSTIN	Walter George	c.1848	1921	*Deputy Clerk of the County Council,* 1889; *Deputy Clerk of the Peace,* 1890. Subsequently Clerk of the Peace and of the County Council, see above.
1909	1918	HART	Ernest Sidney Walter	1870	1957	Subsequently Clerk of the Peace and of the County Council, see above.
1919	1935	RADCLIFFE	Clifford Walter	1888		Subsequently Clerk of the Peace and of the County Council, see above.
1935	1938	ENSOR	Alick Charles Davidson	1907		*Elected to Society, October* 1935. *Deputy Clerk of the Peace only.* Solicitor (admitted 1928). Subsequently Clerk of the Peace for London, *q.v.*
1935	1955	GRAVES	Arthur Glendower	1893		*Deputy Clerk of the County Council,* 1935; *Deputy Clerk of the Peace,* 1938. Subsequently Clerk of the Peace, see above.
1955		DENNIS	John Newman	1913		*Elected to Society, July* 1955. *Deputy Clerk of the County Council only.* Forest School; Solicitor (admitted 1936). Captain, Royal Artillery, 1939–45 War.
1958		SHOOLBRED	Claude Frederick	1901		*Elected to Society, March* 1959. *Deputy Clerk of the Peace only.* Harrow School and Pembroke College, Cambridge; Barrister-at-law, Middle Temple (called 1925). Author of " *Lotteries and the Law* " and " *The Law of Gaming and Betting.*"

MIDDLESEX—CITY AND LIBERTY OF WESTMINSTER

From	To	Surname	Forenames	Birth	Death	Biographical Notes
CLERKS	**OF THE PEACE**	**from c.1620**				
c.1620	1632	OAKELEY	Richard			Possibly admitted to Middle Temple, 1613, and Secretary to the Lord Keeper.
1633	c.1637	OAKELEY	John			
c.1644	1650	JACKSON	John			
1650	c.1654	ROWE	Samuel			
c.1661	1681	LEWIS	Thomas			
1681	1682	MARSHALL	Ralph			
1682	1689	HARDISTY	John			
1689	1692	OVERTON	Benjamin			
1692	1709	SMITH	John		1709	Possibly identical with John Smith, Clerk of the Peace for Middlesex, 1683–89. Previously Deputy Clerk of the Peace.
1710	1729	MIDDLETON	David		1729	
1729	1778	FORBES	Peter			Of St. Marylebone; Treasurer of Trophy Money, 1724.
1779	1802	VAUGHAN	Thomas			
1803	1857	VAUGHAN	Thomas Wright			On his resignation, the execution of the duties of the office devolved on the Clerk of the Peace for Middlesex, pursuant to 7 & 8 Victoria, c. 71.
1857	1889	NICHOLSON	Sir Richard	1828	1913	Also Clerk of the Peace for Middlesex, see above.
DEPUTY	**CLERKS OF THE PEACE**	**from c.1628**				
c.1628	c.1644	CLIFFE	Anthony			
1690	1692	SMITH	John		1709	Subsequently Clerk of the Peace, see above.
c.1710	c.1715	TAYLOR	William		c.1718	
1729		BOUGH	Launcelot			
1762		HIGGS	John			Of Southampton Buildings, Holborn.
c.1780		CARLETON	Charles Cuthbert			
c.1796	1803	ALLEN	Emanuel		1829	Also Deputy Clerk of the Peace for Middlesex, see above.
1803	1821	STABLE	Lorenzo			Solicitor. Clerk to the Lieutenancy of Middlesex, c. 1807–13; Clerk to the Deputy Lieutenants of Middlesex, c. 1814–21.
1822	1826	ALLEN	Emanuel		1829	See above.
1826	c.1842	GYLBY	John Parker		1843	Solicitor (admitted 1812).
c.1843	1845	ALLEN	Charles Pettitt	1794	1871	Also Deputy Clerk of the Peace for Middlesex, see above.
1845	1853	MAUDE	Arthur Grey			Also Deputy Clerk of the Peace for Middlesex, see above.
1853	c.1860	ALLEN	Charles			Also joint Deputy Clerk of the Peace for Middlesex, see above.
c.1861	c.1867	MAUDE	Arthur Grey			See above.

MONMOUTHSHIRE

From	To	Surname	Forenames	Birth	Death	Biographical Notes
		CLERKS OF THE PEACE from 1540				
1540	1543	HUNTLEY	Hugh			Appointed Clerk of the Peace and Clerk of the Crown in Monmouthshire by letters patent, 25th July, 32 Henry VIII.
1544	1565	WATERS	John			
1566	1567	HOSKYNS (HOISKINS)	Richard			Appears also as Joskyns on the Pipe Roll.
1569	1576	WATERS	John			
1581	1609	RUMSEY	Walter		c.1609	Father of Walter Rumsey of Llanover, the Welsh judge.
1611	1625	WATKINS	Roger		c.1628	
1628		MORGAN	Richard			Of Usk.
1629		VAUGHAN	Richard			Possibly Deputy to Morgan.
1631		MORGAN	Richard			Of Usk.
1635	1639	WATKINS	William			Possibly Receiver General of South Wales, 1642.
1640	1641	WILLIAMS	William			Of Caerleon.
1653	1656	HERBERT	William			
1657	1658	JONES	Samuel			
1662		WILLIAMS	Herbert			
1666	1681	JONES	Herbert		c.1699	
1681	1682	LEWIS	Peregrine			
1685		JONES	Herbert			
1686	1688	LEWIS	Peregrine			
1691	1694	FORTUNE	Walter			Town Clerk of Monmouth.
1695	1717	FORTUNE	John			Town Clerk of Monmouth.
1718	1752	CLYFFORD	Thomas		1752	Of Newport.
1752	1795	MORGAN	Henry	1722	1795	Of Caerleon; Attorney. Also County Treasurer.
1796	1803	KEMEYS	George	1728	1805	Attorney. Clerk to Commissioners of Sewers.
1803	1814	TURTON	Zouch	1759	1814	Also County Treasurer.
1814	1839	JONES	Alexander	1770	c.1850	Solicitor. Recorder of Usk, 1832. Previously Deputy Clerk of the Peace.

From	To	Surname	Forenames	Birth	Death	Biographical Notes
1848	1874	PROTHERO	Charles	1816	1874	Solicitor (admitted 1839). Clerk to the Lieutenancy. Also County Treasurer.
1874	1880	FOX	Charles Burton	1820	1880	*Elected to Society, May* 1855. Solicitor (admitted 1841). Temporarily County Treasurer, 1874. Previously Deputy Clerk of the Peace.
1880	1889	WYATT	Osmond Arthur		1894	*Elected to Society, June* 1880. Barrister-at-law, Inner Temple (called 1839). Clerk to the Lieutenancy.

CLERKS OF THE PEACE AND OF THE COUNTY COUNCIL from 1889

From	To	Surname	Forenames	Birth	Death	Biographical Notes
1889	1894	WYATT	Osmond Arthur		1894	See above.
1894	1916	GUSTARD	Henry Stafford	1843	1916	*Elected to Society, June* 1889. Solicitor (admitted 1865). Clerk to the Lieutenancy; Secretary to the Advisory Committee; Clerk to the Commissioners of Sewers; Portreeve of Usk, 1881. Previously Deputy Clerk of the Peace and of the County Council.
1916	1921	COOPER	Frank Lyndon	1876	1921	*Elected to Society, February* 1917. Solicitor (John Mackrell prize) (admitted 1902). Clerk to the Lieutenancy; Secretary to the Advisory Committee.
1921	1936	HUGHES	Thomas	1869	1936	*Elected to Society, October* 1921. Solicitor (admitted 1891). Clerk to the Lieutenancy; Secretary to the Advisory Committee.
1937		LAWRENCE	Vernon	1899		*Elected to Society, January* 1937. Solicitor (admitted 1933). O.B.E., 1942; C.B.E., 1959. Clerk to the Lieutenancy; Secretary to the Advisory Committee; Clerk of the Magistrates' Courts Committee; Member and Honorary Secretary of Welsh Advisory Council for Civil Aviation; Honorary Secretary to Welsh Counties Committee. Previously County Solicitor and Prosecuting Solicitor, Glamorgan County Council. W/T, R.N.V.R., and Second Lieutenant, Royal Air Force, 1914–18 War.

DEPUTY CLERKS OF THE PEACE prior to 1889

From	To	Surname	Forenames	Birth	Death	Biographical Notes
1732		FORTUNE	William	1705	1756	Of Monmouth.
1745		BAGEHOTT	William		c.1794	Of Abergavenny.
1788		TOMKINS	James			
1795		JENKINS				
1796	1814	JONES	Alexander	1770	c.1850	Subsequently Clerk of the Peace, see above.
c.1839	1848	WADDINGTON	Alexander	c.1798	1874	Recorder of Usk, 1847; Portreeve of Usk, 1844–45 and 1867–73.
1848	1874	FOX	Charles Burton	1820	1880	Subsequently Clerk of the Peace, see above.
1886	1889	GUSTARD	Henry Stafford	1843	1916	Subsequently Clerk of the Peace and of the County Council, see above.

DEPUTY CLERKS OF THE PEACE AND OF THE COUNTY COUNCIL from 1889

From	To	Surname	Forenames	Birth	Death	Biographical Notes
1889	1894	GUSTARD	Henry Stafford	1843	1916	See above.
1942	1951	EVANS	Ernest Godfrey	1887	1951	*Elected to Society, July* 1942. Barrister-at-law, Gray's Inn (called 1928). Captain, Royal Garrison Artillery, 1914–18 War.
1952		WALKER	Kenneth Hamblett	1910		*Elected to Society, January* 1952. Solicitor (admitted 1937). LL.B. (Manchester).

MONTGOMERYSHIRE

From	To	Surname	Forenames	Birth	Death	Biographical Notes
		CLERKS OF THE PEACE from 1542				
1542		THOMAS	William			Appointed Clerk of the Peace and of the Crown for Montgomeryshire, Breconshire and Radnorshire by letters patent, 21st January, 33 Henry VIII.
1545		CLERC	William			Appointed Clerk of the Peace and of the Crown for the same three Counties by letters under the Signet, 21st May, 37 Henry VIII, the offices being in the King's hand by reason of felonies committed by William Thomas, who had fled the realm; the appointment to take effect from the preceding Lady Day and to be confirmed by letters patent after Thomas had been convicted by due course of law. Clerc is called " our well beloved servant " and was possibly the clerk in the privy seal office who was the King's private secretary. If so, he probably held these offices only until Thomas obtained a pardon.
c.1573		WILLIAMS	Humphrey			
1597	1600	LLOYD	Robert			
1602	1604	REYNOLDS	Lewis			
1605	1606	JUKES	George			
1607	1609	WILKES	William			
1620		REYNOLDS	Lewis			
1625	1628	REYNOLDS	Solomon			
1628		GRIFFITH	Owen			
1650	1659	MORRIS	Richard			
1660	1664	MORGAN	Rice			
1668	1671	BOWEN	Richard			
1673	1679	READ	John			
1679	1688	HUGHES	Richard			
1691	1708	DAVIES	John			
1721	1722	FFOULKES	Richard			Attorney.
1722	1743	WILSON	John			
	1744	PRYCE	Edmund			
	1769	EDWARDS	John			

From	To	Surname	Forenames	Birth	Death	Biographical Notes
1781	1808	JONES	Humphrey		1808	Of the family of Jones of Garthmyl (see *Montgomeryshire Historical Collections*, 25, pp. 302 *et seq.*)
1808	1822	JONES	Charles			Younger brother of Humphrey Jones.
1823	1848	JONES	Joseph	1799	1848	Brother of Humphrey and Charles Jones; Solicitor. Mayor of Welshpool, 1838, 1845.
1848	1884	HARRISON	John Pryce	1817	1884	Solicitor.
1884	1889	HARRISON	George Devereux	1847	1916	*Elected to Society, May* 1884. Nephew of John Pryce Harrison; son of Robert Devereux Harrison, Deputy Clerk of the Peace to 1874; Solicitor (admitted 1871). Clerk to the Lieutenancy; Clerk to the Justices, Newtown, Lower Cause and Pool Upper divisions, and Chirbury division of Salop. Previously Deputy Clerk of the Peace.

CLERKS OF THE PEACE AND OF THE COUNTY COUNCIL from 1889

From	To	Surname	Forenames	Birth	Death	Biographical Notes
1889	1910	HARRISON	George Devereux	1847	1916	See above.
1910	1945	HARRISON	George Rowland Devereux	1877	1960	*Elected to Society, June* 1910. Son of George Devereux Harrison; Solicitor (admitted 1902). B.A. (Cantab). Deputy Lieutenant. Clerk to the Lieutenancy; Secretary to the Advisory Committee; Registrar of Welshpool County Court, 1911–55; Mayor of Welshpool, 1920–25, and 1936–37. Montgomeryshire Yeomanry, 1914–18 War; Lieutenant Colonel, Royal Welch Fusiliers, 1925–29; Brevet Colonel, 1929; T.D.
1946		WHITE	Percival Edward	1902		*Elected to Society, April* 1934. Solicitor (admitted 1926). LL.B. (London). Deputy Lieutenant, 1960. Clerk to the Lieutenancy; Secretary to the Advisory Committee; Clerk of the Magistrates' Courts Committee and of the Mid-Wales Police Authority; Joint Clerk of the Denbighshire and Montgomeryshire Joint Fire Committee. Previously assistant solicitor, Dorset and Salop County Councils, Deputy Clerk of the County Council of Salop, and Clerk of the County Council of the Isle of Wight.

DEPUTY CLERKS OF THE PEACE prior to 1889

From	To	Surname	Forenames	Birth	Death	Biographical Notes
1575		WHITTINGHAM	William			
1692	1693	DAVIES	Edward			
	1874	HARRISON	Robert Devereux	1813	1874	Brother of John Pryce Harrison, Clerk of the Peace, 1848–84; Solicitor.
1874	1884	HARRISON	George Devereux	1847	1916	Subsequently Clerk of the Peace, see above.

NORFOLK

From	To	Surname	Forenames	Birth	Death	Biographical Notes
		CLERKS OF THE PEACE from 1390				
1390	1399	CAYLY	Geoffrey			
1400	1401	PYKORN	Stephen			
1401	1404	ASLAK	John			
1406		LYNFORD	John			
1407	1427	ASLAK	John			
1431	1453	WATERMAN	Nicholas			
1458	1493	WAYTE(S)	William			Clerk to Sir John Yelverton, Justice of the King's Bench.
1494	1505	DADE	John		?1506	Clerk of the Peace for Suffolk, 1486–87; possibly John Dade of Witton by Norwich whose Will proved, 1506 (see Norwich Consistory Court, 314–8 Ryxe).
1506		EVERARD	Henry			Appointed Clerk of the Peace and of the Crown for Norfolk and Suffolk by letters patent, 16th March, 21 Henry VII.
1506	1533	SPENCER	Leonard		?1539	Appointed Clerk of the Peace and of the Crown for Norfolk and Suffolk by letters patent, jointly in survivorship with John Heigham, 1st September, 22 Henry VII. Spencer appears to have acted in Norfolk. Town Clerk of Norwich (see Rye, *Norfolk Families*, p. 831); Will of one Leonard Spencer proved, 1539 (see P.C.C. Wills 16 Cromwell).
1506	c.1522	HEIGHAM	John		?1522	See note to Leonard Spencer, above; Heigham appears to have acted in Suffolk, *q.v.*
1513	1516	PAYN	Thomas			This and the following three officers were probably deputies for Leonard Spencer.
1518	1519	ASKETYLL	Thomas			
1519	1529	ROBYNS	Thomas			
1530	1531	HAWE	James			
1533	1551	HAWE	James		1561	Appointed Clerk of the Peace and of the Crown for Norfolk and Suffolk by letters patent, jointly with Sir James Bolayne, on surrender of Leonard Spencer's patent, John Heigham being dead (13th March, 24 Henry VIII). Hawe appears to have acted in Norfolk.
1533		BOLAYNE	Sir James		1561	See note to James Hawe, above; Bolayne appears to have acted in Suffolk, *q.v.*
1554	1557	ATKYNS	John			
1557	1560	ATKYNS	Stephen			
1560	1580	BARON	Matthew			
1580	1583	KNEVETT	Henry			
1584	1616	KNEVETT (KNYVETT)	Edmund			
1616	1617	ALLEYN	Thomas			
1617	1644	ANGUISH	Edmund		1657	Of Great Melton.
1645	1656	BERNERS	Hatton			Of Wiggenhall.
1657	c.1681	BURLEIGH	William		1682	Of Norwich.
1681	1689	MOTHAM	Isaac			Of Hethersett; a non-juror.
1689	1709	PAYNE	William			Of Bramerton; Major of a Company of Foot in the Militia.
1709	1725	HOUGHTON	John			
1725	1735	BERNEY	John		1735	
1735		WESTON	Stephen			
1735	1760	WESTON	Edward			
1760	1767	CASE	Philip			Of King's Lynn; four times Mayor. Previously Deputy Clerk of the Peace.

From	To	Surname	Forenames	Birth	Death	Biographical Notes
1767	1799	FINCH	Peter	c.1726	1807	Probably of Norwich.
1799	1818	STOKES	William		1818	Of Fakenham.
1818	1842	COPEMAN	Robert	1769	1844	*Elected to Society, November* 1819. Of Aylsham; Solicitor. Joint owner, with his brother Peter, of private bank at Aylsham which was absorbed by Gurneys, c.1850.
1842	1868	PARMETER	Robert William			*Elected to Society, November* 1842. Of Aylsham; Solicitor (admitted 1818).
1868	1889	FOSTER	Charles		1906	*Elected to Society, June* 1869. Of Norwich; Solicitor (admitted 1861). Previously Deputy Clerk of the Peace.

CLERKS OF THE PEACE AND OF THE COUNTY COUNCIL from 1889

From	To	Surname	Forenames	Birth	Death	Biographical Notes
1889	1906	FOSTER	Charles		1906	See above.
1906	1922	DAVIES	George Christopher	1849	1922	*Elected to Society, March* 1918. Oswestry Grammar School; Solicitor (admitted 1871). Clerk of the Norfolk Cattle Diseases Committee prior to 1888. As Deputy Clerk of the Peace, published an Index to the Local Government Act 1888 which was recognised as an authority (per *The Times*); author of books with natural history and sporting interests, and in early life a regular contributor to *The Field* and *Blackwood's Magazine*. Previously Deputy Clerk of the Peace and of the County Council.
1922	1944	DAVIES	Hugh Christopher			*Elected to Society, February* 1923. Solicitor (admitted 1900). Previously Deputy Clerk of the Peace and of the County Council.
1944	1956	BROWN	Henry Oswald	1891		*Elected to Society, November* 1924. Solicitor (admitted 1912). LL.B. (London). Previously Deputy Clerk of the Peace and of the County Council.
1956		BOYCE	Frederick Peter	1915		*Elected to Society, November* 1948. Son of Thomas Boyce, Director of Education, Bradford County Borough Council; Solicitor (Clement's Inn prize) (admitted 1939). Previously assistant solicitor, Bradford County Borough and Hertfordshire County Councils and Deputy Clerk of the Peace and of the County Council of Hertfordshire. Lieutenant, R.N.V.R., 1939–45 War.

DEPUTY CLERKS OF THE PEACE prior to 1889

From	To	Surname	Forenames	Birth	Death	Biographical Notes
1543		MYCHELL				
1650	1656	OAKES	Richard			Of Norwich; Attorney.
c.1681	1705	ROLFE	John			
1707		ROLFE	William			
1723		WYTHE	Edmund			
1735	1760	CASE	Philip			Subsequently Clerk of the Peace, see above.
1842	1868	FOSTER	Charles		1906	Subsequently Clerk of the Peace, see above.
c.1888	1889	DAVIES	George Christopher	1849	1922	Subsequently Clerk of the Peace and of the County Council, see above.

DEPUTY CLERKS OF THE PEACE AND OF THE COUNTY COUNCIL from 1889

From	To	Surname	Forenames	Birth	Death	Biographical Notes
1889	1906	DAVIES	George Christopher	1849	1922	See above.
1906	1922	DAVIES	Hugh Christopher			Subsequently Clerk of the Peace and of the County Council, see above.
1923	1944	BROWN	Henry Oswald	1891		Subsequently Clerk of the Peace and of the County Council, see above.
1944		WATERFALL	Christopher William	1906		*Elected to Society, September* 1944. Solicitor (admitted 1931). B.A. (Oxon). Previously assistant solicitor, Warwickshire, Essex and Staffordshire County Councils.

NORTHAMPTONSHIRE

From	To	Surname	Forenames	Birth	Death	Biographical Notes
		CLERKS OF THE PEACE from 1412				
1412	1418	WELDON	John			
1418	1419	DYTTON	John			
1419	1423	WELDON	John			
1423	1424	WELDON	William			
1425	1428	WELDON	John			
1435	1436	WELDON	Thomas			
1447	1479	MERTON	Thomas			Appointed by letters patent, for good service to the King and in Eton College, "Clerk of the Crown or Clerk of the Peace" and King's Attorney in all suits before the Justices of Oyer and Terminer in the County. His Will, dated 1481, is preserved (*Archdeaconry of Northampton Wills*, 1467–1506, no. 62); bequeathed sums to many religious houses, residue to his wife Alice, for whom see Baker, *History of Northamptonshire*, I, p. 494.
1480	1490	CHAUNCY	John			His Will, undated, is preserved (*op. cit.*, no. 334); left Latimers Tower, Northampton to his son Anthony; houses in Abington Street, Northampton to his wife Jane for life, remainder to their daughter Agnes, and residue of his lands to his eldest son John, who married Joan, daughter and heiress of Thomas Merton (see Baker, *op.cit.*).
1490	1507	HASILWODE	Edward			Probably son of Thomas Haselwood; died without issue and buried in London; his brother Edmund was Warden of the Fleet prison (see *The Genealogist*, I, pp. 43–44).
1508	1511	BOYVILL	George		1519	Son and heir of Richard Boyvill of Burton Latimer; married Laurentia, daughter of Thomas Burdon, 1501; inherited from his father lands in Burton Latimer and Little Oxendon under Will proved 1511; sold Manor of Little Oxendon to Andrew Palmer, 1515; owned land at Ashley.
1512	1525	WARNER	Edward			
1526	1529	GENT	William			Possibly of Norton.
1531	1537	BRETEN	Christopher			Probably Squire of Teeton who was buried in 1556; of ancient family which owned Teeton from twelfth to eighteenth centuries.
1537	1548	JOSKYN	James			Appointed Clerk of the Peace and of the Crown for Northamptonshire and Leicestershire by letters patent, 26th June, 29 Henry VIII. Also Clerk of the Wardrobe of Robes and of the King's Beds in England.
1549	1553	GENT	William			Also paid as Clerk of the Justices, 1538–39 and 1546, possibly as deputy for Joskyn.
1553	1580	FREEMAN	Henry			Possibly husband of Elizabeth, daughter of George and granddaughter of Henry Gage and Margaret Boyvill, the sister of George Boyvill, Clerk of the Peace, 1508–11. One Henry Freeman of Irchester made Will, proved 1586, leaving at least three sons, one daughter.
1583	1585	FREEMAN	Thomas			Under Sheriff, 1560.
1586		SHUTE	Richard			

NORTHAMPTONSHIRE (*Continued*)

From	To	Surname	Forenames	Birth	Death	Biographical Notes
1587	1610	GAGE	Robert	1542	1615/6	Third son of George Gage (see note to Henry Freeman, Clerk of the Peace, 1553–80); married Anne, daughter of Robert Pemberton of Rushden, 1570/1; six sons, four daughters; lawyer. On his mother's death, inherited moiety of Manor of Raunds, known as Gage's Manor, 1577; lessee of other moiety and of lands in Geddington and Brixworth. Buried at Raunds (monument).
1611	1622	GAGE	John		1649	Of Raunds; eldest son of Robert Gage; married Jane, daughter of Richard Goodwin of Eaton Socon, Bedfordshire; seven sons. Receiver of the Honor of Higham Ferrers, 1624; deputy Steward of Higham Ferrers Hundred, and other Duchy of Lancaster Courts, 1637.
1623	1642	GRAY	Francis		1658	Of Wellingborough; married Alice, daughter and co-heiress of John Page of Rushden. Appointed Deputy Feodary, Coroner, Escheator and Clerk of the Markets for the Duchy of Lancaster within Northamptonshire, 1637. An ardent Royalist, deprived of office, 1642, when he was seized by Captain Francis Sawyer, Parliamentarian, and all Quarter Sessions records carried off, great damage being done at Wellingborough at the time; appears eventually to have come to terms with Parliament. Bought Gage's Manor, and other lands near Wellingborough, 1655.
1646	1660	GUY	Robert			Of Isham; married Mary Sawyer of Kettering, 1644; several children; bought Holdenby Manor, Isham, from Viscount Cullen, 1646.
1660	1666	GORSTELOW	Thomas	1610	1668	Of East Carlton; son of Leonard Gorstelow of Rockingham and Carlton; married Catherine Smith.
1667	1670	IRELAND	William			Of Sutton Bassett, son of William Ireland, the elder.
1671		PICKMER	Francis	1626	c.1679	Of Kingsthorpe, second son of Samuel Pickmer; married Bridget, daughter of William Lane of Quinton, 1657; Attorney, of St. Sepulchre's parish, Northampton.
1672	1678	CHYBNALE (CHIBNELL)	Godfrey	1649/50	1678	Son of Thomas Chybnale of Sherington, Buckinghamshire; Emmanuel College, Cambridge, matriculated 1669; admitted Gray's Inn, 1671. Lord of the Manor, Orlingbury; also owned property at Pytchley; appears as Deputy Clerk of the Peace, 1671–72.
1680	1692	DUCKETT	Joseph			Of All Saints' Parish, Northampton.
1692	1738	HORTON	John			Of Kettering; Attorney. Steward of several Manors in that district; possibly inherited a paper mill at Yardley Gobion, 1723, and died intestate, 1738/9.
1738	1747	SMITH	Thomas		1747	
1748		HOLLED	Thomas		?1787	Possibly son of the Rev. Knightley Holled, Rector of Barby.
1749	1754	BROOKE	Arthur		1754	Of Kettering; second son of Arthur Brooke of Great Oakley; married Mary, daughter of Zaccheus Isham, D.D., Prebendary of St. Paul's Cathedral and Canon of Canterbury Cathedral, 1722, Rector of Solihull, Warwickshire; two daughters. Ancestor of Baron Brooke of Oakley, Chairman of Northamptonshire County Council, 1925–44. Captain in Duke of Montagu's Regiment.
1754	1769	ROGERS	Timothy	1701	1769	Fifth son of Timothy Rogers, Usher of the Free School, Northampton. Under Sheriff. Buried at St. Peter's, Northampton.
1769	1788	MORGAN	Charles		1788	Of St. Giles', Northampton. Clerk to the Lieutenancy, 1779. His Will, dated 1788, appoints his wife Frances as executrix.

From	To	Surname	Forenames	Birth	Death	Biographical Notes
1788	1823	SMYTH	Christopher	1736	1825	Son of the Rev. William Smith, Rector of Emberton, Buckinghamshire; married Anne, daughter of Samuel Hartshorn, attorney of Northampton, 1762; acquired parts of Manors of Little Houghton and Brafield, 1801. Under Sheriff.
1823	1846	MARKHAM	Charles	1778	1846	*Elected to Society, May 1828.* Eldest son of John Markham, Clerk to the Lieutenancy to 1803; Rugby School; married Eliza Mary Packharness; nine children. Attorney (admitted 1800). Clerk to the Lieutenancy, 1803. Buried in St. Giles' Church, Northampton.
1846	1889	MARKHAM	Henry Philip	1816	1904	*Elected to Society, November 1846.* Second son of Charles Markham; married Edith Alexander, 1855; one son, two daughters. Attorney (admitted 1838). Deputy Lieutenant, 1895. Clerk to the Lieutenancy, 1846; Mayor of Northampton, 1861–62.

CLERKS OF THE PEACE AND OF THE COUNTY COUNCIL from 1889

From	To	Surname	Forenames	Birth	Death	Biographical Notes
1889	1904	MARKHAM	Henry Philip	1816	1904	See above.
1904	1933	MILLINGTON	Herbert Ashlin	1868	1933	*Elected to Society, May 1904.* *Vice-Chairman and Honorary Treasurer, 1932–33.* Son of Herbert Millington, Headmaster of Bromsgrove School; Solicitor (admitted 1892). O.B.E., 1918. Clerk to the Lieutenancy; Secretary to the Advisory Committee. Previously Deputy Town Clerk of Richmond, Surrey, and Town Clerk of Great Yarmouth.
1934	1939	MARTIN	Hubert Sinclair	1891		*Elected to Society, October 1930.* *Honorary Treasurer, 1938–56.* Solicitor (admitted 1913). LL.B. (London). Clerk to the Lieutenancy; Secretary to the Advisory Committee. Previously Deputy Clerk of the Peace and of the County Council of East Sussex; subsequently Clerk of the Peace and of the County Council of East Sussex, *q.v.*
1939		TURNER	John Alan	1903		*Elected to Society, November 1932.* Solicitor (admitted 1929). Radley College and Exeter College, Oxford; B.A. O.B.E., 1943. Clerk to the Lieutenancy; Secretary to the Advisory Committee; Clerk of the Magistrates' Courts Committee. Previously assistant solicitor, Ipswich County Borough Council, and Deputy Clerk of the Peace and of the County Councils of Oxfordshire and of Warwickshire.

DEPUTY CLERKS OF THE PEACE AND OF THE COUNTY COUNCIL from 1889

From	To	Surname	Forenames	Birth	Death	Biographical Notes
1889	1904	MARKHAM	Christopher Alexander	1860	1937	*Elected to Society, May 1888.* Son of Henry Philip Markham, Clerk of the Peace, 1846–1904; Solicitor (admitted 1887). Antiquary; editor of *Northamptonshire Notes and Queries.*
1938	1944	GODBER	Geoffrey Chapman	1912		*Elected to Society, March 1941.* Solicitor (Clifford's Inn prize) (admitted 1936). LL.B. (London). Subsequently Clerk of the Peace and of the County Council of Salop, *q.v.*
1944	1947	BROUGHTON	Arthur Stanesby	1907		*Elected to Society, October 1945.* Solicitor (admitted 1928). Previously assistant solicitor, Walsall County Borough Council and Deputy Clerk of the Peace and of the County Borough Council of Blackburn.
1947	1953	SKINNER	Alan Frank	1913		*Elected to Society, March 1947.* Solicitor (honours) (admitted 1937). B.A., LL.B. (Cantab). Subsequently Clerk of the Peace and of the County Council of West Suffolk, *q.v.*
1953		JONES	Owen Meurig	1918		*Elected to Society, November 1953.* Solicitor (admitted 1947). Previously assistant solicitor, Breconshire and Northamptonshire County Councils. Captain, Royal Artillery, 1939–45 War; M.C.

NORTHUMBERLAND

From	To	Surname	Forenames	Birth	Death	Biographical Notes
CLERKS OF THE PEACE from 1673						
1673	1674	CROW	Patrick			
1681	1684	NEWTON	Joseph		1687	Counsellor-at-law; entered Lincoln's Inn, 1676.
1684	1697	PYE	John			
1697	1698	FEATHER-STONHALGH	Ralph			
1698	1708	ORD	John			Attorney.
1708	1737	ORD	Thomas		1737	Son of John Ord.
1737	1742	GOWLAND	Samuel		1742	Entered Gray's Inn, 1708.
1742	1759	DENTON	Christopher		1759	Entered Gray's Inn, 1744; Deputy Clerk of the Pipe in H.M. Exchequer.
1759	1767	CUTHBERTSON	George		1767	Attorney. Town Clerk of Newcastle-upon-Tyne.
1768	1775	FORSTER	Collingwood	1714	1775	Attorney.
1775	1781	DAVIDSON	Thomas	1723	1781	Attorney. Clerk to the Lieutenancy.
1782	1818	DAVIDSON	John	1750	1818	Son of Thomas Davidson; Attorney.
1818	1823	DAVIDSON	Thomas	1754	1823	Brother of John Davidson; Attorney. Receiver of Stamp Duties for Newcastle, Northumberland and Berwick-upon-Tweed.
1823	1843	THORP	Robert	1771	1843	Attorney.
1843	1875	DICKSON	William	1799	1875	*Elected to Society, May* 1845. Solicitor (admitted 1821). Clerk to the Justices, East and North Coquetdale divisions, 1831.
1875	1889	SANDERSON	Stephen	1830	1915	*Elected to Society, June* 1876. Of Berwick-upon-Tweed; Solicitor (admitted 1851). Deputy Lieutenant. Registrar, Berwick County Court. Clerk of the Peace, Berwick-upon-Tweed.
CLERKS OF THE PEACE AND OF THE COUNTY COUNCIL from 1889						
1889	1915	SANDERSON	Stephen	1830	1915	See above.
1916	1928	FORSTER	Charles Davison	1850	1936	*Elected to Society, June* 1916. Solicitor (admitted 1874). Clerk to the Lieutenancy, 1899–1916; resigned that office on appointment as Clerk of the Peace and of the County Council. Previously Deputy Clerk of the Peace and of the County Council.
1928	1946	CARTER	Charles Harold	1886	1946	*Elected to Society, October* 1920. Solicitor (admitted 1914). Clerk to the Lieutenancy from 1930; Secretary to the Advisory Committee. Previously assistant solicitor, Devon County Council, and Deputy Clerk of the Peace and of the County Council of Essex.
1946		HARVEY	Ernest Philip	1905		*Elected to Society, November* 1932. Grandson of Herbert Cranmer Harvey, Deputy Clerk of the County Council, 1891–92; Solicitor (admitted 1928). Clerk to the Lieutenancy; Secretary to the Advisory Committee; Clerk of the Magistrates' Courts Committee. Previously Deputy Clerk of the Peace and of the County Council.
DEPUTY CLERKS OF THE PEACE AND OF THE COUNTY COUNCIL from 1889						
1891	1892	HARVEY	Herbert Cranmer	1843	1920	*Deputy Clerk of the County Council only.* Solicitor (admitted 1869). M.A. (Cantab). Clerk to the Lieutenancy, 1892–94 and 1897–99.
1892	1916	FORSTER	Charles Davison	1850	1936	Subsequently Clerk of the Peace and of the County Council, see above.
1932	1946	HARVEY	Ernest Philip	1905		Subsequently Clerk of the Peace and of the County Council, see above.
1947		HURLEY	Clement Woods	1915		*Elected to Society, March* 1947. Solicitor (admitted 1937). Lieutenant Colonel, Royal Artillery, 1939–45 War; later Colonel, T.A.; O.B.E. (Mil.), T.D.

NOTE: earlier records for Northumberland are no longer extant. The Court of Quarter Sessions had no settled meeting place until the early nineteenth century and it is not known where the early records of the Clerk of the Peace were kept. They may have been in the office of the Town Clerk of Newcastle-upon-Tyne when it was destroyed by fire in 1639, or they may have been lost when Newcastle was occupied in 1644 by Scottish troops after a three months' siege. The Pipe Rolls at the Public Record Office do not contain any earlier references to Northumberland.

NOTTINGHAMSHIRE

From	To	Surname	Forenames	Birth	Death	Biographical Notes
		CLERKS OF THE PEACE from 1400				
1400	1403	STACY	Walter			
1403	1409	MERSTON	Richard			
1415	1418	TAILLARD	Walter			
1418	1435	MANCHESTER	John			
1435	1452	BRYDDE	John			
1455	1476	BYNGHAM	Thomas			
1476	1489	ORSTON	Thomas			
1501	1518	WARREN (WAREN)	William			
1518	1524	ROBERTSON	William			
1526	1531	BEVERCOTES	Richard			
1532	1537	SMYTH	Henry			
1537		PRESTON	Thomas			Appointed Clerk of the Peace and of the Crown in Nottinghamshire and Derbyshire by letters patent, 4th July, 29 Henry VIII.
1538	1546	BOUNE	Edward			Possibly Deputy for Thomas Preston; also Clerk of the Peace for Derbyshire, 1539–44.
1555	1564	TOWNERAWE	Henry			
1567	1603	WRIGHTE	Lawrence			
1603	1604	LACOCK	George			
1605	1606	LACOCK	James			
1618	1635	LACOCK	George			
1640	1641	BUTLER	Robert			
1652		KEATLEWELL	Timothy			
1653	1658	BRISTOWE	Thomas			
1660		LOVELL	George			
1662	1697	CONDE	John		1697	
1697	1705	WYLDE	Francis		1705	
1705	1727	BANKS	Joseph		1727	Of Sheffield; Attorney. Member of Parliament for Grimsby, 1714–21; for Totnes, 1722–27; great-grandfather of Sir Joseph Banks, the Lincolnshire naturalist.
1728	1733	BANKS	Robert		1733	Of Bawtry.
1733	1745	BRISTOWE	William		1745	Of Besthorpe.
1745	1762	LUGG	Adam		1762	Of Gainsborough and Newark; Attorney. Previously Deputy Clerk of the Peace.
1762	1781	HURST	John		1781	Of East Retford.
1782	1795	BROUGH	Job		1795	Solicitor; Town Clerk of Newark.
1795	1806	BROUGH	Job Charlton		1806	Son of Job Brough; Barrister-at-law, Recorder of Newark.

NOTTINGHAMSHIRE (*Continued*)

From	To	Surname	Forenames	Birth	Death	Biographical Notes
1806	1843	GODFREY	Edward Smith		1843	Of Newark; Solicitor.
1843	1858	HURST	William			Of Newark; Solicitor.
1858	1889	BURNABY	Thomas Fowke Andrew		1893	*Elected to Society, May* 1845. Of Newark; Solicitor (admitted 1831). Clerk to the Lieutenancy; Registrar, Newark Borough Court of Record. Previously Deputy Clerk of the Peace.

CLERKS OF THE PEACE AND OF THE COUNTY COUNCIL from 1889

From	To	Surname	Forenames	Birth	Death	Biographical Notes
1889	1893	BURNABY	Thomas Fowke Andrew		1893	See above.
1893	1904	HIND	Jesse	1842	1919	*Elected to Society, June* 1894. Solicitor (admitted 1865). Justice of the Peace, 1907. Clerk to the Lieutenancy, 1893–1918.
1904	1921	COPNALL	Henry Hampton	1862	1921	*Elected to Society, May* 1904. Solicitor (admitted 1888). Clerk to the Lieutenancy, 1919–21. Previously Deputy Clerk of the Peace and of the County Council.
1921	1954	MEABY	Kenneth George Tweedale	1883		*Elected to Society, June* 1916. Solicitor (admitted 1907). Deputy Lieutenant, 1941; C.B.E., 1942. Justice of the Peace, 1954. Clerk to the Lieutenancy, 1921– ; Secretary to the Advisory Committee; Clerk of the Magistrates' Courts Committee. Previously Deputy Clerk of the Peace and of the County Councils of Devon and of Durham. R.N.V.R., 1914–18 War.
1954	1960	NORTON	George	1912	1960	*Elected to Society, March* 1954. *Clerk of the Peace only.* Solicitor (admitted 1938). LL.B. (London). Secretary to the Advisory Committee; Clerk of the Magistrates' Courts Committee.
1954		DAVIS	Alan Robert	1916		*Elected to Society, March* 1954. *Clerk of the County Council,* 1954; *Clerk of the Peace,* 1960. Solicitor (admitted 1938). Secretary to the Advisory Committee and Clerk of the Magistrates' Courts Committee, 1960. Major, Royal Artillery, 1939–45 War.

DEPUTY CLERKS OF THE PEACE prior to 1889

From	To	Surname	Forenames	Birth	Death	Biographical Notes
1733	1745	LUGG	Adam		1762	Subsequently Clerk of the Peace, see above.
1837		TALLENTS	William Edward			*Elected to Society, November* 1837.
1838	1858	BURNABY	Thomas Fowke Andrew		1893	Subsequently Clerk of the Peace, see above.

DEPUTY CLERKS OF THE PEACE AND OF THE COUNTY COUNCIL from 1889

From	To	Surname	Forenames	Birth	Death	Biographical Notes
1891	1904	COPNALL	Henry Hampton	1862	1921	Subsequently Clerk of the Peace and of the County Council, see above.
1947	1951	BREWIS	George Oldfield	1909		*Elected to Society, May* 1939. *Deputy Clerk of the County Council only.* Solicitor (admitted 1931). Subsequently Clerk of the Peace and of the County Council of Bedfordshire, *q.v.*
1954		BROCKBANK	James Tyrrell	1920		*Elected to Society, November* 1954. *Deputy Clerk of the County Council,* 1954; *Deputy Clerk of the Peace,* 1960. Solicitor (admitted 1949). Captain, Inns of Court Regiment, 1939–45 War.

OXFORDSHIRE

From	To	Surname	Forenames	Birth	Death	Biographical Notes
CLERKS OF THE PEACE from 1392						
	1392	BEEK	William			Possibly member of family of Beek (Beke) of Earley, Whiteknights, Reading, Berkshire, and plaintiff in a fine at Kidlington, 1415.
1393	1407	FELMERSHAM	William			Possibly the William Felmersham who was party to deed relating to Manor of Heythrop, 1422, and who appeared in transactions with Abbot of Osney, 1425 and 1437.
1422	1440	FELMERSHAM	John			Possibly the John Felmersham who held Bignell Manor, near Bicester, as tenant of Humphrey, Earl of Stafford, 1439.
1441	1454	WALDYENE	Thomas			
1458	1464	HAUTMONT	John			Duchy of Cornwall bailiff of Watlington, 1452; Under Sheriff, 1458.
1467	1469	SAMWELL	John		c.1500	One John Samwell took 60-year lease of Cottisford Manor from Eton College, 1469. Probably commemorated by mutilated brass in Cottisford Church.
1471	1495	FARYNGDON	John			One John Faryngdon possessed tenements at Eton, conveyed for foundation of College by King Henry VI, 1441.
1495	1498	STOUGHTON	Gilbert			Possibly Bencher of Inner Temple; party to sale of Manor of Holton, 1513; one of the Judges at Gaol Delivery for Wallingford Castle, 1515. Subsequently Justice of the Peace.
1506		CONUSER (COUNCER)	William			Appointed Clerk of the Peace and of the Crown for life by letters patent, 21st November, 22 Henry VII.
1512	1516	ANDREWS	Richard			Also appears to have acted in 1521, possibly as Deputy to his successor; Clerk of the Peace for Berkshire, 1520–23. One Richard Andrews of Hailes, Gloucestershire, received many grants of land in Oxfordshire at the Dissolution.
1519	1528	CRIPS (CRISPE)	Richard			Possibly member of the family of Crispe, of Cobcote near Thame. One Richard Crips was Auditor for Studley Priory for the *Valor Ecclesiasticus*, 1534.
1528		EDMUNDS	William			Possibly acting Clerk only during a vacancy in office, 1527/8. Member of Parliament for Reading, 1522–23; Clerk of the Peace for Berkshire, 1523–41; Mayor of Reading, 1540 and 1550.
1536	1538	WASHEBORNE	Richard			Appointed Clerk of the Peace and of the Crown by letters patent, 18th July, 28 Henry VIII.
1550	1558	BURY	James	1502	1558	Lord of the Manor of Hampton Poyle; Commissioner appointed to enquire into state of Royal Manor of Woodstock, 1551. By his Will, proved 1558, bequeathed all his law books to his nephew John.
1560	1590	MERCER	William		1590	Tenant of lands in Royal Manor of Ewelme. Bequeathed £5 to his servant (probably clerk) Richard Stevens who succeeded him as Clerk of the Peace.
1590	1641	STEVENS (STEPHENS)	Richard		c.1641	Freeman of Oxford and elected Town Clerk, 1613, during stewardship of Lord Knollys, whose lawyer he probably was. Made survey of woods in Royal Manor of Ewelme, 1621; received grants of hereditaments in the Manor, 1627. Richard Stevens of Cottisford was leaseholder of Cottisford Manor, 1627–41.
1646	1652	SPRIGGE	William		c.1654	Lawyer of Banbury, appearing in deeds from 1621 to 1652. Probably acted for Lord Saye and Sele, *Custos Rotulorum*, 1642. Possibly father of Joshua and William Sprigge, the Puritan pamphleteers.
1653	1654	STAMPE	Edward			One Edward Stampe was Steward to Whorwood family of Headington Manor from 1614. A Mr. Stampe gave 30/- towards cost of beautifying and repairing the Lower Guild Hall, Oxford, 1652.
1657	1658	TWYFORD	Edward			One Edward Twyford was lessee of Earl of Downe's sequestered lands in Oxfordshire, 1650. Edward Twyford of Burford joined in sale of the Earl's lands at Enstone, 1653. Edward Twyford of Northmoor was concerned in property transactions, 1662 and 1668.
1662	1691	STEVENS (STEPHENS)	Richard			Possibly related to Richard Stevens, Clerk of the Peace, 1590–1641, and lawyer to Knollys family; may have lived at Henley-on-Thames. Steward of the Manors of Great and Little Milton, c. 1676–88; deputy to John, Lord Lovelace, Steward of the Manor of Woodstock, 1677. Richard Stevens of Henley-on-Thames was Steward of Manors of Shiplake, 1682, and of Rotherfield Greys, 1684.

OXFORDSHIRE (Continued)

From	To	Surname	Forenames	Birth	Death	Biographical Notes
1691	1694	PRINCE	Edward		1694	Apprenticed to John Paynton, Town Clerk of Oxford; admitted to practise in City courts, 1673. Member of City Council, 1675; Coroner, 1677; elected Town Clerk, but approval of appointment refused by King Charles II, 1681; became Town Clerk in 1688, with approval of King James II. Died in London; buried in St. Martin's Church, Oxford.
1694	1716	CLERKE	Richard	1659	c.1716	Sixth son of Sir John Clerke, Baronet, of North Weston, Thame. His brother, Francis Clerke, was Member of Parliament for the County, 1710–15, and Justice of the Peace, c. 1689–1715; his grandson, Francis Clerke, was High Sheriff, 1750. Other members of this family also held office as High Sheriff.
1716	1759	DISTON	William		1759	Appears as witness to deed, 1695. Died while the County was without a *Custos Rotulorum*, and Quarter Sessions appointed Edward Ryves (see below) as Acting Clerk from August to December, 1759.
1759	1762	HARMOOD	Harry		1792	Of Lincoln's Inn Fields and Stockbridge, Hampshire; appointed by Earl of Northington, Lord Keeper of the Great Seal, the post of *Custos Rotulorum* being vacant; exercised his office by Deputy. Clerk and Treasurer of the Basingstoke-Stockbridge Turnpike Trust, 1756–60; Trustee, 1760–92. Justice of the Peace, Hampshire, 1772.
1763	1767	RYVES	Edward		1767	Town Clerk of Woodstock, 1752–67; other members of this family also held that office. See also note to William Diston, Clerk of the Peace, 1716–59.
1767	1777	WALKER	Thomas	c.1723	1804	Exercised office by Deputy. Town Clerk of Oxford, from c. 1759, and of Woodstock, 1767–1804; Receiver General of Land Tax for the County, 1768–1804; Steward and Agent to Duke of Marlborough, c. 1767–97; principal partner in the University and City Bank, Oxford. Previously Deputy Clerk of the Peace.
1777	1781	ELERS	Paul	1700	1781	Barrister-at-law, Middle Temple. Justice of the Peace, 1746–77. Becoming impoverished, was offered post of Clerk of the Peace by Duke of Marlborough as favour to Lord Harcourt, whom Elers had assisted at Oxfordshire election of 1754; exercised the office by Deputy. His father and uncle had come to England with the Prince of Orange, and set up pottery at Bradwell near Burslem, Staffordshire, afterwards moving to Chelsea and working with the Wedgwoods.
1781	1815	TAUNTON	Sir William (Elias)	1744	1825	Son of the Rev. Elias Taunton, Justice of the Peace, 1755–65. Clerk to the Lieutenancy, c. 1778–1815; Town Clerk of Oxford, 1795–1825; gave a charity to the City; knighted on the occasion of the Prince Regent's visit to Oxford, 1814. Previously Deputy Clerk of the Peace. His eldest son, William Elias Taunton, became Recorder of Oxford, 1806, Justice of the Peace, 1822, and Puisne Judge of the King's Bench, 1830, and was knighted the same year.
1815	1831	TAUNTON	Thomas Henry	1775	1831	*Elected to Society, November* 1815. Second son of Sir William Taunton; Abingdon School and Pembroke College, Oxford; Solicitor. Clerk to the Lieutenancy, 1828–31; Assistant Town Clerk of Oxford.
1831	1881	DAVENPORT	John Marriott	1809	1882	*Elected to Society, June* 1831. Solicitor (admitted 1830). F.S.A. Clerk to the Lieutenancy; Under Sheriff, 1853–75; Secretary to Bishops of Oxford, 1855–77; Deputy Registrar of Diocese, 1849–82; Registrar of Court of Probate for Oxfordshire, Berkshire and Buckinghamshire. See Plate VI.
1881	1889	DAVENPORT	Thomas Marriott	1841	1913	*Elected to Society, June* 1869. *Honorary Treasurer,* 1871–1913. Second son of John Marriott Davenport; Rugby School and Pembroke College, Oxford; M.A. Solicitor (admitted 1867). Clerk to the Lieutenancy; Under Sheriff, 1875–1911; Registrar of the Probate Court; Diocesan Registrar. Previously Deputy Clerk of the Peace.

CLERKS OF THE PEACE AND OF THE COUNTY COUNCIL from 1889

From	To	Surname	Forenames	Birth	Death	Biographical Notes
1889	1913	DAVENPORT	Thomas Marriott	1841	1913	See above. Also Secretary to the Advisory Committee.
1913	1928	ROSE	James	1855	1936	*Elected to Society, February* 1914. Exeter College, Oxford; M.A. Solicitor (admitted 1880). Clerk to the Lieutenancy; Secretary to the Advisory Committee; Under Sheriff, 1919–28; Secretary to Bishop of Oxford; Diocesan Registrar. Previously Deputy Clerk of the Peace and of the County Council.

From	To	Surname	Forenames	Birth	Death	Biographical Notes
1928	1953	SCOTT	Francis Gerald	1888		*Elected to Society, April 1924.* Solicitor (admitted 1919). Deputy Lieutenant. Clerk to the Lieutenancy; Secretary to the Advisory Committee; Clerk of the Magistrates' Courts Committee; Under Sheriff. Member of Local Government Sub-Committee, Nuffield College Social Reconstruction Survey, 1942. Previously Deputy Clerk of the Peace and of the County Council of East Sussex. Major, Royal Artillery, 1914–18 War; M.C.; Croix de Guerre.
1953		BURKITT	Gerald Gale	1911		*Elected to Society, July 1946.* Solicitor (first class honours, Clifford's Inn prize) (admitted 1934). LL.B. (Birmingham). Clerk to the Lieutenancy; Secretary to the Advisory Committee; Clerk of the Magistrates' Courts Committee; Under Sheriff. Previously Deputy Clerk of the Peace and of the County Council. Major, General List, 1939–45 War.

DEPUTY CLERKS OF THE PEACE prior to 1889

From	To	Surname	Forenames	Birth	Death	Biographical Notes
1717	c.1720	CHETTLE	William		1745	Attorney; practised in Oxford City courts from 1698. Member of City Council, 1703–18; Coroner, 1716–45; Town Clerk of Oxford, 1718–45.
c.1720	1738	WHITEHEAD	Peter			
1738	c.1759	BULLEY	Thomas		1769/70	
1759	c.1762	WALKER	Thomas	c.1723	1804	Subsequently Clerk of the Peace, see above.
c.1762	c.1767	MORRELL	James			
1768	1781	TAUNTON	William Elias	1744	1825	Subsequently Clerk of the Peace, see above.
1869	1881	DAVENPORT	Thomas Marriott	1841	1913	Subsequently Clerk of the Peace, see above.

DEPUTY CLERKS OF THE PEACE AND OF THE COUNTY COUNCIL from 1889

From	To	Surname	Forenames	Birth	Death	Biographical Notes
1913	1913	ROSE	James	1855	1936	Subsequently Clerk of the Peace and of the County Council, see above.
1913	1918	DAVENPORT	Hugh Nares	1886	1918	*Elected to Society, February 1914.* Third surviving son of Thomas Marriott Davenport, Clerk of the Peace, 1881–1913. Oriel College, Oxford; M.A. Major, Oxfordshire and Buckinghamshire Light Infantry, 1914–18 War; M.C.; killed in action.
1928	1928	HOLCROFT	Edward Stanley	1884		*Elected to Society, November 1933.* Solicitor (admitted 1907). Subsequently Deputy Clerk, later Clerk, of the Peace and of the County Council of Essex, *q.v.*
1932	1933	TURNER	John Alan	1903		*Elected to Society, November 1932.* Solicitor (admitted 1929). B.A. (Oxon). Subsequently Clerk of the Peace and of the County Council of Northamptonshire, *q.v.*
1934	1946	CHATTERTON	John Arthur	1905		*Elected to Society, March 1934.* Solicitor (admitted 1929). Subsequently Clerk of the Peace and of the County Council of Leicestershire, *q.v.*
1946	1953	BURKITT	Gerald Gale	1911		Subsequently Clerk of the Peace and of the County Council, see above.
1953		WALTON	Hugh Merscy	1912		*Elected to Society, July 1953.* *Deputy Clerk of the Peace only.* Solicitor (admitted 1950). M.A. (Oxon et Cantab). County Archivist and assistant solicitor, Oxfordshire County Council.
1953	1959	ATKINSON	Jack	1917		*Elected to Society, July 1953.* *Deputy Clerk of the County Council only.* Solicitor (admitted 1946). LL.B. (Bristol). Subsequently Clerk of the Peace and of the County Council of East Sussex, *q.v.*
1959		HOLDEN	Thomas Geoffrey	1920		*Elected to Society, October 1959.* *Deputy Clerk of the County Council only.* Solicitor (admitted 1947). LL.B. (Cantab). Previously assistant solicitor, Cambridgeshire, Essex, and Nottinghamshire County Councils.

PEMBROKESHIRE

From	To	Surname	Forenames	Birth	Death	Biographical Notes
CLERKS OF THE PEACE from 1541						
1541		MOFFET	Robert			Appointed Clerk of the Peace and of the Crown for Pembrokeshire, Cardiganshire and Carmarthenshire by letters patent, 9th December, 33 Henry VIII; Groom of the Chamber.
c.1573		GARNANCE	John			
c.1628		GWYNNE	David			
	c.1734	PHILLIPS	James			Died before 14th January 1734.
1734	1783	OWEN	Charles		1783	
1783	1793	PARRY	George			
1793	1805	GWYNNE	John			
1805	1834	REES	Henry		1834	
1834	1843	PAYNTER	William Evans		1844	Solicitor.
1843	1855	LEACH	Edward		1855	Solicitor.
1856	1889	OWEN	John		1897	
CLERKS OF THE PEACE AND OF THE COUNTY COUNCIL from 1889						
1889	1897	OWEN	John		1897	See above.
1897	1911	GEORGE	William Davies		1911	*Elected to Society, June* 1905. Solicitor (admitted 1877). Clerk of the Peace for Haverfordwest. Justice of the Peace.
1912	1939	WHEATLEY	Robert Albert	1873	1954	*Elected to Society, May* 1908. *Vice-Chairman,* 1935–39. Solicitor (admitted 1897). M.A. B.C.L. (Oxon). Secretary to the Advisory Committee; Clerk of the Peace for Haverfordwest and Justice of the Peace for that town from 1915. High Sheriff of Pembrokeshire, 1940. Previously Deputy Clerk of the Peace and of the County Council of Durham.
1940	1949	BUFTON	William Evan	1906		*Elected to Society, May* 1939. Solicitor (admitted 1932). LL.B. (Wales). Secretary to the Advisory Committee; Clerk of the Peace for Haverfordwest. Subsequently Clerk of the Peace and of the County Council of Denbighshire, *q.v.*
1950		UNDERWOOD	Henry Louis	1909		*Elected to Society, June* 1945. Son of Henry Laurence Underwood, Clerk of the Peace and of the County Council of Staffordshire, 1933–42; Solicitor (admitted 1934). M.A. (Cantab). Secretary to the Advisory Committee; Clerk of the Magistrates' Courts Committee; Clerk of the Peace for Haverfordwest until abolition of office in 1951. Previously Deputy Clerk of the Peace and of the County Council of Durham. Major, Intelligence Corps, 1939–45 War.
DEPUTY CLERKS OF THE PEACE prior to 1889						
c.1840	c.1858	LANNING	Robert			Solicitor.
c.1880		JAMES	William Vaughan			Solicitor.
DEPUTY CLERKS OF THE PEACE AND OF THE COUNTY COUNCIL from 1889						
1907	1913	GEORGE	Thomas Henry Marshall	1883		*Elected to Society, May* 1912. Son of William Davies George, Clerk of the Peace and of the County Council, 1897–1911. Solicitor (admitted 1907). Subsequently Deputy Clerk of the Peace and of the County Council of Wiltshire, *q.v.*
1948		ROBERTS	Evan Wynne	1912		*Elected to Society, January* 1950. Solicitor (admitted 1935). Merchant Navy, 1939–45 War.

RADNORSHIRE

From	To	Surname	Forenames	Birth	Death	Biographical Notes
		CLERKS OF THE PEACE from 1542				
1542	1545	THOMAS	William			Appointed Clerk of the Peace and of the Crown for Radnorshire, Breconshire and Montgomeryshire by letters patent, 21st January, 33 Henry VIII.
1545		CLERC	William			Appointed Clerk of the Peace and of the Crown for the same three Counties by letters under the Signet, 21st May, 37 Henry VIII, the offices being in the King's hand by reason of felonies committed by William Thomas, who had fled the realm; the appointment to take effect from the preceding Lady Day and to be confirmed by letters patent after Thomas had been convicted by due course of law. Clerc is called "our well beloved servant" and was possibly the clerk in the privy seal office who was the King's private secretary. If so, he probably held these offices only until Thomas obtained a pardon.
c.1573			John ap Owen			
1621		JONES	Griffith			
1844		BANKS	Richard			Solicitor.
c.1885	1889	STEPHENS	William			*Elected to Society, June 1885.* Of Presteign; Solicitor (admitted 1834). Clerk to the Lieutenancy; Coroner.
		CLERKS OF THE PEACE AND OF THE COUNTY COUNCIL from 1889				
1889	1890	STEPHENS	William			See above.
1890	1901	WOOD	Edward			*Elected to Society, June 1890.* Solicitor (admitted 1881).
1901	1931	VAUGHAN	Hugh Vaughan		1937	*Elected to Society, June 1901.* Solicitor (admitted 1875). Father of Hilda Vaughan the authoress, who married Charles Morgan, the novelist.
1931	1945	MOSELEY	Gilbert Watson	1879	1953	*Elected to Society, September 1931.* Solicitor (admitted 1902). Clerk to the Lieutenancy; Secretary to the Advisory Committee. Previously Deputy Clerk of the Peace and of the County Council.
1945	1958	PARKER	Philip	1893		*Elected to Society, October 1945.* Solicitor (admitted 1921). Deputy Lieutenant. Clerk to the Lieutenancy; Secretary to the Advisory Committee; Clerk of the Magistrates' Courts Committee. Lieutenant, 1st Battalion, Herefordshire Regiment, 1914–18 War.
1958		LANE	Douglas Charles Swancott	1919		*Elected to Society, July 1958.* Solicitor (admitted 1950). Clerk of the Magistrates' Courts Committee.
		DEPUTY CLERKS OF THE PEACE AND OF THE COUNTY COUNCIL from 1889				
1902	1931	MOSELEY	Gilbert Watson	1879	1953	Subsequently Clerk of the Peace and of the County Council, see above.
1952	1955	PEARMAIN	Edmund Alfred	1915		Solicitor (admitted 1937). Subsequently appointed to New Zealand Government Land Service. Royal Air Force, 1939–45 War; D.F.C.

RUTLAND

From	To	Surname	Forenames	Birth	Death	Biographical Notes
CLERKS	**OF THE PEACE**		**from 1390**			
1390	1392	GURNEYS	John			
1433	1435	KYRKEBY	John			
1514		WALDRAM	Thomas			
c.1575		CATESBY	Michael			Of Seaton.
1577	1589	FAWLKENER	Anthony			
1597		LACY	Henry			
1599		BARNBY	John			
1656		SCLATER	John			
	1742	LOVE				
1742	1756	LEPLA	James			
1757	1765	RIDLINGTON				
1766	1769	COOMBES	E.			Previously Deputy Clerk of the Peace.
1769	1786	BAYLEY	Isaac			
1786	1809	PARKE	Samuel			Failed in 1786 to deliver the estreats to the Exchequer on the second Monday after the morrow of All Souls, and again on three occasions later in the month when solemnly called to deliver the same, "in contempt of the Court and to the bad example of other Clerks of the Peace." Amerced and assessed by the Barons in the total sum of £17 10s. 0d. Previously Deputy Clerk of the Peace.
1809	1848	ADES	William			
1849	1888	ADAM	Benjamin			*Elected to Society, May 1859.* Solicitor (admitted 1834). Clerk to the Lieutenancy.
1888	1889	ADAM	Benjamin Addington			*Elected to Society, November 1888.* Son of Benjamin Adam; Solicitor (admitted 1872). Clerk to the Lieutenancy.

CLERKS OF THE PEACE AND OF THE COUNTY COUNCIL from 1889

From	To	Surname	Forenames	Birth	Death	Biographical Notes
1889	1931	ADAM	Benjamin Addington			See above. Also Secretary to the Advisory Committee.
1932	1951	DALTON	Robert Cecil	1891	1951	*Elected to Society, January 1932.* Solicitor (admitted 1914). Clerk to the Lieutenancy; Secretary to the Advisory Committee. Captain, Leicestershire Regiment, 1914–18 War; M.C.
1951		BOND	Alan	1902		*Elected to Society, May 1951.* Barrister-at-law, Middle Temple (called 1935). LL.B. (London). O.B.E., 1948. Clerk to the Lieutenancy; Secretary to the Advisory Committee; Coroner. Previously Chief Constable of Rutland.

DEPUTY CLERKS OF THE PEACE prior to 1889

From	To	Surname	Forenames	Birth	Death	Biographical Notes
	1766	COOMBES	E.			Subsequently Clerk of the Peace, see above.
	1786	PARKE	Samuel			Subsequently Clerk of the Peace, see above.
1788		COOMBES	John			
1796		BRIGGS	John			

SALOP

From	To	Surname	Forenames	Birth	Death	Biographical Notes
CLERKS OF THE PEACE from 1391						
1391	1412	OTELEY	Richard			
1416	1435	RODENHURST	John			
1446	1453	BYSSHOP	William			Of Charlton. In office before 1446, when he received grant for life by letters patent of office of Clerk of the Peace and Keeper of the Records, etc., touching the keeping of the Peace and the hearing and determining of divers felonies, etc., "taking the usual fees as he has hitherto had." (28th December, 25 Henry VI.)
1462	1466	SALTER	John			
1490		SALTER	John			
1496	1507	GRAVENOR	Rowland			
1511	1512	SKRYMSHER	Thomas			
1514	1518	HORDE (HORTE)	Alan			
1526	1531	DAYE	William			
1536	1545	HOLT	Nicholas			
1550	1551	SKRYMSHYRE	Thomas			
1553	1555	POWELL	William			
1562	c.1573	SALTER	Thomas			
1576	1587	MITTON	Adam			
1588	1589	HATTON	Francis			
1590	1593	SALTER	Thomas			
1593	1595	HATTON	Francis			
1596	1597	HOLLAND	George			
1598	1610	WILKES	William			
1610	1616	BOWDLER	Samuel			
1616	1617	POWELL	Hugh			
1618	1629	BOWDLER	Samuel			
1631	1659	HARRIES	Richard			Called Robert in the Pipe Roll entry for 1655–56; younger brother of Sir Thomas Harries of Tong, knight and baronet, serjeant-at-law.
1659	1672	CLARKE	Richard			

151

From	To	Surname	Forenames	Birth	Death	Biographical Notes
1676	1691	JENKINS	Richard		1697	Son of Thomas Jenkins of Pimperne, Dorset. Officially attached to the celebrated royalist Lord Colepepper at St. Germains, when Ambassador Extraordinary to Emperor of Russia and the United Provinces, 1649; he was "employed in business of trust and importance and demeaned himself faithfully diligently and discreetly" (see Blakeway, *Sheriffs of Shropshire*, p. 177). Muster Master General of County Militia by 1685.
1691	1696	ADAMS	William			
1696	1718	LACON	John		1718	Grandson of Sir Francis Lacon, Sheriff of Salop in 1612. First attended Sessions as Clerk of the Peace, Michaelmas 1696, but did not produce his appointment (dated 21st February 1697/8) until 1703. At Michaelmas Sessions 1712, articles exhibited against him alleging a breach of a condition of his appointment "that you shall well demean and behave yourselfe in the said office" (perhaps for using threatening language). The articles discharged, January 1712/3.
1718	1737	SKRYMSHER	John		1737	Of Shrewsbury; son of Richard Skrymsher of Forton, Staffordshire; admitted burgess of Shrewsbury free, 1687 (see *Shrewsbury Burgess Roll*, p. 267.)
1737	1779	BALDWYN	Richard	c.1708	1779	
1779	1802	WINGFIELD	Thomas	1721	1802	Mayor of Shrewsbury, 1767.
1802	1833	LOXDALE	Joseph, the elder	1759	1846	*Founder member of Society, March* 1810. Second surviving son of Thomas Loxdale, burgess of Shrewsbury, 1750 and Mayor, 1774, and grandson of Joseph Loxdale, Mayor of Stafford, 1745; Attorney. Steward of Shrewsbury Corporation and Deputy Recorder; Regimental Clerk to the Shropshire Militia, 1789 (see N.L.W. Castle Hill MSS, 765); Mayor of Shrewsbury, 1797; Borough magistrate, 1828. Previously Deputy Clerk of the Peace. Father of twelve children, of whom Joseph was Mayor of Shrewsbury, 1830, James was Town Clerk and Common Clerk, 1833, and John succeeded him as Clerk of the Peace.
1833	1872	LOXDALE	John	1799	1885	*Elected to Society, May* 1830. Fourth son of Joseph Loxdale; Solicitor (admitted 1821). Clerk to the Lieutenancy; Commissioner of property and income tax; Trustee of Shrewsbury School; Justice of the Peace, 1872. When County Finance Committee appointed in 1839, claimed the right as Clerk of the Peace to be employed as its Secretary. The Solicitor-General, Sir William Follett, decided that "there was no such right, though it was customary to appoint the Clerk of the Peace to be Secretary to any Committee of Magistrates". Loxdale was appointed, but not as of right. Previously Deputy Clerk of the Peace.
1872	1886	PEELE	George de Courcy	1836	c.1886	Solicitor (admitted 1859). Clerk to the Lieutenancy; Clerk to Committee of Visitors of County Asylum; Bailiff of Shrewsbury School.
1886	1889	PEELE	Edmund Cresswell	1844	1911	*Elected to Society, June* 1886. Brother of George de Courcy Peele; Solicitor (admitted 1868). Justice of the Peace; Deputy Lieutenant. Clerk to the Lieutenancy; Under Sheriff; Clerk to the Burial Board; Clerk to the Justices, Upper Munslow division; Registrar and Deputy Judge, Shrewsbury Borough Court of Record; Burgess of Shrewsbury, 1866; Town Clerk, 1869–90. Previously County Treasurer. Colonel, 1st Shropshire and Staffordshire Artillery Volunteers; V.D.

SALOP (*Continued*)

From	To	Surname	Forenames	Birth	Death	Biographical Notes

CLERKS OF THE PEACE AND OF THE COUNTY COUNCIL from 1889

From	To	Surname	Forenames	Birth	Death	Biographical Notes
1889	1911	PEELE	Edmund Cresswell	1844	1911	See above. Also Secretary to the Advisory Committee; Mayor of Shrewsbury, 1891–92 and 1896–97.
1911	1926	CROWTE	Frederick	1874	1926	*Elected to Society, November* 1911. Solicitor (admitted 1908). Clerk to the Lieutenancy; Secretary to the Advisory Committee. Previously Deputy Clerk of the Peace and of the County Council.
1926	1933	JOHNSON	Arthur Ainslie	1889	1933	*Elected to Society, December* 1923. Solicitor (admitted 1912). Clerk to the Lieutenancy; Secretary to the Advisory Committee; Clerk to the Committee of Visitors of the County Mental Hospital. Previously Deputy Clerk of the Peace and of the County Council of Berkshire. Major, Northumberland Fusiliers, 1914–18 War; O.B.E. (Mil.) 1919; Despatches (3 times).
1933	1943	EDGE	William Leonard	1885	1943	*Elected to Society, October* 1932. Barrister-at-law, Gray's Inn (called 1932). Clerk to the Lieutenancy; Secretary to the Advisory Committee; Clerk to the Committee of Visitors of the County Mental Hospital.
1944		GODBER	Geoffrey Chapman	1912		*Elected to Society, March* 1941. *Honorary Secretary, 1953– ; Vice-Chairman, 1960– .* Solicitor (Clifford's Inn prize) (admitted 1936). LL.B. (London). Clerk to the Lieutenancy; Secretary to the Advisory Committee; Clerk of the Magistrates' Courts Committee, and to the Walker Trust. Clerk to the Committee of Visitors of the County Mental Hospital until 1948; Member of the Committee thereafter. Assistant Commissioner, Local Government Boundary Commission, 1949; Member of Probation Advisory Board, 1949–55; of Child Care Advisory Council, 1953–56; of Committee of Enquiry into Inland Waterways, 1956; of Inland Waterways Redevelopment Advisory Committee, 1959, and of Waterways Sub-Commission, British Transport Commission, 1959. Previously Deputy Clerk of the Peace and of the County Council of Northamptonshire.

DEPUTY CLERKS OF THE PEACE prior to 1889

From	To	Surname	Forenames	Birth	Death	Biographical Notes
1657		CLARKE	Richard			
1723	1737	BASKERVYLE	Robert			
1747		LOXDALE	Thomas			
1784	1792	LOXDALE	Joseph, the elder	1759	1846	Son of Thomas Loxdale. Subsequently Clerk of the Peace, see above.
1792		WINGFIELD	George			
1820		LOXDALE	Joseph, the younger			*Elected to Society, November* 1820. Son of Joseph Loxdale the elder, Clerk of the Peace, 1802–33.
1830	1833	LOXDALE	John	1799	1885	Subsequently Clerk of the Peace, see above.
1843		PEELE	Joshua John			*Elected to Society, January* 1849.

DEPUTY CLERKS OF THE PEACE AND OF THE COUNTY COUNCIL from 1889

From	To	Surname	Forenames	Birth	Death	Biographical Notes
1904	1911	CROWTE	Frederick	1874	1926	Subsequently Clerk of the Peace and of the County Council, see above.
1933	1938	WHITE	Percival Edward	1902		*Elected to Society, April* 1934. *Deputy Clerk of the County Council only.* Solicitor (admitted 1926). LL.B. (London). Subsequently Clerk of the Peace and of the County Council of Montgomeryshire, *q.v.*
1943		WHITLEY	John Manners	1904		*Elected to Society, April* 1943. Solicitor (admitted 1933). M.A. (Cantab).

SOKE OF PETERBOROUGH

From	To	Surname	Forenames	Birth	Death	Biographical Notes
		CLERKS OF THE PEACE from 1700				
1700	1704/5	WHINYATES	Charles	1658/9	1704/5	Of Chellaston, Derbyshire; married Elizabeth, daughter of Humphrey Orme and widow of William Parker. Feoffee of Peterborough City lands, 1683; Churchwarden, St. John's, Peterborough, 1684/5. Buried in Peterborough Cathedral (monument).
1705	1717	WYCHE	Richard		c.1730	Of Stamford; married Mrs. Elizabeth Parker of Peterborough, 1701. Town Clerk of Stamford.
c.1736	1767	TRYCE	Richard	1694/5	1767	Steward of the Courts and Receiver of Revenues of Bishop of Peterborough; Steward, Receiver General and Registrar of the Dean and Chapter of Peterborough; Steward, Judge and Clerk of the Court of Piepowder, 1730. First Lieutenant of the Peterborough Volunteer Corps raised by Earl Fitzwilliam, 1745. Buried in Peterborough Cathedral (inscription).
1767	1788	STRONG	Isaac	1720	1790	Third son of Isaac Strong of Chatteris, Cambridgeshire; married Elizabeth, daughter of Daniel Delarue, 1752. Father of William Strong, Archdeacon of Northampton, b. 1756, d. 1842. Previously Deputy Clerk of the Peace. Ensign, Peterborough Volunteer Corps, 1745.
1788	1800	SMITH	William			
1800	1801	BOWKER	William		1801	
1801		EDMUNDS	George			
	1820	ATKINSON	John			
1820	1840	ATKINSON	Thomas			
1840	1875	LAWRENCE	William			
1876	1889	DEACON	Leonard John	1828	1903	*Elected to Society, June 1873.* Attorney (admitted 1853). Bailiff of the Liberty. Previously Deputy Clerk of the Peace. Officer Commanding, 1st Northamptonshire Royal Engineers (Volunteers), 1869–91.
		CLERKS OF THE PEACE AND OF THE COUNTY COUNCIL from 1889				
1889	1903	DEACON	Leonard John	1828	1903	See above.
1903	1918	DEACON	Walter John, the elder	1861	1918	*Elected to Society, May 1904.* Son of Leonard John Deacon; Solicitor (admitted 1884). Secretary to the Advisory Committee; Bailiff of the Liberty. Previously Deputy Clerk of the Peace and of the County Council. Officer Commanding, 1st Northamptonshire Royal Engineers (Volunteers), 1891–1907.
1918	1945	DEACON	Walter John, the younger	1885	1945	*Elected to Society, June 1923.* Son of Walter John Deacon, the elder; Solicitor (admitted 1910). Secretary to the Advisory Committee; Bailiff of the Liberty; Steward of the Manors of Farcet and Gidding. Lieutenant, King's African Rifles, 1914–18 War.
1946		SMITH	Eric Pope	1908		*Elected to Society, July 1946.* Solicitor (honours) (admitted 1931). Secretary to the Advisory Committee; Bailiff of the Liberty. Previously assistant solicitor, Nottinghamshire County Council.
		DEPUTY CLERKS OF THE PEACE prior to 1889				
1736		STRONG	William			
1756		STRONG	Isaac	1720	1790	Subsequently Clerk of the Peace, see above.
	1866	BELL	William Lawrence			Solicitor (admitted 1862).
1867	1876	DEACON	Leonard John	1828	1903	Subsequently Clerk of the Peace, see above.
1888	1889	DEACON	Walter John, the elder	1861	1918	Subsequently Clerk of the Peace and of the County Council, see above.
		DEPUTY CLERKS OF THE PEACE AND OF THE COUNTY COUNCIL from 1889				
1889	1903	DEACON	Walter John, the elder	1861	1918	See above.
1918	1947	GILLINGS	Charles Edwin	1884	1951	Rose from junior clerk in the office.
1947		THOMAS	John Henwood	1912		*Elected to Society, June 1947.* Solicitor (admitted 1936). Previously assistant solicitor, Norfolk County Council. Private, Royal Sussex Regiment, later Lieutenant, D.C.L.I., attached King's African Rifles, 1939–45 War.

SOMERSET

From	To	Surname	Forenames	Birth	Death	Biographical Notes
		CLERKS OF THE PEACE from 1389				
1389	1398	BEYVYN	John			Steward of Dunster; Member of Parliament, 1373.
1405	1428	VEELL	Robert			One Robert Veel was escheator of Somerset and Dorset, 1412, and founder of Ilchester almshouse, 1426.
1431	1437	CULLIFORD	Edward			Probably of Bridgwater; Member of Parliament for Bridgwater, 1430.
1437	1447	BOCHELL	William			
1463	1466	LEGH	John			
1486	1524/5	CLAVELSHEY	Cuthbert		1524/5	The inquisition taken after his death is among Chancery Inquisitions *post mortem* for 16 Henry VIII.
1527	1533	CUFFE	John			
1533	1559	DYER	John		1559	Appointed Clerk of the Peace and of the Crown by letters patent, 8th June, 25 Henry VIII; of Wincanton; elder brother of Sir James Dyer, Judge, Member of Parliament and Speaker, b. 1512, d. 1582.
1559/60	1594	MARTIN	Adam		1596	Of Hinton St. George; see pedigree in *Wiltshire Visitation Pedigrees*, 1623 (Harleian Society, 105/6, 1954).
1595	1607	POPHAM	Thomas			
1607	1609	WHITE	Edward		1609	Of Bridgwater.
1609	c.1611	WYKES	Nicholas		1611	Of Wells.
1609	1610	GIBBENS	John		1610	Jointly with Nicholas Wykes. Of Taunton Castle; Keeper of the Gate of Taunton Castle under the Bishop of Winchester.
1611	1627	WYKES	Edward		1644	Son of Nicholas Wykes; Barrister-at-law, Middle Temple (called 1625). Recorder of Wells. Will proved, 1647.
1613	c.1641	BROWNE	Christopher			Jointly with Edward Wykes, 1613–27. Originally of West Coker, subsequently of Chilthorne Domer. Will proved, 1646.
1638	c.1639	HOPKINS	Matthew			Jointly with Christopher Browne.
1647	1649/50	PESTOR	William			
1647	1657	HAGGATT	John			Jointly with William Pestor, 1647–50.
1668		GAPE	Thomas			
1673	c.1677	BENNETT	John			
1677	1690	BENNETT	Philip, the elder	1610	1690	Of South Brewham. Previously Deputy Clerk of the Peace.
1677	1690	BENNETT	Philip, the younger	1637	1725	Son of Philip Bennett the elder; of Wincanton; probably acted jointly with his father. Previously, and subsequently, Deputy Clerk of the Peace.
1689		MALET	John			For one session only.

SOMERSET (*Continued*)

From	To	Surname	Forenames	Birth	Death	Biographical Notes
1690	1706	CHEEKE	Edward		1706	
1706	1724	BENNETT	Philip, the younger	1637	1725	Re-appointed: see above.
1724	1740	RING	William, the elder			Subsequently Deputy Clerk of the Peace.
1740	1745	RING	William, the younger		1745	Son of William Ring, the elder; of Walcot.
1745	1768	DONNE	John		1768	Of Crewkerne; previously Steward for the Manors of Earl Poulett.
1768	1770	KIRKPATRICK	James		1770	Of St. Mary Magdalen, Taunton.
1770	1782	EWEN	Michael		1782	Nephew and executor of Sir Michael Foster, Clerk of the Peace for Wiltshire, 1729–36; of Marlborough, Wiltshire; Attorney. Chief Steward to Seymour family (Earls of Hertford, later Dukes of Somerset). Also Clerk of the Peace for Wiltshire, 1743–82.
1782	1784	BRYANT	Robert		1784	Of Ilminster; succeeded John Donne, Clerk of the Peace, 1745–68, as Steward for Manors of Earl Poulett.
1784	1803	STAPLE	John		1803	Of Chard.
1803	1804	COLES	James		1804	Of Taunton.
1804		BRYANT	Robert Jeane	1759	1804	Of Ilminster; eldest son of Robert Bryant, Clerk of the Peace, 1782–84. Steward for Manors of Earl Poulett.
1804	1816	COLES	James			Of Taunton; resigned apparently to take Holy Orders.
1816	1846	COLES	Edward		1846	*Elected to Society, November* 1814. Of Taunton. Previously Deputy Clerk of the Peace.
1846	1877	LOVELL	Edwin		1877	*Elected to Society, November* 1846. Of Dinder; son of Joseph Lovell (né Teek); Eton College; Attorney. Deputy Steward to his elder brother Edward, Deputy Clerk of the Peace, 1847–57, *q.v.*
1877	1889	DUNN	William		1903	*Elected to Society, June* 1878. Of Frome. Solicitor (admitted 1854).

CLERKS OF THE PEACE AND OF THE COUNTY COUNCIL from 1889

From	To	Surname	Forenames	Birth	Death	Biographical Notes
1889	1903	DUNN	William		1903	See above.
1903	1905	BENNETT	Harry Macaulay	1863		*Elected to Society, May* 1904. Of Frome; son of Henry Edward Bennett of Sparkford; Solicitor (admitted 1888). B.A. Clerk to the Lieutenancy.
1905	1927	SIMEY	George Iliffe		1927	*Elected to Society, June* 1893. Solicitor (admitted 1892). Clerk to the Lieutenancy; Secretary to the Advisory Committee. Previously Deputy Clerk of the Peace and of the County Council of Durham.
1927	1952	KING	Harold	1887	1960	*Elected to Society, October* 1921. Solicitor (admitted 1912). Clerk to the Lieutenancy; Secretary to the Advisory Committee; Clerk of the Magistrates' Courts Committee. Previously assistant solicitor, Yorkshire (North Riding) County Council, and Deputy Clerk of the Peace and of the County Council of Durham. Captain, Royal Artillery, 1914–18 War.
1952		RICKARDS	Ernest Stanley	1907		*Elected to Society, September* 1944. Solicitor (admitted 1930). M.A. (Cantab). Clerk to the Lieutenancy; Secretary to the Advisory Committee; Clerk of the Magistrates' Courts Committee. Previously assistant solicitor, Surrey, Yorkshire (North Riding) and Somerset County Councils, and Deputy Clerk of the Peace and of the County Council of Somerset.

SOMERSET (*Continued*)

From	To	Surname	Forenames	Birth	Death	Biographical Notes
		DEPUTY CLERKS OF THE PEACE prior to 1889				
1607		BOND	T.			
1607		SAWARD	John			
c.1623	1627	ARUNDEL	Thomas			
1632	c.1635	CHUTE	Robert			Steward for Dean and Chapter of Wells of lands in Somerset.
1655	1667	YEAMANS	Thomas			
1668	1672	GRESLEY	Ferrars			
1673	1676	BENNETT	Philip, the elder	1610	1690	Subsequently Clerk of the Peace, see above.
1673	1677	BENNETT	Philip, the younger	1637	1725	Subsequently Clerk of the Peace, see above.
1690	1706	BENNETT	Philip, the younger	1637	1725	See above.
1719	1726	DAY	Bartholomew			
1734		RING	Richard			
1741		RING	William, the elder			Appointed Deputy Clerk of the Peace by his son who succeeded him as Clerk.
1765		GODDARD	William			
1770	1782	WARRY	George			Officiated during Clerkship of Michael Ewen, who appears to have acted only nominally for Somerset; of Chard; died before October 1784.
1794	1810	EDWARDS	Charles		1813	Of Chard; Attorney.
1810	1816	COLES	Edward		1846	Subsequently Clerk of the Peace, see above.
1847	1857	LOVELL	Edward	1804/5	1857	Elder brother of Edwin Lovell, Clerk of the Peace, 1846–77; Attorney. Steward for Bishop of Bath and Wells and Steward of Wells Court of Record from 1837.
1864		FOSTER	William John Slade			Of Wells; Attorney (admitted 1838).
		DEPUTY CLERKS OF THE PEACE AND OF THE COUNTY COUNCIL from 1889				
1915	1943	OLDFIELD	Norman	1877	1943	Solicitor (admitted 1899). M.B.E., 1918.
1915	1924	MEEK	Thomas William			Jointly with Norman Oldfield.
1944	1952	RICKARDS	Ernest Stanley	1907		Subsequently Clerk of the Peace and of the County Council, see above.
1952		JONES	Ronald Laughton	1904		*Elected to Society, November 1952.* *Deputy Clerk of the Peace only.* Solicitor (admitted 1928).
1952		WALLEN	Leonard Paul	1916		*Elected to Society, November 1952.* *Deputy Clerk of the County Council only.* Solicitor (honours) (admitted 1939). LL.B. (London). Previously assistant solicitor, Bristol City and Warwickshire County Councils. Lieutenant Colonel, Royal Artillery, 1939–45 War; M.C., T.D.

STAFFORDSHIRE

From	To	Surname	Forenames	Birth	Death	Biographical Notes
CLERKS OF THE PEACE from 1400						
1400	1433	WELENHALE	Roger			
1434	1435	ASSHEBY	John			
1436	1440	BEDULFF	John			
1440	1458	CLERK	Roger			
	1458	HEGON	John			
1458		YORK	William, the younger			Serjeant of the King's cellar; appointed Clerk of the Peace for life by letters patent, 13th January, 36 Henry VI.
1458		BARBOUR	Henry			Underclerk of the King's kitchen, appointed on the surrender by William York of his patent, 27th March, 36 Henry VI.
1464	1469	STRETHAY	John			
1471	1473	BRENNER (BREMER)	Thomas			
1475	1478	STRETHAY	John			
1492	1504	WELLYS	Thomas			
1504	1516	HASSALL	Richard			
1517	1518	HORDE (WHORDE)	Robert			Also occurs as William.
1519	1537	WITHALL (WHITHALGH)	William			
1537	1546	BOTHE	William			Appointed Clerk of the Peace and of the Crown at all Sessions of the Peace by letters patent, 10th April, 28 Henry VIII.
1548	1551	WOLRYCHE	James			
1552		CHATTERTON	John			
1553		THYCKENES	Robert			
1554	1563	CHATTERTON	John			
1564	1565	FLETCHER	Thomas			
1566	1576	BARROLL	William			Appears as "friend" in Will of Walter, first Earl of Essex.
1576		PENNAUNT	Edward			Occurs in this year with William Barroll as Deputy Clerk.
1577		ARCHEBOLD	John			
1579	1585	BARROLL	William			
1586	1587	BLACKWELL	Nicholas			
1587	1588	BAGOTT	Anthony	1558	1622	Educated Trinity College, Cambridge with Robert Devereux, second Earl of Essex; served with him and took part in his rebellion, 1601; pardoned 1602; married Katherine Lowe of Tamhorn; his letters are a main source of information on Essex's early life.
1588	1589	TREU	William			Married Margaret, sister of Anthony Bagott his predecessor, clandestinely; in frequent attendance on Robert, second Earl of Essex; referred to as "Keeper of Chartley House".
1589	1602/3	LYNACRE	John			Married Mary, daughter of Thomas Skrymsher of Johnson Hall.
1603	1617	IRONMONGER	William		1626	Of Chatcull.
1617	1626	WOLSELEY	Robert	1557	1646	Also occurs as John; Clerk of the King's letters patent; created Baronet, 1628.

158

STAFFORDSHIRE (*Continued*)

From	To	Surname	Forenames	Birth	Death	Biographical Notes
1626	c.1643	CROMPTON	William			
1645	1655	BENDY	William		c.1655	Of Kingswinford and Lincoln's Inn; Member of Staffordshire Parliamentary Committee and of Committee for Sequestrations.
c.1655	1660	BAGNALL	Thomas			
1660	1680	ALPORT	William	c.1628	1682	Of Cannock; Barrister-at-law, Gray's Inn; described as "decrepit of his hands".
1680	c.1687	WALKER	Timothy			
c.1687	1694	FORSTER	John			
1694	1703	NOBLE	Michael	c.1650	c.1708	Barrister-at-law, Middle Temple.
1703	1718	DOLPHIN	John		1724	Of Shenstone; Attorney in Stafford. Steward to Duchess of Hamilton and Earl of Uxbridge; Mayor of Stafford, 1714; Member of Parliament (Tory) for Stafford Borough, 1722. Previously Deputy Clerk of the Peace.
1718	1743	DOLPHIN	Henry		c.1744	Son of John Dolphin; Attorney in Stafford. Bought Footherley Hall.
1743	1746	LEVETT	Theophilus	1693	1746	Town Clerk and Coroner of Lichfield, 1721. Also County Treasurer. Friend of Samuel Johnson; uncle of Matthew Boulton, the engineer.
1746	1748	BARBOR	Robert			Of Somerford.
1748	1751	BOURNE	John			Of Newcastle-under-Lyme; Attorney. Town Clerk of Newcastle-under-Lyme, 1713–48; twice Mayor.
1751	1786	FERNIHOUGH	Thomas	c.1726	1799	Of Newcastle-under-Lyme; married Honor Sneyd of Keele. Town Clerk of Newcastle, 1748–85. Also County Treasurer. Previously Deputy Clerk of the Peace.
1786	1792	FENTON	Thomas	1737	1792	
1792	1804	HINCKLEY	Thomas	1745	1817	Of Lichfield; Attorney. His family was known to Samuel Johnson and connected by marriage to the Seward family.
1804	1862	HINCKLEY	Arthur	1781	1862	Eldest son of Thomas Hinckley; of Lichfield; Attorney. Acted by Deputy.
1862	1873	HAND	Robert William			*Elected to Society, May 1852.* Of Stafford; Solicitor (admitted 1836). Previously Deputy Clerk of the Peace.
1873	1889	BLAKISTON	Matthew Folliott		1906	*Elected to Society, May 1875.* Solicitor (senior prizeman) (admitted 1858). Clerk to the Lieutenancy; Under Sheriff; Town Clerk of Hanley, 1869–73; Town Clerk of Stafford from 1875. Secretary to the Potteries Chamber of Commerce and the Potteries Manufacturers' Association; Honorary Solicitor, North Staffordshire Provident Association; Honorary Secretary, Staffordshire Rifle Association. Captain, Staffordshire Artillery Volunteers. Previously Deputy Clerk of the Peace.

CLERKS OF THE PEACE AND OF THE COUNTY COUNCIL from 1889

From	To	Surname	Forenames	Birth	Death	Biographical Notes
1889	1906	BLAKISTON	Matthew Folliott		1906	See above.
1907	1933	JOY	Richard Eustace	1866	1940	*Elected to Society, April 1907.* Uppingham School and Worcester College, Oxford; M.A. Solicitor (admitted 1893). Clerk to the Lieutenancy.
1933	1942	UNDERWOOD	Henry Laurence	1876	1942	*Elected to Society, June 1916.* Solicitor (admitted 1901). M.A., LL.B. (Cantab). Clerk to the Lieutenancy. Previously Deputy Clerk of the Peace and of the County Council.

From	To	Surname	Forenames	Birth	Death	Biographical Notes
1942		EVANS	Thomas Henry	1907		*Elected to Society, November 1938.* Solicitor (admitted 1930). LL.M. (Liverpool). Deputy Lieutenant, 1947; C.B.E., 1957. Clerk to the Lieutenancy; Clerk of the Magistrates' Courts Committee; Member of Committee on Consolidation of Highway Law, 1958, and of Interdepartmental Committee on Business of Criminal Courts, 1958. Previously Deputy Clerk of the Peace and of the County Council.

DEPUTY CLERKS OF THE PEACE prior to 1889

From	To	Surname	Forenames	Birth	Death	Biographical Notes
1576		BARROLL	William			See note to Edward Pennaunt, Clerk of the Peace in 1576, above.
1589		BAGOTT	Anthony	1558	1622	Also occurs as Clerk of the Peace, 1587–88.
c.1596	c.1601	MARTEN	John		1635	Attorney.
1617	c.1622	DRAKEFORD	Richard	c.1576	1639	Of Forebridge, Stafford; Head Bailiff and twice Mayor of Stafford, occasionally designated Clerk of the Peace.
1623	1626	ASTON	Edward			Of Bishton; officer in King's jewel house; possibly the second son of Sir Edward Aston of Tixall, knight, and brother of Sir Walter Aston, later created Baron Aston for his part in negotiations for marriage of Charles, Prince of Wales to the Infanta Maria.
1626	1657	THORLEY	George			Solicitor for Sequestrations, c. 1644; appears to have acted as Clerk of the Peace, 1642–47 and 1654.
1664	1686	BABBINGTON	Zacchary	c.1611	1687	Of Whittington; grandson of Zacchary Babbington, Chancellor of Lichfield; brother of Matthew Babbington, Chaplain to King Charles I; admitted Inner Temple, 1646.
1668		BYRD	Edward			
1695	1702	DOLPHIN	John		1724	Subsequently Clerk of the Peace, see above.
1746		NOEL	Walter			
1748		FERNIHOUGH	Thomas	c.1726	1799	Subsequently Clerk of the Peace, see above.
1757	1758	BROOKES	William			
c.1783	c.1790	DICKENSON	John		1819	Coroner. Also County Treasurer from 1786.
1792	1795	COLLINS	John			
1795	1828	KEEN	William		1828	Of Stafford; Attorney.
1828	1851	KEEN	George			Of Stafford; Attorney. Under Sheriff; Secretary to Bishop of Lichfield.
1851	1862	HAND	Robert William			Subsequently Clerk of the Peace, see above.
1862	1873	BLAKISTON	Matthew Folliott		1906	Subsequently Clerk of the Peace, see above.

DEPUTY CLERKS OF THE PEACE AND OF THE COUNTY COUNCIL from 1889

From	To	Surname	Forenames	Birth	Death	Biographical Notes
1907	1908	PARR	Thomas Henning			Barrister-at-law, Inner Temple (called 1892). Subsequently King's Counsel and Recorder of Salisbury.
1915	1933	UNDERWOOD	Henry Laurence	1876	1942	Subsequently Clerk of the Peace and of the County Council, see above.
1933		PHILLIPS	George Godfrey	1900		Barrister-at-law, Gray's Inn (called 1925). Subsequently entered Colonial Service; C.B.E., 1943.
1934	1938	HAYWARD	Tom Christopher	1904		*Elected to Society, January 1934.* Solicitor (admitted 1929). B.A. (Cantab). Subsequently Clerk of the Peace and of the County Council of West Sussex, *q.v.*
1938	1942	EVANS	Thomas Henry	1907		Subsequently Clerk of the Peace and of the County Council, see above.
1942		TILDESLEY	Arthur	1895		*Elected to Society, July 1942.* Barrister-at-law, Gray's Inn (called 1940). North Staffordshire Regiment, 1914–18 War.

SUFFOLK

From	To	Surname	Forenames	Birth	Death	Biographical Notes
		CLERKS OF THE PEACE from 1392				
1392	1402	DOWE (DOWVE)	Thomas			
1404	1407	FYNCHYNG-FELD	John			Appointed Clerk and King's Attorney before Justices of the Peace in Suffolk, Essex and Hertfordshire by letters patent, 11th March, 5 Henry IV; Feodary of the Duchy of Lancaster for Essex, Hertfordshire and Kent, 1399–1401 (see Somerville, *Duchy of Lancaster*, I, p. 609).
1408	1447	WODE	Robert			Bailiff of Ipswich, 1434, 1437, 1443, 1446; Claviger, 1439, 1442 (see Bacon, *Annals of Ipswich*, pp. 97–138); Coroner, 1430 (see Copinger, *Suffolk Records*, III, p. 264); Bailiff of the Liberty of St. Etheldreda; owned property at Shirous Hill and Shirhouspitts.
1448	1453	BERNARD	John			Possibly Under Sheriff of Norfolk, 1460.
c.1456	1474	DENE	Robert			See *Paston Letters*, ed. Gardiner, I, p. 370.
1477	1486	CHEKE	John		1493	Writ issued to him and others to deliver Ipswich gaol of prisoners, 1487; probably grantee of 20/- yearly "for his Council and to be of Council with this town (Ipswich) during life", 1488 (see Bacon, *op. cit.*, p. 158); possibly identical with John Cheke "at Debenham" (see Copinger, *op. cit.*, II, p. 216). Will proved, 1492/3 (see Norwich Consistory Court, 70–71 Typpes).
1486	1487	DADE	John		?1506	Clerk of the Peace for Norfolk, 1494–1505; possibly John Dade of Witton by Norwich whose Will proved, 1506 (see Norwich Consistory Court, 314–8 Ryxe).
1489	1505	HEIGHAM	John		?1522	Possibly second son of Thomas Heigham of Hunston (see Hervey, *Visitation of Suffolk*).
1506		EVERARD	Henry			Appointed Clerk of the Peace and of the Crown for Suffolk and Norfolk by letters patent, 16th March, 21 Henry VII.
1506	c.1522	HEIGHAM	John		?1522	Appointed Clerk of the Peace and of the Crown for Suffolk and Norfolk by letters patent, jointly in survivorship with Leonard Spencer, 1st September, 22 Henry VII; Heigham appears to have acted in Suffolk. Probably identical with John Heigham, Clerk of the Peace, 1489–1505.
1506	1533	SPENCER	Leonard		?1539	See note to John Heigham, above; Spencer appears to have acted in Norfolk, *q.v.*
1518	1537	BAGARD	John			Probably deputy to Heigham, Spencer and Bolayne.
1533	1537	BOLAYNE	Sir James		1561	Appointed Clerk of the Peace and of the Crown for Suffolk and Norfolk by letters patent jointly with James Hawe, on surrender of Leonard Spencer's patent, John Heigham being dead (13th March, 24 Henry VIII); Bolayne appears to have acted in Suffolk. Of Blickling and Salle, Norfolk; married Elizabeth Wood of East Marsham; no issue; buried at Blickling; Will proved, 1561 (see P.C.C. Wills 35 Loftes).
1533	1537	HAWE	James			See note to Sir James Bolayne, above; Hawe appears to have acted in Norfolk, *q.v.*
1537	1557	ACRES	John			Appointed Clerk of the Peace and of the Crown for Suffolk by letters patent.
1559	1581	FREMAN	John			
1582	1584	ALMAN	John		1585	Of Bury St. Edmunds; Will proved, 1585 (see P.C.C. Wills 15 Brudenell).
1585	1587	ASHFELD	Edmund		?1603	Possibly third son of John Ashfeld of Stowlangtoft, who was pensioner, Corpus Christi College, Cambridge, 1554; admitted Gray's Inn, 1561; (?) knighted, 1570 (see Venn, *Alumni Cantabrigienses*, and Foster, *Gray's Inn*). Will of one Edmund Ashfield proved, 1603 (see P.C.C. Wills 29 Bolein).
1588	1598	FOREST	John			
1599		FRENCHE	George			

L

From	To	Surname	Forenames	Birth	Death	Biographical Notes
1600	1622	MILLICENT (MILLESON)	Edmund		1623	Will proved, 1623 (see P.C.C. Wills 129 Swann). Testator requested *Custos Rotulorum* to grant office of Clerk of the Peace to his brother-in-law, Robert Dickenson and another in trust to pay testator's debts and provide his children's portions; trustees to surrender patent on testator's son Borrowdale reaching age of 21, to whom the office to be granted. Meanwhile a clerk to be appointed from among named persons as successor to a Mr. Grimwade whom Milleson had employed for over 50 years. In return, testator promised *Custos Rotulorum* a piece of plate worth £20 out of profits of the office each year, and to his Receiver, Solicitor and other servants a gold ring worth £1 out of the first year's profits.
1623	1636	SLEGGE	Roger			
1638	1639	ANDREWS	George			
1642	1651	COLLINS (COLLYNE)	Richard			
1652	1657	HAWARD (HAYWARD)	Philip		?1665	Possibly son of Philip Hayward of Carlton; pensioner, Caius College, Cambridge, 1637/8, Scholar, 1639–42; B.A.; of Carlton Colville (see Venn, *Alumni Cantabrigienses*); Will proved, 1665 (Archdeaconry of Suffolk, no. 47).
1660	1681	CLARKE	Robert		1697	Attorney of Ipswich at Crown Pleas, 1647. Town Clerk, 1660; numerous references in Ipswich Corporation records, *e.g.*, subscribed to Solemn League and Covenant, 1664/5; to present petition with others, for new town charter, 1684. Will proved, 1697 (Archdeaconry of Suffolk, no. 84).
1681	1691	COVELL	Thomas	1634	1715	Second son of William and Alice Covell of Horringer; brother of John Covell, Master of Christ's College, Cambridge. Drew up survey of Ickworth, 1665, published by Lord John Harvey. Possibly Alderman, Bury St. Edmunds, 1687/8, and removed by the King's order, 1688. Will proved, 1715 (Archdeaconry of Sudbury, Goodwin VI, 3 and 60).
1691	1700	PIGEON	Charles	1637	1700	Probably son of Henry Pigeon; Bury Grammar School and Christ's College, Cambridge (Sizar, 1653/4); admitted, Gray's Inn, 1656. Buried at Boxted (monumental inscription).
1700	c.1726	BRITIFFE	Robert	?1663	1749	Probably son of Edmund Britiffe of Baconsthorpe, Norfolk; pensioner, Caius College, Cambridge, 1679/80; admitted Middle Temple, 1682. Member of Parliament for Norwich, 1715–34; Recorder, 1737–43. Will proved, 1749/50 (see P.C.C. Wills 363 Lisle).
1726	1748	COCKSEDGE	Henry		1762	Recorder of Thetford. Will proved, 1762 (see P.C.C. Wills 96 St. Eloy); bequeathed his law and statute books to his successor and grandson Henry Collett.
1748	1802	COLLETT	Henry		1803	Of Woodbridge and Westerfield; grandson of Henry Cocksedge; son of William Collett of Woodbridge; Bury Grammar School. Previously Deputy Clerk of the Peace.
1802	1807	JENKIN	Abraham	c.1747	1807	Of Long Sutton, Lincolnshire, later of Brandon and Bury St. Edmunds; married Mary, daughter of Sir John Cullum of Hawsted Place; Solicitor. Town Clerk of Bury St. Edmunds, 1787–1802; Burgess of the Common Council, 1796; Chief Burgess, 1805; Alderman, 1806–07. Buried at Hawsted; Will proved, 1807 (see P.C.C. Wills 506 Lushington).
1807	1842	BORTON	James	1771	1847	*Elected to Society, November* 1813. Younger son of John Borton of Diss; Solicitor. Under Sheriff; fined £5 at Woodbridge Sessions, 1805, for neglecting to attend his duty in that office; Proctor of the Archdeaconry of Sudbury. Burgess of the Common Council of Bury St. Edmunds, 1805; Chief Burgess, 1817; Alderman, 1818–19 and 1824–25; Coroner of the Liberty of St. Edmund. Secretary of the Suffolk Hospital Association.
1842	1872	BORTON	John Henry	1800	1872	*Elected to Society, November* 1829. Eldest son of James Borton; Bury Grammar School; Solicitor (admitted 1821). Burgess of the Common Council, Bury St. Edmunds, 1824. Previously Deputy Clerk of the Peace.
1872	1889	CHERRY	James	1817	1900	Barrister-at-law, Middle Temple (called 1855). Poor Law Auditor.

SUFFOLK (*Continued*)

| --- | --- | --- | --- | --- | --- | --- |

DEPUTY CLERKS OF THE PEACE prior to 1889

From	To	Surname	Forenames	Birth	Death	Biographical Notes
1684		WARD	Anthony			
1690		COVELL	John		1694	Eldest surviving son of William Covel(l) of Horningsheath; nephew of Thomas Covell, Clerk of the Peace 1681–91. Bury Grammar School and Christ's College, Cambridge (sizar 1679); admitted Inner Temple, 1681/2. Burgess of the Common Council, Bury St. Edmunds, 1688; Town Clerk, 1688/9. Buried at Horringer. Administration of his goods granted, 1696.
1694	1696	KIPLING	William		1696	
1707	1726	CARTER	John			
1726		BRINKLEY	William		1730	Of Bury St. Edmunds; Attorney. Administration of his goods granted to his widow Mary.
1727	1745	COLLETT	William			Of Woodbridge. Under Sheriff.
1746	1748	COLLETT	Henry		1803	Son of William Collett. Subsequently Clerk of the Peace, see above.
1784	c.1802	NOTCUTT	Thomas			Town Clerk of Ipswich, 1779.
1829	1842	BORTON	John Henry	1800	1872	Subsequently Clerk of the Peace, see above.

EAST SUFFOLK

CLERKS OF THE PEACE AND OF THE COUNTY COUNCIL from 1889

From	To	Surname	Forenames	Birth	Death	Biographical Notes
1889	1900	CHERRY	James	1817	1900	Previously Clerk of the Peace for Suffolk, see above; also Clerk of the Peace and of the County Council of West Suffolk, 1889–1900. Revising Barrister for East Suffolk.
1901	1924	COBBOLD	Alfred Townshend	1852	1934	*Elected to Society, June 1897.* Solicitor (admitted 1876). O.B.E., 1920. Clerk to the Lieutenancy. Also Clerk of the Peace and of the County Council of West Suffolk, 1901–24. Previously and subsequently Deputy Clerk of the Peace and of the County Council.
1924	1947	OAKES	Sir Cecil	1884	1959	*Elected to Society, October 1920.* *Honorary Secretary, 1935–47; Vice-Chairman, 1943–44; Chairman, 1944–47.* Solicitor (admitted 1907). C.B.E., 1938; knighted, 1943; Deputy Lieutenant. Clerk to the Lieutenancy. Member of Royal Commission on Justices of the Peace, 1946. Previously Deputy Clerk of the Peace and of the County Council; subsequently Chairman, later Deputy Chairman, of Quarter Sessions for East and West Suffolk; Councillor, later Alderman, East Suffolk County Council. Major, Cheshire Regiment, 1914–18 War.
1947		LIGHTFOOT	George Cecil	1906		*Elected to Society, January 1944.* *Honorary Secretary, Golfing Society, 1950.* Solicitor (admitted 1930). B.A. (Oxon). Clerk to the Lieutenancy. Member of Home Office Departmental Committee on the Probation Service, 1959. Previously assistant solicitor, East Sussex County Council, and Deputy Clerk of the Peace and of the County Council.

DEPUTY CLERKS OF THE PEACE AND OF THE COUNTY COUNCIL from 1889

From	To	Surname	Forenames	Birth	Death	Biographical Notes
1890	1894	WESTHORP	Sterling	1825	1895	Solicitor (admitted 1847). Clerk to the Justices, Samford division. Councillor, Ipswich Borough Council, 1862; Alderman, 1875; Mayor, 1884–85. Also Deputy Clerk of the Peace and of the County Council of West Suffolk.
1894	1901	COBBOLD	Alfred Townshend	1852	1934	Subsequently Clerk of the Peace and of the County Council, see above. Also Deputy Clerk of the Peace and of the County Council of West Suffolk, 1894–1901 and 1924–34.
1920	1924	OAKES	Cecil	1884	1959	Subsequently Clerk of the Peace and of the County Council, see above.
1924	1934	COBBOLD	Alfred Townshend	1852	1934	Re-appointed Deputy and Honorary Consultant Clerk of the Peace for life, after serving as Clerk, in order to secure a pension to him, the Local Government and Other Officers' Superannuation Act, 1922, not having been adopted.

EAST SUFFOLK (*Continued*)

From	To	Surname	Forenames	Birth	Death	Biographical Notes
1935	1943	DAVIS	Guy Heath	1904		*Elected to Society, March* 1935. Solicitor (admitted 1929). Subsequently Clerk of the Peace and of the County Council of Gloucestershire, *q.v.*
1943	1947	LIGHTFOOT	George Cecil	1906		Subsequently Clerk of the Peace and of the County Council, see above.
1947		HUTCHISON	Sir Peter	1907		*Elected to Society, June* 1947. 2nd Baronet. Solicitor (admitted 1933). M.A. (Oxon). Previously assistant solicitor, Warwickshire County Council. Flight-Lieutenant, Royal Air Force, 1939–45 War.

WEST SUFFOLK

CLERKS OF THE PEACE AND OF THE COUNTY COUNCIL from 1889

From	To	Surname	Forenames	Birth	Death	Biographical Notes
1889	1900	CHERRY	James	1817	1900	Previously Clerk of the Peace for Suffolk, see above. Also Clerk of the Peace and of the County Council of East Suffolk, 1889–1900.
1901	1924	COBBOLD	Alfred Townshend	1852	1934	*Elected to Society, June* 1897. Solicitor (admitted 1876). O.B.E., 1920. Clerk to the Lieutenancy. Also Clerk of the Peace and of the County Council of East Suffolk, 1901–24. Previously and subsequently Deputy Clerk of the Peace and of the County Council.
1924	1953	MUNSEY	Laurence George Hensman	1888		*Elected to Society, April* 1920. Solicitor (honours) (admitted 1912). Clerk of the Magistrates' Courts Committee. President, Suffolk and North Essex Law Society, 1938. Previously assistant solicitor, with Solicitors and Parliamentary Agents to Westminster City Council; assistant solicitor, Essex County Council, and Deputy Clerk of the Peace and of the County Council of West Suffolk. Lieutenant, Inns of Court Regiment, (British Salonika Force), 1914–18 War.
1953		SKINNER	Alan Frank	1913		*Elected to Society, March* 1947. Son of Horace Wilfrid Skinner, C.B.E., Clerk of the Peace and of the County Council of Derbyshire, 1930–50; Solicitor (honours) (admitted 1937). M.A., LL.B. (Cantab). O.B.E., 1946. Secretary to the Advisory Committee; Clerk of the Magistrates' Courts Committee. Previously assistant solicitor, Derbyshire and Nottinghamshire County Councils, and Deputy Clerk of the Peace and of the County Council of Northamptonshire.

DEPUTY CLERKS OF THE PEACE AND OF THE COUNTY COUNCIL from 1889

From	To	Surname	Forenames	Birth	Death	Biographical Notes
1890	1894	WESTHORP	Sterling	1825	1895	Solicitor (admitted 1847). Clerk to the Justices, Samford division. Councillor, Ipswich Borough Council, 1862; Alderman, 1875; Mayor, 1884–85. Also Deputy Clerk of the Peace and of the County Council of East Suffolk.
1894	1901	COBBOLD	Alfred Townshend	1852	1934	Subsequently Clerk of the Peace and of the County Council, see above. Also Deputy Clerk of the Peace and of the County Council of East Suffolk, 1894–1901 and 1924–34.
1903	1906	WILSON	Rowland Holt			*Deputy Clerk of the Peace only.* Solicitor (admitted 1869). Coroner; Clerk to the Justices, Thingoe and Thedwastre divisions.
1907	1918	GROSS	Charles James		1918	*Deputy Clerk of the Peace only.* Solicitor (admitted 1886).
1920	1924	MUNSEY	Laurence George Hensman	1888		Subsequently Clerk of the Peace and of the County Council, see above.
1924	1934	COBBOLD	Alfred Townshend	1852	1934	See note to corresponding appointment in East Suffolk, above.
1953		JEFFERSON	Charles	1902		*Elected to Society, March* 1954. Solicitor (honours) (admitted 1930). Previously assistant solicitor, Surrey and West Suffolk County Councils.

SURREY

From	To	Surname	Forenames	Birth	Death	Biographical Notes
CLERKS OF THE PEACE from 1390						
1390	1392	CROWE	Thomas			
1395	1396	COGGERE	John			Also Clerk of the Peace for Sussex, 1392–97.
1401	1402	CURTEYS	Thomas			Also Clerk of the Peace for Sussex, 1401–c.08.
1406	1417	VYNCENT	John			
1418	1427	HIPPERON	John			Possibly Member of Parliament for Guildford, 1413 and 1422 (see Manning and Bray, *History of Surrey*, I, p. 43).
1427	1467	ELIOT (ELYOT)	Thomas		1467	Of Wonersh; Filacer for Surrey and Sussex (see Manning and Bray, *op. cit.*, I, p. 619; II, pp. 111, 114).
1483	1488	WELBEK	Richard		1488	Of Putney and the Middle Temple; on commission of enquiry for Surrey.
1488	1506	SKYNNER	John, the elder	c.1447	c.1520	Of Reigate and Lincoln's Inn; Member of Parliament for Reigate; Under Sheriff for Surrey and Sussex; subsequently Justice of the Peace (see Wedgewood, *Parliament 1439–1509*, p. 772 and Hooper, *Reigate*, pp. 115–6).
1507	1522	SKYNNER	John, the younger			Son of John Skynner the elder; possibly Member of Parliament for Reigate, 1529, and Justice of the Peace.
1523	1530	HILL	Richard		? 1550/1	Possibly Lord of the Manors of Downe (Sutton) in Shere and Gosterwood in Wotton (see *V.C.H.* III, pp. 116, 157).
1535	1538	CARLETON	John		c.1552	Held lands at Esher, Pyrford, Stoke D'Abernon and Walton-on-Thames, also lands in Berkshire, Cambridgeshire and Oxfordshire, sometimes jointly with his wife Joyce; Charity Commissioner (see Surrey Arch. Coll. XXV).
1542	1546	ELYOTT	Thomas		?1548	Appointed Clerk of the Peace and of the Crown by letters patent, 28th November, 34 Henry VIII. Possibly of Bramley, lessee for 99 years of Shalford Rectory (see *V.C.H.* III, p. 58) and Member of Parliament for Guildford, 1547–48 (see Manning and Bray, *op. cit.*, I, p. 171).
1550	1554	STOUGHTON	Anthony			Of Stoke next Guildford.
1554	1555	STOUGHTON	John			Of Stoke next Guildford.
1555	1572	ELIOT	Richard		c.1609	Of Albury and Reigate; inherited Manors of Hartswood in Buckland, Bures in Horley, and Reigate rectory.
1573	1617	AUSTEN	George		1621	Of Shalford; probably Mayor of Guildford, 1579, 1588; Member of Parliament for Haslemere, 1597; for Guildford, 1602–03; benefactor of Guildford grammar school.
1618	1635	CAMPION	John		?1665	Possibly of Arlington, Devon, at his death.
1644	1645	EVERARD	Anthony			
1650	1652	DYER	William			
1653	1660	LAUNDER	John			Possibly of Mortlake, and Lord of the Manor of Farncombe in Godalming until 1675 (see *V.C.H.* III, p. 33). Ordered, unsuccessfully, to deliver Sessions Rolls, etc., to Henry Byne, Michaelmas 1660.
1660	1675	BYNE	Henry	1628	1697	Of Carshalton; Lord of the Manor of Woldingham (see *V.C.H.* IV, pp. 187–8). Deputy Sheriff and Collector of Hearth Tax, 1662–63; Receiver of Eighteen Months Tax, 1673.
1675	1678	SNOW	Charles		1680	Son and heir of John Snow of Tydd St. Giles, Cambridgeshire; of the Middle Temple.

SURREY (*Continued*)

From	To	Surname	Forenames	Birth	Death	Biographical Notes
1678	1680	WYNNE	Robert			Possibly Barrister-at-law, Inner Temple, and of Denbighshire family.
1681	1689	ABELL	Humfrey			Of St. Dunstan's in the West; later of Ham in Kingston and of West Molesey; possibly third son of William Abell of Baginton, Warwickshire, and admitted to Middle Temple, 1687.
1689	1700	SMYTHE	William			Of the Inner Temple.
1701	1706	CORBETT	Edward	?1678		Possibly of Lincoln's Inn, son and heir of Edward Corbett of Blakland in Bobbington, Staffordshire (see *Staffordshire Pedigrees 1664–1700*, Harleian Society, LXIII, p. 58).
1706	1742	CORBETT	Robert		1742	Probably son of Edward Corbett; admitted Lincoln's Inn, 1721/2. Receiver General in Surrey; Collector of 4½ *per cent.* duty in Barbados 1703–05. Previously Deputy Clerk of the Peace.
1742	1751	MILLER	Thomas		1751	Of Guildford. Also County Treasurer.
1751	1754	WILLIAMS	Richard			Of West Clandon. Also County Treasurer.
1754		CHETWOOD	John		c.1755	Possibly son of John Chetwood of Wellington, Somerset; Barrister-at-law, Middle Temple. His appointment disputed, and in office only from January to March.
1754		TARRANT	Thomas			Of Ashtead.
1755	1763	LAWSON	John	1707	1764	Second son of James Lawson of Preston, Lancashire; of Wimbledon and of the Middle and Inner Temples. Buried in Wimbledon churchyard. (See Manning and Bray, *op. cit.*, III, p. 279, and *Monumental Inscriptions in St. Mary's Church, Wimbledon*, p. 48).
1763	1804	LAWSON	Francis			Son of John Lawson; Queen's College, Oxford; of Wimbledon; Barrister-at-law, Inner Temple. Previously Deputy Clerk of the Peace.
1804	1837	LAWSON	Charles John			*Founder Member of Society, March* 1810. *Honorary Treasurer,* 1811–35. Son of Francis Lawson; Barrister-at-law, Middle Temple (called 1798, Bencher 1839, Reader 1843). Justice of the Peace, Kent, 1838. Previously Deputy Clerk of the Peace.
1837	1839	LAWSON	Frederick William	c.1813	1839	*Elected to Society, November* 1837. Of North Clay, Kent; Barrister-at-law. Buried at Wimbledon.
1839	1848	LAWSON	Charles John		1848	
1848	1865	GREIG	Woronzow	c.1806	1865	*Elected to Society, November* 1849. Grandson of Sir Samuel Greig (1735–88), Admiral of the Russian fleet and son of Mary, daughter of Sir William Fairfax, better known as Mary Somerville (1780–1872); Barrister-at-law, Inner Temple (called 1830). F.R.S.
1865	1871	MARSHALL	Henry	c.1795	1874	*Elected to Society, June* 1868. Of Godalming; Solicitor (admitted 1816). Clerk to the Lieutenancy, 1840–70. Six times Mayor of Godalming between 1836 and 1863. Joint Clerk of Guildford, Godalming and Farnham County Courts; later Registrar of Guildford County Court.
1871	1889	WYATT	Sir Richard (Henry)	1823	1904	*Elected to Society, June* 1872. Solicitor (admitted 1851). Knighted, 1886. Deputy Lieutenant. Clerk to the Lieutenancy; Parliamentary Agent to the Treasury; High Sheriff of Merioneth, 1885. Justice of the Peace, Kent, Merioneth, and Cinque Ports. See also list of Clerks of the Peace for the County of London.

From	To	Surname	Forenames	Birth	Death	Biographical Notes

CLERKS OF THE PEACE AND OF THE COUNTY COUNCIL from 1889

From	To	Surname	Forenames	Birth	Death	Biographical Notes
1889	1904	WYATT	Sir Richard (Henry)	1823	1904	See above.
1904	1927	WEEDING	Thomas Weeding	1847	1929	*Elected to Society, June 1905.* Solicitor (admitted 1870). Justice of the Peace, 1878. Deputy Chairman of Quarter Sessions, 1889–91. Deputy Lieutenant, 1927. Clerk to the Lieutenancy; Member of the Chertsey Board of Guardians. Previously Deputy Clerk of the Peace and of the County Council. Played cricket for Surrey, 1865–66, 1868 (against the Australian Aboriginals in the first match played in England against a Colonial team), and 1874. His daughter, Daphne, became member of Surrey County Council (1934–58) and Chairman of the County Records and Ancient Monuments Committee (1945–58).
1927	1950	AUKLAND	Dudley	1887	1950	*Elected to Society, October 1927.* Solicitor (admitted 1909). LL.M. (Liverpool). Clerk to the Lieutenancy. Previously Deputy Town Clerk, Liverpool. Captain, 5th Battalion, South Lancashire Regiment (T.A.), 1914–18 War.
1951	1956	GRAHAM	Ernest	1886		*Elected to Society, July 1946.* *Clerk of the Peace only.* Barrister-at-law, Inner Temple (called 1923). M.A. (Oxon). Deputy Lieutenant. Clerk to the Lieutenancy; Secretary to the Advisory Committee; Clerk of the Magistrates' Courts Committee. Brought to Kingston most of the Quarter Sessions records left at Newington by Sir Richard Wyatt (see above). Previously in Indian Civil Service, 1909–22, and Deputy Clerk of the Peace.
1951	1952	GOODERIDGE	Thomas William Wade	1887		*Elected to Society, January 1948.* *Clerk of the County Council only.* Solicitor (admitted 1910). Previously assistant solicitor, Essex and Hertfordshire County Councils, and Deputy Clerk of the County Council. Lieutenant, Royal Artillery, 1914–18 War (prisoner of war, 1918); Brevet Major, Royal Artillery (T.A.), 1920–32.
1952		RUFF	William Willis	1914		*Elected to Society, March 1951.* *Clerk of the County Council only.* Solicitor (admitted 1937). Previously assistant solicitor, Scarborough and Heston and Isleworth Borough Councils, and Deputy Clerk of the County Council. Major, Royal Signals, 1939–45 War.
1956		NOPS	Geoffrey Austin	1913		*Elected to Society, March 1956.* *Clerk of the Peace only.* Son of Sir Wilfrid Nops, LL.B., Clerk of the Central Criminal Court and Clerk of the Peace for the City of London; Magdalen College, Oxford, M.A., B.C.L.; Barrister-at-law, Middle Temple (called 1937). Clerk to the Lieutenancy; Secretary to the Advisory Committee; Clerk of the Magistrates' Courts Committee. Previously Deputy Clerk of the Peace. Royal Artillery, 1939–45 War.

DEPUTY CLERKS OF THE PEACE prior to 1889

From	To	Surname	Forenames	Birth	Death	Biographical Notes
c.1690		SHUTE	Richard			
1691		DRAKE	Ralph			
1691		REYNOLDS	John			Jointly with Ralph Drake.
c.1699	1703	MAIDMAN (MAYDMAN)	Edward			
1704	1705	ROLFE	John			
1706	1706	CORBETT	Robert		1742	Subsequently Clerk of the Peace, see above.
c.1711	1712	MAIDMAN	Edward			
1713	c.1749	PEYTO	Thomas			

SURREY (*Continued*)

From	To	Surname	Forenames	Birth	Death	Biographical Notes
1751	1754	AKEHURST	Alexander			Of Leatherhead; appointed by Richard Williams, Clerk of the Peace 1751–54, for the period of his clerkship.
1760	1762	LAWSON	Francis			Subsequently Clerk of the Peace, see above.
c.1779	1788	SQUIRE	Francis			
1792	1803	LAWSON	Charles John			Subsequently Clerk of the Peace, see above.
c.1809		LAWSON	J.			Of Guildford.
c.1813		LAWSON	D.			Of King's Bench Walk, Temple.
c.1840	c.1848	ONSLOW	Richard			*Elected to Society, May* 1841. Barrister-at-law, Middle Temple.
c.1853	1871	SMALLPEICE	William Haydon	1815	1872	Of Guildford; Solicitor (admitted 1835). Clerk to the Guildford Borough Justices.
1871		HELPS	Arthur			

DEPUTY CLERKS OF THE PEACE AND OF THE COUNTY COUNCIL from 1889

From	To	Surname	Forenames	Birth	Death	Biographical Notes
1891	1904	WEEDING	Thomas Weeding	1847	1929	Subsequently Clerk of the Peace and of the County Council, see above.
1909	1928	NARES	Ramsey	1861	1934	*Elected to Society, March* 1922. *Vice Clerk of the County Council*, 1909; *Deputy Clerk of the Peace*, 1912. Solicitor (admitted 1884).
1928	1932	WILLIAMS	Harold Beck	1889		*Elected to Society, May* 1928. Solicitor (admitted 1912); Barrister-at-law, Middle Temple (called 1933); King's Counsel, LL.D. (London). Deputy Chairman of Surrey Quarter Sessions, 1955–56 and of Middlesex Quarter Sessions. Lieutenant, Hampshire Regiment, 1914–18 War.
1932	1946	WILLWAY	Alfred Cedric Cowan	1898		*Elected to Society, October* 1932. *Deputy Clerk of the Peace only.* Barrister-at-law, Inner Temple (called 1924). B.A. (Oxon). Justice of the Peace; Deputy Lieutenant, 1950; C.B., 1953. County Councillor, 1952–59; Chairman of Quarter Sessions from 1955. Second Lieutenant, Royal Engineers, 1914–18 War; Brigadier, Chief Signal Officer, 1939–45 War; T.D., 1940; C.B.E. (Mil.) 1944.
1932	1948	ROGERS	George Foster	1888		*Elected to Society, October* 1932. *Deputy Clerk of the County Council only.* Solicitor (admitted 1927). O.B.E., 1941.
1946	1951	GRAHAM	Ernest	1886		*Deputy Clerk of the Peace only.* Subsequently Clerk of the Peace, see above.
1948	1951	GOODERIDGE	Thomas William Wade	1887		*Deputy Clerk of the County Council only.* Subsequently Clerk of the County Council, see above.
1951	1956	NOPS	Geoffrey Austin	1913		*Deputy Clerk of the Peace only.* Subsequently Clerk of the Peace, see above.
1951	1952	RUFF	William Willis	1914		*Deputy Clerk of the County Council only.* Subsequently Clerk of the County Council, see above.
1952		WAITE	Alan Charles Victor	1915		*Elected to Society, May* 1952. *Deputy Clerk of the County Council only.* Solicitor (admitted 1940).
1956		RUSHWORTH	Victor Henry	1916		*Deputy Clerk of the Peace only.* Solicitor (admitted 1961). LL.B. (London).

SUSSEX

From	To	Surname	Forenames	Birth	Death	Biographical Notes
		CLERKS OF THE PEACE from 1392				
1392	1397	COGGERE	John			Also Clerk of the Peace for Surrey, 1395–96.
1401	c.1408	CURTEYS	Thomas			Also Clerk of the Peace for Surrey, 1401–02.
c.1408	1424	WANNOK	Simon			
1424	c.1449	WELLYS	Henry			
c.1450	1455	BAKER	Thomas			
1463	1467	FAGGER	William			
1474	1494	BAKER	Thomas			
1497	1521	BOWYER	William			
1521	1530	MICHELL	John			
1532		BYSSHOP	John			
1535	1555	BYSSHOP	Thomas			An occupant of the office who obtained a grant for life by letters patent, 29th January, 29 Henry VIII.
1555	1557	STAPLETON	William			
1559	1560	BYSSHOP	Thomas			
1564	1566	BOWYER	William			
1571	1578	TURNER	John			
1581	1606	AYNSCOMBE	Thomas			Possibly two persons, son succeeding father. One Thomas Aynscombe "probably of Buxted, Sussex" matriculated 1585, admitted to Inner Temple 1588, called 1598 (see Venn, *Alumni Cantabrigienses* and Comber, annotated copy of Berry's *Sussex Genealogies*, pp. 98, 200). Will of Thomas Aynscombe of Mayfield, Sussex, proved 1605/6 in Peculiar Court of the Deanery of South Malling (ref. C.30) and also in Prerogative Court of Canterbury (see P.C.C. Wills 48 Stafford).
1608	1615	RAVENS-CROFTE	John	c.1571	1615	Probably in office from 1606. Will of John Ravenscroft of Horsham, Sussex, proved 1617 (see P.C.C. Wills 52 Weldon).
1615	1640	THOMAS	William		1640	Possibly William Thomas who was admitted to Gray's Inn, 1600 (see Foster, *Admissions to Gray's Inn* and Venn, *op. cit.*) Comber, *op. cit.*, describes him as descended out of Wales, buried at West Dean, and with family entries in parish registers of All Saints, Lewes (see pp. 291, 299). Will proved 1640 (see P.C.C. Wills 32 Coventry).
1640	1660	ALCOCK	William			Possibly William Alcock of the Friars, Lewes, whose daughter Hannah baptised 1635 and married 1660 at All Saints, Lewes (see Comber, *op. cit.*, p. 177).
1661	1668	SHELLEY	Timothy			Of Sullington, or of Champneys in the neighbouring parish of Thakeham; probably held office until 1671. Great-great-great-grandfather of Percy Bysshe Shelley, the poet (see Comber, *op. cit.*, p. 66). Will proved 1671 in Court of the Archdeaconry of Chichester (STC I/25 f. 28 v).
1678	1713	WHEELER	William			Of Storrington. Will proved 1713 in Court of the Archdeaconry of Chichester (STC I/31 p. 397).
1713	1725	MANNING	Richard			
1725	1730	MOORE	Richard			
1731	1736	YOUNG	Richard			
1736	1756	SEARLE	Robert			Will of Robert Searle of Midhurst, (who held lands in Storrington also) proved 1756 in Court of the Archdeaconry of Chichester (STC I/40 p. 1).
1756	1775	MICHELL	James			
1775	1806	ELLIS	William			Possibly of Horsham.
1806	1832	LANGRIDGE	William Balcombe	1757	1845	*Founder Member of Society, March* 1810. Of Lewes; Solicitor.

SUSSEX (*Continued*)

From	To	Surname	Forenames	Birth	Death	Biographical Notes
1832	1865	LANGRIDGE	William Vidler		1866	*Elected to Society, November 1832.* Of Lewes; only son of William Balcombe Langridge; Solicitor.
1866	1882	LANGRIDGE	William Kirby Johnson		1882	*Elected to Society, June 1863.* Son of William Vidler Langridge; Solicitor (admitted 1859). Previously Deputy Clerk of the Peace.
1882	1889	MERRIFIELD	Frederic	c.1828	1924	*Elected to Society, May 1883.* Probably third son of John Merrifield of the Middle Temple. Barrister-at-law, Middle Temple (called 1863).

DEPUTY CLERKS OF THE PEACE prior to 1889

From	To	Surname	Forenames	Birth	Death	Biographical Notes
1669	1671	SHELLEY	Timothy			
1671	1678	WHEELER	William			
1711	1730	SEARLE	Robert			References to him occur in the years 1711–12, 1715–20 and 1730.
1745	1763	SCUTT	William			References to him occur in the year 1756 as Clerk of the Peace, but probably only Acting Clerk.
1767	1770	FARNES	Thomas			Attended Court in West Sussex only.
1773		TUTTÉ	Randolph		1778	Probably son of William Tutté of Chichester. Treasurer of the tax made for conveying vagrants, etc., in the West Part of Sussex. Died at Bath.
1773	1775	TURNER	Chatfield			
1782	1784	WALLER	Samuel			
1806		ELLIS	William			
1863	1866	LANGRIDGE	William Kirby Johnson		1882	Subsequently Clerk of the Peace, see above.

EAST SUSSEX

CLERKS OF THE PEACE AND OF THE COUNTY COUNCIL from 1889

From	To	Surname	Forenames	Birth	Death	Biographical Notes
1889	1914	MERRIFIELD	Frederic	c.1828	1924	*Elected to Society, May 1883.* *Vice-Chairman, 1907–10; Chairman, 1910–14.* Previously Clerk of the Peace for Sussex, see above. Also Clerk of the Peace and of the County Council of West Sussex, 1889–1913.
1914	1938	McILVEEN	Hugh John Turnly	1879	1939	*Elected to Society, June 1914.* *Honorary Treasurer, 1933–38.* Solicitor (admitted 1902). Previously Deputy Town Clerk of Birmingham. R.A.S.C., 1914–18 War.
1939	1959	MARTIN	Hubert Sinclair	1891		*Elected to Society, October 1930.* *Honorary Treasurer, 1938–56; Vice-Chairman, 1953–56; Chairman, 1956–58.* Solicitor (admitted 1913). LL.B. (London). C.B.E., 1945. Secretary to the Advisory Committee; Clerk of the Magistrates' Courts Committee. Assistant Commissioner, Local Government Boundary Commission, 1947. Previously Deputy Town Clerk, Great Yarmouth; Assistant Town Clerk, Birmingham; Deputy Clerk of the Peace and of the County Council, and Clerk of the Peace and of the County Council of Northamptonshire. Major, R.F.A., 1914–18 War; Order of the Nile.
1959		ATKINSON	Jack	1917		*Elected to Society, July 1953.* Solicitor (admitted 1946). LL.B. (Bristol). Secretary to the Advisory Committee; Clerk of the Magistrates' Courts Committee. Previously assistant solicitor, Cheltenham Borough and Hampshire County Councils, and Deputy Clerk of the County Council of Oxfordshire. Lieutenant Colonel, Royal Marines, 1939–45 War.

DEPUTY CLERKS OF THE PEACE AND OF THE COUNTY COUNCIL from 1889

From	To	Surname	Forenames	Birth	Death	Biographical Notes
1909	1913	de MONT-MORENCY	Frank Raymond		1913	*Elected to Society, November 1907.* Solicitor (admitted 1903). Also Deputy Clerk of the Peace and of the County Council of West Sussex, 1907–13.
1913	1915	DARKE	Hugh Cuff		1916	Also Deputy Clerk of the Peace and of the County Council of West Sussex, 1913–14. Major, R.F.A., 1914–18 War; died on active service.

From	To	Surname	Forenames	Birth	Death	Biographical Notes
1915	1919	HARRIS	George Montagu			*Elected to Society, April* 1918. Winchester College and New College, Oxford; Barrister-at-law, Middle Temple (called 1893). O.B.E., 1918. Secretary, County Councils Association, 1902–19. Subsequently President, Town Planning Institute, 1927–28; President, International Union of Local Authorities, 1936–48; Alderman, Oxford City Council, 1937–45; Author of Works on Local Government.
1922		FOVARGUE	Reginald West			
1924	1928	SCOTT	Francis Gerald	1888		*Elected to Society, April* 1924. Solicitor (admitted 1919). Subsequently Clerk of the Peace and of the County Council of Oxfordshire, *q.v.*
1928	1930	SEAGER	John Edward	1884	1938	Subsequently Deputy Clerk, later Clerk, of the Peace and of the County Council of West Sussex, see below.
1930	1933	MARTIN	Hubert Sinclair	1891		Subsequently Clerk of the Peace and of the County Council of Northamptonshire and later of East Sussex, see above.
1934		EDWARDS	William Richard	1906		*Elected to Society, April* 1934. Solicitor (admitted 1929).

WEST SUSSEX

CLERKS OF THE PEACE AND OF THE COUNTY COUNCIL from 1889

From	To	Surname	Forenames	Birth	Death	Biographical Notes
1889	1913	MERRIFIELD	Frederic	c.1828	1924	*Elected to Society, May* 1883. *Vice-Chairman,* 1907–10; *Chairman,* 1910–14. Previously Clerk of the Peace for Sussex, see above. Also Clerk of the Peace and of the County Council of East Sussex, 1889–1914.
1913	1931	THORNELY	Samuel	1867	1932	*Elected to Society, June* 1894. *Instituted "Periodical Circular",* 1897; *Editor,* 1897–1931. Eldest son of Frederick Thornely of Helsby, Cheshire; Solicitor (admitted 1890). Clerk to the Lieutenancy; Secretary to the Advisory Committee. On the purported termination of his offices of Clerk of the Peace and of the County Council, sued Chairman of Standing Joint Committee for, and obtained, declaration, that the offices were freehold (*Thornely v. Leconfield* [1925] 1 K.B. 236; *Leconfield v. Thornely* [1926] A.C. 10). Previously solicitor, Hampshire County Council and Clerk of the Peace and of the County Council of Worcestershire, *q.v.* Died at Helsby, Cheshire.
1932	1938	SEAGER	John Edward	1884	1938	*Elected to Society, January* 1928. *Editor, "Periodical Circular",* 1931–33. Solicitor (admitted 1909). Clerk to the Lieutenancy; Secretary to the Advisory Committee. Previously Deputy Clerk of the Peace and of the County Council of East Sussex, and of West Sussex.
1939		HAYWARD	Tom Christopher	1904		*Elected to Society, January* 1934. *Vice-Chairman,* 1956–58; *Chairman,* 1958–61; *Chairman of 150th Anniversary Dinner,* 1960. Solicitor (admitted 1929). B.A. (Cantab). C.B.E., 1946. Clerk to the Lieutenancy; Secretary to the Advisory Committee; Clerk of the Magistrates' Courts Committee, and of the West Sussex River Board. Assistant Commissioner, Local Government Boundary Commission, 1947. Previously Deputy Clerk of the Peace and of the County Council of Staffordshire.

DEPUTY CLERKS OF THE PEACE AND OF THE COUNTY COUNCIL from 1889

From	To	Surname	Forenames	Birth	Death	Biographical Notes
1907	1913	de MONT-MORENCY	Frank Raymond		1913	*Elected to Society, November* 1907. Solicitor (admitted 1903). Also Deputy Clerk of the Peace and of the County Council of East Sussex, 1909–13.
1913	1914	DARKE	Hugh Cuff		1916	Also Deputy Clerk of the Peace and of the County Council of East Sussex, 1913–15. Major, R.F.A., 1914–18 War; died on active service.
1930	1932	SEAGER	John Edward	1884	1938	Subsequently Clerk of the Peace and of the County Council, see above.
1934		ROBINSON	Arthur Desmond	1906		*Elected to Society, October* 1937. *Deputy Clerk of the County Council,* 1934; *of the Peace,* 1937. Solicitor (admitted 1930).

WARWICKSHIRE

From	To	Surname	Forenames	Birth	Death	Biographical Notes
		CLERKS OF THE PEACE from 1402				
1402	1425	STRETHAY	Philip		c.1448	Of Strethay, near Lichfield, Staffordshire; son of William de Strethay, Clerk of the Sessions of South Wales, who was granted bailiwick of Hundred of Pirehill, Staffordshire, for long service in that office. Mainpernor for persons sued by Prior of Wenlock, 1404; attorney in England for Thomas Roche, 1406; joint tenant of reversion to part of estates of Elizabeth, widow of Nicholas de Audley, Chief Justice of South Wales, who died 1391; also of lands in Strethay.
1425	1454	CAMPION	John			Of Gaydon; received into Guild of Holy Cross, Stratford-upon-Avon, to act as legal representative, 1424; given breakfast by Stratford-upon-Avon Corporation, 1432; Commissioner to deliver Warwick gaol of Prior of Wootton, 1431, and of Richard Reynold, 1432; Commissioner for an inquisition for wrongful entry, 1449; property dealings in Stratford-upon-Avon, 1454; pardoned for not producing a defendant at Coventry, 1454.
1454	1469	WEST	John		c.1478	Of Solihull; granted Clerkships of the Sessions of the Peace and of Justices of Oyer and Terminer for life by letters patent, wherein grantee described as "attendant in the King's service in the company of the King's clerk, Thomas Greswold, coroner and attorney in the King's Bench"; Mainpernor to whom were committed lands of Robert Aderne, attainted, 1453; specially admitted to Lincoln's Inn, 1465; granted offices of coroner and attorney in the King's Bench by letters patent, 1467; received yearly grant of £10 from the Exchequer, commencing 1469; named in commissions of array, to hold inquisitions, and to deliver gaols of named prisoners, 1470–78; reversion of his offices of coroner and attorney in the King's Bench granted to John Werall, 1478.
1469	1470	DURANT (DERAUNT)	Edward	1425	1480	Of Bredon Cross, Worcestershire (formerly Warwickshire); probably officer of central law court, 1453. Member of Parliament for Lostwithiel, Cornwall, 1453–54; elector in Warwickshire, 1455; attorney in law suits in Warwickshire, 1459; Under Sheriff, 1460; Member of Parliament for Warwick Borough, 1467; attorney in King's Bench, 1473. Mainpernor for William Hugford, 1478. Probably the Edward Durant who was party to final concords relating to Ullenhall, 1450–51, and to Kenilworth, 1466–67.
1472		HEDLEY	Richard			Possibly the Richard Hedley who, with his wife Alice, was made member of Guild of the Holy Cross at Stratford-upon-Avon, 1442–43.
1473	1511	BOTELER	John			Appointment as Clerk of the Peace and of the Crown confirmed by letters patent, 22nd December, 22 Henry VII. Probably of Solihull, and party to final concords relating to lands mostly in Solihull and Coventry, 1481–1506. Commissioner to inquire of payments anciently due to the Crown in Warwickshire, 1486.
1516	1549	HAWES	Richard			Appointment as Clerk of the Peace and of the Crown confirmed by letters patent, 23rd November, 29 Henry VIII. Auditor named in commission to inquire about tenths of spiritualities in Warwickshire and Coventry, 1535; auditor of possessions of College of St. Mary's, Warwick, up to time of its dissolution, 1546–47; probably identical with Richard Hawses, tenant of house in West Street, Warwick, belonging to St. Mary's, 1546–47.
1549	1557	EDGWORTH	Robert		1559	Probably the Robert Edgworth enrolled with Margaret his wife in the Guild of Knowle, 1526; pardoned for having acquired without licence properties in Warwick, Coten, Myton, etc., from John Beaufo of Emscot, 1530; tenant of lands in Claverdon belonging to late prior of Pinley, 1544; devised lands in Warwick, Preston Bagot, etc., with tithes of Knowle, and buried in St. Mary's, Warwick, 1559.
1558	1560	UNDERHILL	William			Of Idlicote; second son of Edward Underhill of Ettington. Admitted to Inner Temple, 1551; Attorney in Common Pleas; acquired New Place, Stratford-upon-Avon, 1567, which was later sold by his son to William Shakespeare; bought Manors of Idlicote and Loxley, 1568; buried at Lower Ettington.
1560	1567	HILL	William			Possibly the William Hill, brother to Sir Rowland Hill, lessee of Manor of Honiley, 1553.

THE SHIRE HALL, WARWICK

1829

From	To	Surname	Forenames	Birth	Death	Biographical Notes
1567	1575	FISHER	John		c.1590	Of Warwick, son of Thomas Hawkins, *alias* Fisher (said by Dugdale to have sold fish at the market cross in Warwick); bailiff of Warwick, 1564–65, 1580–81; Member of Parliament for Warwick Borough, 1572–83, 1584–85; Town Clerk and Deputy Recorder of Warwick, 1580–88; compiler of the *Book of John Fisher* and in part of the *Black Book of Warwick*.
1575	1595	JEFFEREYS	John			Of Wolverton; concerned with John Fisher, see above, in affray at Myton tithe barn, 1576 (Fisher says of him "he might be reckoned *qui interturbat omnia*"); Town Clerk, 1586–1603, and Steward, 1596–1603, of Stratford-upon-Avon.
1595	1604	NORTON	John			
1604	1605	HUNT	Thomas			Possibly Thomas Hunt, Attorney, who acted in a local dispute near Stratford-upon-Avon, 1598, and who, with others, brought a Chancery action against the bailiff and burgesses of Warwick for breaches of trust concerning Henry VIII's and other charities, 1613.
1605	1606	NORTON	John			
1606	1617	GOSSE	George			
1618	1625	HUNT	Thomas			
1625	1628	NORTON	John		1635	Possibly identical with, or son of, John Norton, Clerk of the Peace, 1595–1604 and 1605–06; Clerk to Warwick Borough Justices, 1613–15; Steward and Deputy Recorder of Warwick.
1628	1649	GIBBON(S)	William			Possibly the William Gibbons who, with others, bought the Manor of Moreton Bagot, 1629.
1649	1659	BOUNE	Abraham			Of Coventry; active Parliamentarian during Civil War; Receiver for the County of Warwick of the Revenue of the King, Queen and Prince, 1643; Clerk to the Committee of Safety for the County of Warwick and the City and County of Coventry, 1643; Clerk to the Committee for Sequestrations in Warwickshire; Advocate to the Court Martial sitting at Coventry, 1646.
1659	1668	DIGHTON (DEIGHTON)	Thomas		c.1668	Of Stratford-upon-Avon; son of Thomas Dighton of Ashby-de-la-Zouch; married Margaret Smith at Stratford-upon-Avon, 1628; Attorney; Commissioner to take oaths of witnesses in suit against Corporation of Stratford-upon-Avon, 1634. Acted by Deputy at end of his period of office.
1668	1675	CHALLONER	William, the elder		c.1701	Of Stratford-upon-Avon; son of Thomas Challoner, postmaster of Stone, Staffordshire; grandson of Robert Challoner of Stone, innkeeper; married Elizabeth, daughter of Thomas Dighton, his predecessor; his appointment presumably lapsed on death of Basil, Earl of Denbigh, the *Custos Rotulorum*, 1675; Attorney for the County at assize, 1676; Attorney of Stratford-upon-Avon Court of Record, 1677.
1676		SMITH	Thomas			Possibly the Thomas Smith who was bailiff of Barlichway Hundred, 1673–75, 1679; possibly dismissed for inefficiency—the Sessions records were badly kept by him.
1676	c.1701	CHALLONER	William, the elder		c.1701	Re-appointed by Edward Viscount Conway, the succeeding *Custos Rotulorum*.
c.1701	1719	CHALLONER	William, the younger	c.1670	1719	Of Stratford-upon-Avon, son of William Challoner, the elder; married Anne Palmer, 1696; Attorney of Stratford-upon-Avon Court of Record, 1699; owned property at Stratford-upon-Avon and at Tittensor, Staffordshire.
1719	1720	FULLER	William			
1720	1731	HUNT	Joseph			Possibly of Stratford-upon-Avon; apparently not of the Hunt family of Tanworth, see below.
1731	1748	MASON	Bartlett		1748	Of Old Stratford; one of fourteen children of Nathaniel Mason, of whom he and one brother, Thomas, reached maturity; Deputy Steward and Clerk of the Peace for Borough of Stratford-upon-Avon, 1732–48; Attorney of Stratford-upon-Avon Court of Record, 1738; with his brother Thomas, who owned Mason Croft (now the Shakespeare Institute), granted licence to rebuild seat in Guild Chapel, Stratford-upon-Avon, 1736.

WARWICKSHIRE (*Continued*)

From	To	Surname	Forenames	Birth	Death	Biographical Notes
1748	1772	BEARDSLEY	John		1772	Of Warwick; acted as Sheriff's deputy in proclaiming accession of King George III at Warwick and elsewhere, 1761; admitted to Gray's Inn, 1766; buried at St. Mary's, Warwick.
1772	1789	HEWITT	Joseph	1725	1813	Of Coventry; probably third son of William Hewitt, Mayor of Coventry in 1744; Attorney; Town Clerk of Coventry and Clerk to Justices, 1752–80; Coroner, 1752–79; Deputy Clerk of the Peace for Coventry, c. 1773–76; probably enabled to retire from office by the death in 1789 of his wealthy brother, Viscount Lifford, Lord Chancellor of Ireland.
1789	1802	HUNT	Charles Henry	1763	1817	Of Stratford-upon-Avon; second son of William Hunt, descended from the Hunt family of Beaumonts in Tanworth; married Catherine Oakes; Attorney. Town Clerk of Stratford-upon-Avon, 1783–92; bought Nash's House, 1785, and adjoining site of New Place, 1790 (see notes to William Underhill, 1558–60, above); sold the same, 1807; bought Manors of Loxley and Wolverton, and property at Walford, 1789–96. Commenced banking business in Stratford-upon-Avon, c. 1790; declared bankrupt, 1800.
1802	1819	HUNT	Thomas	1768	1837	*Represented at first meeting of Society, March* 1810. Of Stratford-upon-Avon; fourth son of William Hunt; married Rebecca Maria Beaumont; admitted to Lincoln's Inn, 1788. Town Clerk of Stratford-upon-Avon, 1792–1818; Coroner for the County; owned a table inlaid with wood from Shakespeare's mulberry tree, now in New Place Museum. Previously Deputy Clerk of the Peace.
1821	1873	HUNT	William Oakes	1795	1873	*Elected to Society, May* 1827. Of Stratford-upon-Avon; eldest son of Thomas Hunt; Solicitor (admitted 1817). Town Clerk of Stratford-upon-Avon, 1818–64; clerk to various turnpike trusts; steward of Manor of Henley-in-Arden; concerned in purchase of Shakespeare's Birthplace and in formation of Shakespeare's Birthplace Trust, to which he presented the Stratford portrait of Shakespeare, on discovering it among his family possessions, 1862. Previously Deputy Clerk of the Peace.
1873	1874	HUNT	Henry Oliver		1874	Of Stratford-upon-Avon; third son of Thomas Hunt; Solicitor (admitted 1836). Coroner for the County, 1837; Town Clerk of Stratford-upon-Avon, 1864–74. Previously Deputy Clerk of the Peace.
1874	1889	FIELD	Algernon Sydney	1813	1907	*Elected to Society, May* 1875. Of Leamington; son of the Rev. William Field; his paternal grandmother was Anne Cromwell, great-great-granddaughter of the Protector; Solicitor (admitted 1834). Clerk to the Justices, Kenilworth division, 1841–77; to the Leamington Borough Justices, 1844–70.

CLERKS OF THE PEACE AND OF THE COUNTY COUNCIL from 1889

From	To	Surname	Forenames	Birth	Death	Biographical Notes
1889	1904	FIELD	Algernon Sydney	1813	1907	See above. Died aged 94; buried at Lillington.
1904	1926	FIELD	Edward	1850	1926	*Elected to Society, November* 1888. Of Leamington; second son of Algernon Sydney Field, his predecessor; Rugby School and Wadham College, Oxford; B.A. Solicitor (admitted 1877). Clerk to the Lieutenancy; Secretary to the Advisory Committee; Clerk to the Justices, Kenilworth division, 1877; first Clerk to the Warwickshire and Coventry Joint Committee for Tuberculosis, 1914. Previously Deputy Clerk of the Peace and of the County Council.
1926	1927	FIELD	Sydney Riach	1882	1927	*Elected to Society, February* 1918. Of Leamington; eldest son of Edward Field; Rugby School and Trinity College, Oxford; Solicitor (admitted 1908). Clerk to the Lieutenancy; Secretary to the Advisory Committee; Clerk to the Warwickshire Insurance Committee, 1912–13; to the Warwickshire Local Pensions Committee, 1913; to the Visiting Justices of Private Lunatic Asylums and Mental Deficiency Institutions, 1913; to the Warwickshire and Coventry Joint Committee for Tuberculosis, 1926. Previously Deputy Clerk of the Peace and of the County Council. Enlisted while at Oxford and served in South African War; Captain, 4th South Midland (Howitzer) Brigade, 1914–18 War; wounded 1916. Died at Helouan near Cairo, and buried there.

From	To	Surname	Forenames	Birth	Death	Biographical Notes
1927		STEPHENS	Sir (Leon) Edgar	1901		*Elected to Society, October 1926.* *Honorary Secretary, 1947–53; Vice-Chairman, 1952–53; Chairman, 1953–56; Honorary Treasurer, 1956– ; Founder and first Secretary of Golfing Society, 1932–50; Author of Brochure for Society's 150th Anniversary Dinner, 1960; Editor of "The Clerks of the Counties, 1360–1960"; designed and presented to Society the Coat of Arms granted to them by letters patent from the Kings of Arms, 1960.* Son of William Edgar Stephens, O.B.E., F.S.A., Town Clerk of Great Yarmouth; Felsted School and Trinity Hall, Cambridge; M.A., LL.B. Barrister-at-law, Middle Temple (called 1924). C.B.E., 1945; Deputy Lieutenant, 1950; knighted, 1960. L.M.T.P.I.—Chairman of Midlands Branch of Town Planning Institute, 1947–48; F.S.A., 1943; Member of Master of the Rolls' Archives Committees, 1945–56; of Departmental Committee on Magistrates' Courts Bill and of Lord Chancellor's Rule Committee, 1952–60; of Historical Manuscripts Commission, 1959. Clerk to the Lieutenancy; Secretary to the Advisory Committee; Clerk of the Magistrates' Courts Committee; of the Warwickshire and Coventry Joint Committee for Tuberculosis, 1927–48; of the War Zone Courts (Midland Region) 1939–45, and Honorary Secretary of the Warwickshire War Relief Committee, 1939–46. Previously legal assistant, Warwickshire County Council, and Deputy Clerk of the Peace and of the County Council. Coxed Cambridge University boat, 1921 and 1922.

DEPUTY CLERKS OF THE PEACE prior to 1889

From	To	Surname	Forenames	Birth	Death	Biographical Notes
1613		COLLINS	Francis			
1716		GOODWIN	John			
1730		HUNT	Joseph, the younger			
1800	1802	HUNT	Thomas	1768	1837	Subsequently Clerk of the Peace, see above.
1803		HOBBS	Robert			Of Stratford-upon-Avon.
1818	1820	HUNT	William Oakes	1795	1873	Subsequently Clerk of the Peace, see above.
1865	1873	HUNT	Henry Oliver		1874	Subsequently Clerk of the Peace, see above.
1878	1889	FIELD	Edward	1850	1926	Subsequently Clerk of the Peace and of the County Council, see above.

DEPUTY CLERKS OF THE PEACE AND OF THE COUNTY COUNCIL from 1889

From	To	Surname	Forenames	Birth	Death	Biographical Notes
1889	1904	FIELD	Edward	1850	1926	See above.
1905	1913	FIELD	Henry			Of Leamington; son of Algernon Sydney Field, Clerk of the Peace, 1874–1904; Solicitor (admitted 1877). B.A.
1913	1926	FIELD	Sydney Riach	1882	1927	Subsequently Clerk of the Peace and of the County Council, see above.
1926	1927	STEPHENS	Leon Edgar	1901		Subsequently Clerk of the Peace and of the County Council, see above.
1927	1933	MOON	Richard Lovering	1903		*Elected to Society, May 1927.* Son of Walter Moon, Town Clerk of Liverpool; Solicitor (admitted 1926). Subsequently Clerk of the Peace and of the County Council of Gloucestershire, *q.v.*
1934	1939	TURNER	John Alan	1903		*Elected to Society, November 1932.* Solicitor (admitted 1929). B.A. (Oxon). Subsequently Clerk of the Peace and of the County Council of Northamptonshire, *q.v.*
1939		WILLIS	Robert Metherell	1908		*Elected to Society, January 1939.* Solicitor (admitted 1930). Previously assistant solicitor, Warwickshire County Council.

WESTMORLAND

From	To	Surname	Forenames	Birth	Death	Biographical Notes
		CLERKS OF THE PEACE from 1421				
1421	1431	BATY	Thomas			
1540	1545	ARROWSMITH	George			
1554	1575	MIDDELTON	John			
1582	1584	PHILIPSON	Miles			
1592	1593	LINACRE	John			
1596	1609	AYREY (AYRE)	John			
1619	1628	PICKERING	Thomas			
1669	1678	ROWLANDSON	Richard			
1678	1681	FOTHERGILL	George		1681	Receiver of rents of Crown lands in Westmorland, Lancashire and Cumberland.
	1688	HUDSON				
	1702	BAYNES	Richard		1744	Dismissed by Quarter Sessions, Easter 1702, for misdemeanour in execution of office.
1702	1706	CARLETON	Thomas			Appointed immediately on dismissal of Richard Baynes.
1706	1729	BAYNES	Richard		1744	Reinstated as order for his dismissal quashed in the Queen's Bench, Trinity 1706 (2 Raymond's Reports 1265).
1729	1736	CARLETON	William	1704	1736	Steward to Lord Thanet.
1736	1744	WILKIN	William			
1744	1750	WORDSWORTH	Richard		1760	Attorney. Steward to Henry Viscount Lonsdale, 1728–38; Alderman of Appleby Borough. Grandfather of William Wordsworth, the poet; uncle by marriage of his two successors.
1750	1760	ROBINSON	John	1727	1802	Appleby Grammar School. Freeman of Appleby, 1750, Alderman, 1755; Mayor, 1760–61; Justice of the Peace. Member of Parliament for Westmorland, 1764–74; for Harwich, 1774–1802; Secretary to the Treasury, successively under Duke of Grafton and Lord North; Surveyor General of H.M. Woods and Forests, 1788 (appointed by William Pitt the younger). Lieutenant Colonel, Westmorland Militia. When Secretary to the Treasury and accused of bribery, he was "named" in the House of Commons by Sheridan in the words "I could name him as soon as I could say Jack Robinson." See plate V.
1763	1776	ROBINSON	Joseph	1734	1776	Brother of John Robinson; Solicitor.
1776	1778	NICHOLSON	John			
1778	1780	WHEATLEY	George			Of Lowther; principal agent to James, Earl of Lonsdale, 1789–1800.
1780	1792	NICHOLSON	Joshua	1759	1792	Of Appleby; Solicitor.
1792	1797	TATHAM	Henry		1797	
1798	1799	SAUL	George		1799	
1799	1812	RICHARDSON	John		1812	Alderman of Carlisle; Receiver-General for Westmorland; principal agent to William, Earl of Lonsdale, 1800–12. Previously Deputy Clerk of the Peace.
1812	1838	STEPHENSON	Richard Shepherd		1838	Attorney. Town Clerk and Coroner, Appleby.

From	To	Surname	Forenames	Birth	Death	Biographical Notes
1839	1888	BELL	John	1801	1888	*Elected to Society, June 1886.* Son of James Bell, Captain in the Westmorland Militia; Caius College, Cambridge; married at Gretna Green, 1847; Barrister-at-law, Lincoln's Inn (called 1835). Commissioner of Bankrupts for Westmorland; Deputy Judge of Appleby County Court; seven times Mayor of Appleby, 1863–76. Gazetted Ensign in Westmorland Militia, and served in France, 1814, apparently at the age of twelve; Lieutenant, 1820; drew Army pension of £100 p.a. for seventy years.
1888	1889	BOLTON	John	1838	1924	*Elected to Society, November 1888.* Solicitor (admitted 1863). Clerk to the Justices, Windermere division, 1869–78, and Kendal division, 1878–88; also to Kendal Borough Justices, 1878–88; Town Clerk, Kendal, 1874–1908; Clerk to Sleddall Almshouses and to Kendal Reservoir Commissioners; Under Sheriff. Ensign, Westmorland Rifle Volunteers, 1860.

CLERKS OF THE PEACE AND OF THE COUNTY COUNCIL from 1889

From	To	Surname	Forenames	Birth	Death	Biographical Notes
1889	1916	BOLTON	John	1838	1924	See above. Also President, Westmorland Law Society, 1891–1914.
1916	1918	MILNE	Alexander	1855		*Elected to Society, June 1916.* Solicitor (admitted 1877). Clerk to Guardians of Kendal Union and Assessment Committee, and to Kendal Rural Sanitary Authority, 1882–1916.
1919	1950	GREENWOOD	Harry Bordley	1879	1952	*Elected to Society, March 1919.* Trinity College, Cambridge; M.A., LL.B. Solicitor (admitted 1903). O.B.E., 1951. Clerk to the Lieutenancy; Secretary to the Advisory Committee; Under Sheriff, 1917–52; Clerk to Governors of Kendal High School and of Kendal Grammar School. Previously Clerk of South Westmorland R.D.C. Lieutenant, Border Regiment, 1914–18 War.
1950		HIMSWORTH	Kenneth Stephenson			*Elected to Society, November 1950.* Solicitor (admitted 1938). M.A. (Cantab), LL.B. (London). Clerk to the Lieutenancy; Secretary to the Advisory Committee; Clerk of the Magistrates' Courts Committee, and of the Lake District Planning Board. Previously Deputy Clerk of the County Council.

DEPUTY CLERKS OF THE PEACE prior to 1889

From	To	Surname	Forenames	Birth	Death	Biographical Notes
c.1619	1628	WARD	George			
1671	1672	WHEELER	William			
1745		ROBINSON	Daniel			
1755		ROBINSON	Joseph			
1792		RICHARDSON	John		1812	Subsequently Clerk of the Peace, see above.
1794		YEOWARD	William			Re-appointed in 1797 and 1799.

DEPUTY CLERKS OF THE PEACE AND OF THE COUNTY COUNCIL from 1889

From	To	Surname	Forenames	Birth	Death	Biographical Notes
1948	1950	HIMSWORTH	Kenneth Stephenson			*Deputy Clerk of the County Council only.* Subsequently Clerk of the Peace and of the County Council, see above.
1959		RODGERS	Frederick Harrod			*Deputy Clerk of the County Council, 1959; Deputy Clerk of the Peace, 1960.* Solicitor (admitted 1939). LL.B. (Liverpool).

WILTSHIRE

From	To	Surname	Forenames	Birth	Death	Biographical Notes
		CLERKS OF THE PEACE from 1390				
1390	c.1409	COLLING-BOURNE	Richard			Member of Parliament for Marlborough, 1402; Escheator, 1403.
c.1409	1411	LAMBARD	John			Member of Parliament for Wilton, 1413; Coroner; Verderer in Groveley Wood.
1412		HORN				
1417	1420	HARDEN	Richard			
1421	1444	GILES	John			Member for several Boroughs in Wiltshire, attending seven Parliaments.
1444	1458	UFFENHAM	John			Father and son of this name; the father was Member of Parliament for Wilton, 1441–50, and also Coroner, 1449, dying c. 1481.
1461	1481	CHAFFIN	John			
1481	1483	HAMPTON	John			Member for New Salisbury in four Parliaments, 1483–95; Coroner, 1486; Justice of the Peace, 1494.
1486	1513	CHAFFIN	Thomas			
1516	1520	BULKLEY	Charles			Of Salisbury; Justice of the Peace, 1526; Sheriff, 1545–46.
1523	1525	CHAFFIN	Leonard			
1537	c.1567	DYSMERS	Christopher			Appointed Clerk of the Peace and of the Crown by letters patent, 3rd July, 29 Henry VIII.
c.1567	1580	BERINGTON	Walter			Second son of William Berington, of Reading; admitted Gray's Inn, 1547; possibly also Clerk of the Crown for Wiltshire.
1580	1581	STRENSHAM	Robert	1535	1605	Son of George Strensham, afterwards Mayor of Faversham, Kent; elected Fellow, All Souls College, Oxford, 1563; Bachelor of civil and canon law, 1568; married Frances Wightman of Harrow-on-the-Hill, 1578; possibly also Clerk of the Crown for Wiltshire; buried at Ospringe.
1581	1582	STAPLES	William			
1582	1587	STRENSHAM	Robert	1535	1605	Re-appointed; see above.
1587	1588	STAPLES	William			
1588	1596	APPLEFORD	Daniel			
1597	1626	KENT	John	c.1559	1630	Son of Roger Kent of Coppenhall, Cheshire; married Mary, daughter of Thomas Wiatt of Calne; Town Clerk, Coroner, and Mayor (1602) of Devizes; Member of Parliament for Devizes, 1597–98, 1621, 1624; Steward to Earl of Hertford. The forename appears as William in the Pipe Rolls from 1597 to 1600.
1626	1645	FRAMPTON	George			Possibly Steward to Sir Francis Seymour.
1646	1658	COLES	William			Of the Close, Salisbury. Previously Deputy Clerk of the Peace.
1658	1659	BARNABY	Gabriel			Of Salisbury.
1659	1660	PORDAGE	Samuel	1633	c.1691	Son of John Pordage, astrologer and mystic. Minor poet; Chief Steward to Philip, Earl of Pembroke.

PLATE XI

THE COUNTY COURTS, DEVIZES, WILTSHIRE

1836

WILTSHIRE (*Continued*)

From	To	Surname	Forenames	Birth	Death	Biographical Notes
1660	1696	BOWMAN	Seymour			Of Salisbury; Member of Parliament for Old Sarum, 1660; Freeman of Salisbury, 1685.
1697	1729	EDGELL	James			Of Warminster; also County Treasurer, 1703–13; Under Sheriff; Steward to Thomas, Viscount Weymouth. Previously Deputy Clerk of the Peace.
1729	1736	FOSTER	Michael	1689	1763	Born at Marlborough; matriculated, Exeter College, Oxford, 1705; Barrister-at-law (called 1713); married Martha, daughter of James Lyde of Stantonwick, Somerset, 1725; Recorder of Bristol, 1735; Serjeant-at-law, 1736; Puisne Judge of King's Bench, 1745; knighted 1745; buried at Stanton Drew, Somerset.
1736	1743	HAWKES	William			Of Marlborough; married Hannah, sister of Sir Michael Foster. Also County Treasurer, 1741–43. Previously Deputy Clerk of the Peace.
1743	1782	EWEN	Michael		1782	Nephew and executor of Sir Michael Foster; of Marlborough; Attorney. Chief Steward of Seymour family (Earls of Hertford, later Dukes of Somerset); also Clerk of the Peace for Somerset, 1770–82.
1782	1796	TURNER	John			
1796	1824	SWAYNE	James			Steward to Herbert family of Wilton (Earls of Pembroke and Montgomery).
1824	1864	SWAYNE	John	1777		*Elected to Society, May* 1846. Solicitor. Previously Deputy Clerk of the Peace.
1864	1875	MERRIMAN	William Clark		c.1878	*Elected to Society, June* 1865. Solicitor (admitted 1827). Town Clerk of Marlborough, 1841–63.
1875	1889	MERRIMAN	Robert William	1836	1924	*Elected to Society, June* 1876. Son of William Clark Merriman; Marlborough Grammar School and Winchester College; Solicitor (admitted 1860). Town Clerk of Marlborough, 1863–87; Registrar of Marlborough County Court, 1877–1912; antiquarian, publishing in *Wiltshire Gazette* and *Wiltshire Archaeological and Natural History Magazine*. Previously Deputy Clerk of the Peace.

CLERKS OF THE PEACE AND OF THE COUNTY COUNCIL from 1889

From	To	Surname	Forenames	Birth	Death	Biographical Notes
1889	1912	MERRIMAN	Robert William	1836	1924	See above. Subsequently Justice of the Peace, 1913.
1912	1940	BOWN	William Langsdale	1869	1942	*Elected to Society, October* 1912. Solicitor (admitted 1892). Clerk to the Lieutenancy; Secretary to the Advisory Committee. Previously Deputy Clerk of the Peace and of the County Council.
1940	1960	STRINGER	Philip Austin Selborne	1895		*Elected to Society, March* 1929. Solicitor (admitted 1922). Deputy Lieutenant. Clerk to the Lieutenancy; Secretary to the Advisory Committee; Clerk of the Magistrates' Courts Committee. Previously assistant solicitor, Essex County Council, and Deputy Clerk of the Peace and of the County Council of Cambridgeshire. Captain, Essex Regiment, 1914–18 War.
1960		HARRIES	Robert Paschal	1919		*Elected to Society, May* 1953. Solicitor (admitted 1946). Clerk to the Lieutenancy; Secretary to the Advisory Committee; Clerk of the Magistrates' Courts Committee. Previously assistant solicitor, Wiltshire County Council, and Deputy Clerk of the Peace and of the County Council. Captain, Royal Artillery, 1939–45 War; Despatches.

WILTSHIRE (*Continued*)

From	To	Surname	Forenames	Birth	Death	Biographical Notes
DEPUTY CLERKS OF THE PEACE prior to 1889						
1626	1658	BENNETT	Francis			Deputy to George Frampton, and later to William Coles, at times during their Clerkships.
1626	1645	COLES	William			Deputy to George Frampton at times during his Clerkship.
1646	1658	CHAMPION	John			Deputy to William Coles at times during his Clerkship.
1660	1696	SAMBROOKE	Francis			This and the following five Deputies all acted as such to Seymour Bowman at times during the latter's Clerkship.
		BENNETT	Thomas			Of Salisbury.
		CONSTABLE	Robert			Of Warminster.
		GOUGH	John			
		EYRES	Thomas			
	1697	EDGELL	James			Subsequently Clerk of the Peace, see above.
1730	1736	HAWKES	William			Subsequently Clerk of the Peace, see above.
1818	1824	SWAYNE	John	1777		Subsequently Clerk of the Peace, see above.
1862	1864	JUDD	James Edward			
1865	1875	MERRIMAN	Robert William	1836	1924	Subsequently Clerk of the Peace, see above.
DEPUTY CLERKS OF THE PEACE AND OF THE COUNTY COUNCIL from 1889						
1900	1912	BOWN	William Langsdale	1869	1942	Subsequently Clerk of the Peace and of the County Council, see above.
1913	1946	GEORGE	Thomas Henry Marshall	1883		*Elected to Society, May 1912.* *Deputy Clerk of the Peace only after 1941.* Son of William Davies George, Clerk of the Peace and of the County Council of Pembrokeshire, 1897–1911; Solicitor (admitted 1907). Previously Deputy Clerk of the Peace and of the County Council of Pembrokeshire.
1941	1949	HEY	William Leonard			*Elected to Society, March 1941.* *Deputy Clerk of the County Council only.* Solicitor (admitted 1905). Previously assistant solicitor, Wiltshire County Council.
1949	1953	WOOD	Wilfred Knoyle	1914		*Elected to Society, January 1949.* Solicitor (Fowler prize) (admitted 1937). Commander, R.N.V.R., 1939–45 War.
1953	1960	HARRIES	Robert Paschal	1919		Subsequently Clerk of the Peace and of the County Council, see above.
1960		BUTLER	Dennis William Langford	1926		*Elected to Society, October 1960.* Solicitor (admitted 1951). Royal Marines, 1945–47.

WORCESTERSHIRE

From	To	Surname	Forenames	Birth	Death	Biographical Notes
CLERKS OF THE PEACE from 1391						
1391	1397	LYNDRES	Robert			
1403	1418	OSENEY	Richard			Son of Thomas and Matilda Oseney; Member of Parliament for Worcester, 1406, 1425; seven times Bailiff between 1430 and 1457; King's Attorney.
1419	1427	FORTHEY	John			Member of Parliament for Worcester, 1420–22, 1429, 1431; Escheator for County, 1433.
1436	1442	BYKERSTAFF	John			Member of Parliament for Worcester, 1442.
1447	1464	TOUNLAY	Robert			
1474		GRAFTON	John			Son of Richard Grafton; of Grafton Flyford; Member of Parliament for Worcester, 1472.
1485	1502	KNOTTESFORD	James			
1505	1511	RUDHALE	John		?1530	Possibly the John Rudhale who married Isabella Whittington.
1515	1517	STEDE	John			
1517	1535	SALWAY	Richard			
1537	1542	RUSSELL	Henry			Appointed Clerk of the Peace and of the Crown by letters patent, 3rd July, 29 Henry VIII.
1543	1546	SHELDON	Richard			
1549	1556	MORE	William			
1557	1569	CHILD	William			
1569	1571	BUTLER	Richard			
1573	1585	LITTLETON	George		1600	Son of Roger Littleton; of Groveley; Barrister-at-law, Inner Temple (admitted 1574, called 1583). Member of Parliament for Droitwich, 1586–87; buried at Bromsgrove.
1591	1595	WELLS	Edward			
1599	1622	SYMONDS	Thomas			
1623		MAYNARD	Thomas			
1626	1633	COVENTRY	William			
1634	1640	WALKER	Francis			
1647	1652	COVENTRY	Thomas	?1606	?1661	Possibly the Thomas Coventry who married, 1627, Mary, youngest daughter of Sir William Craven, Lord Mayor of London in 1611. Member of Parliament for Droitwich, 1625–26; for Worcestershire, 1628–29; Member of Council of the Marches of Wales, 1633.
1653	1656	WALKER	Francis			
1656	1660	SYMONDS	Thomas			Of Pershore.
1660	1680	TWITTY	Thomas			
1681	1689	TWITTY	George			
1690	1700	COOKES	Edward			
1700	1719	TURNER	John			
1720	1753	WOLLEY	Richard			
1760	1806	SOLEY	John			Possibly Recorder of Bewdley.
1807	1838	BLAYNEY	Thomas			*Represented at first meeting of Society, March* 1810. Attorney.
1839		DOMVILLE	Henry Barry			
1843	1889	MARCY	William Nichols	1810	1894	*Elected to Society, May* 1845. Son of George Marcy, planter, and Elizabeth née Nichols; born Jamaica, B.W.I.; Solicitor (admitted 1834). Town Clerk, Bewdley, 1833–73; Deputy Recorder, Bewdley, 1833; four times Mayor, 1873–81.

WORCESTERSHIRE (*Continued*)

From	To	Surname	Forenames	Birth	Death	Biographical Notes

CLERKS OF THE PEACE AND OF THE COUNTY COUNCIL from 1889

From	To	Surname	Forenames	Birth	Death	Biographical Notes
1889	1894	MARCY	William Nichols	1810	1894	See above.
1895	1913	THORNELY	Samuel	1867	1932	*Elected to Society, June 1894.* *Instituted "Periodical Circular", 1897; Editor, 1897–1931.* Eldest son of Frederick Thornely of Helsby, Cheshire; Solicitor (admitted 1890). Previously Solicitor, Hampshire County Council, and Deputy Clerk of the Peace and of the County Council of Worcestershire; subsequently Clerk of the Peace and of the County Council of West Sussex, *q.v.* Served in 2nd Battalion, Cheshire Regiment (22nd Foot) and Worcestershire Regiment (Captain, Honorary Major) 1887–1912; during his military service he organised courts on the Rand, South Africa, first as Crown Prosecutor, later as Crown Solicitor, 1900, and sat frequently as member of Courts Martial.
1914	1942	BIRD	Clifford Henry	1879	1960	*Elected to Society, February 1914.* Son of the Rev. Benwell Bird, of Plymouth; Plymouth College; Solicitor (admitted 1901). Clerk to the Lieutenancy from 1929. Justice of the Peace for Devonshire, 1944.
1942		SCURFIELD	William Russell	1908		*Elected to Society, January 1938.* Son of Harold Scurfield, M.D., D.P.H.; Malvern College; Solicitor (admitted 1930). LL.B. (London). Clerk to the Lieutenancy; Clerk of the Magistrates' Courts Committee. Previously assistant solicitor, Durham County Council, and Deputy Clerk of the Peace and of the County Council of Durham.

DEPUTY CLERKS OF THE PEACE prior to 1889

From	To	Surname	Forenames	Birth	Death	Biographical Notes
1627	1656	WALKER	Francis			
1701	1708	ASTLEY (ASHLEY)	John			
1713	1721	WATKINS	John			
1754	1764	THORNELOE	J.			
1765	c.1787	SOCKETT	Richard			
1788	c.1790	MENCE	Richard Mugg			
1805	1814	MENCE	Nathaniel			
1815	1827	HILL	George			*Elected to Society, November 1823.* Attorney. Coroner.
1827	1830	BARNEBY (BURNABY)	Richard			Proposed as a member of the Society without his knowledge, and elected, but declined to accept membership, 1827.
1830	1838	BEST	James			
1839	1852	HELM	Charles Augustus			*Elected to Society, November 1842.* Attorney. Steward to the Bishop of Worcester.

DEPUTY CLERKS OF THE PEACE AND OF THE COUNTY COUNCIL from 1889

From	To	Surname	Forenames	Birth	Death	Biographical Notes
1893	1894	THORNELY	Samuel	1867	1932	Subsequently Clerk of the Peace and of the County Council, see above.
1900		SEACOME	Robert Owen			*Elected to Society, May 1900.* Acting Clerk during absence of Samuel Thornely in South Africa.
1910	1912	THORNLEY	Hubert Gordon	1884		*Elected to Society, June 1911.* Solicitor (admitted 1906). Subsequently Clerk of the Peace and of the County Council of Yorkshire (North Riding), *q.v.*
1930	1944	KENT	Godfrey Lawrence Dunsterville	1875	1947	*Elected to Society, May 1930.* Son of Captain G. Kent of Kempsey; Worcester Royal Grammar School.
1944		PHELIPS	James Henry Caswall	1911		*Elected to Society, September 1944.* Son of Canon A. H. Phelips, of Pershore; Solicitor (admitted 1937). M.A. (Oxon). Previously assistant solicitor, Portsmouth City and Warwickshire County Councils. Captain, Royal Artillery, 1939–45 War.

YORKSHIRE, EAST RIDING

From	To	Surname	Forenames	Birth	Death	Biographical Notes
CLERKS OF THE PEACE from c.1363						
c.1363		BRUYS	Robert			See Yorkshire Archaeological Society, *Record Series*, 100, p. xxiv.
c.1394	c.1396	de PRESTON	Henry		1406	
c.1422	c.1426	RYLLINGTON	William		1427	
c.1428	c.1464	DAVYSON	Robert		c.1464	Clerk of the Crown for Yorkshire.
1507		ROKEBY	Thomas			
c.1514	c.1528	MARSHALL	William			Appears to have acted in part of the North Riding also.
c.1545	c.1546	ANDREW	William			
c.1564	c.1565	COWPER	Gabriel			
c.1575	c.1586	BETHEL	Hugh			
1589		BROWNE	Richard			
c.1595	c.1609	BLACKALLER	Robert		1612	
c.1610	1611	POTTES	Thomas			
	c.1649	SCOTT	John			Described as "lately Clerk of the Peace" in this year.
c.1647	c.1651	BRADFORD	William			
1657	1658	BLACKBEARD	Richard			
1661		HAWKINS	Peter			
c.1662	1679	BLANSHARD	Richard			
1679	1713	MACE	Thomas		1713	Town Clerk of York, 1699–1713.
1713	1736	HARLAND	Richard			Subject of a series of attempts to remove him from office, 1715–17, for neglecting the laws against Papists, failing to make necessary returns of non-jurors and not residing within County; Quarter Sessions ordered his discharge from office, 10th April 1716; also accused of failing to keep proper Sessions records and of failing to deliver records "not being in process" to the *Custos Rotulorum*.
1736	1746	APPLETON	Robert, the elder			Of Beverley; Attorney. Previously Deputy Clerk of the Peace, and re-appointed Deputy by his son after his retirement from the Clerkship.
1746	1787	APPLETON	Robert, the younger		1787	Son of Robert Appleton, the elder; Attorney. Clerk to Commissioners of Sewers. Previously Deputy Clerk of the Peace.
1787	1827	JOHNSON	Richard William		1827	Of Darlington; Attorney.
1828	1843	HOWARD	Hon. William	1781	1843	Second son of fifth Earl of Carlisle; Barrister-at-law. Member of Parliament for Morpeth, 1806–32; for Sutherlandshire, 1837.
1843	1882	LEEMAN	George	1809	1882	*Elected to Society, November 1849.* Solicitor (admitted 1835). Deputy Lieutenant, North Riding of Yorkshire. Member of Parliament for York, 1865–68 and 1871–80. Lord Mayor of York, 1853, 1860 and 1870. Chairman of North Eastern Railway and of York, Newcastle and Berwick Railway; Chairman of Railway Association; inveterate opponent of George Hudson "the railway king"; his statue in white marble stands outside York railway station.
1882	1889	BICKERSTETH	John Joseph	1850	1932	*Elected to Society, May 1883.* Marlborough and Christ Church, Oxford; B.A. Barrister-at-law, Inner Temple (called 1875). Registrar, East Riding Deeds Registry.
CLERKS OF THE PEACE AND OF THE COUNTY COUNCIL from 1889						
1889	1925	BICKERSTETH	John Joseph	1850	1932	See above. M.B.E., 1917; O.B.E., 1920; C.B.E., 1926; Deputy Lieutenant; Hon. LL.D. (Leeds). Major, 4th Battalion, East Riding Volunteer Regiment, 1914–18 War.
1925	1932	PROCTER	John Robert	1865	1947	*Elected to Society, June 1896.* Solicitor (admitted 1887). Clerk to the Lieutenancy; Secretary to the Advisory Committee; Clerk to the North Eastern Sea Fisheries District Committee; Registrar, East Riding Deeds Registry. Previously Deputy Clerk of the Peace and of the County Council.

From	To	Surname	Forenames	Birth	Death	Biographical Notes
1932	1940	MACDONALD OF THE ISLES	Sir Godfrey (Middleton Bosville)	1887	1951	*Elected to Society, January* 1932. 15th Baronet; 22nd Chief of Sleat; Eton College and Magdalen College, Oxford; M.A. Barrister-at-law, Inner Temple (called 1912). M.B.E., 1918. Clerk to the Lieutenancy; Secretary to the Advisory Committee; Registrar, East Riding Deeds Registry. Previously Deputy Clerk of the Peace and of the County Council. British Red Cross Society, 1914–18 War; Despatches.
1940		STEPHENSON	Thomas	1889		*Elected to Society, November* 1934. *Clerk of the County Council only after* 1959. C.B.E., 1943. Clerk to the Lieutenancy; Secretary to the Advisory Committee; Clerk of the Magistrates' Courts Committee; Clerk to the North Eastern Sea Fisheries District Committee. Previously Deputy Clerk of the Peace and of the County Council.
1959		WHITLEY	Raymond Archer	1908		*Elected to Society, April* 1946. *Clerk of the Peace only.* Solicitor (admitted 1934). B.A. (Oxon). Also Deputy Clerk of the County Council; Registrar, East Riding Deeds Registry. Previously Deputy Clerk of the Peace and of the County Council of Merioneth, assistant solicitor, Gloucestershire County Council and Deputy Clerk of the Peace and of the County Council of Yorkshire (East Riding).

DEPUTY CLERKS OF THE PEACE prior to 1889

From	To	Surname	Forenames	Birth	Death	Biographical Notes
c.1708	1709	KILVINGTON	John		1709	
1711	1725	LUND	John			
1725	1726	WILKINSON	Edward			
1726	1736	APPLETON	Robert, the elder			Subsequently Clerk of the Peace, see above.
1736	1746	APPLETON	Robert, the younger		1787	Subsequently Clerk of the Peace, see above.
1747		APPLETON	Robert, the elder			Re-appointed: see above.
c.1780	1785	ELLIS	William		1785	Town Clerk of Beverley.
1785	1827	LOCKWOOD	John	1755	1827	Solicitor. Mayor of Beverley, 1805, 1812, 1814, 1818. Clerk to Commissioners of Sewers; to Militia of East Riding and of Kingston-upon-Hull; to White Cross—Beverley Turnpike Trust; to Ottringham Drainage Commissioners; and to Committee for Internal Defence of the East Riding.
1827	1843	SHEPHARD	Henry John		1848	Solicitor. Clerk to the Lieutenancy. Also County Treasurer, 1803–48. Mayor of Beverley, 1825.
1843	1865	CLARK	William Fox	1816	1865	Solicitor. Lord Mayor of York, 1861–63.
1869	1889	WILKINSON	Joseph	1823	1900	Solicitor (admitted 1844). Clerk to the Lieutenancy; Town Clerk and Clerk of the Peace of York, 1864–86.
c.1872	1883	LEEMAN	Joseph Johnson	1842	1883	Jointly with Joseph Wilkinson. Second son of George Leeman, Clerk of the Peace, 1843–82; Solicitor (admitted 1865). Deputy Lieutenant, West Riding of Yorkshire. Joint Clerk to the Lieutenancy; Member of Parliament for York, 1880–83.

DEPUTY CLERKS OF THE PEACE AND OF THE COUNTY COUNCIL from 1889

From	To	Surname	Forenames	Birth	Death	Biographical Notes
1889	1900	WILKINSON	Joseph	1823	1900	See above.
1892	1925	PROCTER	John Robert	1865	1947	Subsequently Clerk of the Peace and of the County Council, see above.
1926	1931	MACDONALD	Godfrey Middleton Bosville	1887	1951	Subsequently Clerk of the Peace and of the County Council, see above.
1932	1940	STEPHENSON	Thomas	1889		Subsequently Clerk of the Peace and of the County Council, see above.
1940	1946	BEAUMONT	Richard Melville	1909		*Elected to Society, March* 1942. Solicitor (admitted 1932). Registrar, East Riding Deeds Registry.
1946		WHITLEY	Raymond Archer	1908		*Deputy Clerk of the County Council only after* 1959. Clerk of the Peace from 1959, see above.

YORKSHIRE, NORTH RIDING

From	To	Surname	Forenames	Birth	Death	Biographical Notes
		CLERKS OF THE PEACE from 1361				
1361		GRETHEUED	Thomas		?1402/3	Clerkship inferred from his appearance as King's Attorney in Traverse; see Yorkshire Archaeological Society, *Record Series*, 100, p. 113; and his status met the provisions of the Act 34 Edw. III, c.1. A substantial tenant in the Honor of Richmond, which made John of Gaunt as Earl of Richmond dominant magnate of the Riding; thrice a Commissioner of Oyer and Terminer regarding Royal lands in Yorkshire, 1359–60; (see *Calendar of the Patent Roll, Edw. III*, 1358–61, pp. 321, 404, 412, 467). Lived in Stanwick, perhaps until c. 1403, when his widow was claiming dower.
c.1395	1420	ASCOUGH	John		1425	Tenant of the Nevilles, appointed when that family was obtaining control of Richmondshire—by lease in 1395; by grant of the Honor in 1399. Great-nephew of William Ayscough, Bishop of Salisbury and Confessor to King Henry VI; father of Sir William Ayscough, Justice of the King's Bench, and of Robert, Archdeacon of Colchester; John lived at Cowling Hall, Bedale, which his successor R. A. Wotherspoon, ignorant of the coincidence, bought, on appointment as Clerk of the Peace and of the County Council in 1960. (See M'Call, *Early History of Bedale*; pedigrees in Harleian Society 50; and Clay, *Dugdale's Visitation of Yorkshire*, II, p. 375).
1425	1426	GRENEFELD	John		?1464	Probably Serjeant-at-law, of Barnbow and Barwick-in-Elmet; a Royal servant brought in from the Honor of Pontefract to serve the interests of John, Duke of Bedford, when the latter received the Earldom of Richmond at Ralph Neville's death in 1425 (see Somerville, *Duchy of Lancaster*, I, pp. 454, 516; Surtees Society, 30, p. 74; 45, p. 327; 57, pp. 53–4; Yorkshire Archaeological Society, 50, p. 105; and Lumb, *Barwick-in-Elmet*).
1444		WELTDEN	Thomas	1408	1470	Member of an influential Northumbrian family, as were his two successors. The curiously brief tenures probably reflect their concern with greater affairs (Thomas, January–October 1444; Richard, December 1444–August 1445, and Robert, October 1445–April 1446). Thomas was Member of Parliament for Northumberland, 1460–61.
1444	1445	WELTDEN	Richard			Twice Member of Parliament for Newcastle-on-Tyne; his tremendous practice in the eastern counties appears in the Patent, Close and Fine Rolls; Receiver of the Honor of Richmond, 1443–44, having previously acted as man of business to Christopher Conyers, who in 1436 received extensive privileges after Bedford's death. In Surtees Society, 130, pp. 139, 149, is a clear suggestion that Richard was again acting as Clerk of the Peace in 1455–56. Elizabethan heralds saw the Weltden arms in Catterick Church. Pedigree in *History of Northumberland*, 10 (1914), at pp. 327–332.
1445	1446	WELTDEN	Robert			
1455	1456	WYGHALL	John		1468	Of Thirkleby, near Thirsk.
c.1464	c.1466	DANBY	John		1466	Of Leake, near Northallerton; nephew of Sir Robert Danby of Thorp Perrow, etc., Chief Justice of the Common Pleas; Commissioner for the Archbishop of York on a Ripon dispute, 1461 (see Surtees Society, 74, pp. 288–9).
1488	1490	DANBY	Thomas			Grandson of Sir Robert Danby, the Chief Justice; left the law for the church; presented to a family living, the Rectory of Terrington, and granted a dispensation from Pope Alexander VI (Borgia) absolving him from consequences of his legal activities and particularly the writing of indictments upon which persons had been condemned, 1492; passed through minor orders to become a priest, 15th March 1493/4.

From	To	Surname	Forenames	Birth	Death	Biographical Notes
1508	c.1511	BURNAND (BYRNAND)	George		?1550	Appointed Clerk of the Peace and Clerk of the Crown in the North Riding for life by letters patent, 11th October, 24 Henry VII; undocumented except for his death, and notice of his heirs as tenants at Aldborough in 1564, though his family is well documented in the 14–17th centuries, especially about Boroughbridge, Knaresborough and York. One George Birnaund occurs, 1512, in list of persons who, at the demise of the Crown, had been indebted to King Henry VII (see *Letters and Papers, Foreign and Domestic, Henry VIII, I.*, Pt. I, p. 680; inadequate pedigree in Harleian Society, Vol. 94, p. 90).
c.1515	c.1528	MARSHALL	William			Also Clerk of the Peace in the East Riding. Both Marshall and Gower (see below) acted, sometimes over the same period, possibly as deputies of Burnand, in different divisions.
c.1515	c.1528	GOWER	Robert		?1546	Probably the fourth son of Sir John Gower of Stittenham, and so grandson of a Baron of the Exchequer; his wife was granddaughter of Sir Robert Danby, Chief Justice of the Common Pleas.
1534	c.1567	NORTON	Robert		?1571	Appointed by letters patent, 22nd December, 26 Henry VIII; probably graduated B.A. (Cantab), early same year; lived at Thormanby. The forename appears in the Pipe Rolls as John and Thomas also.
c.1571	1572/3	BRAND	Wilfrid		1572/3	In office by January 1570/1; lived at Sutton-under-Whitestoncliffe, near Thirsk, where his house was broken into, 1569; Will, proved 1572/3, preserved at York. A son and namesake, intended for the law, became a merchant and was Chamberlain of York, 1588.
1575		THORNETON	Richard		1591	Clerk of the Peace to the Archbishop of York for his Liberty of Ripon; known for this year only from *State Papers Domestic (Elizabeth)* 12/104. Lived at Ripon and buried there.
c.1582	1603	DAVYLLE	Christopher		1606	Second son of William Davylle of Coxwold; matriculated Jesus College, Cambridge, 1568; admitted, Inner Temple, 1573; signed his pedigree at the Visitation of 1584–85 (ed. Jos. Foster 1875, p. 215). In 1597–98 was busy with private conveyancing for Archbishop Hutton. Absences in 1600 noticed in Quarter Sessions, and a possible disability indicated on the Pipe Roll of 1600–01, though he reappears on that of 1602–03. Under Sheriff, 1605–06.
1596	1597	BESSON	Anthony		1613	Acted for nine months, possibly as Deputy to Davylle. Under Sheriff, 1587–88 and 1590–91. Admitted, Gray's Inn, as one of the Attorneys of the Star Chamber, 1595, and lived at York; but shortly afterwards developed interests in his native Wensleydale, buying property there and founding Yorebridge Grammar School; forfeited to the Treasury forty shillings penalty, 1602, as a bondsman for the Yorkshire Sheriff of 1590–91; took out King James I's general pardon, 1604; organised the opposition of Wensleydale tenants to Ludovic Stuart, Duke of Lennox (later of Richmond), which came to a head in 1606. Justice of the Peace, 1606. Finally moved south and died on his Manor of Byram near Pontefract.
1597	1601	HILL	Stephen		1642	Appears in the Pipe Rolls of 1597–98 and 1600–01, possibly as Deputy to Davylle; see also below, 1615–28.
1604	1615	BRADLEY	William		1638	Of York; probably admitted from Barnard's Inn to Gray's Inn, 1594. Impoverished in later life; about the time of his death was receiving compassionate payments from the Court of Quarter Sessions.
1615	1628	HILL	Stephen		1642	Of York; Attorney; admitted, Inner Temple, 1608. Under Sheriff 1595–96. Listed for knighthood at accession of King Charles I, and paid £10 composition for failing to take up the honour, c. 1630–32. A prisoner was tried at Quarter Sessions for slanderously suggesting that Hill shared illegal profits from land transactions, 1624.

From	To	Surname	Forenames	Birth	Death	Biographical Notes
1628	1632	YOWARD	Ralph	1600	1641	Lord of the Manor of Westerdale; admitted Inner Temple, 1620. Took livery of his father's Crown lands, 1622; listed for knighthood at King Charles I's coronation and later paid £12 composition for having failed to present himself. Pedigree in Clay, *Dugdale's Visitation of Yorkshire*, 3, pp. 318–9. See also *V.C.H.*, II, pp. 415–6.
1632	1633	MOORE	James	c.1598	1666	Served one quarter only; see below, 1635–45.
1633	1634	YOWARD	Ralph	1600	1641	Restored to office at Epiphany 1632/3 and drew a full year's fees.
1635	?1645	MOORE	James	c.1598	1666	Saw service in Bohemia before 1623; subsequently settled at Angram Grange in Coxwold with his father-in-law Michael Askwith. Attorney, of Clifford's Inn and possibly Gray's Inn. In his official capacity, helped to raise money for the King at the beginning of the Civil War; although he conformed as soon as the Royalists lost control of the Riding, receiving protections from Leven and Fairfax at the fall of York in 1644, his estate was sequestered and he was fined £138 (see *Composition Papers*, SP 23/3 and 23/77). His testimony in favour of Lord Fauconberg was received in 1653, but three years later, at Thirsk Quarter Sessions, Moore with five other local attorneys was presented as "not fitt to be allowed to practise according to ye Lord Protector's last Declaration." Justice of the Peace, Ripon. Pedigree in Clay, *Dugdale's Visitation of Yorkshire*, 3, p. 496.
1645	1660	HOLBORNE	Robert		1679	Parliamentarian; previously Clerk to Commission of Pious Uses. Nominee of Thomas Lord Fairfax, for whom he was steward of the Buckingham Manors of Kirbymoorside etc., c. 1652–60. Bought a prebendal house in York Close and other confiscated church properties, 1647. Only known residence in York, and buried there (see *Register of Holy Trinity, York*).
1660	1681	MOORE	William	1631	1681	Second son of James Moore, Clerk of the Peace 1635–45. Indicted at Quarter Sessions for refusing his clients a bill of costs: case removed into King's Bench on *certiorari*, 1655–56. Received special payment on Lord Treasurer's warrant for services re North Riding Hearth Money, 1665 (see *Cal. Treasury Books*, 1660–67, p. 671). On marriage in 1649 settled at his wife's home, Howe in Pickhill; but in 1674 bought the Manor of Oswaldkirk, wherein his father had a leasehold, and moved thither.
1681	1689	CHAMBER	Allan	c.1615	1690	From Westmorland; Barrister-at-law, Inner Temple (Bencher). Grandson and father of Recorders of Kendal; great-grandfather of Mr. Justice Chambre (1739–1823). Settled at Coxwold on marrying a daughter of James Moore, supra. Memorial tablet at Coxwold. Pedigree in Clay, *op. cit.*, 3, p. 415.
1689	1736	FRANKLAND	Henry	1668	1736	Third son of Sir William Frankland of Thirkleby, first Baronet; nephew of Thomas, Earl Fauconberg, the Lord Lieutenant. Admitted Sidney Sussex College, Cambridge, 1684; entered Lincoln's Inn, 1685; lived and was buried at Sowerby, near Thirsk.
1736	1762	PRESTON	James, the elder		1762	Of Malton; Steward and Bailiff of the Borough; Land Steward and political Agent of the Rockingham-Fitzwilliam interest; Captain of Militia and noted racehorse owner; left a stable of 21. While dying after an accident at York Races, begged the Marquess of Rockingham, the Lord Lieutenant, to continue his offices in his young son (see North Riding Militia papers; Turton, *North York Militia* (1907), and Rockingham *Correspondence*).
1762	1787	PRESTON	James, the younger	1745	1787	Son of James Preston, the elder; sworn Clerk of the Peace at age of sixteen. Of Malton; Bailiff of the Borough. Admitted Gray's Inn, 1765. Justice of the Peace 1769 and 1780; occasionally Clerk or Deputy Clerk of Assize at York c. 1772–3. Another devotee of the turf; popular; but left his affairs in disorder when killed by a fall from his horse after Beverley Races.

From	To	Surname	Forenames	Birth	Death	Biographical Notes
1787	1796	WAILES	William	1731	1796	Born at Husthwaite, where he was associated with Henry, Earl Fauconberg, the Lord Lieutenant; Attorney, at York. Subsequently settled in Northallerton as Deputy Registrar of Deeds, 1761–72; Deputy Steward of the Bishop of Durham's Manor of Northallerton, 1776–80.
1796	1816	STOCKDALE	Robert	c.1737	1816	Lived and died at Knaresborough, West Riding, which his family had represented in Parliament, being lords of Bilton until impoverished by South Sea Bubble; bought parts of Manor of Sinnington, 1796, which he used as an official and electoral qualification.
1816	1849	TOPHAM	Lupton	1778	1849	Of the Caldberg family; lived at Middleham; Attorney. First Clerk of the Peace to receive, from Michaelmas 1837, a salary of £600 p.a., in place of £20 p.a. "for keeping the Rolls" plus fees—then about £500 p.a. Deputy Sheriff, c. 1826–49.
1849	1889	YEOMAN	Thomas Lawrence	1819	1901	Of the Woodlands family of Whitby; Barrister-at-law, Inner Temple (called 1846). M.A. (Cantab). Hon. Major, 1st Volunteer Battalion, Yorkshire Regiment. Nephew to Thomas, 2nd Earl of Zetland, K.G., K.T., the Lord Lieutenant, who is said to have given him the Clerkship upon condition that he appointed Thomas Tudor Trevor (see below) "to look after things for him" as Deputy. Paid by fees till 1859; then by salary of £889 p.a., without allowance for clerks.

CLERKS OF THE PEACE AND OF THE COUNTY COUNCIL from 1889

From	To	Surname	Forenames	Birth	Death	Biographical Notes
1889	1898	YEOMAN	Thomas Lawrence	1819	1901	See above.
1898	1915	TREVOR	William Charles	1843	1919	*Elected to Society, May* 1875. Son of Charles Trevor, Controller of Legacy and Succession Duties, Somerset House, and of Olivia (née Lindo), cousin of Benjamin Disraeli; Harrow School; Solicitor (admitted 1866). Clerk to the Lieutenancy, 1897–1919; Clerk to the Justices, Langbaurgh East division, 1872–1903. Previously Deputy Clerk of the Peace. Commissioned in 1st North Riding Artillery Volunteer Corps, 1862. His elder brother was Sir (Charles) Cecil Trevor, C.B.; his sister Katherine married Ralph Disraeli; two of his uncles were Canon George Trevor, D.D., and Thomas Tudor Trevor, Deputy Clerk of the Peace (see below).
1916	1960	THORNLEY	Sir Hubert (Gordon)	1884		*Elected to Society, June* 1911. *Vice-Chairman,* 1944–47; *Chairman,* 1947–50. Solicitor (admitted 1906). O.B.E., 1920; Deputy Lieutenant, 1941; C.B.E., 1949; knighted, 1958. Clerk to the Lieutenancy 1919– ; Clerk of the Magistrates' Courts Committee; Registrar, North Riding Deeds Registry; Vice-Chairman, North Riding Territorial and Auxiliary Forces Association, 1941–46; Assistant Commissioner, Local Government Boundary Commission, 1947; County Alderman, 1960. Previously Deputy Clerk of the Peace and of the County Council of Worcestershire and assistant solicitor, Essex County Council.
1960		WOTHERSPOON	Robert Andrew	1912		*Elected to Society, July* 1951. Solicitor (admitted 1937). Clerk to the Magistrates' Courts Committee; Registrar, North Riding Deeds Registry. Previously assistant solicitor, Buckinghamshire, Wiltshire and Hertfordshire County Councils, and Deputy Clerk of the Peace and of the County Council of Derbyshire. Flying Officer, Royal Air Force, 1939–45 War.

DEPUTY CLERKS OF THE PEACE prior to 1889

From	To	Surname	Forenames	Birth	Death	Biographical Notes
c.1608		WOODD	William			Possibly a man so named who compounded, 1630–2, for not taking knighthood.
c.1653		YORKE	Ralph		?1631	Probably of Coxwold; indicted in 1653 for malpractice.

From	To	Surname	Forenames	Birth	Death	Biographical Notes
c.1673	c.1693	JACKSON	Robert			Perhaps the same "Mr. Jackson of Oulston" named in Quarter Sessions papers as late as 1708.
c.1681		HODGSON	Edward			Possibly Town Clerk of Ripon c. 1661–74.
c.1723	c.1737	CLOSE	John			Of Oulston in Coxwold; had charge of a part-time Deeds Registry at Thirsk and Northallerton, 1726, eight years prior to the North Riding Registry Act, 8 George II, c. 6.
1727		JACKSON	James			Of Furnival's Inn; Attorney of the Common Pleas.
c.1743		GOULTON	Christopher			Of Husthwaite; acted as Solicitor to Quarter Sessions.
c.1757		CONYERS	William			
c.1761	1765	SKEPPER	George	1732		Deputy Sheriff, 1762; *de facto* Clerk of the Peace in minority of James Preston the younger; Clerk of the Monk-Bridge to Scarborough Turnpike Trust.
1765	1785	WARTER	Robert			
1786	1790	BIRCH	Joseph			Of New Malton, where his private practice provided a second office for Quarter Sessions business. (William Wailes, the Clerk of the Peace, worked at Northallerton.)
1796		WAILES	William	1764		Son of his namesake, Clerk of the Peace, 1787–96; acted briefly as Deputy Clerk while his father was dying of dropsy, 1796. Clerk to the Justices of Allertonshire; Clerk to the Lieutenancy, c. 1796–8.
1792	1809	EWBANK	Thomas			Of New Malton. Thomas Paul "junior" (see below) was Ewbank's clerk in 1798, but Paul seems to have performed some of the acts of the Deputy before he clearly obtained the office in 1810. Possibly an elder Thomas Paul was co-deputy with Ewbank, 1797–1807.
1797	1818	PAUL	Thomas		c.1835	Of Malton and Oldstead Grange in Byland; Deputy Sheriff 1818–26. See note to Thomas Ewbank, above.
1819	c.1830	WAILES	William	1798	1844	Nephew of William Wailes, Deputy Clerk in 1796. No further appointment of a Deputy until 1837.
1837	1843	TOPHAM	Edward Charles	1813	1892	Third son of Lupton Topham, Clerk of the Peace, 1816–49; entered the Church, 1843, and as the Rev. E. C. Topham, M.A., became Rector of Hauxwell and Rural Dean.
1843	1849	TOPHAM	John	1812	1888	Second son of Lupton Topham, Clerk of the Peace, 1816–49; Attorney (admitted 1836). Clerk of Indictments, c. 1840; Clerk to the Visiting Justices from 1845; Deputy Sheriff, 1850.
1849	1872	TREVOR	Thomas Tudor	1816	1872	Uncle of William Charles Trevor, Clerk of the Peace and of the County Council, 1898–1915; M.A., Trinity College, Dublin. Of Guisborough; Attorney (admitted 1841). Clerk to the Justices, Langbaurgh East division.
1872	1889	TREVOR	William Charles	1843	1919	Subsequently Clerk of the Peace and of the County Council, see above.

DEPUTY CLERKS OF THE PEACE AND OF THE COUNTY COUNCIL from 1889

From	To	Surname	Forenames	Birth	Death	Biographical Notes
1889	1898	TREVOR	William Charles	1843	1919	See above; designated "Clerk Assistant" of the County Council.
1933	1954	PETERS	John Brown Meharry	1891		*Elected to Society, November 1934.* *Deputy Clerk of the County Council only.* Solicitor (admitted 1920). Previously assistant solicitor, Newcastle County Borough and Yorkshire (North Riding) County Councils.
1954		WHEELER	Malcolm Hele	1908		*Elected to Society, March 1954.* Solicitor (admitted 1936). B.A. (Oxon). Previously assistant solicitor, Huntingdonshire and Yorkshire (North Riding) County Councils.

YORKSHIRE, WEST RIDING

From	To	Surname	Forenames	Birth	Death	Biographical Notes
CLERKS OF THE PEACE from 1395						
1395	1399	LACY	Thomas			
1399	1411	SCOT	William			
1415	1426	TYLNEY	John			Feodary of Tickhill, 1411–12 (see Somerville, *Duchy of Lancaster*, I, p. 531); executor of Sir Robert Waterton of Methley.
1443	1451	DYNELEY	Henry			
1517	1520	MANSFIELD	William			
1526	1527	BRADFORD	Walter			
1530	1551	BROWNE	Henry			
1552	1555	GREEN	John			
1556	1587	BROWN	Stephen			
1589	1593	TINDALL	George			
1594	1615	CARTWRIGHT	William			
c.1632		RADCLIFFE	Charles			
1637	1646	BENSON	Robert		1676	Deposed by Parliamentarians; subsequently Clerk of Assize, Northern Circuit, and Deputy Lord Treasurer; his son was Chancellor of the Exchequer and Ambassador to Spain, created Lord Bingley in 1718.
1647	1648	HARRYSON	William			Captain in Parliamentary Army, 1649.
1648		THOMSON	Thomas			Temporary appointment by the Justices only.
c.1649	1651	WHARTON	William			
1655	1658	RICHARDS	Alexander			
1661	1666	CLAPHAM	Richard			Uncle or brother of Sir Christopher Clapham, Lord of the Manor of Wakefield.
1667	1681	PEABLES	John	1630	1684	Grandson of Chaplain to King Charles I; Gentleman of the Privy Chamber; Lord of the Manor of Dewsbury Rectory; known as "the Devil of Dewsbury" on account of persecution of non-conformists.
1681	1688	SIMPSON	William			
1689	1717	SHELTON	Theophilus		1717	Related by marriage to Lord Fairfax, Parliamentary General; appointed "Treasurer of the Riding", 1702; first Registrar, West Riding Deeds Registry, 1704.
1717	1733	WICKHAM	William	1663	1733	Of Ulleskelf; resided in London.
1733	1759	PULLEYN	Thomas	1701	1759	Clerk to the Lieutenancy, 1757.
1760	1765	PLACE	Thomas		1765	Clerk to the Lieutenancy.
1765	1772	CROWLE	William		1772	Clerk to the Lieutenancy.
1773	1789	FENTON	Richard	1708	1789	Clerk to the Lieutenancy; related to Robert Boyle, the scientist.
1789	1827	WYBERGH	Thomas		1827	Clerk to the Lieutenancy.
1827	1865	ELSLEY	Charles Heneage		1865	*Elected to Society, May* 1828. Clerk to the Lieutenancy until 1858 or later.
1865	1866	DIXON	Benjamin			*Elected to Society, April* 1853. Temporary appointment only; previously and subsequently Deputy Clerk of the Peace.

YORKSHIRE, WEST RIDING (*Continued*)

From	To	Surname	Forenames	Birth	Death	Biographical Notes
1866	1884	HAMMERTON	John		1884	Of family long established at Hellifield Peel.
1884	1889	DARWIN	Francis Alvey Rhodes	1852	1937	*Elected to Society, June 1885.* Son of Francis Darwin, Chairman of Quarter Sessions, of Creskeld Hall, Pool-in-Wharfedale. Barrister-at-law, Inner Temple (called 1877).

CLERKS OF THE PEACE AND OF THE COUNTY COUNCIL from 1889

From	To	Surname	Forenames	Birth	Death	Biographical Notes
1889	1929	DARWIN	Francis Alvey Rhodes	1852	1937	See above.
1929	1943	McGRATH	Sir (Joseph) Charles	1871	1951	*Elected to Society, October 1923.* *Vice-Chairman, 1939–43.* Solicitor (admitted 1901). Hon. LL.D; knighted 1933. Previously Deputy Clerk of the Peace and of the County Council.
1943		KENYON	Bernard	1904		*Elected to Society, July 1941.* Solicitor (admitted 1928). B.A. (Cantab). Clerk to the Lieutenancy; Secretary to the Advisory Committee; Clerk of the Magistrates' Courts Committee; Registrar, West Riding Deeds Registry. Previously Deputy Clerk of the Peace and of the County Council.

DEPUTY CLERKS OF THE PEACE prior to 1889

From	To	Surname	Forenames	Birth	Death	Biographical Notes
c.1661	c.1681	HOPKINSON	John	1611	1682	Of Lofthouse; celebrated genealogist.
1729	1734	COWPER	Richard			
1736		JOHNSON	Alan			
1772		SAMBOURNE	Thomas			Of New Malton.
1793		WELLS	John			Of Wakefield.
1794		SKELTON	John			Of Leeds.
1821		FOLJAMBE	Thomas			Of Wakefield; Solicitor.
1826	1865	DIXON	Benjamin			Subsequently Clerk of the Peace, see above.
1864		DIXON	John Henry			Jointly with Benjamin Dixon.
1866		DIXON	Benjamin			Re-appointed after temporary service as Clerk of the Peace.
1885	1889	DIXON	William Vibart	1850	1930	*Elected to Society, June 1885.* Son of Benjamin Dixon, Clerk of the Peace, 1865–66; Solicitor (admitted 1873).

DEPUTY CLERKS OF THE PEACE AND OF THE COUNTY COUNCIL from 1889

From	To	Surname	Forenames	Birth	Death	Biographical Notes
1889	1923	DIXON	William Vibart	1850	1930	See above. O.B.E., 1918; K.B.E., 1924.
1923	1929	McGRATH	Joseph Charles	1871	1951	Subsequently Clerk of the Peace and of the County Council, see above.
1930	1940	JONES	Reginald Cecil	1877	1940	
1941	1943	KENYON	Bernard	1904		Subsequently Clerk of the Peace and of the County Council, see above.
1951		JACKMAN	Trevor Bromley	1906		*Elected to Society, May 1951.* *Deputy Clerk of the Peace only.* Solicitor (admitted 1928). Lieutenant Colonel, 1939–45 War; M.B.E. (Mil.) 1943; O.B.E. (Mil.) 1945; Despatches; T.D., 1950; Officer of American Legion of Merit, 1945.
1951		McVICAR	Sidney James	1909		*Elected to Society, May 1951.* *Deputy Clerk of the County Council only.* Solicitor (admitted 1931). O.B.E., 1946.

ADDENDA

The following changes have taken place since the 31st December, 1960:

County	Surname	Forenames	Biographical Notes
Anglesey	JONES	William	See page 51. Retired 1961.
,,	DAVIES	Idris	See page 51. Appointed Clerk of the Peace and of the County Council, Secretary to the Advisory Committee and Clerk of the Magistrates' Courts Committee.
,,	WILLIAMS	Robert Thomas David	*Elected to Society, December* 1960. Appointed Deputy Clerk of the Peace and of the County Council. Solicitor (admitted 1949). B.A. (Wales), LL.B. (London). Previously assistant solicitor, Wolverhampton County Borough and Ilford Borough Councils. Flight Lieutenant, Royal Air Force, 1939–45 War. (Born 1920).
Breconshire	JOLLY	Albert	See page 57. Died 1961.
Denbighshire	JONES	Sir William	See page 74. Died 1961.
,,	ROWLANDS	William John	See page 74. Retired 1961.
,,	JONES	David Evan Alun	*Elected to Society, July* 1961. Appointed Deputy Clerk of the Peace and of the County Council. Solicitor (admitted 1952). LL.B. (Wales). Previously assistant solicitor, City of Exeter, Ilford Borough and Southampton County Borough Councils, and Berkshire and Surrey County Councils. Flight Lieutenant, Royal Air Force, 1939–45 War. (Born 1925).
Dorset	BRUTTON	Charles Phipps	See page 81. Retired 1961.
,,	TEMPLEMAN	Arthur Cowley	See page 81. Appointed Clerk of the Peace and of the County Council, Clerk to the Lieutenancy, Secretary to the Advisory Committee and Clerk of the Magistrates' Courts Committee.
,,	SIMMONS	John	*Elected to Society, March* 1961. Appointed Deputy Clerk of the Peace and of the County Council. Solicitor (admitted 1948). M.A., LL.B. (Cantab). Previously assistant solicitor, Loughborough Borough, Bristol County Borough and Devon County Councils. Captain, Royal Signals, 1939–45 War. (Born 1922).
Durham	HOPE	James Kenneth	See page 83. Retired 1961.
,,	BROCKBANK	James Tyrrell	See page 144. Appointed Clerk of the Peace and of the County Council of Durham, Secretary to the Advisory Committee, Clerk of the Magistrates' Courts Committee and Clerk of the Durham Police Authority.
Hampshire	WHEATLEY	George Andrew	See page 96. *Appointed Honorary Secretary of Society,* 1961.
Isle of Ely	OLLARD	John William Arthur	See page 107. Died 1961.
Merioneth	OWEN	Hugh John	See page 126. Died 1961.
Nottinghamshire	CUST	Edwin	*Elected to Society, July* 1961. Appointed Deputy Clerk of the Peace and of the County Council. Solicitor (admitted 1950). M.A. (Cantab). Previously assistant solicitor, St. Helens, Gloucester and Southport County Borough Councils, and Berkshire and Nottinghamshire County Councils. Sub-Lieutenant, Fleet Air Arm, 1939–45 War. (Born 1923).
Salop	GODBER	Geoffrey Chapman	See page 153. *Appointed Chairman of Society,* 1961 *and relinquished offices of Vice-Chairman and Honorary Secretary.* C.B.E., 1961.
,,	JONES	William Neville Pritchard	*Elected to Society, May* 1961. Appointed Second Deputy Clerk of the County Council. Son of William Jones, Clerk of the Peace and of the County Council of Anglesey, 1940–61; Solicitor (admitted 1950). M.A. (Cantab). Previously assistant solicitor, Cumberland, Wiltshire and Salop County Councils. Captain, Royal Welch Fusiliers, 1939–45 War. (Born 1923).
West Sussex	HAYWARD	Tom Christopher	See page 171. *Relinquished office of Chairman of Society,* 1961.
Yorkshire, North Riding	WHEELER	Malcolm Hele	See page 189. Died 1961.
,,	BECKETT	Ronald Arthur	*Elected to Society, May* 1961. Appointed Deputy Clerk of the Peace and of the County Council. Solicitor (admitted 1949). LL.B. (Liverpool). Previously assistant solicitor, Poole Borough and Yorkshire (North Riding) County Councils. Captain, Royal Artillery, 1939–45 War. (Born 1920).
Yorkshire, West Riding	KENYON	Bernard	See page 191. *Appointed Vice-Chairman of Society,* 1961.

PART II

THE SOCIETY OF CLERKS OF THE PEACE OF COUNTIES AND OF CLERKS OF COUNTY COUNCILS

A RETROSPECT
OF THE ACTIVITIES OF THE SOCIETY
FROM 1810 TO 1960

1810   First recorded Meeting of Clerks of the Peace (27th March) held at Gray's Inn Coffee House – Clerks of the Peace for Essex, Salop, Surrey and Sussex present, also representatives from Cheshire, Warwickshire and Worcestershire; Provisions of Parliamentary Elections Act, 1780 (20 George III cap. 17) considered – proposed application to Parliament for modification of duties and penalties devolving on Clerks of the Peace decided upon, but abandoned after two adjourned meetings for lack of support from Clerks of the Peace in general; Following resolutions passed at meeting held on 13th November:—

> *"RESOLVED that it is the Opinion of this Meeting that it would be mutually beneficial to Clerks of the Peace in the Execution of their Office by a Communication of the Practice of their respective Counties and by the Opportunity afforded of considering any Bills in their progress thro' Parliament which are likely to affect the Interest of Clerks of the Peace if a Meeting of the Clerks of the Peace were held in London once a year.*

> *"RESOLVED that the Clerks of the Peace now present will Assemble Annually at the Gray's Inn Coffee House in Holborn on the second Tuesday after the Morrow of All Souls being the day next after the Day on which the Estreats are required to be delivered into the Exchequer when it is Apprehended many Clerks of the Peace come to Town and that the Clerks of the Peace of every County in England and Wales be invited to join the Meeting".*

1811   Annual Meeting at Gray's Inn Coffee House, 12th November; £2 2s. 0d. membership fee fixed; All Clerks of the Peace for the Counties considered eligible as members – Deputy Clerks to be admitted by ballot; Clerk of the Peace for Surrey (C. J. Lawson) appointed Honorary Treasurer; Absentees from meetings to pay 7s. 0d. to the general fund.

1812   No business recorded.

1813   Procedure for admission of Deputy Clerks (by ballot) agreed upon; An "Annual Dinner" to be provided at a cost of 10s. 6d. each member.

1814   Clerk of the Peace for Kent (J. F. Claridge) appointed Honorary Secretary; Minute Book to be kept; Committee of Clerks of the Peace (Home Counties) appointed – "to take care of the interests of the Society in regard to any Bills in Parliament"; Special meetings of Society to be held when necessary.

1815   Question about fees Clerks of the Peace might claim in criminal cases raised and considered.

1816   Rules of Society formulated and agreed – to be printed and sent to each member.

1817   Membership fees revised to £3 3s. 0d. on admission and thereafter £1 1s. 0d. *per annum;* Fine for absence from meetings reduced to 5s. 0d.

1818   No business recorded.

1819   Annual Dinner in future to be at 6 p.m., preceding Annual Meeting for business at 8 o'clock.

1820   The Committee appointed to consider Parliamentary Bills authorised to expend up to £10 10s. 0d. in the carrying out of their functions; Payment of arrears of membership subscriptions called for.

1821   No business recorded.

1822   Clerk of the Peace for Buckinghamshire (T. Tindal) appointed Honorary Secretary in succession to J. F. Claridge, deceased; Clerks of the Peace (Home Counties) Committee to consider recent legislation in regard to fees to be taken by Clerks of the Peace.

1823   Tables of fees, as adopted or proposed for several Counties, to be considered – members' observations on this matter invited; Investment of £200 of Society's funds decided upon; Meetings now to be held twice yearly; Charge for Annual Dinner reduced to 7s. 6d.

1824   Arrangements to be made by Honorary Treasurer for obtaining copies of Parliamentary Bills affecting Clerks of the Peace and for their circulation to members.

1825   Rules of Society to be reprinted and circulated to members and to those Clerks of the Peace who were not members; For non-attendance at Annual Meeting without excuse, Chairman (R. Sherrard) fined a " half dozen bottles of Claret".

1826   Place of meeting changed to Albion Tavern, Aldersgate Street; Opinion of Counsel to be taken upon liability of defendant's Attorney (in misdemeanour at Quarter Sessions) to pay fees due to Clerk of the Peace.

1827   Clerks of the Peace (Fees) Act (57 George III cap. 91) considered – procedure thereunder for prescribing table of fees questioned – Opinion of Counsel to be taken on this; A uniform table of fees favoured; Home Counties designated as Essex, Kent, Surrey, Sussex, Hertfordshire, Buckinghamshire and Cambridgeshire; Three members called upon to pay a total of £35 2s. 0d. arrears of subscription and fines for absence.

1828   Parliamentary Bills (Alehouses Licensing and Offences against the Person) considered – Clerks of the Peace (Home Counties) Committee to watch progress of these Bills; The Isle of Ely considered to come within the description of a County so as to entitle Clerk of the Peace for that Liberty to be a member; Clerk of the Peace for City of Westminster regarded as ineligible for membership.

1829   Traverse fee – payment demanded by Clerk of the Peace for Wiltshire before a trial allowed to proceed – derogatory reference to that Clerk of the Peace in particular and to all Clerks of the Peace in general in the "*Morning Chronicle*" – Society decided that the Clerk of the Peace for Wiltshire not having thought proper to answer the charge alleged against him, and so much time having elapsed since the attack was made in the paper, it was "not expedient to take notice of the matter"; Clerks of the Peace for the Divisions of Lincolnshire considered eligible for membership of Society.

1830   Procedure on returns of Clerks' bills and fees to Committee of the House of Commons discussed and decisions about the making of the returns made – Clerks of the Peace (Home Counties) Committee empowered to take steps to safeguard rights and interests of Clerks of the Peace in the matter.

1831   Clerk of the Peace for City of London elected (by ballot) to membership "notwithstanding the Rules of the Society"; Attention of Home Counties Committee directed "to obtaining a due remuneration for the Clerks of the Peace for the trouble which may be imposed upon them in any further Reform Bill".

1832   Clerk of the Peace for City of London made a member of the Committee of Home Counties.

1833   Poor Law Removal Act (3 & 4 William IV cap. 40) considered and resolutions passed; Rules and list of members to be reprinted.

1834   Annual Meeting to be held in May; Home Counties Committee empowered to appoint Agent – Agent to report all orders of the Houses of Parliament and all Bills in Parliament relating to the office of Clerk of the Peace; Time of meeting changed to 5 p.m., dinner at 7 p.m., no business relating to Society to be transacted after dinner.

1835   Two meetings of Home Counties Committee at Nichols Hotel to appoint Agent – Mr. St. George Burke of Counsel appointed; Registration of Voters Bill discussed – Committee of five set up to press for amendments in Bill to secure reasonable remuneration; "Dinner including everything but wine" to cost 10s. 0d.; C. J. Lawson resigned office of Honorary Treasurer, C. P. Allen (Deputy Clerk of the Peace for Middlesex) appointed.

RETROSPECT

1836   Registration of Voters Bill again discussed – two members to wait on Attorney-General with proposed amendments.

1837   Mr. St. George Burke's services discontinued; Deputy Clerk of the Peace for Middlesex resigned having been appointed County Treasurer for Middlesex but continued in his office of Honorary Treasurer of Society as an honorary member.

1838   Clerk of the Peace for Buckinghamshire (T. Tindal) resigned and replaced as Honorary Secretary by his son, A. Tindal, newly appointed as Clerk of the Peace for Buckinghamshire; Clerk of the Peace for the West Riding of Yorkshire resigned in consequence of the distance of his residence from London.

1839   Two meetings – no business recorded.

1840   Lord John Russell's Bill for registration of voters at Parliamentary elections discussed – copies to be obtained and sent to all members – Home Counties Committee asked to inspect Bill.

1841   Home Counties Committee met at Law Institution, Chancery Lane – Registration Bill discussed – Clerks of the Peace asked to approach *Custodes Rotulorum* to get alterations made.

1842   Minutes of meeting of Home Counties Committee approved.

1843   Arrangements to be made "to move place of meeting to some House further to the West of London" – three members (A. Tindal, C. G. Parker and J. M. Davenport) to agree on convenient meeting place.

1844   Meeting place changed to Freemasons' Tavern, Great Queen Street; Bill to regulate appointment and payment of Clerks of the Peace discussed – Home Counties Committee to prepare statement of objections – "voluminous observations" received on the Bill from members.

1845   Several meetings of Home Counties Committee on Clerks of the Peace Bill – Parliamentary Agents consulted as to mode of presenting objections – personal interview by three members with Home Secretary; Clerks of the Peace outside Society asked to pay £2 2s. 0d. each to Society for obtaining alterations to the Bill.

1846   Rules and List of Clerks of the Peace to be reprinted and circulated among members.

1847   Meeting place changed to Law Club, Chancery Lane; Parliamentary votes to be sent to Honorary Secretary.

1848   Voluntary fine of £1 3s. 0d. for non-attendance sent by Clerk of the Peace for Northumberland (W. Dickson); New trustees for Society appointed – trustees to audit Treasurer's accounts, "which have not been audited for many years".

1849   Summary Jurisdiction Act (11 & 12 Victoria, cap. 43) discussed at Special Meeting; Committee of eight set up to frame table of fees for Clerks of the Peace – two printed copies of revised table sent to Secretary of State with covering letter.

1850   Special Meeting called to consider Bill to set up County Financial Boards – decided not "to prosecute any measures on County Financial Boards Bill as it was under consideration by Select Committee"; C. Pemberton made honorary member on retirement as Clerk of the Peace for Cambridgeshire after 57 years in office.

1851   County Rates and Expenditure Bill discussed – communication to be sent to Secretary of State on right of appeal to him on fixing salaries; Bill on Registration of Assurances considered; Criminal Justice Administration Act (14 & 15 Victoria, cap. 55) – Society proposed salary be paid to include all fees received from County Rate.

1852   Fine ruling altered – members to pay only after failure to give notice of non-attendance.

1853   County Financial Boards Bill discussed – Petition on Bill to be presented to House of Commons asking that Clerks of the Peace should *ex officio* become Clerks of the Boards or alternatively should receive compensation; Case prepared and submitted to Counsel for decision on matters arising from *R. v. The Governors and Guardians of Kingston-upon-Hull*, as to the expenses allowable to Clerks of the Peace in relation to duties in respect of registration of Parliamentary voters.

1854   *R. v. The Governors and Guardians of Kingston-upon-Hull* again considered – deputation waited on Under Secretary of State and discussed case – he recommended that memorial on the subject be sent to Secretary of State for Home Affairs; Memorial subsequently sent to Lord Palmerston with the names of forty Clerks of the Peace appended.

1855 Criminal Justice Bill discussed – Society thanked Committee appointed to examine Bill for their efforts to obtain a compensation clause for loss of emoluments by Clerks of the Peace under the Bill – Committee also asked to press for a fixed salary.

1856 Two meetings held – seven and eight members present respectively; in each case "no business was transacted and the Meeting adjourned to dinner".

1857 November meetings abandoned "in consequence of the paucity of Members who lately attended the half-yearly meetings"; Honorary Secretary to send out notices to all members and Clerks of the Peace who were not members pointing out advantages of Society, together with a copy of the Rules.

1858 Fourteen attended meeting on 12th May – "there being no business to transact at this Meeting the Members present adjourned to dinner".

1859 Honorary Secretary (A. Tindal) named as member of Commission to inquire into cost of prosecutions and other matters; Committee of five appointed to prepare uniform table of fees to be paid to Clerks of the Peace; Clerk of the Peace for Rutland admitted without entrance subscription owing to limited nature of the emoluments of his office.

1860 Committee for general and financial purposes appointed – to audit Honorary Treasurer's accounts – to settle sum out of funds sufficient to indemnify Honorary Secretary for acting as Commissioner as aforesaid; Clerk of the Peace for Wiltshire (J. Swayne) signified his desire to cease to be a member in consequence of his advanced age of 83 years.

1861 Date of future meetings to be fixed by General Purposes Committee.

1862 Members to pay 10s. 0d. towards cost of Annual Dinner – balance to be defrayed out of funds; As far as practicable Annual Meetings to be held on the first Tuesday in June.

1863 No business transacted other than election of a member.

1864 County Voters Registration Bill considered – deputation waited on Mr. Dodson, the Member of Parliament introducing the Bill – they pressed for adoption of amending clauses to provide proper remuneration for Clerks of the Peace.

1865 Clerk of the Peace for Northamptonshire (H. P. Markham) gave notice at meeting held on 13th June, that at the next meeting he would move "that each member be at liberty to introduce one friend at the Annual Dinner of the Society".

1866 Society expunged Rule for the payment of a fine of 5s. 0d. by each member of Society absent from the Annual Meeting.

1867 Valuation of Property Bill examined – Meeting agreed with clauses whereby Clerks of the Peace became *ex officio* Clerks of the proposed County Valuation Boards.

1868 Twenty attended annual meeting; Registration of Voters Bill discussed – new scheme examined.

1869 Fifteen attended meeting – no business recorded other than election of members.

1870 No business recorded.

1871 Local Stamp Act, 1869, discussed; Grant of £50 made to three unmarried daughters of the late Clerk of the Peace for Kent (H. A. Wildes), they being unprovided for; Honorary Treasurership – C. P. Allen resigned owing to failing health – Deputy Clerk of the Peace for Oxfordshire (T. M. Davenport) appointed.

1872 The Clerks of the Peace and the Justices' Clerks' Salaries and Fees Bill considered – Executive Committee asked to wait on Home Secretary to represent the views of the Clerks of the Peace.

1873 Annual Meeting to be fixed earlier in the year, as near as possible to re-assembly of Parliament after the Easter Recess; Gratuity of £5 5s. 0d. granted to Honorary Secretary's clerk for his services; Juries Bill considered.

1874 Registration of Voters Act, 1868, discussed; Injury to County bridges "by locomotive engines and other ponderous machines" considered; Question of fees on deposit of Parliamentary plans of railways and other undertakings raised; Adulteration of Food and Drugs Act, 1872 – Public Analysts discussed – minute reads "the subject was considered a dead letter".

RETROSPECT

1875 Treasury Minute on the subject of examination, prior to repayment, of the account of costs incurred by Counties in prosecutions at Assizes and Sessions opposed – Executive Committee to protest to Secretary of State; Local Authorities' Loans Bill subjected to severe criticism by meeting as regards proposal to appoint auditors – "Is it to be expected that Counties and Boroughs will give up their independence, and put themselves under the Local Government Board, without a struggle?"

1876 Highway Bill, Valuation Bill and Prisons Bill discussed but no resolutions passed.

1877 Public Record Office Act, 1877, discussed – especially "that part of it by which the County Records would be liable to be removed to the Record Office in the Rolls" – three members, T. M. Davenport, A. Tindal and H. P. Markham to draw up Bill having for its object the removal from the Record Office and elsewhere of all Inclosure Awards and their return to County muniment rooms.

1878 Prisons Act, 1877, discussed – no action taken – matter left to Executive Committee; Executive Committee reported that they had drawn up Bill for transfer from the Record Office to the Clerks of the Peace of all Inclosure Awards now in that Office – Earl Spencer had taken charge of the Bill.

1879 The Clerks of the Peace of Boroughs proposed for membership – proposal negatived; Highways Act discussed – meeting decided that the extra work imposed by the Act entitled Clerks of the Peace to make professional charges; Clerks of the Peace to send in future to Honorary Secretary copies of every bye law and other printed County papers when issued – the Secretary to circulate them to other Counties.

1880 Highways and Locomotives (Amendment) Act, 1878, considered – Honorary Secretary asked to obtain returns from all Clerks on various aspects of the Act including the "class of persons appointed to survey Main Roads", and their remuneration.

1881 Death of A. Tindal, Honorary Secretary since 1838, reported to meeting – Clerk of the Peace for Hertfordshire and Middlesex (R. Nicholson) appointed; Question of the power of a Clerk of the Peace to appoint a deputy without the consent of the *Custos Rotulorum* considered – meeting decided it undesirable not to obtain his concurrence.

1882 Motion that Society should possess an album of photographs of past and present members defeated; Death of J. M. Davenport, "for upwards of fifty years Clerk of the Peace for Oxfordshire"; Quarter Sessions Procedure (Amendments) Bill considered but no action taken; R. Nicholson appointed Chairman of Society, and subsequently re-appointed annually until 1910.

1883 Aspects of Contagious Diseases (Animals) Act, 1878, considered; Question of revising and raising assessments under County Rate Basis Act, 1842, discussed; Home Office returns – meeting considered making representations to Home Secretary about onerous duties of Clerks in making returns – decided not to press the matter.

1884 Corrupt and Illegal Practices Prevention Act, 1883, referred to Executive Committee for examination; Legal power of County to take over a bridge repairable either *ratione tenurae* or by prescription discussed – no formal resolution made; Following question answered in the negative:—"If the Clerk of the Peace has a sufficient Deputy, can the Justices raise any objections or interfere with the Clerk of the Peace on account of his being unable from ill health to discharge his duties in person or of his non-residence in the County, there being no other cause for complaint against him?"

1885 Registration Act, 1885 – complimentary fee of £10 10s. 0d. "paid to Mr. Nicholson's clerk for his efficient services" in connection with the Act; Police Superannuation Fund considered but no action taken; Register of voters – members asked to make returns as to remuneration of the Clerk of the Peace.

1886 Revised Rules adopted – Executive Committee to be appointed annually; Municipal Corporations Act, 1883 – question of weekly rate for maintenance of lunatics considered – case on question to be submitted to Counsel; Resolution passed by meeting congratulating Sir Richard Wyatt and Sir Richard Nicholson on their having received the honour of knighthood.

1887 Question of "extraordinary charges" payable out of Police Rate under the County Police Act considered; Resolution on question as to how costs incurred by Justices, or by the Police in relation to proceedings brought against them, should be met, to be brought to notice of Society of Chairmen of Quarter Sessions; Responsibility and power of Clerks of the Peace as to accommodation of prisoners awaiting trial discussed; Poem entitled "A Lay from Cornwall for the Jubilee of Queen Victoria" by Clerk of the Peace for Cornwall (H. S. Stokes) submitted to meeting.

1888   Three meetings held; Local Government (England and Wales) Bill discussed, particularly as it affected Clerks of the Peace, and alterations suggested – Committee of Society to see if alterations could be implemented; Sir Richard Nicholson presented with three silver bowls by the Society in appreciation of services rendered especially in connection with the Local Government Act, 1888.

1889   Meeting considered action to be taken to hasten registration proceedings to allow more time for printing the register of Parliamentary voters – resolution sent to Local Government Board; Scale of costs for Returning Officers discussed; Sections of the Local Government Act, 1888, considered.

1890   Attention of meeting called to the Superannuation (Officers of County Councils) Bill; County Registers of Electors – meeting pressed for extension of time for preparation; Local Government Act, 1888, section 119(2) discussed – meeting of opinion that Clerks of the Peace in office on 1st April 1889 could not be required, against their will, to undertake the duties of County Accountant.

1891   Rules of Society altered – Clerks and Deputy Clerks to be proposed and seconded in writing before meeting, ballot to be held at meeting, two black balls to exclude candidate; Repairs to footpaths by the side of main roads discussed – meeting told that Bill would be introduced "to define what County Councils have to pay for footpaths".

1892   Question of the inconvenience and delay arising from the system of audit of County Council accounts discussed – resolution passed that attention of President of the Local Government Board should be drawn to the inconvenience caused; Small Agricultural Holdings Bill referred to Executive Committee.

1893   Registration of Electors (Amendment) Bill – report received from Executive Committee – many resolutions passed by meeting; Inquiry on amounts to be paid for travelling expenses after Second Class fares had been abolished.

1894   Parochial Electors (Registration Acceleration) Bill discussed – meeting doubted if its provisions could be carried out; Local Government Act, 1894 – correspondence and papers read to meeting; Fees on appointment of Justices of the Peace – Society could not recommend any particular fee.

1895   Registration Order, 1895, considered; Extra remuneration to Clerks of County Councils for bringing the Local Government Act, 1894, into operation – Society decided it was a matter for the Standing Joint Committees; Practice at opening of Quarter Sessions – it appeared that in fourteen Counties the Proclamation against Vice was read; County records – on a question whether County records could be placed in the hands of a neighbouring authority for safe custody, Society decided that the Lord Lieutenant, as *Custos Rotulorum*, had no right to part with the custody of the records; Justices of the Peace Bill considered – members of Society to ask Members of Parliament for the Counties to move the striking out of clause 4, which placed Clerks of the Peace under a penalty for failing to keep record of Justices attending Quarter Sessions.

1896   Decided "that it is desirable that a circular should be issued for the information of Members of the Society" which "should contain information on points of law and practice of interest to Members"; Education Bill examined and referred to Executive Committee; Signatures of Clerks of the Peace – Society informed that in nine counties Clerk signed with surname only, and in eight counties with Christian and surname; Public Auditors – Society decided that they had no control over County Council expenditure unless it was contrary to law and they could not object to reasonableness of any item which County Councils thought proper to incur.

1897   First issue of Periodical Circular – Clerk of the Peace for Worcestershire (S. Thornely) appointed Editor; Local Government (County Council Clerks) Bill – report by Executive Committee received and adopted; Prevention of Cruelty to Children Act, 1894 – cost of prosecutions considered.

1898   Appointment and payment of staffs in offices of Clerks of the Peace and Clerks of County Councils considered – Society informed some staffs appointed and paid by Councils, others appointed and paid by Clerks; County bridges – meeting of opinion that there was no legal obligation to alter County bridges to make them strong enough to carry traction engines.

1899   Resolution of regret on death of F. C. Hulton, Clerk of the Peace for Lancashire and one of the founders of the County Councils Association; Local Authorities' Servants' Superannuation Bill considered – referred to Executive Committee; Meeting of opinion that the County Council alone could appoint a County Solicitor but that, if they so desired, the Standing Joint Committee could appoint their own Solicitor; Annual Dinner 1900 – members asked whether dinner should be at Greenwich, Richmond or London.

RETROSPECT

1900   Local Authorities' Officers' Superannuation Bill discussed – proposed that the rights of Clerks of the Peace and of County Councils should be saved; Treasurers' vouchers and Jury Lists – questions asked as to how long they should be kept – the general practice appeared to be indefinitely; Deposit of light railway plans – fees charged considered – it was usual to obtain a fee when possible; Incorrigible rogues – inquiry made as to "what number of strokes can a Court order in the case of whipping being given and with what instrument are the strokes to be inflicted".

1901   Bills promoted by Municipal Corporations – attention of Society drawn to clauses giving powers of visiting and other powers outside area of Borough as to milk supply and infectious diseases; Fees allowed to Counsel in criminal cases at Quarter Sessions considered – Honorary Secretary stated return setting out fees had been issued a few years before; Justices' Property Qualification Oath considered.

1902   Stamp duties on main road maintenance contracts discussed – agreement drawn up by Clerk of the Peace for Durham inserted in Minutes; Taxation Order, 1901, considered – no action taken; Register of Electors – questions asked; Attention of meeting called to question of appointment of a Deputy by a Franchise Coroner; Summary Jurisdiction Act, 1879, section 17 – disposal of fines discussed.

1903   Education Act, 1902 – provisions considered and opinions given – memorandum forwarded to Board of Education and copy of Board's reply submitted; Poor Prisoners' Defence Bill considered; Four members named to give evidence before Departmental Committee on Main Roads; Local Government Act, 1894, sections 16(1) and 26(4) examined; Question of the fine payable by County Councillors on resigning discussed; Inclosure Awards – attention of meeting drawn to circular letter from Secretary of the Board of Agriculture asking for a return of all Inclosure Awards deposited or enrolled with Clerks of the Peace.

1904   Death of H. P. Markham, Clerk of the Peace for Northamptonshire and a member of Society for fifty-eight years; Motor Car Act, 1903 – Society of the opinion that all driving licences taken out by a person after conviction should be endorsed, without limit as to time; Question of appointment of the Crier of the Court of Quarter Sessions considered – the appointment appeared to vary from County to County; Licensing Act, 1904, considered – recommendations sent to Home Secretary relating to various details of the Act; Proposal put forward, but not proceeded with, that Society should meet every month.

1905   Decided that all members should be elected with voting papers – a cross to be treated as a black ball; County Councils Association – arrangements proposed to prevent overlapping of work – suggestion that Secretary of Association should attend meetings of Society not approved; Election of County Aldermen – discussion as to whether the reading out of voting papers should include names of voters; Attention of meeting called to position of Clerks of the Peace appointed since the Local Government Act, 1888.

1906   Clerks of the Peace and County Councils Bill discussed – Society disapproved of proposal to divide the offices; Education Bill discussed – resolutions passed and copies sent to President of the Board of Education; Points under the Licensing Act, 1904, discussed; Highway Act, 1835 – definition of Parish discussed; Riot (Damages) Act, 1886, section 3(2) discussed.

1907   Workmen's Compensation Act, 1906 – various aspects discussed; Criminal Appeal Act, 1907, discussed with regard to shorthand notes; Probation of Offenders Act, 1907, and Smallholdings and Allotments Act, 1907, considered; F. Merrifield appointed first Vice-Chairman of the Society.

1908   Attention of meeting called to the lack of support given to the Periodical Circular; Home Office ruling submitted that Clerks of the Peace and of County Councils must provide and pay the staff they require; Report with respect to the collection of Local Taxation Licence Duties submitted; Criminal Appeal Act, 1907 – arrangements for engaging shorthand writers discussed; Date and hour of meeting – resolved that Executive Committee try and arrange Annual Meeting on the day before a meeting of Executive Council of County Councils Association.

1909   Local Government Act, 1888, section 54 – discussion on methods of opposition to confirmation of Provisional Orders for extension of boundaries of County Boroughs; Questions asked about vendors' costs of conveying land under the Education Act, 1902, and the Smallholding and Allotments Act, 1908; Children Act, 1908 – various sections considered; Quarter Sessions subpoenas – discussion as to whether to issue subpoenas in the name of the *Custos Rotulorum*, the King, or the Chairman of Quarter Sessions.

1910   Centenary Dinner held at Princes' Restaurant, Piccadilly on 1st June; Resignation of Sir Richard Nicholson as Chairman and Honorary Secretary – "now . . . that all hope of regaining any portion of my sight is gone" – succeeded as Chairman by F. Merrifield – appointment of Honorary Secretary deferred; C. E. Longmore appointed Vice-Chairman; Conveyance of land by County Councils – discussion on practice of conveying as beneficial owner, and of undertaking safe custody of retained deeds; Children's Act, 1908 – provision of places of detention discussed; Correspondence on the question of stamps on contracts for repair of main roads considered; Attention of meeting drawn to circular issued by Law Society on the subject of alleged improper practice of Clerks of the Peace at Quarter Sessions.

1911   C. E. Longmore appointed Honorary Secretary; Clerks of the Peace and County Councils Bill discussed, and resolutions passed; Opinion of Mr. W. O. Danckwerts submitted as to tenure of office of Clerks of the Peace appointed after 1888; Qualification of Justices of the Peace considered – meeting agreed that a naturalized alien could be appointed to the Commission; Locomotive Act, 1898 – after considerable discussion meeting decided that a threshing machine was a wagon within the meaning of the Act; Special meeting held to discuss Report of Joint Committee of the Houses of Lords and Commons as to adjustments under the Local Government Acts, 1888 and 1894; C. E. Longmore appointed C.B.

1912   National Insurance Act, 1911 – administrative provisions discussed; Shops Act, 1911 – attention of Society drawn to certain provisions; Presentation of silver to S. Thornely as editor of Periodical Circular; Franchise and Regulation Bill considered, especially clause 38 affecting the duties which would devolve upon Registration Officers; Police (Weekly Rest Day) Act, 1910 – opinion given on a provision in section 1 of the Act; Local Government Officers' Superannuation Bill – resolved that progress of Bill should be watched.

1913   Local Government (Adjustments) Bill considered – provisions of Bill referred to Executive Committee; Discussion on railless traction and motor-buses; Shops Act, 1912, discussed; Inquiry made as to the appointment of Chief Constables; Death of Sir Richard Nicholson, former Chairman of Society; Sir Charles Longmore, Vice-Chairman and Honorary Secretary, congratulated on his becoming a K.C.B.

1914   Local Government (Adjustments) Act, 1913, and Mental Deficiency Act, 1913, discussed; Presentation of silver tea and coffee service to F. Merrifield, retiring Chairman; Sir Charles Longmore appointed Chairman and W. J. Freer appointed Vice-Chairman and Honorary Treasurer.

1915   Annual dinner suspended owing to War; Staffs of Clerks of the Peace – attention called to position of staff who had been refused permission to enlist – letter from Prime Minister on subject read to meeting; Society considered matters connected with members' duties as Clerks to the Lieutenancy and of the Peace due to the War.

1916   Naval and Military War Pensions Act, 1915, considered; Locomotive Act, 1898 – discussion on width of tyres of the driving wheels required under the Act; Sir Charles Longmore, Clerk of the Peace for Hertfordshire, presented with grandfather clock to commemorate his being Chairman of Society for the year 1914–15 and at the same time being President of the Law Society and in command of the 2nd Battalion of the Hertfordshire Regiment; Congratulations tendered to Sir Harcourt Clare on the honour of knighthood conferred on him.

1917   Vote of condolence – Capt. L. W. Crouch, Deputy Clerk of the Peace for Buckinghamshire, having been killed in action at the Battle of the Somme; Report of Speaker's Conference to Prime Minister on Electoral Reform considered; Grand Juries (Suspension) Bill and Representation of the People Bill discussed; Society decided that no liability attached to Standing Joint Committee to pay for false teeth supplied to police constable; Elections and Registration Act, 1915 – Society considered question of election of Alderman on a casual vacancy; Col. C. E. F. Copeman appointed C.M.G., J. J. Bickersteth appointed M.B.E. in the Birthday Honours List.

1918   Representation of the People Act, 1918 – ten meetings held and resolutions sent to Local Government Board; Miss B. Haynes attended meeting in July as representative of Clerk of the Peace for Warwickshire; Appeal made for comforts for road construction and quarrying companies in France; Maternity and Child Welfare Bill – Society to watch Bill especially regarding inspection of midwives; Members requested to urge County Councils to oppose Bill on Smallholding Colonies; Members of Society were appointed during the year to the following honours – O.B.E.: W. V. Dixon, E. T. Gardom, C. C. Hodgson, W. B. Prosser (New Year Honours List); Dr. E. W. Maples, H. A. Millington (Birthday Honours List); G. M. Harris (November) – M.B.E.: W. O. Jones (New Year Honours List); E. S. W. Hart (Birthday Honours List).

1919   Special Police Grants discussed; Question of pensions for Clerks of the Peace and their staffs referred to Executive Committee; Status of Standing Joint Committees and appointment of Clerks of the Peace and County Council discussed – resolution sent to County Councils Association; Heavy expenditure incurred by Society in connection with the Representation of the People Act, 1918 – each member in consequence to pay for his dinner at Annual Meeting; Land Settlement (Facilities) Act, 1919, and Housing, Town Planning, etc., Act, 1919, considered; G. H. Etherton and H. J. C. Neobard appointed O.B.E. in the New Year Honours List.

RETROSPECT

1920   Ministry of Agriculture and Fisheries Act, 1919, discussed – Mr. Lawrence Weaver, C.B.E., Director General of Land Settlement, attended January meeting to explain circular issued under the Act; Annual subscription raised to £3 3s. 0d. (Deputy Clerks £2 2s. 0d.); Report of Civil Service National Whitley Council Cost of Living Committee and circular letter from Ministry of Health discussed; Opinion of Society given on aspects of the Women Jurors (Criminal Cases) Rules; Question of erecting houses under the Housing Acts, 1890 to 1919, for County Council employees considered; A. T. Cobbold, N. J. H. Hallett, A. Tabrum, H. G. Thornley, J. J. Bickersteth, P. R. Longmore and H. A. Tilby appointed O.B.E. in the New Year Honours List.

1921   Agriculture Bill and Law of Property Bill discussed; Letter on paying County Council workmen by cheque read to meeting; Attention drawn to draft orders made under Ministry of Health Act, 1919; Periodical Circular to be issued biennially, instead of annually; Opinion given on Criminal Justice Administration Act, 1914, section 10; Ecclesiastical Tithe Rentcharge (Rates) Act, 1920 discussed; Rating of railways – Society decided that question of assessments should be dealt with by County Councils Association; Sir Thomas Franklen congratulated on the honour of knighthood conferred on him.

1922   Great Northern Railway Bill, 1922, discussed – Society opposed to clause 31 (provisions as to rating of railways); Memoranda submitted on cases committed for trial at Quarter Sessions but triable only at Assizes; Gas Regulation Act, 1920 – appointment of gas examiner discussed; Chairman reported on his interviews with Government Departments regarding reports of Committee on National Expenditure; Local Government and Other Officers' Superannuation Bill – Society informed it had been introduced into the House of Commons and supported by Mr. Neville Chamberlain and Mr. Arthur Henderson – Bill considered; County Agricultural Committees – work of Smallholdings Sub-Committees reviewed.

1923   Juries Act, 1922, considered – instructions given by Under Sheriffs summoning Jurors submitted; Petrol pumps – form of agreement for erection considered; Royal Commission on County Boroughs reported on and terms of reference given; Local Government and Other Officers' Superannuation Act, 1922 – question of inclusion of Registration Officers' fees; Powers of Chief Constables discussed; Points raised about Orders declaring highways to be main roads; Rating and Valuation and several other Bills considered.

Rating of railways, 1924–25 – memorandum considered; Attention of Society drawn to paragraph in the *Justice of the Peace* on the bias of officers of Courts of Justice; Question of robes worn by Clerks of the Peace discussed – correct dress should be wig and robes of King's Counsel; Opinion submitted on dismissal of married women teachers; Question of contested election of Chairman of County Council considered; Tenure of office of Clerk of the Peace discussed, and note submitted by Sir Charles Longmore; Consideration given to judgment of Mr. Justice Swift in *Thornely v. Leconfield and another*, (subsequently reversed by Court of Appeal) – members of Society contributed to expenses incurred by the Clerk of the Peace for West Sussex in prosecuting his appeal and before the House of Lords; Sir William Dixon (honorary member) congratulated on the honour of K.B.E. conferred on him in the Birthday Honours List.

1925   Chairman reported that County Councils Association intended to press for legislation giving County Councils control over their Clerks – negotiations with the Association; E. S. W. Hart elected Chairman and Honorary Secretary; Presentation of silver tea kettle and Morland engravings to Sir Charles Longmore, retiring Chairman and Honorary Secretary; Census 1926 – Society decided they would assist; Local Government Act, 1888, section 65 (1) – opinion given on compulsory purchase of land, and also on expenses of construction and maintenance of County bridges; Representation of the People Act, 1918 – residence abroad, and position of nurses discussed; Land Charges Act, 1925 – Land Charges Rules considered.

1926   Rating and Valuation Act, 1925 – various aspects considered; Memorandum submitted by Chairman with regard to prescription of building lines; Performing Animals Act, 1925 – memorandum considered; Marking of jurors discussed; Representation of the People Acts and Economy (Miscellaneous Provisions) Bill reported on by Chairman; County Council elections – discussion on whether an ex-police officer should be disqualified as a candidate – general opinion in the negative; Roadside wastes – report on campaign against ancient encroachments brought to notice of Society; Training and supply of midwives – interpretation of Ministry instructions discussed; Powers and duties of Chairman of Quarter Sessions – questions raised by member; Office of Clerk of the Peace – draft Bill prepared by sub-committee of County Councils Association considered; J. J. Bickersteth appointed C.B.E. in the Birthday Honours List.

1927   Office of Clerk of the Peace – Chairman reported representatives of County Councils Association had agreed to the provisions of the proposed Clerks of the Peace Bill practically in the form approved by Society; Milk and Dairies Order, 1926, considered; Election of County Alderman – notice of vacancy – enquiry as to signing by two County electors; Clerks of the Peace – pensions – memorandum submitted by Chairman; Question of stage plays licences for "Mystery Plays" in Essex discussed; Clerks of the Peace – robing at Council meetings – some members wore wigs and gowns, others did not; Poor Prisoners' Defence Act, 1903 – correspondence considered; Town Planning Schemes – discussion on protection of County Council property; Sir George Etherton congratulated on the honour of knighthood conferred on him in the New Year Honours List.

1928   Education Acts – school attendance – refusal of ratepayers in Dorset to send children to another school; Local taxation prosecutions – power of police officer to prosecute on behalf of County Council discussed; Local Land Charges Rules, 1927 – views of members regarding the parts of the register to be kept by Clerk read to Society; County Council staff – question raised about inquiry into organisation of various administrative departments, with or without the aid of an expert; Rating and Valuation Act, 1925, section 9 – issue of precepts discussed; Quarter Sessions – cost of criminal prosecutions – correspondence read and view of Society given.

1929   Society invited to give evidence before Royal Commission on Local Government with regard to Clerks of the Peace – draft memorandum of evidence submitted to members; Sections of the Local Government Act, 1929, considered; Representation of the People Acts – residence, absent voters' lists, and other aspects discussed; Question of Annual Dinner always being held in London considered; Highways Act, 1835 – correspondence read on the diversion of highways in a Quarter Sessions borough; Highway obstructions – trees discussed and decision of Altrincham County Court submitted; Local Government Act, 1929 – transfer of road officers discussed.

1930   Local Government (Clerks) Bill – considered at several meetings; Local Government Act, 1929 – various aspects discussed – opinion of Counsel given on highway diversions and transfer of road properties and liabilities; Criminal Justice Administration Act, 1914 – allocation of fines and fees considered; *R. v. Keepers of the Peace and Justices of the County of Somerset* – validity of second Order containing details of taxed costs upheld, notwithstanding earlier Order stating costs to be taxed; Presentation of silver salvers made to W. J. Freer, Vice-Chairman and Honorary Treasurer of Society, on completion of fifty years as member; Invitation to give evidence before Departmental Committee on Local Government Officers accepted.

1931   Local Government Act, 1929 – report by Chairman on superannuation provisions of transferred officers – review of County Districts discussed; Representation of the People Acts, 1918 to 1928 – letter considered on registration of absent voters; Election of County Councillors – correct day for lodging nominations discussed; Local Government (Clerks) Act, 1931 – Chairman thanked for his services in connection with Act; Officers' salaries – question of salary cuts owing to financial condition of country discussed; J. E. Seager appointed editor of Periodical Circular – S. Thornely thanked for acting as editor for thirty-four years.

1932   Sir John Anderson, G.C.B. – letter read thanking Society for best wishes on his appointment as Governor of Bengal; Presentation of grandfather clock and the *Encyclopaedia Britannica* to the Chairman (E. S. W. Hart) in recognition of his services to Society, particularly in reference to the passing of the Local Government (Clerks) Act, 1931; Constitution of Society – recommendations discussed – title of Society changed – Rules amended; Misfeasance on highways – negligent repair – judgment of Bristol County Court Judge in *Leech v. Lord Mayor and Corporation of Bristol* submitted; Quarter Sessions – question of robing by Chairman raised; Death of W. J. Freer, a member of Society for fifty-two years and Vice-Chairman and Treasurer for eighteen years – the last of the pre-1889 Clerks; H. A. Millington appointed Vice-Chairman and Honorary Treasurer; Local Government Act, 1929 – registration of births, deaths and marriages – copy of Warwickshire Scheme under section 24 sent to Society; Clerks of the Peace Golfing Society formed; Local Government and Other Officers' Superannuation Act, 1922 – memorandum by Vice-Chairman submitted.

1933   Solicitors' Act, 1932, sections 19 and 21 (concerning articled clerks) considered; Issue of Periodical Circular discontinued; Prosecutions at Quarter Sessions and Assizes in indictable offences – motion carried stating that, except where arrangements were made for an independent person to sit as Clerk of the Court of Quarter Sessions, it was undesirable that the Clerk of the Peace or a member of his staff should act as prosecuting solicitor; Golfing Society – Cup presented to be competed for annually; Probation Officers' reports – practice of sending to Quarter Sessions and Assizes considered; Traffic light signals – discussion as to powers; Sir George Etherton and H. J. T. McIlveen appointed Vice-Chairman and Honorary Treasurer respectively following the death of H. A. Millington; Society congratulated Sir Charles McGrath on the honour of knighthood conferred on him.

1934   Register of Electors – question of supplying copies to British Union of Fascists and Communist Party considered; Rights of Way Act, 1932, section 1(4) – correspondence submitted; Local Government Act, 1933 – various sections discussed; Discussion about salary "cuts" and their restoration; Public Health Acts (Amendment) Act, 1907, section 7 – question asked as to proper tribunal to hear an Appeal; Summary Jurisdiction (Appeals) Act, 1933 – memorandum submitted on granting appeal aid certificates; Standing Joint Committee – Chairman's memorandum as to powers considered; Seal of Lord Lieutenant – discussion as to when used; Poor Prisoners' Defence Act, 1930 – practice in direct conflict with intention of legislature considered – Chairman approached Sir Claud Schuster on matter; Hadow Report on Local Government Officers discussed.

RETROSPECT

1935   Retirement of Sir Ernest Hart, Chairman and Honorary Secretary since 1925 – Society decided that in future these offices should be held separately; Presentation and luncheon given to Sir Ernest Hart; Sir George Etherton, R. A. Wheatley and C. Oakes appointed Chairman, Vice-Chairman and Honorary Secretary respectively; Summary Courts (Social Services) Committee, dispatch of business at common law, revision of block grant formula, weak bridges – all subjects of reports by Executive Committee; Licensing Rules – confirmation of new licences – letter considered on the desirability of greater uniformity in the matter of the Rules; Preservation of County records – correspondence submitted and resolution passed on the undesirability of destroying records of the Court of Quarter Sessions; Air Raid Precautions – circular letter discussed; Memorandum submitted on loose-leaf minute books; Restriction of Ribbon Development Act, 1935 – various points considered; Law Committee established; Society congratulated Sir Ernest Hart on the honour of knighthood conferred on him.

1936   Society express profound sorrow to Royal Family on death of King George V; Superannuation – persons who had been in the permanent employment of a Clerk of the Peace – memorandum from N.A.L.G.O. discussed; Memorandum on Indictments prepared; Maintenance of roads on railway bridges – report submitted on recent judgment of the House of Lords; Hospitals – appropriation – assessment of liable relatives to cost of maintenance – Case and Opinion of Counsel submitted; Solicitors' Practice Rules, 1936, "undercutting" – report given; Local Government policy – letter from County Councils Association deprecating the submission by Officers' Societies to Government Departments of representations on matters of policy; Lunacy Act, 1890, and Poor Law Act, 1930 – correspondence about appeals against Settlement and Removal Orders considered; Society congratulated Sir George Gater on the honour of knighthood and on being elected a fellow of Winchester College.

1937   Trunk Roads Bill submitted; Maidenhead By-pass Bridge – opinion given on the power to build bridge over the Thames; Society appointed representatives to Joint Standing Committee of local authority Clerks' Societies; Representation of the People Acts – support given for broadcast appeal to electorate to complete registration forms; Royal Commission on Local Government in Tyneside area – memorandum considered; Local land charges – letter from Leicester Law Society as to uniformity of practice on issue of certificates read; Disqualification for membership of Local Authorities – letter and memorandum considered; Annual Dinner attended by Duke of Kent; Society agreed to join with the other Clerks' Societies in presenting annually a Local Government Prize to be competed for at the Final Examination of the Law Society.

1938   Local Government Act, 1933, Part XV – custody of parochial documents – orders for preservation discussed; Local Government Act, 1933, section 55 – letter on failure of Parish to elect Parish Council considered – resolution sent to Minister of Health; Police prosecutions at Assizes and Quarter Sessions – memorandum submitted; Restriction of Ribbon Development Act, 1935 – difficulties in administration discussed – summary submitted; Administration of Justice (Miscellaneous Provisions) Bill – attention drawn to Lord Chancellor's amendments; Court of Criminal Appeal – question of Clerk of the Peace representing respondent discussed – letter from Assistant Director of Public Prosecutions submitted; H. S. Martin appointed Honorary Treasurer on the resignation of H. J. T. McIlveen; Departmental Committee on Clerks to Justices – Society agreed to give evidence; Courts of Assize and Quarter Sessions – letter from Home Office on attendance of probation officers considered; Society congratulated C. Oakes on his appointment as C.B.E. in the Birthday Honours List.

1939   Aid Raid Precautions – National Defence – question of Clerks of the Peace serving as Joint Secretaries of Local National Service Committees; Administration of Justice (Miscellaneous Provisions) Act, 1938 – appointment of legally qualified Chairmen – summary submitted; Auxiliary Territorial Service – letter submitted from Ministry of Health as to the desirability of women employees of County Councils enrolling; Alteration of level of highway – resolution passed that County Councils have power to raise level of highways; Civil Defence Bill – clauses discussed; British Records Association – report given on the inspection of local records; Sir Charles McGrath appointed Vice-Chairman; Sir George Gater (honorary member) congratulated upon his appointment as Permanent Secretary of the Colonial Office; Mental Deficiency Act, 1938 – resolution passed on Detention Orders; Standing Joint Committee – question raised as to whether County Council or Quarter Sessions could require Standing Joint Committee to report their proceedings; Annual Dinner cancelled owing to outbreak of War; Society congratulated J. H. Davies on his appointment as C.B.E. in the New Year Honours List.

1940   War service – payment to Superannuation Fund – opinion submitted; Diversion of highway – opinion given on obligation of Clerk of the Peace to investigate title of owners of land over which the highway passes; Summary Jurisdiction (Appeals) Act, 1933 – recovery of costs of Rating Appeals – procedure agreed; Local Elections and Register of Electors (Temporary Provisions) Act, 1939 – Society agreed about election of County Councillors; Solicitors' Bill – various aspects considered; Personal Injuries (Civilians) Scheme – matter considered and Chairman asked to represent Society at a conference.

1941   Dr. E. W. Maples (honorary member) congratulated on his appointment as Vice-Chairman of Executive Council of County Councils Association; Subscriptions reduced for the duration of the War; Discussion regarding projected War Zone Courts – Society endorsed the view that the Clerk of the Peace should be Secretary of the County Advisory Committee; Truck Acts considered; Local Land Charges, Additional Questions – Law Society raised question as to scheduling of abandoned bombs; Standing Joint Committees – letters submitted on propriety of High Sheriff acting as member of Standing Joint Committee; Society congratulated the following members on their respective appointments – H. W. Skinner, Major P. E. Longmore and W. Jones, C.B.E. (Birthday Honours List); E. W. Scorer, H. D. Rowland and G. F. Rogers, O.B.E. (New Year Honours List).

1942   Prevention of Crimes Act, 1871, section 12, and County Police Act, 1839 – Society decided that *ex abundante cautela* prosecutions of assaults on County police officers should be framed under both Acts; F. G. Scott (Clerk of the Peace for Oxfordshire) having been appointed a member of the Local Government Sub-Committee of the Nuffield College Social Reconstruction Survey, it was agreed he should be kept informed of Society's views on Local Government reconstruction; Suspension of County Council elections – reappointment of Committees – Society decided Committees should be appointed for definite periods, afterwards reappointed; Evacuation of school children – question of recovery of billeting charges discussed; Conference on security of tenure – report considered; Cultivation of roadside wastes – opinion submitted; Society congratulated the following members on their respective appointments – K. G. T. Meaby and C. W. Radcliffe, C.B.E.; V. Lawrence and H. C. Marris, O.B.E. (Birthday Honours List), L. G. L. Lewis, M.B.E. (New Year Honours List).

1943   Sir Cecil Oakes congratulated on having received the honour of knighthood – also appointed Vice-Chairman of Society; Compensation (Defence) Act, 1939 – letter submitted on requisitioning school buildings; National Service (Armed Forces) Act, 1939 – position of temporary employees considered; County Treasurers – Society of the opinion that a County Treasurer must be a "natural person" as opposed to a Banking Corporation or a Bank Manager; Deputy Clerks of the Peace – opinion given that they should wear a stuff gown and wig at Quarter Sessions; Land Drainage Act, 1930 – maintenance of water courses – opinion that powers of County Councils as drainage authorities should be strengthened; *Nomina Ministrorum* – members asked if they had used this instrument to summon Quarter Sessions – no member present did so; Society congratulated Sir Eric Salmon on the honour of knighthood conferred on him in the Birthday Honours List, and also T. Stephenson and J. A. Turner on their appointments as C.B.E. and O.B.E. respectively in the New Year Honours List.

1944   Parliamentary Electors (War Time Registration) Act, 1943 – Sir Sylvanus Vivian, the Registrar General, reviewed the new registration procedure to Society; Adjourned Quarter Sessions – discussion; Sir Cecil Oakes, H. G. Thornley and L. E. Stephens appointed Chairman, Vice-Chairman and Assistant Secretary respectively; Public Works (Facilities) Act, 1930 – compulsory purchase Order – note considered about lapse of time after making Order; Deduction of income tax from payments made to Deputy Acting Returning Officers discussed; Solicitors' Practice Rules, 1936, Rule 3, (as to sharing profit costs) considered; Society congratulated Sir George Gater (honorary member) on his appointment as G.C.M.G. in the New Year Honours List.

1945   Presentation of silver tankard made to Sir George Etherton, retiring Chairman; Salaries of Clerks of County Councils – report of sub-committee appointed to meet representatives of County Councils Association received; Land Charges Act, 1935 – letter read on supplying supplementary information to solicitors; Education Act, 1944 – various aspects considered; Joint Planning Committees – points from Opinion of Counsel submitted; Dr. E. W. Maples (honorary member) congratulated on becoming President of County Councils Association; Reinstatement and rehabilitation of local government officers – letter from Ministry of Health considered; Electoral Registration – discussion on present system; Meeting held of Joint Sub-Committee of Society and County Accountants' Society about the Education Act, 1944; Annual Dinner – Society not to revive it until end of the War with Japan; General Election – correspondence read on charges for clerical work; Society congratulated H. S. Martin and L. E. Stephens on their appointments as C.B.E. in the New Year Honours List, and also J. B. Graham and A. H. Joliffe on their appointments as C.B.E. and O.B.E. respectively in the Birthday Honours List.

1946   Police advocacy in courts of summary jurisdiction – statement by Chairman of Worcestershire Quarter Sessions submitted approving the practice; Representation of the People Acts – question of entitlement to local government vote discussed; Amended form of inquiry to accompany requisition for official search in Local Land Charges Register examined; Rating and Valuation Acts, 1925 to 1940 – membership of Assessment Committees – opinion submitted; Relationship of County Council and Education Committee – resolution passed on Clerkship of the Education Committee; Local government staffs – supplementation of service pay discussed; Royal Commission on Justices of the Peace – four members nominated to give evidence – memorandum of evidence prepared – Society recorded their appreciation on appointment of Sir Cecil Oakes as a member of the Royal Commission; Society congratulated T. C. Hayward and J. K. Hope on their appointments as C.B.E. and C. P. Brutton, H. Copland and D. Johns on their appointments as O.B.E. in the New Year Honours List, and W. Jones on his appointment as O.B.E. in the Birthday Honours List.

RETROSPECT

1947   Curtis Report – Chairman requested to put views of Society to Secretary of County Councils Association; Special Committee set up to consider day of week for meeting of Society, and future policy; Execution of warrants of English Courts in Scotland – memorandum submitted; National Scheme of Conditions of Service – letters discussed on subsistence allowances, the Provincial Appeals Committee and other matters; National Health Service Act, 1946 – Case and Opinion submitted on disposal of funds on transfer of mental hospitals under the Act; Local Government boundaries – boundaries of County Boroughs discussed; Presentation to Sir Cecil Oakes on his retirement as Chairman and Honorary Secretary – succeeded by H. G. Thornley as Chairman and by L. E. Stephens as Honorary Secretary; W. L. Platts appointed Vice-Chairman; Status and remuneration of assistant solicitors discussed; Supreme Court Committee on Practice and Procedure – Society asked to prepare draft memorandum and submit it to County Councils Association; Parliamentary and General Purposes and Law Committees appointed; Full rate of membership subscription restored.

1948   Fire Services Act, 1947 – form of management scheme submitted; Society decided that Clerks and Deputy Clerks should be excluded from the joint negotiating machinery proposed by the Local Authority Associations; Judges' Lodgings – discussion on question of duty of County Councils to provide; Report of Special Sub-Committee appointed to consider rules and finances of Society, and the Annual Dinner, presented, and revised rules adopted; Sub-Committee appointed to consider the Representation of the People Bill and empowered to offer advice to County Councils Association; Sign manual of Clerks of the Peace – memoranda submitted; Memorandum of Evidence submitted to Mr. Justice Byrne's Committee on Depositions; Relationship between central departments and the Local Government service – memorandum by the Clerk of the Peace for London considered; Meeting of Joint Standing Committee of Clerks' Associations held; Wild Birds Protection – T. C. Hayward appointed to serve on Home Office Advisory Committee; Memorandum sent to Mr. Justice Lynskey's Working Party on Dispatch of Business in the Supreme Court; Society congratulated G. C. Scrimgeour on his appointment as O.B.E. in the New Year Honours List.

1949   Coroners' Acts – memorandum prepared at request of County Councils Association; Salaries of Clerks of County Councils – agreement reached with County Councils Association to appoint representatives to review existing standards and other related matters; Local Government Manpower Committee – report by Clerk of the London County Council as to progress made; Departmental Committee on Local Land Charges – H. S. Martin appointed to serve on the Committee – V. Lawrence, R. E. Millard and G. A. Wheatley to give evidence – memoranda of evidence prepared; Representation of the People Act, 1948, and Regulations, 1949 – official poll cards – report of meeting held at the Treasury submitted; Town and Country Planning Act, 1947 – memorandum submitted on procedure at public inquiry into development plan objections; Local Government Act, 1933, section 5 – views expressed on election of two Vice-Chairmen of a County Council; Justices of the Peace Bill – Sub-Committee appointed to consider the Bill – Sub-Committee's observations sent to Lord Chancellor's Office and Home Office; County Councils' part in Festival of Britain – address by Secretary of Festival arranged; Society congratulated Sir Howard Roberts and Sir William Jones on the honour of knighthood conferred on them in the Birthday Honours List, and also H. D. Rowland (honorary member) and H. G. Thornley on their appointments as C.B.E. in the New Year Honours List.

1950   Proposals of London Clearing Banks as to operation of County Fund and subsidiary accounts considered; Representation of the People Act, 1948 – discussion at Home Office as to scale of expenses for 1950 Register; Local Government Manpower Committee – simplification of County administration – Sir Howard Roberts reported; Justices of the Peace Act, 1949 – size and chairmanship of Benches – consideration given to proposed Rules; Presentation of silver and Sheffield plate to H. G. Thornley, retiring Chairman; W. L. Platts and Sir Robert Adcock appointed Chairman and Vice-Chairman respectively; "Organisation and Methods" – subject discussed in relation to Local Government administration; Presentation to Sir Sidney Johnson upon his retirement as Secretary of County Councils Association; Mr. J. C. D. Mackley (Secretary of New Zealand Institution of County Clerks) attended meeting of Society by invitation; Society congratulated Sir Robert Adcock on the honour of knighthood conferred on him in the New Year Honours List.

1951   Salaries of Clerks of County Councils – new scales of salaries approved by County Councils Association following discussions between representatives of Association and of Society; Transmission of copies of Probation Orders and documents to Supervising Court – memorandum submitted; Tithe Act, 1936 – question of land within highway boundaries discussed; Magistrates' Courts Committees (Constitution) Regulations, 1951 – draft regulations submitted to Society for observations; National Parks and Access to the Countryside Act, 1949 – liability to repair public paths – Opinion of Counsel submitted; Report of Departmental Committee on Weights and Measures Legislation – recommendation that prosecution should have right of appeal on questions of fact referred to Law Committee of Society; Presentation made to L. E. Stephens for his services as Honorary Secretary of Golfing Society from 1932 – G. C. Lightfoot appointed as his successor; Lord Lieutenancy – special sub-committee set up to consider various questions raised by members of Society; Society congratulated C. L. Burgess and H. B. Greenwood on their appointments as C.B.E. and O.B.E. respectively in the New Year Honours List, and also D. J. Parry on his appointment as C.B.E. in the Birthday Honours List.

1952 Clerks of County Councils acting for police officers and members of the staff – correspondence with Law Society; Society convey their deep sorrow to Royal Family on death of King George VI; Accession of Queen Elizabeth II – letter received showing the correct caption for Quarter Sessions; Magistrates' Association – invitation to Society to nominate three members to serve on Council of Association declined; G. C. Godber appointed Assistant Honorary Secretary; Presentation to W. L. Platts, retiring Chairman; Sir Robert Adcock and L. E. Stephens appointed Chairman and Vice-Chairman respectively; Powers and duties of District Auditors – memorandum submitted; Joint Sub-Committee of Society and of Society of County Treasurers – meeting held to discuss vehicle licensing and registration systems; Special Sub-Committee set up to consider proposed amendments to the Local Government Superannuation Act, 1937; Law Society's Salaried Solicitors Committee – invitation to submit name of member to serve on Committee; Theatres Act, 1843 – question of production of stage plays in a parish church discussed by Law Committee; Statistical Officer of Society, E. R. Davies, appointed.

1953 Coronation of Her Majesty Queen Elizabeth II – seats offered to Society by Ministry of Works; County Council Parliamentary Bills – difficulty as to inclusion of clauses for the benefit of lesser local authorities – County Councils Association advised as to action to be taken; L. E. Stephens and H. S. Martin appointed Chairman and Vice-Chairman respectively, the former being succeeded as Honorary Secretary by G. C. Godber; Meeting of Joint Standing Committee – security of tenure and other matters discussed; Town Development Act, 1952 – overspill problems and boundary extensions discussed; Justices of the Peace Act, 1949, and Local Government Act, 1933, section 180(2) – memorandum on incidence of cost of Magistrates' Courts Committees received; Clergy Discipline Act, 1892, section 5(4) – correspondence on this section passed to Law Committee; Presentation of silver cigarette case to Mr. R. Hedges in recognition of the valuable services rendered by him over many years as clerk to Honorary Secretary; Society invited to nominate two representatives for co-option to Central Council of Magistrates' Courts Committees; Standing Joint Committees – question of appointing County Treasurer expressly to act also as Treasurer of Standing Joint Committee discussed by Parliamentary and General Purposes Committee; Society congratulated Sir Clifford Radcliffe on the honour of knighthood conferred on him in the New Year Honours List.

1954 R.I.B.A. Form of Contract as adapted for the use of Local Authorities – report given on discussions between Society and Society of County Architects as to amendment of the form; Retirement of Clerk with Justices – Society expressed opinion that Clerks of the Peace should not retire with the Justices as a matter of course; Recovery of charges for local authority services – opinion of Society given on existing law; Architectural copyright – correspondence received from County Architects' Society; Adoption of cycle tracks as repairable highways – views of Society sought by County Councils Association; Representation of the People Acts – note submitted from Home Office on meeting of the electoral conference held at Home Office on 13th July 1954; Town and Country Planning Act, 1947 – validity of condition restricting the felling of trees discussed; Agricultural workers' cottages – joint opinion received on conditions restricting the use of a house to a particular class of occupier; Society congratulated C. P. Brutton on his appointment as C.B.E. in the New Year Honours List.

1955 Salaries of Clerks and Deputy Clerks – agreement with representatives of County Councils Association regarding salary scales – memorandum prepared by the Clerk of the West Riding County Council on the subject of negotiating machinery submitted and considered; Land Charges Departmental Committee under chairmanship of Mr. Justice Roxburgh – draft memorandum of evidence prepared for County Councils Association; 150th anniversary of formation of Society – Society accepted the suggestion of Chairman of his intention to prepare a Brochure upon Society and its past history; Representation of the People Act, 1949 – scales of fees payable to Registration Officers and Acting Returning Officers – representatives appointed to negotiate with Home Office; First United Nations Congress on prevention of crime and treatment of offenders – invitation from Home Office for Honorary Secretary to attend; Quarter Sessions – minuting of criminal business discussed; Society addressed by Director-General of Civil Defence; Sheriffs Act, 1887 – question of whether Act disqualifies a Justice of the Peace from acting when High Sheriff considered by Law Committee; Road Traffic Acts, 1930 to 1933 – responsibility for the provision and maintenance of traffic signs considered.

1956 H. G. Thornley congratulated on completing forty years service as Clerk of the Peace and of the County Council of the North Riding of Yorkshire; Local Government Act, 1933, section 281(4) – custody and preservation of Parish documents discussed; Road Traffic Act, 1934, section 23 – powers of County Councils to light roads considered by Parliamentary and General Purposes Committee; Reciprocal arrangements between Weights and Measures authorities – correspondence laid before Law Committee; Presentation of Royal Worcester dinner service to L. E. Stephens, retiring Chairman; H. S. Martin and T. C. Hayward appointed Chairman and Vice-Chairman respectively, the former being succeeded as Honorary Treasurer by L. E. Stephens; Salaries of Clerks and Deputy Clerks of County Councils – discussions with representatives of County Councils Association as to the revision of salary ranges – case submitted to Counsel on the question of forming a trade union; "Organisation and Methods" investigation into electoral registration work – Treasury proposal accepted and representatives appointed to serve on Working Party; Execution of contracts of local authorities – opinion submitted; Quarter Sessions – correspondence submitted regarding new rules for drafting indictments; Report on planning conditions affecting highways presented by Committee of representatives of Society, County Surveyors' Society and County Planning Officers' Society; Recruitment of university graduates discussed.

RETROSPECT

1957 Salaries of Clerks and Deputy Clerks of County Councils – application to County Councils Association for constitution of a formal joint negotiating committee; Annual Dinner – invitations to be sent to ladies only if holding office as Chairman or Vice-Chairman of a County Council, or if by virtue of their office included among Society's official guests; Local Government – functions of County Councils and County District Councils – special committee appointed; Re-organisation of local government and finance – report as to Departmental control approved for submission to County Councils Association; Reception held for American Bar Association Convention at Middlesex Guildhall; Libel insurance – memorandum submitted about policies designed to cover liability of Councils, their members and officers, for damages awarded against them in actions for libel; Care of records and archives – memorandum submitted to Ministry of Housing and Local Government; Consolidation of highway law – memorandum to be prepared; Re-organisation of local government and finance – proposal to abolish special grant for registration of electors discussed, and representations made to County Councils Association; Local Government Bill – compensation for loss of office – representatives appointed to consider draft regulations; Society congratulated T. H. Evans on his appointment as C.B.E. in the New Year Honours List.

1958 Representation of the People Act, 1949 – note submitted about proposals affecting Returning Officers' fees and expenses considered at meeting between the Home Office, the Treasury, the Society and the Society of Town Clerks; Departmental Committee on Proceedings before Examining Justices – evidence submitted on behalf of Society; Local Government Bill – compensation to officers – report submitted; Public Records Bill – summary of provisions prepared; Salaries of Clerks and Deputy Clerks of County Councils – negotiating machinery – decision taken to form an Association of Clerks and Deputy Clerks for the purpose of dealing with the terms and conditions of employment and with a view to its registration as a trade union; Presentation of wristlet watch to H. S. Martin, retiring Chairman; T. C. Hayward and C. P. Brutton appointed Chairman and Vice-Chairman respectively; Chief Officers and policy – correspondence with County Councils Association; Town and Country Planning Act, 1947, section 23 – enforcement notices – caravan sites – unsatisfactory nature of enforcement provisions of the Act discussed with representatives of Ministry; Interdepartmental Committee on business of the criminal courts – Society invited to submit memorandum of evidence; Local Government Act, 1958 – re-organisation of local government and finance, and Local Government Commission – matters referred to Special Sub-Committee set up in 1957; Offices of Clerk of the Peace and Clerk of the County Council – consideration given to questions raised in memorandum by B. Kenyon; Society congratulated Sir Hubert Thornley on the honour of knighthood conferred on him in the New Year Honours List.

1959 Arrangements to be made under the Public Records Act, 1958 – discussions with Government Departments concerned; Local Government Act, 1933, section 76 (interest of members in contracts, etc.) – duty of Clerks considered; Departmental Committee on Probation Service – Society congratulated G. C. Lightfoot on his appointment as member of Committee – Sub-Committee of Society appointed to prepare and submit memorandum of evidence; Local Government Act, 1958, section 58 – the question of the making and content of financial regulations discussed; Statutory Committees of Local Authorities – views of Society sought by County Councils Association on relaxation of central government controls; Memorandum submitted on attendance of Chief Constable at the Civil Meeting of Quarter Sessions; Legal Aid and Advice Act, 1949 – implementation of sections 21–23 considered at request of Home Office; Justices of the Peace Act, 1949, section 25(2) (c) (indemnification against costs or damages) – L. E. Stephens nominated to serve on Working Party set up by Lord Chancellor and Home Secretary; Prosecution fees to Counsel at Quarter Sessions – Society considered a suggested fee table circulated by General Council of the Bar; Office of Deputy Lieutenant – note by Honorary Secretary submitted; Society congratulated V. Lawrence and T. G. Randall on their appointments as C.B.E. in the New Year Honours List and Birthday Honours List respectively.

1960 Society offered sincere congratulations to the Queen and Prince Philip on the birth of Prince Andrew; Local Government Act, 1958 – review of County boundaries – progress of reviews outlined by members; Betting and Gaming Act, 1960, section 10 – Home Office assured of co-operation of members in furnishing statistical information; Royal Commission on Police – Society decided not to submit memorandum of evidence; Census of Population, 1961 – Society's comments on draft circular sought by Registrar General; Recruitment of university graduates – report of special sub-committee approved; Public Bodies (Admission to Meetings) Bill, Corporate Bodies (Contracts) Act, 1960 – revision of model Standing Orders considered; Local Government Act, 1958, section 60(2) – compensation for loss of office – draft Regulations considered; G. C. Godber appointed Vice-Chairman; Society congratulated Sir Edgar Stephens on the honour of knighthood conferred on him in the New Year Honours List, and G. A. Wheatley on his appointment as C.B.E. in the Birthday Honours List; Society's 150th Anniversary Dinner held at the Mansion House, London, on Wednesday, the 14th December, by kind permission of the Lord Mayor – 275 members and their guests attended, including the Lord High Chancellor, the Lord Chief Justice of England, the Master of the Rolls, the Minister of Housing and Local Government, thirteen of Her Majesty's Lieutenants for the Counties, and the Permanent Secretaries of the Ministries closely associated with the Society; Armorial Bearings of Society – the Duke of Norfolk (Lord Lieutenant of Sussex), who was a guest of the Chairman, handed over to him, during the proceedings, a Grant of Arms by the Kings of Arms to be borne henceforth by the Society.

CHAIRMEN OF THE SOCIETY, 1810-1960
and
PLACE OF MEETINGS AND OF ANNUAL DINNERS

Year	Date of Meeting	Chairman	Place of Meeting	Annual Dinner
1810	27th March	William Bullock (Essex)	Gray's Inn Coffee House	
	15th May	,,	,,	
	13th November	,,	,,	Gray's Inn Coffee House (a)
1811	12th November	Charles John Lawson (Surrey)	,,	,,
1812	7th November	Charles John Lawson (Surrey) in the absence of Henry Collingwood Selby (Middlesex)	,,	,,
1813	16th November	William Burnet (Dorset)	,,	,,
1814	15th November	Joseph Loxdale (Salop)	,,	,,
1815	14th November	John Fellows Claridge (Kent)	,,	,,
1816	12th November	Thomas Tindal (Buckinghamshire)	,,	,,
1817	11th November	Christopher Pemberton (Cambridgeshire)	,,	,,
1818	17th November	John Carter (Coventry)	,,	,,
1819	16th November	James Borton (Suffolk)	,,	,,
1820	14th November	Edward Coles (Somerset)	,,	,,
1821	13th November	Thomas Henry Taunton (Oxfordshire)	,,	,,
1822	12th November	Robert Copeman (Norfolk)	,,	,,
1823	11th November	Edward Bloxsome (Gloucestershire, Deputy Clerk)	,,	,,
1824	25th May	Thomas Tindal (Buckinghamshire) in the absence of Henry Collingwood Selby (Middlesex)	,,	
	16th November	Thomas Tindal (Buckinghamshire) in the absence of Robert Sherard (Huntingdonshire)	,,	,,
1825	31st May	Thomas Tindal (Buckinghamshire) in the absence of Robert Sherard (Huntingdonshire)	,,	

(a) Although there are frequent references in the Society's Minutes to the Annual Dinners held between 1810 and 1875, there is no specific mention of the places where the Dinners were held. As they were always on the same day as the Annual Meetings, it may be assumed, however, that Dinner was provided in those years at the place of meeting.

THE CLERKS OF THE COUNTIES, 1360—1960

Year	Date of Meeting	Chairman	Place of Meeting	Annual Dinner
1825–26(a)	15th November 30th May	Charles George Parker (Essex) ,,	Gray's Inn Coffee House ,,	Gray's Inn Coffee House
1826–27	14th November 29th May	William Scudamore (Kent, Deputy Clerk) ,,	Albion Tavern, Aldersgate Street ,,	Albion Tavern, Aldersgate Street
1827–28	13th November 27th May	Theed Pearse (Bedfordshire) ,,	,, ,,	,,
1828–29	11th November 26th May	Thomas Tindal (Buckinghamshire) Charles John Lawson (Surrey) both in the absence of William Budd (Berkshire)	,, ,,	,,
1829–30	17th November 23rd March* 11th May	John Samuel Story (Hertfordshire) Thomas Tindal (Buckinghamshire) in the absence of John Samuel Story John Samuel Story (Hertfordshire)	,, Wright's Hotel in the Adelphi Albion Tavern, Aldersgate Street	,,
1830–31	16th November 21st June	Charles Markham (Northamptonshire) ,,	,, ,,	,,
1831–32	15th November 8th May	William Oakes Hunt (Warwickshire) ,,	,, ,,	,,
1832–33	13th November 14th May	Charles Heneage Elsley (Yorkshire, West Riding) Charles John Lawson (Surrey) in the absence of Charles Heneage Elsley	,, ,,	,,
1833–34	12th November 13th May	James Borton (Suffolk) in the absence of John Henry Borton (Suffolk, Deputy Clerk) ,,	,, ,,	,,
1834–35	11th November 12th May 17th November	Hugh Jackson (Isle of Ely) ,, ,,	,, ,, ,,	,, ,,
1836(b)	10th May 15th November	John Hardwick Hollway (Lincolnshire, Parts of Lindsey) ,,	,, ,,	,,
1837	9th May 14th November	William Forbes (Lincolnshire, Parts of Kesteven) ,,	,, ,,	,,
1838	8th May 13th November	Francis Thirkill (Lincolnshire, Parts of Holland) ,,	,, ,,	,,
1839	14th May 12th November	John Loxdale (Salop) William Vidler Langridge (Sussex) in the absence of John Loxdale	,, ,,	,,
1840	12th May 10th November	John Marriott Davenport (Oxfordshire) ,,	,, ,,	,,

*Special Meeting.

(a) A second meeting in May having been introduced in 1824, it was decided in November 1825 to appoint in the future a Chairman for the ensuing year, who would preside at the November (Annual) meeting and at that in the following May.

(b) Commencing with the year of office 1836, Chairmen of the Society were appointed in the previous November for the meetings in the following calendar year.

CHAIRMEN, MEETINGS AND ANNUAL DINNERS

Year	Date of Meeting	Chairman	Place of Meeting	Annual Dinner
1841	11th May	Charles Pettitt Allen (honorary member)	Albion Tavern, Aldersgate Street	
	2nd November	Charles George Parker (Essex)	„	Albion Tavern, Aldersgate Street
1842(a)	3rd May	Robert Copeman (Norfolk)	„	„
	1st November	John Marriott Davenport (Oxfordshire)	„	
1843	2nd May	Thomas Tindal (honorary member)	„	„
	7th November	William Vidler Langridge (Sussex)	„	
1844	15th May	Acton Tindal (Buckinghamshire)	Freemasons' Tavern, Great Queen Street	Freemasons' Tavern, Great Queen Street
	13th November	„	„	
1845	26th March*	John Marriott Davenport (Oxfordshire)	Law Institution, Chancery Lane	
	14th April*	„	„	
	14th May	Henry Atkinson Wildes (Kent)	Freemasons' Tavern, Great Queen Street	„
	12th November	„	„	
1846	13th May	George Bowes Morland (Berkshire)	„	„
	11th November	„	„	
1847	12th May	Richard Onslow (Surrey)	„	„
	10th November	„	Law Club, Chancery Lane	
1848	10th May	Charles Augustus Helm (Worcestershire, Deputy Clerk)	„	Law Club, Chancery Lane
	8th November	„	„	
1849	16th January*	Acton Tindal (Buckinghamshire)	Law Institution, Chancery Lane	
	9th May	Robert William Parmeter (Norfolk)	Law Club, Chancery Lane	„
	14th November	„	„	
1850	6th March*	John Marriott Davenport (Oxfordshire)	„	
	8th May	Theed Pearse (Bedfordshire)	Law Institution, Chancery Lane	Law Institution, Chancery Lane
	13th November	„	„	
1851	25th March*	John Marriott Davenport (Oxfordshire)	„	
	14th May	William Oakes Hunt (Warwickshire)	„	„
	19th September*	John Marriott Davenport (Oxfordshire)	„	
	12th November	Acton Tindal (Buckinghamshire)	„	
1852	12th May	John Marriott Davenport (Oxfordshire)	„	„
	10th November	„	Law Club, Chancery Lane	
1853	11th April*	„	Law Institution, Chancery Lane	
	11th May	William Nichols Marcy (Worcestershire)	Law Club, Chancery Lane	Law Club, Chancery Lane
	11th November	George Bowes Morland (Berkshire)	„	
1854	7th February*	Acton Tindal (Buckinghamshire)	Law Institution, Chancery Lane	
	10th May	Thomas Fowke Andrew Burnaby (Nottinghamshire, Deputy Clerk)	Law Club, Chancery Lane	„
	15th November	„	„	

*Special meeting.

(a) From 1842 onwards, the Annual Meeting was that held in May, not November.

THE CLERKS OF THE COUNTIES, 1360—1960

Year	Date of Meeting	Chairman	Place of Meeting	Annual Dinner
1855	9th May	John Marriott Davenport (Oxfordshire) in the absence of Thomas Woodham (Hampshire, Deputy Clerk)	Law Club, Chancery Lane	Law Club, Chancery Lane
	14th November	Thomas Woodham (Hampshire, Deputy Clerk)	,,	
1856	14th May	John Swayne (Wiltshire)	,,	,,
	12th November	,,	Gray's Inn Coffee House	
1857	13th May	Henry Philip Markham (Northamptonshire)	Law Institution, Chancery Lane	Law Institution, Chancery Lane
	11th November	John Marriott Davenport (Oxfordshire) in the absence of Henry Philip Markham	,,	
1858	12th May	John Marriott Davenport (Oxfordshire) in the absence of Arthur Grey Maude (Middlesex, Deputy Clerk)	,,	,,
1859	10th February*	Woronzow Greig (Surrey)	,,	
	11th May	John Marriott Davenport (Oxfordshire) in the absence of William Ffooks (Dorset)	,,	,,
1860	9th May	John Cleave (Herefordshire)	,,	,,
1861	8th May	Woronzow Greig (Surrey)	Trafalgar Hotel, Greenwich	Trafalgar Hotel, Greenwich
1862	17th June	John Hardwick Hollway (Lincolnshire, Parts of Lindsey)	,,	,,
1863	2nd June	Hugh Robert Evans (Cambridgeshire) in the absence of William Freer (Leicestershire)	Law Institution, Chancery Lane	Law Institution, Chancery Lane
1864	7th June	John Marriott Davenport (Oxfordshire) in the absence of Hugh Robert Evans (Cambridgeshire)	,,	,,
1865	13th June	John Marriott Davenport (Oxfordshire) in the absence of Charles Metcalfe (Isle of Ely)	,,	,,
1866	12th June	John Marriott Davenport (Oxfordshire) in the absence of Robert William Hand (Staffordshire)	,,	,,
1867	11th June	Joshua John Peele (Salop, Deputy Clerk)	,,	,,
1868	9th June	John Marriott Davenport (Oxfordshire)	,,	,,
1869	8th June	John Marriott Davenport (Oxfordshire) in the absence of John Barber (Derbyshire)	,,	,,
1870	14th June	John Marriott Davenport (Oxfordshire) in the absence of Charles Burton Fox (Monmouthshire)	,,	,,
1871	20th June	George Riddiford (Gloucestershire)	,,	,,

*Special Meeting.

216

CHAIRMEN, MEETINGS AND ANNUAL DINNERS

Year	Date of Meeting	Chairman	Place of Meeting	Annual Dinner
1872	11th June	John Marriott Davenport (Oxfordshire)	Law Institution, Chancery Lane	Law Institution, Chancery Lane
1873	10th June	,,	,,	,,
1874	23rd April	,,	,,	,,
1875	6th May	Richard Nicholson (Hertfordshire and Middlesex)	,,	,,
1876	15th June	John Marriott Davenport (Oxfordshire)	Inns of Court Hotel	Trafalgar Hotel, Greenwich
1877	7th June	,,	,,	Inns of Court Hotel
1878	13th June	,,	,,	Trafalgar Hotel, Greenwich
1879	5th June	,,	,,	Inns of Court Hotel
1880	3rd June	,,	,,	The Albion, Aldersgate Street
1881	16th June	Thomas Fowke Andrew Burnaby (Nottinghamshire)	,,	Inns of Court Hotel
1882–1910		Sir Richard Nicholson (Hertfordshire, Middlesex and London) (a)	38 Spring Gardens, S.W. (1882–83) (2 meetings); Law Institution, Chancery Lane (1884–85) (2 meetings); Inns of Court Hotel (1885–93) (12 meetings); Guildhall, Westminster (1894–1910) (30 meetings)	Trafalgar Hotel, Greenwich (1882); *No record*, 1883; Albion Hotel, Aldersgate Street (1884); Inns of Court Hotel (1885–86); Trafalgar Hotel, Greenwich (1887–89); Ship Hotel, Greenwich (1890–97); Grand Summer Dining Room, Crystal Palace (1898); Ship Hotel, Greenwich (1899) Albion Hotel, Aldersgate Street (1900–04); Conservative Club, St. James' Street (1905); Princes Restaurant, Piccadilly (1906–10)
1910–14		Frederic Merrifield (East and West Sussex)	Guildhall, Westminster (1910–11) (2 meetings); Westminster Palace Hotel (1911–14) (6 meetings)	Princes Restaurant, Piccadilly (1911–12); Claridge's (1913)
1914–25		Sir Charles (Elton) Longmore, K.C.B. (Hertfordshire) (b)	Guildhall, Westminster (60 meetings)	Claridge's (1914); *No dinners*, 1915–18; Law Society's Hall, Chancery Lane (1919); Claridge's (1920–24)

(a) The practice of appointing the same Chairman for a long series of years may be said to have commenced with the appointment in 1882 of Mr. (later Sir) Richard Nicholson. Single annual meetings continued until 1902, with the exception of 1885 (2 meetings), 1888 (3 meetings) and 1889 (2 meetings). Thereafter the number varies. One meeting only was held in each of the years 1910, 1913, 1915, 1916 and 1940; in others it has been as low as two or as high as eleven (in 1918). During Sir Richard Nicholson's Chairmanship, the Chair was taken in his absence by Matthew Folliott Blakiston (Staffordshire) at one meeting and by Frederic Merrifield (East and West Sussex) at thirteen meetings and three Annual Dinners (including the centenary Dinner in 1910) towards the end of the period.

(b) During Sir Charles Longmore's Chairmanship, the Chair was taken in his absence by William Jesse Freer (Leicestershire) at two meetings.

THE CLERKS OF THE COUNTIES, 1360—1960

Year	Chairman	Place of Meeting	Annual Dinner
1925–35	Sir Ernest (Sidney Walter) Hart, M.B.E. (Middlesex) (a)	Guildhall, Westminster (61 meetings)	Claridge's (1925–28); Hotel Metropole, Northumberland Avenue (1929); Claridge's (1930); *No dinner*, 1931; Claridge's (1932–34)
1935–44	Sir George (Hammond) Etherton, O.B.E., D.L. (Lancashire) (b)	Guildhall, Westminster (40 meetings)	Dorchester Hotel, Park Lane (1935–36); Claridge's (1937–38); *No dinners*, 1939–44
1944–47	Sir Cecil Oakes, C.B.E. (East Suffolk) (c)	Guildhall, Westminster (10 meetings); 84 Eccleston Square, S.W. (2 meetings)	*No dinners*
1947–50	Hubert Gordon Thornley, C.B.E. (Yorkshire, North Riding)	Guildhall, Westminster (6 meetings); County Hall, S.E.1 (8 meetings)	*No dinner*, 1947; Claridge's (1948–49)
1950–52	Walter Leslie Platts (Kent)	Guildhall, Westminster (8 meetings); County Hall, S.E.1. (4 meetings)	Claridge's
1952–53	Sir Robert Adcock, C.B.E., D.L. (Lancashire) (d)	Guildhall, Westminster (1 meeting); County Hall, S.E.1. (4 meetings)	Claridge's
1953–56	Leon Edgar Stephens, C.B.E., D.L. (Warwickshire)	Guildhall, Westminster (13 meetings); County Hall, S.E.1 (2 meetings)	Claridge's
1956–58	Hubert Sinclair Martin, C.B.E. (East Sussex) (e)	Guildhall, Westminster (9 meetings); County Hall, S.E.1 (1 meeting)	Claridge's
1958–	Tom Christopher Hayward, C.B.E. (West Sussex) (f)	Guildhall, Westminster (11 meetings); County Hall, S.E.1 (3 meetings)	Claridge's (1958–59); The Mansion House (1960)

(a) During Sir Ernest Hart's Chairmanship, the Chair was taken in his absence by Sir George Etherton (Lancashire) at two meetings, and by William Jesse Freer (Leicestershire), Herbert Ashlin Millington (Northamptonshire), Hubert Gordon Thornley (Yorkshire, North Riding), Hugh John Turnly McIlveen (East Sussex) and Edward William Maples (Herefordshire) at one meeting each.

(b) During Sir George Etherton's Chairmanship, the Chair was taken in his absence by Robert Albert Wheatley (Pembrokeshire) at three meetings and by Hubert Gordon Thornley (Yorkshire, North Riding) at one meeting.

(c) During Sir Cecil Oakes' Chairmanship, the Chair was taken in his absence by Hubert Gordon Thornley (Yorkshire, North Riding) at one meeting.

(d) During Sir Robert Adcock's Chairmanship, the Chair was taken in his absence by Leon Edgar Stephens (Warwickshire) at one meeting, and at the Annual Dinner in 1952.

(e) During Mr. H. S. Martin's Chairmanship, the Chair was taken in his absence by Hubert Gordon Thornley (Yorkshire, North Riding) at one meeting.

(f) During the period from June 1958 to December 1960, the Chair was taken in the Chairman's absence by Charles Phipps Brutton (Dorset) at two meetings, and at the Annual Dinner in 1958.

OTHER OFFICERS OF THE SOCIETY, 1810-1960

Vice Chairmen

1907–1910 Frederic Merrifield (East and West Sussex)

1910–1914 Sir Charles (Elton) Longmore, K.C.B. (Hertfordshire)

1914–1932 William Jesse Freer (Leicestershire)

1932–1933 Herbert Ashlin Millington, O.B.E. (Northamptonshire)

1933–1935 Sir George (Hammond) Etherton, O.B.E. (Lancashire)

1935–1939 Robert Albert Wheatley (Pembrokeshire)

1939–1943 Sir Charles McGrath (Yorkshire, West Riding)

1943–1944 Sir Cecil Oakes, C.B.E. (East Suffolk)

1944–1947 Hubert Gordon Thornley, O.B.E. (Yorkshire, North Riding)

1947–1950 Walter Leslie Platts (Kent)

1950–1952 Sir Robert (Henry) Adcock, C.B.E., D.L. (Lancashire)

1952–1953 Leon Edgar Stephens, C.B.E., D.L. (Warwickshire)

1953–1956 Hubert Sinclair Martin, C.B.E. (East Sussex)

1956–1958 Tom Christopher Hayward, C.B.E. (West Sussex)

1958–1960 Charles Phipps Brutton, C.B.E. (Dorset)

1960– Geoffrey Chapman Godber (Salop)

Honorary Treasurers

1811–1835 Charles John Lawson (Surrey)

1835–1871 Charles Pettitt Allen (Deputy Clerk, Middlesex until 1837; thereafter honorary member)

1871–1913 Thomas Marriott Davenport (Deputy Clerk, later Clerk, Oxfordshire)

1914–1932 William Jesse Freer (Leicestershire)

1932–1933 Herbert Ashlin Millington, O.B.E. (Northamptonshire)

1933–1938 Hugh John Turnly McIlveen (East Sussex)

1938–1956 Hubert Sinclair Martin, C.B.E. (Northamptonshire, later East Sussex)

1956– Sir (Leon) Edgar Stephens, C.B.E., D.L. (Warwickshire)

Honorary Secretaries

1814–1822 John Fellows Claridge (Kent)

1822–1838 Thomas Tindal (Buckinghamshire)

1838–1880 Acton Tindal (Buckinghamshire)

1881–1910 Sir Richard Nicholson (Hertfordshire, Middlesex and London)

1910–1911 *Office vacant*

1911–1925 Sir Charles (Elton) Longmore, K.C.B. (Hertfordshire)

1925–1935 Sir Ernest (Sidney Walter) Hart, M.B.E. (Middlesex)

1935–1947 Sir Cecil Oakes, C.B.E. (East Suffolk)

1947–1953 Leon Edgar Stephens, C.B.E., D.L. (Warwickshire)

1953– Geoffrey Chapman Godber (Salop)

TIEN · LE · DROICT

PLATE XII

THE ARMORIAL BEARINGS OF THE SOCIETY

To commemorate their 150th Anniversary, the Society applied for and received a Grant of Armorial Bearings from the Kings of Arms, which was formally handed to the Chairman of the Society, Mr. T. C. Hayward, C.B.E., at the Anniversary Dinner by His Grace the Duke of Norfolk, K.G., G.C.V.O., Her Majesty's Lieutenant for the County of Sussex and Earl Marshal of England.

The Coat of Arms is shown in the illustration opposite and its blazon is as follows:—

" *Quarterly Azure and Argent in the first and fourth quarters a Lion passant guardant Or and in the second and third quarters a Dragon rampant Gules on a Chief Sable two Quill Pens in saltire points downward also Argent*
" *And for the Crest On a Wreath of the Colours An Ancient Crown Or Jewelled proper* "

The Grant is signed and sealed by the Kings of Arms as follows:—

G. R. Bellew,	J. D. Heaton-Armstrong,	Aubrey J. Toppin,
Garter	Clarenceux	Norroy and Ulster
(L.S.)	(L.S.)	(L.S.)

and an Endorsement states that the Grant is recorded in the College of Arms, London, by J. R. B. Walker, Lancaster Herald and Registrar.

As will be seen from the illustration, the four quarters of the shield bear alternately a lion passant guardant or, representing England, and a dragon rampant gules, representing Wales. The chief reflects the interests of the Society, having a sable background signifying the black silk gown of a Clerk of the Peace and two quill pens in saltire, symbolic instruments or weapons of the lawyer's trade. The ancient crown, forming the crest, alludes to the historic connection between the offices of Clerk of the Peace and Clerk of the Crown discussed above on pages 29 to 35, which persisted until the reign of King Henry VIII.

The motto adopted by the Society " *Tien Le Droict,*" in the Norman French spelling familiar to the early Clerks of the Peace and of the Crown, can but have been their aim and object and that of their successors throughout the intervening centuries. Similarly it may be considered not to be inappropriate for the Clerks of the Peace and of County Councils of to-day. The Arms were designed by and were the gift of the Honorary Treasurer of the Society.

THE ACTIVITIES OF THE CLERKS OF THE PEACE GOLFING SOCIETY FROM 1932 to 1960

The Clerks of the Peace Golfing Society was formed in 1932 and held its first annual meeting the following year at the New Highwood Golf Club, Bexhill-on-Sea. It also played in that year its first two matches, one against the Ministry of Health at Sunningdale and the other against the Society of Town Clerks at Hollinwell. Good fellowship was the main objective of the founders of the Society. The new body was to be a social adjunct to the main Society, with the object of affording Clerks and Deputy Clerks of the Counties, at an annual meeting to be held in different parts of England and Wales, an opportunity of for-gathering informally and of getting to know one another better than was possible in the more austere atmosphere of their professional meetings in London. Apart from the period covered by the Second World War, the Society has held its annual meeting each year with unfailing regularity. It was to be for players and non-players; for present and honorary members of the main Society: golf—as was emphasized at the start—was to be the excuse for an enjoyable week-end.

The annexes give details of the twenty-two annual meetings which have been held, together with a full list of members—a hundred and twenty-one in all—who have been present at these meetings, as well as the names of the winners of the three Cups competed for annually, and of the winners of the Bogey Competition for which the main Society provide the first prize. Details are also given of twenty-one matches played against the Ministry of Health Golfing Society, four against the Society of Town Clerks and three against the Society of County Clerks in Scotland.

The pattern set for the first annual meeting at Bexhill by the then Honorary Secretary has remained virtually unaltered during the intervening years, and his successor since 1950 has never felt any wish to alter the traditional arrangements. Except in 1960, when the Society met at North Berwick, the meetings have involved annual visits in turn to places in Wales and the North, East and South of England which provide the essentials of a com-fortable hotel, nearby golf course (generally demanding rather more skill than is possessed by the members), and opportunities for non-players to relax for two or three days in the way that suits them best. In the evening there is the formal dinner party, at the end of which certain business is transacted and the members are then free to occupy themselves at bridge and noisier games or in talk until the small hours. The " business " never varies. On the first evening an auction-sweep of all the golfers competing for the Society Challenge Cup is held. Since the War, a percentage of the takings has been devoted each year to the Royal Air Force Benevolent Fund as the golf meeting usually embraces " Battle of Britain Sunday ", and this has resulted in a total sum of more than £130 being handed over to that cause. On the second evening, the Society attempts to decide the venue and date of the next annual meeting and of the matches to be played during the ensuing year, in an atmosphere imposing exceptional demands on the presiding Chairman (an atmosphere which on the occasion of the first visit to Harlech in 1938 was unforgettably dissipated in the music of the harp and Penillion singing). On the third and last evening the gathering is generally smaller and more peaceful, some having had to depart for home refreshed and ready for more orthodox pursuits in their County and Shire Halls. It has been found, however, that several members have been able after their return to reconcile a renewed devotion to work with a wish to record the spirit of the occasion in verse, and two such efforts are also included in the annexes.

Two caricatures specially commissioned for the Golfing Society and given by " Giles ", as well as four group photographs, are here reproduced. An attempt has been made in the selection of the latter to include as many as possible of the Clerks of the Counties and of their Deputies who have attended the annual meetings since 1933. At the end of this section is a sketch of the device embroidered on the Society's tie produced at the wish of the members present at Alwoodley in 1958. Earlier Clerks of the Peace undoubtedly lived by the maxim " The Pen is mightier than the Sword ", but their successors felt able to introduce a different symbol in recognition of the good fellowship engendered and fostered by their own Golfing Society then approaching its twenty-first annual meeting.

From the beginning, the members of the Clerks of the Peace Society have been free to take part in the activities of the Golfing Society, but no attempt is ever made to persuade them to do so. Those who attend pay no annual subscription, since the principle followed is for the expenses arising on each occasion to be defrayed by the individuals participating at the time, and they are bound by no formal Rules as there are none. Neither is there any executive committee to run the Society's affairs; only a small Golfing Committee whose main purpose is to give help to the Honorary Secretary when he needs it. The Golfing Society continues on its way without a constitution, without minutes, and completely flexible, and perhaps on that account the more able to achieve the aims and objects of its founders twenty-eight years ago, as interpreted in the eyes of their successors.

PLATE XIII

SIR HUBERT THORNLEY

CLERK OF THE PEACE FOR THE NORTH RIDING OF YORKSHIRE

1916-1960

GOLFING SOCIETY

Annexe I

Honorary Secretaries and Members of the Golfing Committee

| Honorary Secretaries: | L. Edgar Stephens ... ... | 1932–1950 |
| | G. C. Lightfoot ... ... | 1950– |

Golfing Committee:	Sir Robert Adcock, C.B.E., D.L. ...	1953–1956
	J. E. Blow	1953–
	C. P. Brutton, C.B.E.	1953–1960
	Vernon Lawrence, C.B.E.	1955–
	G. C. Lightfoot	1947–
	H. J. T. McIlveen	1932–1937
	H. A. Millington, O.B.E.	1932–1933
	F. G. Scott, M.C., D.L.	1938–1952
	Sir Edgar Stephens, C.B.E., D.L.	1932–

Annexe II

Annual Meetings, 1933 to 1960, and number of Members attending

Year	Club	Number attending
1933	New Highwood Golf Club, Bexhill-on-Sea, Sussex	14
1934	Royal Porthcawl Golf Club, Porthcawl, Glamorganshire	10
1935	Hunstanton Golf Club, Hunstanton, Norfolk	21
1936	Royal Lytham and St. Annes Golf Club, St. Annes-on-the-Sea, Lancashire	24
1937	Tadmarton Heath Golf Club, Tadmarton, Oxfordshire	25
1938	Royal St. David's Golf Club, Harlech, Merionethshire	24
1940	Ferndown Golf Club, Ferndown, Dorset	17
1946	Woodhall Spa Golf Club, Woodhall Spa, Lincolnshire	31
1947	Woodhall Spa Golf Club, Woodhall Spa, Lincolnshire	41
1948	Woodhall Spa Golf Club, Woodhall Spa, Lincolnshire	35
1949	Royal St. George's Golf Club, Sandwich, Kent	34
1950	Ganton Golf Club, Ganton, Yorkshire	30
1951	Royal St. David's Golf Club, Harlech, Merionethshire	36
1952	Sheringham Golf Club, Sheringham, Norfolk	41
1953	Hayling Golf Club, Hayling Island, Hampshire	37
1954	Royal Lytham and St. Annes Golf Club, St. Annes-on-the-Sea, Lancashire	37
1955	Woodhall Spa Golf Club, Woodhall Spa, Lincolnshire	41
1956	Royal Porthcawl Golf Club, Porthcawl, Glamorganshire	34
1957	Parkstone Golf Club, Parkstone, Dorset	28
1958	Alwoodley Golf Club, near Leeds, Yorkshire	29
1959	Hunstanton Golf Club, Hunstanton, Norfolk	32
1960	New Club, North Berwick, East Lothian, Scotland	18

THE CLERKS OF THE COUNTIES, 1360—1960

Annexe III

Present and past Members of the Society who have attended Annual Meetings,
or have played in Matches, during the period from 1933 to 1960

(The number in brackets after a name represents the number of attendances
at an Annual Meeting)

Sir Robert Adcock, C.B.E., D.L. (8)

Dudley Aukland (4)

A. C. Aylward (4)

C. H. Bird

J. E. Blow (14)

F. P. Boyce (2)

J. K. Boynton (3)

G. O. Brewis (6)

H. O. Brown (1)

C. P. Brutton, C.B.E. (10)

W. E. Bufton (4)

G. G. Burkitt (1)

F. D. V. Cant (10)

J. E. R. Carson (2)

H. Carswell (1)

C. H. Carter (4)

J. A. Chatterton (7)

H. W. Cleaver (6)

H. Copland, O.B.E. (4)

Guy R. Crouch, M.C., D.L. (12)

W. L. Dacey (Honorary) (4)

E. R. Davies (5)

H. C. Davies

A. R. Davis (1)

J. N. Dennis (2)

W. R. Edwards

Sir George Etherton, O.B.E., D.L. (5)

H. A. Foley, M.C. (13)

D. G. Gilman (6)

G. C. Godber (7)

K. Goodacre (1)

J. B. Graham, C.B.E., D.L. (6)

H. B. Greenwood (1)

R. N. D. Hamilton (5)

R. C. Hansen (4)

E. P. Harvey (11)

T. C. Hayward, C.B.E. (8)

A. C. Hetherington, M.B.E. (12)

C. G. Hickson (1)

E. S. Holcroft (7)

J. K. Hope, C.B.E., D.L. (6)

C. W. Hurley, O.B.E. (8)

Sir Peter Hutchison, Bt. (3)

P. D. Inman (8)

C. Jefferson (4)

H. Jevons (1)

R. John (1)

Gwilym T. Jones (5)

O. M. Jones (1)

R. L. Jones (2)

Sir William Jones, C.B.E. (2)

William Jones, O.B.E. (2)

D. W. Jones-Williams, M.C. (9)

Eustace Joy

PLATE XIV

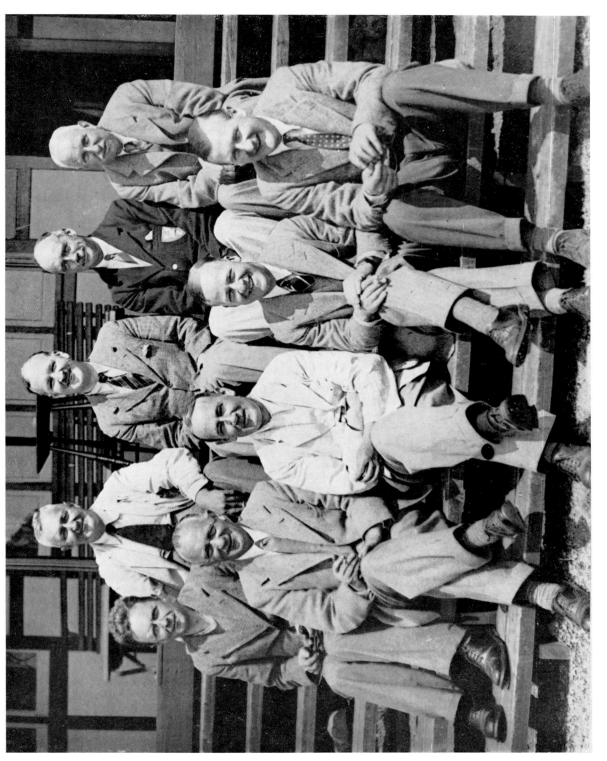

MEMBERS AT THE ANNUAL MEETING OF THE GOLFING SOCIETY, PORTHCAWL, 1934

The names, reading from left to right (with the County they represent) are as follows : *Front Row* : J. B. Kelly (Huntingdonshire) ; H. J. Owen (Merioneth) ; H. Rowland (Glamorgan) ; L. E. Stephens (Warwickshire) ; R. L. Moon (Gloucestershire). *Back Row* : K. G. T. Meaby (Nottinghamshire) ; G. R. Crouch (Buckinghamshire) ; D. Auckland (Surrey) ; H. L. Underwood (Staffordshire).

PLATE XV

MEMBERS AT THE ANNUAL MEETING OF THE GOLFING SOCIETY, HARLECH, 1938

The names, reading from left to right (with the County they represent) are as follows : *Front Row* : H. L. Underwood (Staffordshire) ; W. L. Platts (Kent) ; H. J. Owen (Merioneth) ; H. G. Thornley (Yorkshire, North Riding) ; L. E. Stephens (Warwickshire) ; F. G. Scott (Oxfordshire) ; C. H. Carter (Northumberland). *Back Row* : L. P. New (Bedfordshire) ; J. A. Turner (Warwickshire) ; C. P. Brutton (Dorset) ; G. R. Crouch (Buckinghamshire) ; E. W. Maples (formerly Hereford-shire) ; J. B. Graham (Bedfordshire) ; Cecil Oakes (East Suffolk) ; E. P. Harvey (Northumberland) ; P. E. Longmore (Hertfordshire) ; J. B. Kelly (Huntingdon-shire) ; H. Rowland (Glamorgan) ; E. S. Holcroft (Essex) ; H. J. C. Neobard (Berkshire) ; V. Lawrence (Monmouthshire) ; R. C. Hansen (Herefordshire).

PLATE XVI

MEMBERS AT THE ANNUAL MEETING OF THE GOLFING SOCIETY, WOODHALL SPA, 1947

The names, reading from left to right (with the County they represent) are as follows : *Front Row* (sitting) : H. S. Martin (East Sussex) ; R. H. Adcock (Lancashire); H. J. Owen (Merioneth) ; L. E. Stephens (Warwickshire) ; Sir Cecil Oakes (formerly East Suffolk) ; H. G. Thornley (Yorkshire, North Riding) ; W. L. Platts (Kent) ; E. W. Scorer (Lincolnshire, Parts of Lindsey) ; H. Rowland (formerly Glamorgan) ; F. G. Scott (Oxfordshire). *Middle Row* : J. E. McComb (Lancashire) ; J. M. Whitley (Salop) ; J. H. Thomas (Soke of Peterborough) ; A. C. Hetherington (Cumberland) ; E. P. Smith (Soke of Peterborough) ; R. C. Hansen (Herefordshire) ; V. Lawrence (Monmouthshire) ; T. C. Hayward (West Sussex) ; J. A. Turner (Northamptonshire) ; J. K. Hope (Durham) ; H. J. C. Neobard (Berkshire) ; R. C. Millard (Buckinghamshire) ; G. C. Godber (Salop) ; G. T. Jones (Caernarvonshire) ; P. E. White (Montgomeryshire). *Back Row* : E. T. Verger (Cornwall) ; H. Upton (Durham) ; J. E. Blow (Lincolnshire, Parts of Kesteven) ; J. B. Graham (Bedfordshire) ; G. R. Crouch (Buckinghamshire) ; A. N. Moon (Hertfordshire) ; H. A. Foley (formerly Buckinghamshire) ; W. Jones (Denbighshire) ; J. B. Kelly (Huntingdonshire) ; F. D. V. Cant (Herefordshire).

PLATE XVII

MEMBERS AT THE ANNUAL MEETING OF THE GOLFING SOCIETY, HUNSTANTON, 1959

The names, reading from left to right (with the County they represent) are as follows : *Front Row* (sitting) : R. A. Pearson (Lincolnshire, Parts of Kesteven) ; E. P. Harvey (Northumberland) ; V. Lawrence (Monmouthshire) ; H. A. Foley (formerly Buckinghamshire) ; L. E. Stephens (Warwickshire) ; G. C. Lightfoot (East Suffolk) ; H. J. Owen (formerly Merioneth) ; F. G. Scott (formerly Oxfordshire) ; J. B. Kelly (formerly Huntingdonshire). *Middle Row* : C. W. Hurley (Northumberland) ; W. H. Jones (Flintshire) ; F. D. V. Cant (Herefordshire) ; E. J. Roberts (Lincolnshire, Parts of Holland) ; D. W. Jones-Williams (Merioneth) ; D. G. Gilman (Derbyshire) ; J. M. Whitley (Salop) ; C. W. Waterfall (Norfolk) ; P. Hutchison (East Suffolk) ; J. A. Laverack (Huntingdonshire) ; G. O. Brewis (Bedfordshire). *Back Row* : A. F. Skinner (West Suffolk) ; R. A. Whitley (Yorkshire, East Riding) ; J. A. Chatterton (Leicestershire) ; E. R. Davies (Berkshire) ; W. E. Bufton (Denbighshire) ; R. A. Wotherspoon (Derbyshire) ; C. Jefferson (West Suffolk) ; R. N. D. Hamilton (Buckinghamshire) ; M. H. Wheeler (Yorkshire, North Riding).

GOLFING SOCIETY

J. B. Kelly (20)

B. Kenyon (2)

J. A. S. Laverack (4)

Vernon Lawrence, C.B.E. (16)

L. G. L. Lewis, M.B.E. (3)

G. C. Lightfoot (14)

D. H. Lines (1)

P. E. Longmore, C.B.E. (1)

C. V. Lucas (1)

C. P. H. McCall, M.B.E. (6)

J. E. McComb (1)

Sir Charles McGrath (2)

H. J. T. McIlveen (2)

Dr. E. W. Maples, O.B.E. (3)

H. C. Marris, O.B.E. (2)

H. S. Martin, C.B.E. (13)

J. H. Martin (1)

K. Tweedale Meaby, C.B.E., D.L. (1)

R. E. Millard (13)

H. A. Millington, O.B.E. (1)

A. Neville Moon (8)

R. L. Moon (3)

L. G. H. Munsey (1)

H. J. C. Neobard, O.B.E., D.L. (6)

L. P. New (6)

G. Norton (1)

Sir Cecil Oakes, C.B.E., D.L. (13)

J. H. Oldham (2)

Hugh J. Owen, D.L. (21)

R. A. Pearson (7)

G. R. S. Pepler (2)

J. H. C. Phelips (1)

W. L. Platts (7)

E. S. Rickards (4)

E. J. Roberts (2)

E. W. Roberts (3)

H. Rowland, C.B.E. (19)

W. W. Ruff (3)

E. W. Scorer, O.B.E. (5)

F. G. Scott, M.C. (16)

J. D. Scott (3)

G. C. Scrimgeour, D.S.O., O.B.E., M.C. (12)

W. R. Scurfield (1)

A. F. Skinner, O.B.E. (7)

Eric P. Smith (4)

Sir Edgar Stephens, C.B.E., D.L. (21)

T. Stephenson, C.B.E. (1)

P. A. Selborne Stringer, D.L. (4)

J. Henwood Thomas (5)

W. S. Thomas (2)

Sir Hubert Thornley, C.B.E., D.L. (10)

J. Alan Turner, O.B.E. (13)

H. L. Underwood (6)

H. Louis Underwood (5)

H. Upton (4)

E. T. Verger (2)

L. P. Wallen (4)

A. C. Walter (1)

H. A. H. Walter (4)

T. V. Walters (1)

C. W. Waterfall (3)

G. A. Wheatley (3)

M. H. Wheeler (6)

P. E. White (5)

J. M. Whitley (3)

R. A. Whitley (11)

R. A. Wotherspoon (5)

THE CLERKS OF THE COUNTIES, 1360—1960

Annexe IV

Winners of main competitions at Annual Meetings

Year	Clerks of the Peace Society Challenge Cup	Henry Rowland Scratch Cup	Veterans Cup	Bogey Competition
1933	H. A. Millington			
1934	H. Rowland			
1935	E. P. Harvey			H. S. Martin
1936	L. G. L. Lewis			C. H. Carter
1937	C. P. Brutton			L. G. L. Lewis
1938	C. P. Brutton			H. W. Cleaver
1940	L. P. New			H. Rowland
1946	F. D. V. Cant			C. P. Brutton
1947	H. S. Martin			A. C. Hetherington
1948	G. C. Lightfoot			G. C. Lightfoot
1949	J. A. Turner			G. C. Lightfoot
1950	G. C. Lightfoot			R. A. Whitley
1951	D. W. Jones-Williams			A. C. Hetherington
1952	R. A. Whitley			H. L. Underwood
1953	L. E. Stephens			G. C. Lightfoot
1954	{ A. C. Hetherington { G. C. Lightfoot		J. B. Kelly	E. P. Harvey
1955	M. H. Wheeler	F. D. V. Cant	H. A. Foley	M. H. Wheeler
1956	G. C. Lightfoot	G. C. Lightfoot	H. A. Foley	H. A. Foley
1957	E. S. Rickards	J. H. Martin	H. A. Foley	L. P. Wallen
1958	D. W. Jones-Williams	D. W. Jones-Williams	L. E. Stephens	C. Jefferson
1959	G. C. Lightfoot	G. C. Lightfoot	L. E. Stephens	{ D. W. Jones-Williams { G. C. Lightfoot
1960	R. N. D. Hamilton	G. C. Lightfoot	H. A. Foley	A. C. Hetherington

GOLFING SOCIETY

Annexe V

*Results of matches played by the Society against the
Golfing Societies of the following Bodies*

Year	Place	Opponents	Result
1933	Sunningdale	Ministry of Health	Lost
1933	Hollinwell	Society of Town Clerks	Lost
1934	Walton Heath	Ministry of Health	Won
1934	Hollinwell	Society of Town Clerks	Won
1935	Wentworth	Ministry of Health	Lost
1935	Hollinwell	Society of Town Clerks	Lost
1936	Sunningdale	Ministry of Health	Lost
1937	Addington	Ministry of Health	Lost
1937	Sunningdale	Society of Town Clerks	Won
1938	Berkshire	Ministry of Health	Lost
1939	Bramshot	Ministry of Health	Won
1946	Walton Heath	Ministry of Health	Halved
1947	Sunningdale	Ministry of Health	Won
1948	Sunningdale	Ministry of Health	Won
1949	Moor Park	Ministry of Health	Lost
1950	Walton Heath	Ministry of Health	Lost
1951	Sunningdale	Ministry of Health	Lost
1952	Sunningdale	Ministry of Health	Lost
1953	Swinley Forest	Ministry of Health	Lost
1954	Swinley Forest	Ministry of Health	Lost
1954	Royal Lytham and St. Annes	Society of County Clerks in Scotland	Lost
1955	Old Troon	Society of County Clerks in Scotland	Lost
1956	Walton Heath	Ministry of Health	Won
1957	St. George's Hill	Ministry of Health	Halved
1958	Camberley Heath	Ministry of Health	Lost
1959	Camberley Heath	Ministry of Health	Lost
1960	Worplesdon	Ministry of Health	Won
1960	Gullane	Society of County Clerks in Scotland	Won

Annexe VI

" *Oop for t' Coop,*" *or a Hymn of Hunstanton*
21st September 1935

Prologue
(*after* " *Ruddigore* ")

There stood a band of brothers
   On the big 1st Tee,
Carefree of office bothers
   Each and all a C. of P.
Each one tense and all excited
   (Even those that had been knighted)
Took a little ball to smite it—
   Off the big 1st Tee.

   Sing hey—
     Lack-a-day,
Let the tears fall free
For that little band of brothers
   On the big 1st Tee.

Now firstly let me mention our Chairman, good Sir George,
He did not claim to play the game, he only came to gorge,
He said he knew of nobody who at the game was poorer
Tho' this was much refuted by the much reputed Scorer.
With mental reservations to refrain from " looking-up ",
Each other member of the Gang had sworn to win the Cup.
Among the keen protagonists was Mr. Neobard
Determined he to hit the ball and hit it very hard
It gives me pain so I'll refrain from mentioning his score,
But it didn't ruffle " Neo ", he just murmured " What a bore "!
Bold Rowland of Glamorgan he sought to emulate
The doughty deeds of yester year, but oh! I grieve to state
His efforts were in vain, Alas! his score was merely " mush "
So he lingers on the laurels that he gained in far Portrush.
All a-blowin' and a-glowin' came another out of Wales,
And at golfing competitions Hughie Owen rarely fails,
T'would be ungenerous to state how many strokes he took,
And as other favourites failed him, it quite spoiled " his little book ".
A knightly oath to keep the true and straight and narrow path
Was sworn before Commissioner by sprightly Charles McGrath,
But even he quite failed to place West Riding on the map,
Tho' to frighten his opponents, he wore a " plus-four " cap!
Now Underwood was understood to be a darkish horse
But, slashing right and left of him, was rarely on the course.
Stout J. B. G. from Bedfordshire, tho' unsuccessful he,
Was more than satisfied to beat his humble Deputy.
Poor Kelly found a rendezvous in Bunker No. 1,
And Holcroft quite agreed with him that golfing wasn't fun.
C. H. Carter was a starter but he couldn't stay the pace,
Tho' as you'll hear hereafter his County won the race.
Sir George was most disconsolate and was even heard to heave a

PLATE XVIII

SIR EDGAR STEPHENS

CLERK OF THE PEACE FOR WARWICKSHIRE

FROM 1927

GOLFING SOCIETY

Sigh of pain and anguish at the card returned by Cleaver.
H. C. Marris merely muttered, as the rain it fell in showers,
" I'm good at cutting golf balls, but I'm better cutting flowers ".
Lanky Lewis out of Essex, at the end of the day's play,
Wished to God he'd gone to Clacton for his fortnight's holiday.
Came a Colonel out of Buckingham, a lawyer eke was he,
But I'm afraid a golfer he will never, never be,
For very rarely did he do a hole in under seven,
And, Man Alive! at No. 5, he took at least eleven!
The same sad story could I tell, the multitude of strokes
Amassed by Edgar Stephens, L. P. New and Cecil Oakes.
Only one—the handsome Harvey—felt that life was really grand,
He dwelleth not in Israel, but in far Northumberland.
He only of that brotherhood kept true and straight a line,
And was proclaimed the winner with a " Nett " of one five nine.

Postscript

I have touched on all the players, but before I take my leave
I really must refer again to Secretary " Steve ",
He owns a " ruddy " putter (christened Ada so 'tis said)
One part of it is made of wood, and twenty parts of lead.
For every artifice in golf for spin, or cut or drag,
He seizes and he squeezes little Ada from his bag.
It matters not the distance from the hole that he may be
With the aid of artful Ada he is on the green in three.
It may be asked why Stephens the Cup did not bring off,
Ah! Ada 'ad a 'eadache and a 'orrid 'acking cough.
He holds a handicap of twelve, he may become a " Plus ",
But if he quits the golfing game, what will become of us ?
He's an organising genius of never flurried mien,
All's well with the Society when he's behind the scene.

Epilogue

Every player told his story
At the 19th Hole,
And their lies were grim and gory
At the 19th Hole.
I don't mean to be unkind
P'raps I'd say (if they don't mind)
That each story was designed
" Merely to give artistic verisimilitude
To an otherwise bald
And unconvincing
statement "
at the
19th
Hole.

Sing hey—
Lack-a-day,
I am in an awful mess
Having ruffled all the feathers
Of the C. of P.G.S.

L. P. NEW.

Annexe VII

Lines by a non-player on the occasion of the meeting of the
Clerks of the Peace Golfing Society at Royal Lytham and St. Annes
19th September 1936

Lock, bolt and bar the County Hall,
In plus-four pocket hide the key,
Take suitcase, club, and one spare ball,
One " third return St. Anne's-on-Sea."
Now there will be—nay, do not scoff—
Some few who do not " golf " or " goff ",
Including one poor witless oaf
Who owns he does not even " goaf,"
Yet we are told we may come too
Although an ineffective crew
Who don't do as the Romans do.
We can resolve if nothing more
We won't get in the way nor bore
We'll step aside when they shout " Fore!"
We'll duck and dodge like anything
The Clubs which the more active swing,
Applaud the ball upon the wing.
We'll get a chance to do our stuff
For we can give them help enough
Retrieving balls from out the " rough "!
We can replace each mangled sod
And smooth the bruised and battered turf
And sing as usefully we plod
A song of larks and thundrous surf.

Remember too, at close of day
The Golfer puts his clubs away,
Removes plus-fours and, as you'll see,
Looks much the same as you and me.
Then altogether we'll go forth
To see this Naples of the North
And, ere we tiptoe up to bed
Perhaps we'll paint old Blackpool red
At any rate there's sure to be
A little clerical Whoopee!

Sir George at Preston (Bless his Soul!)
Has set the festive board and bowl
Oh, what a perfect nineteenth hole!
For there could not—be well assured—
A nobler Bacchus crown the Board
O kindly host, O genial knight
We'll set thy County Hall alight
With rosy flames of gratitude
Exuding rich beatitude
In oriental attitude!

GOLFING SOCIETY

I wonder if we're all aware
That Blackpool has a Pleasure Fair.
Oh brethren! picture to yourselves
The members like gay sportive elves
Up in the roundabouts and swings
Pucklike upon electric wings;
Clerks of the Peace in paper hats
Spiralling down on lightning mats;
While some expert in " drives " and " puts "
Play hell among the coconuts,
And others who are fond of sport,
The shootin', huntin', fishin' sort,
Pot the clay pipes and dancing balls,
Win rock and geegaws at the stalls
In order not to disappoint
The Chairman of their Standing Joint.

So as we, when the time arrives,
Resume our staid, official lives
All reinforced with Blackpool air
We'll show the world how much we care.
We'll swagger home as tanned as blacks
And smite our Chairmen on their backs.
Then when the Council meeting comes
Into our waistcoats stick our thumbs
And shout, " Eh lads, you'll like to see
What Blackpool air has done for me
A gradely time we've had and so
I want to take next time we go
Those who are most among you here
Amenable throughout the year
Provided always that you'll not
Expect Sir George to dine the lot.
Assuming this to be agreed
Come, Mr. Chairman, pray proceed!"

P. E. WHITE.

APPENDICES

The Imprisonment of John Bunyan in Bedford Gaol, 1660–1672.

John Bunyan (1628–1688) was imprisoned in Bedford Gaol in 1660, shortly after the Restoration, as a consequence of the revival of the old Acts of Parliament against Nonconformists, which had not been rigorously enforced during the Protectorate. He was never tried for the offence for which he was arrested, namely of holding a religious service in a private house, as he refused to plead to the charge. Paul Cobb, the Clerk of the Peace for Bedfordshire, some years afterwards wrote—apparently from the legal interest—to Roger Kenyon, the Clerk of the Peace for Lancashire, about Bunyan's appearance before Quarter Sessions, as follows:—

> " *One Bonyon was indicted upon the Statute of 35 Elizabeth for being at a Conventicle. He was in prison, and was brought back into Court and the indictment read to him; and because he refused to plead to it, the Court ordered me to record his confession, and he hath lain in prison upon that conviction, ever since Christmas Sessions, 12 Chas. II. . . And truly, I think it but reasonable that if any one do appear, and afterwards will not plead, but that you should take judgment by* nihil dicit, *or confession.*"

The Justices did not wish to leave Bunyan in prison indefinitely. In view of his obstinacy, they had no alternative but to commit him, and after some weeks they sent Cobb to him, in gaol, in an attempt to persuade him to submit to the Church of England and to secure his submission to the laws. This was unsuccessful but Bunyan says that he thanked Cobb " for his civil and meek discoursing with me ". Subsequently Bunyan endeavoured to appeal to Assizes and persuaded the gaoler to put his name down in the Calendar. As this was not (apparently) legally possible, Cobb deleted it and Bunyan then wrote that Cobb " did discover himself to be one of my greatest opposers ". The position seems, however, to have been that Cobb was obliged to discharge his office and that Bunyan did not understand the legal technicalities involved.

Bunyan did not obtain his release until 1672, when the laws against Nonconformists and Roman Catholics were suspended. An account of the conversation between Cobb and Bunyan was included in the latter's *Grace Abounding to the Chief of Sinners* which was written during the first part of his imprisonment and first published in 1666. It is set out in the three following pages:—

THE CLERKS OF THE COUNTIES, 1360—1960

" The Substance of some Discourse had between the Clerk of the Peace and myself, when he came to admonish me, according to the tenor of that Law by which I was in Prison.

When I had lain in prison other twelve weeks, and now not knowing what they intended to do with me, upon the 3rd of April 1661, comes Mr. Cobb unto me, as he told me, being sent by the justices to admonish me; and demanded of me submittance to the Church of England, &c. The extent of our discourse was as followeth:—

Cobb. When he was come into the house he sent for me out of my chamber; who, when I was come unto him, he said, Neighbour Bunyan, how do you do?

Bun. I thank you, Sir, said I, very well, blessed be the Lord.

Cobb. Saith he, I come to tell you that it is desired you would submit yourself to the laws of the land, or else at the next sessions it will go worse with you, even to be sent away out of the nation, or else worse than that.

Bun. I said that I did desire to demean myself in the world, both as becometh a man and a Christian.

Cobb. But, saith he, you must submit to the laws of the land, and leave off those meetings which you was wont to have; for the statute law is directly against it; and I am sent to you by the justices to tell you that they do intend to prosecute the law against you if you submit not.

Bun. I said, Sir, I conceive that that law by which I am in prison at this time doth not reach or condemn either me or the meetings which I do frequent; that law was made against those that, being designed to do evil in their meetings, making the exercise of religion their pretence, to cover their wickedness. It doth not forbid the private meetings of those that plainly and simply make it their only end to worship the Lord, and to exhort one another to edification. My end in meeting with others is simply to do as much good as I can, by exhortation and counsel, according to that small measure of light which God hath given me, and not to disturb the peace of the nation.

Cobb. Every one will say the same, said he; you see the late insurrection at London, under what glorious pretences they went; and yet, indeed, they intended no less than the ruin of the kingdom and commonwealth.

Bun. That practice of theirs I abhor, said I; yet it doth not follow that, because they did so, therefore all others will do so. I look upon it as my duty to behave myself under the King's government, both as becomes a man and a Christian, and if an occasion were offered me, I should willingly manifest my loyalty to my Prince, both by word and deed.

Cobb. Well, said he, I do not profess myself to be a man that can dispute; but this I say, truly, neighbour Bunyan, I would have you consider this matter seriously, and submit yourself; you may have your liberty to exhort your neighbour in private discourse, so be you do not call together an assembly of people; and, truly, you may do much good to the church of Christ, if you would go this way; and this you may do, and the law not abridge you of it. It is your private meetings that the law is against.

Bun. Sir, said I, if I may do good to one by my discourse, why may I not do good to two? and if to two, why not to four, and so to eight? &c.

Cobb. Ay, saith he, and to a hundred, I warrant you.

Bun. Yes, Sir, said I, I think I should not be forbid to do as much good as I can.

Cobb. But, saith he, you may but pretend to do good, and indeed, notwithstanding, do harm, by seducing the people; you are, therefore, denied your meeting so many together, lest you should do harm.

Bun. And yet, said I, you say the law tolerates me to discourse with my neighbour; surely there is no law tolerates me to seduce any one; therefore, if I may, by the law, discourse with one, surely it is to do him good; and if I by discoursing, may do good to one, surely, by the same law, I may do good to many.

Cobb. The law, saith he, doth expressly forbid your private meetings; therefore they are not to be tolerated.

APPENDIX I

Bun. I told him that I would not entertain so much uncharitableness of that Parliament in the 35th of Elizabeth, or of the Queen herself, as to think they did, by that law, intend the oppressing of any of God's ordinances, or the interrupting any in the way of God; but men may, in the wresting of it, turn it against the way of God; but take the law in itself, and it only fighteth against those that drive at mischief in their hearts and meetings, making religion only their cloak, colour, or pretence; for so are the words of the statute: ' If any meetings, under colour or pretence of religion,' &c.

Cobb. Very good; therefore the king, seeing that pretences are usually in and among people, as to make religion their pretence only, therefore he, and the law before him, doth forbid such private meetings, and tolerates only public; you may meet in public.

Bun. Sir, said I, let me answer you in a similitude: Set the case that, at such a wood corner, there did usually come forth thieves, to do mischief: must there therefore a law be made that every one that cometh out there shall be killed ? May there not come out true men as well as thieves out from thence ? Just thus it is in this case; I do think there may be many that may design the destruction of the commonwealth; but it does not follow therefore that all private meetings are unlawful; those that transgress, let them be punished. And if at any time I myself should do any act in my conversation as doth not become a man and Christian, let me bear the punishment. And as for your saying I may meet in public, if I may be suffered, I would gladly do it. Let me have but meeting enough in public, and I shall care the less to have them in private. I do not meet in private because I am afraid to have meetings in public. I bless the Lord that my heart is at that point, that if any man can lay anything to my charge, either in doctrine or practice, in this particular, that can be proved error or heresy, I am willing to disown it, even in the very market place; but if it be truth, then to stand to it to the last drop of my blood. And, Sir, said I, you ought to commend me for so doing. To err and to be a heretic are two things; I am no heretic, because I will not stand refractorily to defend any one thing that is contrary to the Word. Prove anything which I hold to be an error, and I will recant it.

Cobb. But, goodman Bunyan, said he, methinks you need not stand so strictly upon this one thing, as to have meetings of such public assemblies. Cannot you submit, and, notwithstanding, do as much good as you can, in a neighbourly way, without having such meetings ?

Bun. Truly, Sir, said I, I do not desire to commend myself, but to think meanly of myself; yet when I do most despise myself, taking notice of that small measure of light which God hath given me, also that the people of the Lord, by their own saying, are edified thereby. Besides, when I see that the Lord, through grace, hath in some measure blessed my labour, I dare not but exercise that gift which God hath given me for the good of the people. And I said further, that I would willingly speak in public, if I might.

Cobb. He said, that I might come to the public assemblies and hear. What though you do not preach ? you may hear. Do not think yourself so well enlightened, and that you have received a gift so far above others, but that you may hear other men preach. Or to that purpose.

Bun. I told him, I was as willing to be taught as to give instruction, and I looked upon it as my duty to do both for, said I, a man that is a teacher, he himself may learn also from another that teacheth, as the apostle saith: " Ye may all prophesy, one by one, that all may learn." 1 Co. xiv. 31. That is, every man that hath received a gift from God, he may dispense it, that others may be comforted; and when he hath done, he may hear and learn, and be comforted himself of others.

Cobb. But, said he, what if you should forbear awhile, and sit still, till you see further how things will go ?

Bun. Sir, said I, Wicliffe saith, that he which leaveth off preaching and hearing of the Word of God for fear of excommunication of men, he is already excommunicated of God, and shall in the day of judgment be counted a traitor to Christ.

Cobb. Ay, saith he, they that do not hear shall be so counted indeed; do you, therefore, hear.

Bun. But, Sir, said I, he saith, he that shall leave off either preaching or hearing, &c. That is, if he has received a gift for edification, it is his sin, if he doth not lay it out in a way of exhortation and counsel, according to the proportion of his gift; as well as to spend his time altogether in hearing others preach.

Cobb. But, said he, how shall we know that you have received a gift ?

Bun. Said I, let any man hear and search, and prove the doctrine by the Bible.

Cobb. But will you be willing, said he, that two indifferent persons shall determine the case, and will you stand by their judgment?

Bun. I said, Are they infallible?

Cobb. He said, No.

Bun. Then, said I, it is possible my judgment may be as good as theirs. But yet I will pass by either, and in this matter be judged by the Scriptures; I am sure that is infallible, and cannot err.

Cobb. But, said he, who shall be judge between you, for you take the Scriptures one way, and they another?

Bun. I said, The Scripture should, and that by comparing one scripture with another; for that will open itself, if it be rightly compared. As, for instance, if under the different apprehensions of the word Mediator, you would know the truth of it, the Scriptures open it, and tell us that he that is a mediator must take up the business between two, and " a mediator is not a *mediator* of one, but God is one," and " *there is* one mediator between God and men, [even] the man Christ Jesus." Ga. iii. 20. 1 Ti. ii. 5. So likewise the Scripture calleth Christ a complete, or perfect, or able high priest. That is opened in that he is called man, and also God. His blood also is discovered to be effectually efficacious by the same things. So the Scripture, as touching the matter of meeting together, &c., doth likewise sufficiently open itself and discover its meaning.

Cobb. But are you willing, said he, to stand to the judgment of the church?

Bun. Yes, Sir, said I, to the approbation of the church of God; the church's judgment is best expressed in Scripture. We had much other discourse which I cannot well remember, about the laws of the nation, and submission to government; to which I did tell him, that I did look upon myself as bound in conscience to walk according to all righteous laws, and that whether there was a king or no; and if I did anything that was contrary, I did hold it my duty to bear patiently the penalty of the law, that was provided against such offenders; with many more words to the like effect. And said, moreover, that to cut off all occasions of suspicion from any, as touching the harmlessness of my doctrine in private, I would willingly take the pains to give any one the notes of all my sermons; for I do sincerely desire to live quietly in my country, and to submit to the present authority.

Cobb. Well, neighbour Bunyan, said he, but indeed I would wish you seriously to consider of these things, between this and the quarter-sessions and to submit yourself. You may do much good if you continue still in the land; but alas, what benefit will it be to your friends, or what good can you do to them, if you should be sent away beyond the seas into Spain, or Constantinople, or some other remote part of the world? Pray be ruled.

Jailer. Indeed, Sir, I hope he will be ruled.

Bun. I shall desire, said I, in all godliness and honesty to behave myself in the nation, whilst I am in it. And if I must be so dealt withal, as you say, I hope God will help me to bear what they shall lay upon me. I know no evil that I have done in this matter, to be so used. I speak as in the presence of God.

Cobb. You know, saith he, that the Scripture saith, " the powers that be are ordained of God."

Bun. I said, Yes, and that I was to submit to the king as supreme, also to the governors, as to them that are sent by him.

Cobb. Well then, said he, the King then commands you, that you should not have any private meetings; because it is against his law, and he is ordained of God, therefore you should not have any.

Bun. I told him that Paul did own the powers that were in his day, as to be of God; and yet he was often in prison under them for all that. And also, though Jesus Christ told Pilate, that he had no power against him, but of God, yet he died under the same Pilate; and yet, said I, I hope you will not say that either Paul, or Christ, were such as did deny magistracy, and so sinned against God in slighting the ordinance. Sir, said I, the law hath provided two ways of obeying: The one to do that which I, in my conscience, do believe that I am bound to do, actively; and where I cannot obey actively, there I am willing to lie down, and to suffer what they shall do unto me. At this he sat still, and said no more; which, when he had done, I did thank him for his civil and meek discoursing with me; and so we parted.

O that we might meet in heaven!

Farewell. J.B."

240

APPENDIX II

Dinners at Greenwich

The Society's Minutes show that between 1861 and 1899 the Annual Dinner was held at Greenwich on a number of occasions. The Society first adjourned to dinner there at the " Trafalgar " in 1861 and, in later years down to 1889, they dined at the same tavern on at least seven more occasions, although there is no indication in the Minutes where the Annual Dinner was held for the years from 1863 to 1875. From 1890 to 1897 the Society went regularly to the " Ship " finishing up there finally in 1899 at the close of the century. The members travelled by steamer. The Minutes do not state why the choice was made, but the reason is not hard to guess, when it is realised what a popular resort Greenwich had become during the early nineteenth century and how much the whitebait and other fish dinners were enjoyed by the fashionable London society.

The origin and popularity of the Greenwich Whitebait Dinners is perhaps best explained in the following extracts from an article written by Mr. David Leggatt, the Chief Librarian of the Borough, which appeared in the 1951 Greenwich Festival Guide and is now reproduced with his kind permission.

" . . . At a convenient excursion distance from London, at the end of London's first railway, with good transport by river, Greenwich was well situated to become a popular and fashionable resort; as an additional advantage it possessed a constant supply of the small fry of ' *Clupea harengus* ' and ' *Clupea sprattus* '. It is upon these, commonly known as whitebait, that the gastronomic fame of Greenwich was built . . .

" When the Court was at Greenwich, the town was well supplied with taverns for the refreshment of statesmen, and others with business at Court; it is likely that the whitebait which abounded in the river at flood-tide often appeared on the tables of these taverns. Whitebait had for a long time been regarded as a delicacy; one of the conditions of success being that the fish should go direct from the river into the cauldron. In 1765 the landlord of the ' Ship ' advertised, ' Whitebait is dressed here in the highest perfection all the season '. Pennant, a naturalist and topographer, writing about this time, says that ' Whitebait are esteemed very delicious when fried with fine flour, and occasion, during the season, a vast resort of the lower order of epicures to the taverns contiguous to the places where they are taken '.

" Before long, whitebait at Greenwich was attracting not only ' the lower order of epicures ' but fashionable London society. The waterside taverns of Greenwich, with their weather-board fronts and bow windows commanding views of Greenwich and Blackwall Reaches, became the resort of the man-about-town. In 1842, a company, including George Cruikshank, gathered at the ' Ship ' to welcome Dickens on his return from America. Dickens wrote to a friend afterwards: ' Cruikshank was perfectly wild at the reunion, and after singing all manner of marine songs, wound up the entertainment by coming home (six miles) in a little open phaeton of mine, on his head, to the mingled delight and indignation of the Metropolitan police '. Not long after this orgy, Cruikshank became a teetotaller. Two years later Dickens attended another dinner at Greenwich, this time to celebrate the appearance of 'Martin Chuzzlewit'. Turner, the painter, on a sultry summer day, attended with his throat enveloped in a huge red belcher handkerchief, which nothing would induce him to remove. Carlyle declined an invitation to join the party, declaring that he truly loved Dickens, but that he would prefer to show his love in some other form than that of dining out in the dog-days . . .

" The first inn to become a fashionable resort for London diners-out was probably the ' Crown and Sceptre ', later the clubhouse of the Curlew Rowing and Sailing Club. Wellington was entertained here on his return from Waterloo. Greville, in his ' Memoirs ', writes under date 26th June 1833, of being one of a party taken by Lord Sefton ' in his omnibus and great open carriage ' to dine in a room called the ' Apollo '. As the century advanced, the Lord Mayor, the members of the Royal Academy and Her Majesty's Judges developed the habit of holding fish dinners at one or other of the Greenwich inns.

" The most renowned of these feasts, however, was the Annual Ministerial Dinner. For a long time during the nineteenth century it was the custom for Ministers of the Crown to celebrate the close of the parliamentary session by visiting Greenwich and partaking of a fish dinner which included whitebait. Accounts show that schoolboys breaking-up for their holidays were no more boisterous and light-hearted than legislators on the eve of the recess. These ministerial junketings appear to have been started by Sir Robert Preston, Bt., at one time M.P. for Dover. Sir Robert had what he called a ' fishing cottage ' at Dagenham, where he frequently had as his guest the Rt. Hon. George Rose, Secretary of the Treasury. On Rose's suggestion, Mr. Pitt, the Premier, visited the cottage. Pitt was pleased at the Baronet's hospitality—all three were considered two- or three- bottle men—and became a regular annual visitor.

" When, in course of time, the distance between Westminster and Dagenham proved inconvenient to the Premier, Preston proposed a rendezvous nearer to London, and Greenwich was chosen. Lord Camden joined the group to make a fourth, and soon afterwards Mr. Long, later Lord Farnborough, made a fifth. All were the personal guests of Sir Robert Preston, but as the party grew in size, Camden objected that, as they were dining at a tavern, it was not fair that Preston should pay. So it was arranged that the dinners should be given at Preston's invitation, and he insisted on contributing a buck and champagne, but the rest of the cost was to be defrayed by the guests. The meetings continued on this basis until the death of Pitt, by which time the guests included most of the Cabinet. They were generally held soon after Trinity Monday, just before the end of the Session. By the time Preston died the dinner had become an institution. At one time the Ministers went down river from Westminster by ordnance barge. Later, an ordinary steamer was used.

" During the long period of Tory supremacy, the dinners assumed a semi-political character. When the Tories were in office, the dinners were held at the ' Ship '; the Whigs went to the ' Trafalgar.' The Chief Whip generally took the chair. Waiters were excluded when the dinner had been served, and it was understood that everybody was permitted to say what he liked about his colleagues. All sorts of jokes were perpetrated. The dinners became irregular when Gladstone gained power in the late sixties, but Disraeli's last government kept up the tradition. Forty covers were laid for the dinner in 1878, at which the Earl of Beaconsfield, the Duke of Northumberland, the Lord Chancellor, the Duke of Richmond and Gordon and the Marquis of Salisbury were present. There was then a gap until Lord Rosebery's short term of office. The last of the dinners was held on August 15th 1894, and is described in the *Kentish Mercury* in these words:—

' After a lapse of ten years the Ministerial Whitebait Dinner, which used to be one of the chief social events of every Parliamentary session, was revived by Lord Rosebery at the historic Ship Hotel, Greenwich, on Wednesday evening. Years ago Liberal Cabinets used to dine at the " Trafalgar ", whilst the " Ship " was regarded as the Conservative house. But the " Trafalgar " whose trade went with the decadence of Greenwich as a fashionable resort, has been closed for some years, and so it was to the hospitable " Ship " that our

"DINNER DOWN THE RIVER" BY RICHARD DOYLE (1862)

PLATE XIX

Radical rulers went for their delectable feast. The old house had excelled itself in its desire to do honour to the occasion. The Union Jack and flags of lesser degree surmounted the roof, and from their capheads depended lines of tiny streamers which fluttered gaily in the fresh evening breeze. Around the lawn, fairy lamps were picturesquely grouped, and when darkness crept over the river varied hues lent additional attractiveness. The Victoria Steamboat Association were not to be outdone in a proper appreciation of the event. There were flags everywhere on the pier, and, as an illustration of the united interests which the visitors were supposed to represent, the Union Jack, the Royal Standard, and St. George's Cross floated bravely from the mast heads.' "

Dickens, as already suggested, seems to have found pleasure in dining at Greenwich. In *Our Mutual Friend* he wrote of Bella and her " pa ":—

" ' Where shall we go, my dear ? '
" ' Greenwich!' said Bella valiantly, . . .
" The little expedition down the river was delightful, and the little room overlooking the river into which they were shown for dinner was delightful. Everything was delightful. The park was delightful, the punch was delightful, the dishes of fish were delightful, the wine was delightful . . ."

The drawing by Richard Doyle *Dinner down the River*, dated 1862, here reproduced, convincingly confirms the wise choice of Greenwich for these dinner parties.

The " Trafalgar " still stands today, though the interior has been converted. The " Ship " was destroyed by bombing in the Second World War. Its site was subsequently cleared and used for the dry dock in which the " Cutty Sark " is now preserved.

APPENDIX III

List of persons present
at the 150th Anniversary Dinner of the Society

In the Chair : Tom C. Hayward, Esq., C.B.E.

The Society's Principal Guest : The Rt. Hon. The Lord Mayor of London,
Sir Bernard Waley-Cohen.

1. The Society's Official Guests, and Members' Personal Guests, in alphabetical order:

Harold M. Abrahams, Esq., C.B.E.

J. Roland Adams, Esq., Q.C.

Philip Allen, Esq., C.B.

The Rt. Hon. Lord Ashburton
(H.M. Lieutenant of Hampshire)

Reginald Atkins, Esq.

John Aubrey-Fletcher, Esq.

John Bale, Esq.

G. E. Banwell, Esq., C.B.E., M.C.

Sir Harold Banwell

T. E. Chester Barratt, Esq.

R. Wilson Bartlett, Esq., D.L.

Sir Alfred Bates, M.C., D.L.

Tom Beaumont, Esq.

H. C. Bedwell, Esq.

W. J. Bennett, Esq., C.B.E.

Tristram de la Poer Beresford, Esq.,
K.St.J., Q.C.

Dr. W. T. Bermingham

J. C. Blake, Esq., C.B.

T. M. Bland, Esq., T.D., D.L.
(Chairman of the County Councils
Association)

W. W. Boulton, Esq., C.B.E., D.L.

F. T. Bowen, Esq.

Roderic Bowen, Esq., Q.C., M.P.

Major-General The Viscount Bridgeman,
K.B.E., C.B., D.S.O., M.C. (H.M.
Lieutenant of Shropshire)

S. Britnor, Esq.

P. E. Brodie, Esq., O.B.E.

The Rt. Hon. Henry Brooke, M.P.
(Minister of Housing and Local
Government)

The Rt. Hon. Sir Norman Brooke, G.C.B.

R. E. Brooks, Esq.

R. K. Brown, Esq., O.B.E., T.D., Q.C.

William Brown, Esq., O.B.E.

Group Captain H. E. Bufton, D.S.O., O.B.E.,
D.F.C., A.F.C.

Air Vice-Marshal S. O. Bufton, C.B., D.F.C.

Charles H. A. Butler, Esq.

His Hon. Judge William Lawson Campbell

His Hon. W. K. Carter, Q.C.

The Rt. Hon. Florence E. Cayford
(Chairman of the London County Council)

The Rt. Rev. The Lord Bishop of Chichester

Leonard Childs, Esq., O.B.E., D.L.

Major S. V. Christie-Miller, D.L.

Brigadier Patrick Clapham, O.B.E.

John Cockram, Esq.

C. L. S. Cornwall-Legh, Esq., D.L.

C. Lynton Cox, Esq.

The Rt. Hon. Lord Cozens-Hardy, D.L.

R. S. Crossfield, Esq.

Sir Charles Cunningham, K.B.E., C.B.,
C.V.O.

The Viscount Curzon

W. L. Dacey, Esq.,
(Secretary of the County Councils
Association)

The Rt. Hon. Lord De Ramsey, T.D.
(H.M. Lieutenant of Huntingdonshire)

The Rt. Hon. The Earl of Derby, M.C.
(H.M. Lieutenant of Lancashire)

N. Doodson, Esq.

Edward Du Cann, Esq., M.P.

Sir Michael Duff, Bt., K.St.J.
(H.M. Lieutenant of Caernarvonshire)

Sir James Dunnett, K.C.B., C.M.G.

Victor Durand, Esq., Q.C.

T. V. S. Durrant, Esq.

F. L. Edwards, Esq., C.B., O.B.E.

Sidney Elmitt, Esq.

B. F. L. Elwin, Esq.

Sir Wesley Emberton, D.L.

His Hon. Judge E. Eifion Evans, Q.C.

Sir David Evans, O.B.E.

The Rt. Hon. Lord Evershed
(Master of the Rolls)

G. C. Fardell, Esq., M.B.E.

F. D. Farley, Esq., D.L.

Norman Farmer, Esq., C.B.E.

Major T. P. Farrelly

The Hon. Mr. Justice Finnemore

E. M. T. Firth, Esq., C.B.

Peter Fleetwood-Hesketh, Esq., T.D.

Mrs. M. R. Forbes

Sir Frank Foster, C.B.E.

T. J. W. Foy, Esq.

His Hon. Judge Conolly Gage

The Rt. Hon. The Earl of Gainsborough

Carl Ronald Giles, Esq., O.B.E.

A. E. Gilfillan, Esq., O.B.E.

THE CLERKS OF THE COUNTIES, 1360—1960

F. Blaise Gillie, Esq., C.B.

Sir Fergus Graham, Bt., K.B.E., T.D.
(H.M. Lieutenant of Cumberland)

H. J. Hamblen, Esq., C.B.E.

Sir Henry Hancock, K.C.B., K.B.E., C.M.G.
(Chairman of the Local Government
Commission for England)

A. W. Harrison, Esq.

H. S. Haslam, Esq., O.B.E.

Desmond Heap, Esq.

Dr. G. W. Heckels

Denys T. Hicks, Esq., O.B.E., T.D., D.L.
(President of the Law Society)

V. G. Hines, Esq.

R. R. Meyric Hughes, Esq.

B. H. Hunt, Esq.

Major T. H. Ives

R. L. Jackson, Esq., C.B.E.

F. J. Jenkinson, Esq., O.B.E.

H. C. Johnson, Esq., O.B.E.

Alwyn Hughes Jones, Esq.

J. K. T. Jones, Esq., C.B.E.

R. A. Kidd, Esq., C.B.E.

The Rt. Hon. Viscount Kilmuir, G.C.V.O.
(Lord High Chancellor of Great Britain)

Mr. Sheriff Adam K. Kirk

Geoffrey Lawrence, Esq., Q.C.
(President of the Society of Chairmen and
Deputy Chairmen of Quarter Sessions)

C. E. Leatherland, Esq., O.B.E.

The Viscount Leverhulme, T.D.
(H.M. Lieutenant of Cheshire)

E. N. Liggins, Esq., T.D.

Alan Lubbock, Esq.

A. J. Lyddon, Esq., C.B.E.

Sir Malcolm McAlpine, K.B.E.

Major S. H. Macknelly

Ewart Marlow, Esq., C.B.E., M.C.

Sir Theobald Mathew, K.B.E., M.C.

The Rt. Hon. Lord Merthyr, T.D.

L. R. Missen, Esq., C.M.G., M.C.

The Hon. Ewen E. S. Montagu,
C.B.E., Q.C.

Garth Moore, Esq.

Sir George Mowbray, Bt., K.B.E.

A. A. Muir, Esq.

E. H. Nichols, Esq., T.D.

His Grace The Duke of Norfolk, E.M.,
K.G., G.C.V.O. (H.M. Lieutenant of
Sussex)

His Hon. R. H. Norris

Miss M. O'Conor, O.B.E.

W. H. Openshaw, Esq.

A. G. B. Owen, Esq., C.B.E.

G. A. Pargiter, Esq., D.L., M.P.
(Vice-Chairman of County Councils
Association)

The Rt. Hon. Lord Parker of Waddington
(Lord Chief Justice of England)

A. R. Parr, Esq., O.B.E.

D. T. Peterborough, Esq.

G. Godfrey Phillips, Esq., C.B.E.

Sir John G. Carew Pole, Bt., D.S.O., T.D.

K. H. Potts, Esq.

E. John Powell, Esq., C.B.E.

P. Stanley Price, Esq., Q.C.

The Rt. Hon. John Profumo, O.B.E., M.P.
(Secretary of State for War)

R. J. Proudfoot, Esq.

S. Rhodes, Esq.

E. W. W. Richards, Esq.

Lieut.-Cdr. R. M. Richards, R.N. (Retd.)

Sydney W. L. Ripley, Esq.

Dr. G. Wyn Roberts

B. H. Rockman, Esq., O.B.E., D.L.

Eustace Roskill, Esq., Q.C.

Sir Kenneth Ruddle, T.D., D.L.

Sir John Ruggles-Brise, Bt., C.B.,
O.B.E., T.D. (H.M. Lieutenant of Essex)

R. W. Rule, Esq., O.B.E.

Dame Enid Russell-Smith, D.B.E.

J. Waring Sainsbury, Esq.

Arthur Schmiegelow, Esq.

Philip S. Scorer, Esq.

R. E. Seaton, Esq., C.B.E.

Colonel G. P. Shakerley, M.C., T.D.

Dame Evelyn Sharp, D.B.E.

Sir Reginald Sharpe, Q.C.

J. R. Shaw, Esq.

Lieut.-Col. Sir Herbert Shiner,
D.S.O., M.C., D.L.

W. T. C. Skyrme, Esq., C.B.E., T.D.

F. A. Small, Esq.

Dame Mary Smieton, D.B.E.

P. E. G. Smith, Esq.

C. M. T. Smith-Ryland, Esq.

His Hon. Judge T. F. Southall

F. R. Steele, Esq.

Dr. Duncan Stewart

J. H. Street, Esq.

Sir Austin Strutt, K.C.V.O., C.B.

Alderman and Sheriff Colonel R. H.
Studholme, O.B.E.

R. M. A. C. Talbot, Esq.

Dr. G. W. H. Townsend

Colonel Cennydd Traherne, T.D.,
(H.M. Lieutenant of Glamorgan)

S. E. Trotman, Esq.

Brigadier G. B. Vaughan-Hughes,
M.C., D.L.

Captain Sir Offley Wakeman, Bt.,
C.B.E., D.L.

L. J. Wallach, Esq.

D. P. Walsh, Esq., C.B.

Major R. P. H. Walter

Thomas Waterhouse, Esq., C.B.E.

David Watson, Esq.

His Grace The Duke of Wellington, K.G.
(Governor of the Isle of Wight)

James Westoll, Esq.

Major Simon Whitbread
(H.M. Lieutenant of Bedfordshire)

J. Whittle, Esq.

David G. Widdicombe, Esq.

J. P. Widgery, Esq., Q.C.

Harold B. Williams, Esq., Q.C.

Colonel J. F. Williams-Wynne, D.S.O.
(H.M. Lieutenant of Merioneth)

Dr. J. H. Willis

Dr. T. G. Willis

The Rt. Hon. Lord Willoughby de Broke,
M.C., A.F.C., K.St.J.
(H.M. Lieutenant of Warwickshire)

Sir John Winnifrith, K.C.B.

A. C. Wood, Esq.

E. A. C. Woodcock, Esq.

APPENDIX III

2. Members and Honorary Members of the Society

J. Atkinson, Esq.

A. C. Aylward, Esq.

L. H. Baines, Esq.

M. A. Bains, Esq.

C. G. T. Berridge, Esq.

J. E. Blow, Esq.

A. Bond, Esq., O.B.E.

J. H. N. Bourne, Esq.

G. O. Brewis, Esq.

* H. Oswald Brown, Esq.

W. E. Bufton, Esq.

C. Leo Burgess, Esq., C.B.E.

G. G. Burkitt, Esq.

D. W. L. Butler, Esq.

J. E. R. Carson, Esq.

* Hugh Carswell, Esq.

H. Crossley, Esq.

E. R. Davies, Esq.

A. R. Davis, Esq.

Guy H. Davis, Esq.

J. N. Dennis, Esq.

C. W. Doré, Esq.

T. H. Evans, Esq., C.B.E., D.L.

* H. A. Foley, Esq., M.C.

D. G. Gilman, Esq.

G. C. Godber, Esq.

K. Goodacre, Esq., T.D.

R. N. D. Hamilton, Esq.

W. L. Hann, Esq.

R. P. Harries, Esq.

W. O. Hart, Esq., C.M.G.

E. P. Harvey, Esq.

G. T. Heckels, Esq.

A. C. Hetherington, Esq., M.B.E.

K. S. Himsworth, Esq.

J. K. Hope, Esq., C.B.E., D.L.

C. W. Hurley, Esq., O.B.E., T.D.

Sir Peter Hutchison, Bt.

P. D. Inman, Esq.

C. Jefferson, Esq.

R. John, Esq.

W. Hugh Jones, Esq.

D. W. Jones-Williams, Esq., M.C.

Bernard Kenyon, Esq.

W. E. Lane, Esq.

Vernon Lawrence, Esq., C.B.E.

G. C. Lightfoot, Esq.

J. N. Manson, Esq.

C. P. H. McCall, Esq., M.B.E., T.D.

R. E. Millard, Esq.

A. Neville Moon, Esq., D.L.

* L. G. H. Munsey, Esq.

J. H. Oldham, Esq., T.D.

* Hugh J. Owen, Esq., D.L.

R. P. Owen, Esq.

J. E. Owen-Jones, Esq.

* D. J. Parry, Esq., C.B.E.

R. A. Pearson, Esq.

G. R. S. Pepler, Esq.

W. J. Piper, Esq.

T. G. Randall, Esq., C.B.E.

T. M. H. Rees, Esq.

E. S. Rickards, Esq.

E. J. Roberts, Esq.

* Sir Howard Roberts, C.B.E., D.L.

W. W. Ruff, Esq.

W. W. Sayers, Esq.

C. F. Shoolbred, Esq.

Sir Edgar Stephens, C.B.E., D.L.

G. N. C. Swift, Esq.

W. S. Thomas, Esq.

* Sir Hubert Thornley, C.B.E., D.L.

R. F. G. Thurlow, Esq.

J. Alan Turner, Esq., O.B.E.

H. Louis Underwood, Esq.

E. T. Verger, Esq.

A. C. V. Waite, Esq.

L. P. Wallen, Esq., M.C., T.D.

H. A. H. Walter, Esq.

T. V. Walters, Esq.

C. W. Waterfall, Esq.

G. Andrew Wheatley, Esq., C.B.E.

P. E. White, Esq., D.L.

J. M. Whitley, Esq.

R. M. Willis, Esq.

R. A. Wotherspoon, Esq.

*Honorary member

APPENDIX IV

List of Members of the Society
31st December, 1960

1. Serving Members

		Surname	Forenames	Office held	Address	Date of joining the Society
*†	1	STEPHENS	Sir (Leon) Edgar, C.B.E., D.L., F.S.A.	C.P. and C.C. of Warwickshire	Shire Hall, Warwick (past Chairman) (Hon. Treasurer)	1926
*	2	HOPE	James Kenneth, C.B.E., D.L.	C.P. and C.C. of Durham	Shire Hall, Durham	1927
	3	HANSEN	Richard Claussen	C.P. and C.C. of Herefordshire	Shire Hall, Hereford	1932
*	4	THURLOW	Richard Francis Gardom	C.P. and C.C. of Isle of Ely	County Hall, March	1932
*†	5	BRUTTON	Charles Phipps, C.B.E.	C.P. and C.C. of Dorset	County Hall, Dorchester (past Vice-Chairman)	1932
*†	6	TURNER	John Alan, O.B.E.	C.P. and C.C. of Northampton-shire	County Hall, Northampton	1932
*	7	HARVEY	Ernest Philip	C.P. and C.C. of Northumberland	County Hall, Newcastle-upon-Tyne, 1	1932
*†	8	HAYWARD	Tom Christopher, C.B.E.	C.P. and C.C. of West Sussex	County Hall, Chichester (Chairman)	1934
*	9	CHATTERTON	John Arthur	C.P. and C.C. of Leicestershire	County Offices, Grey Friars, Leicester	1934
*†	10	WHITE	Percival Edward, D.L.	C.P. and C.C. of Montgomery-shire	County Offices, Welshpool	1934
	11	EDWARDS	William Richard	D.C.P. and D.C.C. of East Sussex	County Hall, Lewes	1934
*†	12	BLOW	Joseph Edward	C.P. and C.C. of Lincolnshire, Parts of Kesteven	County Offices, Sleaford	1934
	13	STEPHENSON	Thomas, C.B.E.	C.C. of Yorkshire, East Riding	County Hall, Beverley	1934
*	14	BERRIDGE	Christian Gerard Timperley	C.C. of Essex	County Hall, Chelmsford	1934
	15	LEWIS	Laurence George, M.B.E.	D.C.C. of Essex	County Hall, Chelmsford	1934
*†	16	DAVIS	Guy Heath	C.P. and C.C. of Gloucester-shire	Shire Hall, Gloucester	1935
*†	17	DAVIES	Ellis Roger	C.P. and C.C. of Berkshire	Shire Hall, Reading	1936

*Member of the Parliamentary and General Purposes Committee.
†Member of the Law Committee.

THE CLERKS OF THE COUNTIES, 1360—1960

		Surname	Forenames	Office held	Address	Date of joining the Society
*†	18	LAWRENCE	Vernon, C.B.E.	C.P. and C.C. of Monmouth-shire	County Hall, Newport, Mon.	1937
	19	ROBINSON	Arthur Desmond	D.C.P. and D.C.C. of West Sussex	County Hall, Chichester	1937
*	20	SCURFIELD	William Russell	C.P. and C.C. of Worcestershire	Shire Hall, Worcester	1938
*	21	EVANS	Thomas Henry, C.B.E., D.L.	C.P. and C.C. of Staffordshire	County Buildings, Stafford	1938
	22	WILLIS	Robert Metherell	D.C.P. and D.C.C. of Warwick-shire	Shire Hall, Warwick	1939
*	23	WHEATLEY	George Andrew, C.B.E.	C.P. and C.C. of Hampshire	The Castle, Winchester	1939
*	24	BUFTON	William Evan	C.P. and C.C. of Denbighshire	County Offices, Ruthin	1939
	25	BREWIS	George Oldfield	C.P. and C.C. of Bedfordshire	Shire Hall, Bedford	1939
*	26	SWIFT	George Norman Cyrus	C.P. and C.C. of Cumberland	The Courts, Carlisle	1940
	27	JONES	William, O.B.E.	C.P. and C.C. of Anglesey	County Offices, Llangefni	1941
*†	28	GODBER	Geoffrey Chapman	C.P. and C.C. of Salop	Shire Hall, Shrewsbury (Vice-Chairman and Hon. Secretary)	1941
†	29	BURGESS	Clarkson Leo, C.B.E.	C.P. of London	Sessions House, Newington Causeway, London, S.E.1.	1941
*	30	KENYON	Bernard	C.P. and C.C. of Yorkshire, West Riding	County Hall, Wakefield	1941
	31	CANT	Francis Denis Victor	D.C.P. and D.C.C. of Here-fordshire	Shire Hall, Hereford	1942
*†	32	VERGER	Edward Thomas	C.P. and C.C. of Cornwall	County Hall, Truro	1942
	33	TILDESLEY	Arthur	D.C.P. and D.C.C. of Stafford-shire	County Buildings, Stafford	1942
	34	WALTER	Hugh Albert Harold	C.P. and C.C. of Lincolnshire, Parts of Holland	County Hall, Boston	1942
	35	ROWLANDS	William John	D.C.P. and D.C.C. of Denbigh-shire	County Offices, Ruthin	1942
*	36	BAINES	Leslie Henry	C.P. and C.C. of Isle of Wight	County Hall, Newport, Isle of Wight	1942
	37	WHITLEY	John Manners	D.C.P. and D.C.C. of Salop	Shire Hall, Shrewsbury	1943
*	38	LIGHTFOOT	George Cecil	C.P. and C.C. of East Suffolk	County Hall, Ipswich	1944
	39	WATERFALL	Christopher William	D.C.P. and D.C.C. of Norfolk	County Offices, Thorpe Road, Norwich	1944
*	40	RICKARDS	Ernest Stanley	C.P. and C.C. of Somerset	County Hall, Taunton	1944
†	41	PHELIPS	James Henry Caswall	D.C.P. and D.C.C. of Worces-tershire	Shire Hall, Worcester	1944

*Member of the Parliamentary and General Purposes Committee.
†Member of the Law Committee.

		Surname	Forenames	Office held	Address	Date of joining the Society
*	42	JONES	William Hugh	C.P. and C.C. of Flintshire	County Buildings, Mold	1945
	43	WELLS	Charles Martin Sidney	C.P. and C.C. of Breconshire	County Hall, Brecon	1945
*	44	UNDERWOOD	Henry Louis	C.P. and C.C. of Pembrokeshire	County Offices, Haverfordwest	1945
	45	PHYTHIAN	Charles	C.P. and C.C. of Cambridge-shire	Shire Hall, Cambridge	1945
*†	46	MILLARD	Richard Edward	C.P. and C.C. of Buckingham-shire	County Hall, Aylesbury	1945
	47	MOON	Arthur Neville, D.L.	C.P. and C.C. of Hertfordshire	County Hall, Hertford	1946
	48	WHITLEY	Raymond Archer	C.P. and D.C.C. of Yorkshire, East Riding	County Hall, Beverley	1946
	49	OWEN-JONES	John Eryl	C.P. and C.C. of Caernarvon-shire	County Offices, Caernarvon	1946
*	50	HETHERINGTON	Arthur Carleton, M.B.E.	C.P. and C.C. of Cheshire	County Offices, Chester	1946
	51	SMITH	Eric Pope	C.P. and C.C. of Soke of Peterborough	Clerk of the Peace Office, Peterborough	1946
	52	HANN	William Liddell	D.C.P. and D.C.C. of Cam-bridgeshire	Shire Hall, Cambridge	1946
†	53	BURKITT	Gerald Gale	C.P. and C.C. of Oxfordshire	County Hall, Oxford	1946
	54	KNIGHT	Clifford	D.C.P. and D.C.C. of Leicester-shire	County Offices, Grey Friars, Leicester	1946
*	55	AYLWARD	Anthony Case	C.P. and C.C. of Huntingdon-shire	County Buildings, Huntingdon	1947
	56	DORÉ	Clifford William	D.C.P. and D.C.C. of Cornwall	County Hall, Truro	1947
	57	HURLEY	Clement Woods, O.B.E., T.D.	D.C.P. and D.C.C. of Northum-berland	County Hall, Newcastle-upon-Tyne, 1	1947
*†	58	SKINNER	Alan Frank, O.B.E.	C.P. and C.C. of West Suffolk	Shire Hall, Bury St. Edmunds	1947
	59	THOMAS	John Henwood	D.C.P. and D.C.C. of Soke of Peterborough	Clerk of the Peace Office, Peterborough	1947
	60	ROGERS	Donald George	D.C.P. and D.C.C. of Gloucestershire	Shire Hall, Gloucester	1947
	61	HUTCHISON	Sir Peter, Bt.	D.C.P. and D.C.C. of East Suffolk	County Hall, Ipswich	1947
*	62	GILMAN	Denis George	C.P. and C.C. of Derbyshire	County Offices, Matlock	1947
	63	PEPLER	George Richard Summerland	D.C.P. and D.C.C. of Lincoln-shire, Parts of Lindsey	County Offices, Lincoln	1947
	64	GODSALL	Harold Graham	C.P. and C.C. of Devon	The Castle, Exeter	1947
	65	REES	Thomas Morgan Haydn	D.C.P. and D.C.C. of Flintshire	County Buildings, Mold	1948
	66	JONES-WILLIAMS	Dafydd Wyn, M.C.	C.P. and C.C. of Merioneth	County Offices, Dolgelley	1948

*Member of the Parliamentary and General Purposes Committee.
†Member of the Law Committee.

THE CLERKS OF THE COUNTIES, 1360—1960

		Surname	Forenames	Office held	Address	Date of joining the Society
*	67	BOYCE	Frederick Peter	C.P. and C.C. of Norfolk	County Offices, Thorpe Road, Norwich	1948
	68	DAVIES	Idris	D.C.C. of Anglesey	County Offices, Llangefni	1949
†	69	McCALL	Charles Patrick Home, M.B.E., T.D.	C.P. and C.C. of Lancashire	County Hall, Preston	1949
	70	TEMPLEMAN	Arthur Cowley	D.C.P. and D.C.C. of Dorset	County Hall, Dorchester	1949
	71	CARSON	James Eric Rutherford	C.P. and C.C. of Cardiganshire	County Office, Marine Terrace, Aberystwyth	1949
	72	ROOK	David James	D.C.P. and D.C.C. of Isle of Ely	County Hall, March	1950
	73	ROBERTS	Evan Wynne	D.C.P. and D.C.C. of Pembrokeshire	County Offices, Haverfordwest	1950
	74	GOODWIN	Laurence Eric	D.C.P. and D.C.C. of Durham	Shire Hall, Durham	1950
	75	RANDALL	Terence George, C.B.E.	D.C.C. of London	The County Hall, London, S.E.1.	1950
*	76	HIMSWORTH	Kenneth Stephenson	C.P. and C.C. of Westmorland	County Hall, Kendal	1950
*	77	RUFF	William Willis	C.C. of Surrey	County Hall, Kingston-upon-Thames	1951
	78	INMAN	Peter Donald	D.C.P. and D.C.C. of Lancashire	County Hall, Preston	1951
†	79	BOYNTON	John Keyworth, M.C.	D.C.P. and D.C.C. of Berkshire	Shire Hall, Reading	1951
	80	BOND	Alan, O.B.E.	C.P. and C.C. of Rutland	County Offices, Oakham	1951
	81	JACKMAN	Trevor Bromley, O.B.E., T.D.	D.C.P. of Yorkshire, West Riding	County Hall, Wakefield	1951
	82	McVICAR	Sidney James, O.B.E.	D.C.C. of Yorkshire, West Riding	County Hall, Wakefield	1951
	83	WOTHERSPOON	Robert Andrew	C.P. and C.C. of Yorkshire, North Riding	County Hall, Northallerton	1951
	84	WALKER	Kenneth Hamblett	D.C.P. and D.C.C. of Monmouthshire	County Hall, Newport, Mon.	1952
	85	LUCAS	Charles Vivian	D.C.P. and D.C.C. of Devon	The Castle, Exeter	1952
*	86	JOHN	Richard	C.P. and C.C. of Glamorgan	County Hall, Cardiff	1952
	87	WAITE	Alan Charles Victor	D.C.C. of Surrey	County Hall, Kingston-upon-Thames	1952
	88	PIPER	Walter John	C.P. of Essex	Clerk of the Peace Office, Tindal Square, Chelmsford	1952
	89	GRAHAM	Robert Lawrence	D.C.P. and D.C.C. of Cumberland	The Courts, Carlisle	1952

*Member of the Parliamentary and General Purposes Committee.
†Member of the Law Committee.

APPENDIX IV

	Surname	Forenames	Office held	Address	Date of joining the Society
90	THOMAS	Wynne Simpson	C.P. and C.C. of Carmarthenshire	County Offices, Carmarthen	1952
91	JONES	Ronald Laughton	D.C.P. of Somerset	County Hall, Taunton	1952
† 92	WALLEN	Leonard Paul, M.C., T.D.	D.C.C. of Somerset	County Hall, Taunton	1952
93	HARRIES	Robert Paschal	C.P. and C.C. of Wiltshire	County Hall, Trowbridge	1953
94	ATKINSON	Jack	C.P. and C.C. of East Sussex	County Hall, Lewes	1953
95	WALTON	Hugh Merscy	D.C.P. of Oxfordshire	County Hall, Oxford	1953
96	JONES	Owen Meurig, M.C.	D.C.P. and D.C.C. of Northamptonshire	County Hall, Northampton	1953
97	WALTERS	Tom Vivian	D.C.P. and D.C.C. of Glamorgan	County Hall, Cardiff	1953
98	HECKELS	Geoffrey Thomas	C.P. and C.C. of Kent	County Hall, Maidstone	1954
99	JEFFERSON	Charles	D.C.P. and D.C.C. of West Suffolk	Shire Hall, Bury St. Edmunds	1954
100	WHEELER	Malcolm Hele	D.C.P. and D.C.C. of Yorkshire, North Riding	County Hall, Northallerton	1954
* 101	DAVIS	Alan Robert	C.P. and C.C. of Nottinghamshire	County Hall, West Bridgford, Nottingham	1954
102	JONES	Evan John Lloyd	D.C.P. and D.C.C. of Merioneth	County Offices, Dolgelley	1954
103	ROBERTS	Eric John	D.C.P. and D.C.C. of Lincolnshire, Parts of Holland	County Hall, Boston	1954
104	PEARSON	Reginald Arthur	D.C.P. and D.C.C. of Lincolnshire, Parts of Kesteven	County Offices, Sleaford	1954
105	BROCKBANK	James Tyrell	D.C.P. and D.C.C. of Nottinghamshire	County Hall, West Bridgford, Nottingham	1954
106	MILLS	John Spencer, M.C.	D.C.C. of Essex	County Hall, Chelmsford	1954
* 107	GOODACRE	Kenneth, T.D.	C.P. and C.C. of Middlesex	Middlesex Guildhall, Westminster, London, S.W.1.	1955
108	HAMILTON	Richard Neville Dalton	D.C.P. and D.C.C. of Buckinghamshire	County Hall, Aylesbury	1955
109	LANE	Walter Ernest	C.P. and C.C. of Lincolnshire, Parts of Lindsey	County Offices, Lincoln	1955
110	BAINS	Malcolm Arnold	D.C.C. of Kent	County Hall, Maidstone	1955
111	DENNIS	John Newman	D.C.C. of Middlesex	Middlesex Guildhall, Westminster, London, S.W.1.	1955
* 112	HART	Sir William (Ogden), C.M.G.	C.C. of London	The County Hall, London, S.E.1.	1955

*Member of the Parliamentary and General Purposes Committee.
†Member of the Law Committee.

THE CLERKS OF THE COUNTIES, 1360—1960

	Surname	Forenames	Office held	Address	Date of joining the Society
113	NOPS	Geoffrey Austin	C.P. of Surrey	County Hall, Kingston-upon-Thames	1956
114	PEREGRINE	Gwilym Rees	D.C.P. and D.C.C. of Carmarthenshire	County Offices, Carmarthen	1956
115	MANSON	John Neville	D.C.P. and D.C.C. of Hertfordshire	County Hall, Hertford	1956
116	LAVERACK	John Anthony Smith	D.C.P. and D.C.C. of Huntingdonshire	County Buildings, Huntingdon	1956
117	HOPKINS	Garth	D.C.P. and D.C.C. of Caernarvonshire	County Offices, Caernarvon	1957
118	MARTIN	John	D.C.P. and D.C.C. of Hampshire	The Castle, Winchester	1957
119	OLDHAM	John Hugh, T.D.	D.C.P. of Kent	County Hall, Maidstone	1957
120	SAYERS	Warwick Waghorn	D.C.P. of London	Sessions House, Newington Causeway, London, S.E.1.	1957
121	LANE	Douglas Charles Swancott	C.P. and C.C. of Radnorshire	County Offices, Llandrindod Wells	1958
122	JONES	David Alun Rhagfyr	D.C.P. and D.C.C. of Cardiganshire	County Office, Marine Terrace, Aberystwyth	1958
123	SHOOLBRED	Claude Frederick	D.C.P. of Middlesex	Middlesex Guildhall, Westminster, London, S.W.1.	1959
124	BOURNE	John Hugh Neville	D.C.P. and D.C.C. of Cheshire	County Offices, Chester	1959
125	HOLDEN	Thomas Geoffrey	D.C.C. of Oxfordshire	County Hall, Oxford	1959
126	OWEN	Robert Penrhyn	D.C.P. and D.C.C. of Lancashire	County Hall, Preston	1960
127	SMYTH	Arthur Hugh Manistre	D.C.P. and D.C.C. of Hampshire	The Castle, Winchester	1960
128	CROSSLEY	Harry	D.C.P. and D.C.C. of Derbyshire	County Offices, Matlock	1960
129	LOMAS	James	D.C.P. and D.C.C. of Durham	Shire Hall, Durham	1960
130	BUTLER	Denis William Langford	D.C.P. and D.C.C. of Wiltshire	County Hall, Trowbridge	1960
131	LANG	Gordon Robert	D.C.P. of Leicestershire	County Offices, Grey Friars, Leicester	1960
132	BACKHOUSE	Horace John	D.C.P. and D.C.C. of Bedfordshire	Shire Hall, Bedford	1960
133	WILLIAMS	Robert Thomas David	D.C.C. of Anglesey	County Offices, Llangefni	1960§

§ Effective from 16th January, 1961.

APPENDIX IV

2. Honorary Members

	Surname	Forenames	Office formerly held	Address	Date of joining the Society	Date of election as Hon. Member
1	THORNLEY	Sir Hubert (Gordon), C.B.E., D.L.	C.P. and C.C. of Yorkshire, North Riding	The Register House, Northallerton	1911	1960
2	GEORGE	Marshall	D.C.P. of Wiltshire	138 Bradford Road, Trowbridge	1912	1946
3	MEABY	Kenneth George Tweedale, C.B.E., D.L.	C.P. and C.C. of Nottinghamshire	Burgage Court, Southwell, Notts.	1916	1954
4	SCORER	Eric West, O.B.E.	C.P. and C.C. of Lincolnshire, Parts of Lindsey	Coombe Hurst, Sewell Road, Lincoln	1916	1947
5	RADCLIFFE	Sir Clifford (Walter), C.B.E., D.L.	C.P. and C.C. of Middlesex	53 Wildcroft Manor, Putney Heath, S.W.15	1919	1954
6	MARRIS	Harold Colquhoun, O.B.E.	C.P. and C.C. of Lincolnshire, Parts of Holland	127 Spilsby Road, Boston	1920	1954
7	MUNSEY	Laurence George Hensman	C.P. and C.C. of West Suffolk	" Kenbourne ", Bury St. Edmunds	1920	1953
8	OWEN	Hugh John, D.L.	C.P. and C.C. of Merioneth	The Cottage, Pwllheli, Caernarvonshire	1920	1954
9	RUMSEY	Lucas Eustace	C.P. and C.C. of Leicestershire	Court Cottage, Burwash, Etchingham, Sussex	1922	1946
10	NEOBARD	Harold John Cooke, O.B.E., D.L.	C.P. and C.C. of Berkshire	Calcot, near Reading	1922	1951
11	DAVIES	Hugh Christopher	C.P. and C.C. of Norfolk	The Lodge, Old Lakenham, Norwich	1923	1944
12	JONES	David Griffith	C.P. and C.C. of Caernarvonshire	Woodford, Vaynol Road, Caernarvon	1923	1945
13	WITHYCOMBE	Arthur John	C.P. and C.C. of Devon	Redcot, Exeter	1923	1947
14	FOLEY	Henry Arthur, M.C.	D.C.P. and D.C.C. of Buckinghamshire	Robin Hill, Wendover, Bucks	1924	1945
15	SCOTT	Francis Gerald, M.C., D.L.	C.P. and C.C. of Oxfordshire	The Beeches, Steeple Aston, Oxford	1924	1953
16	HICKSON	Cuthbert Gollan	D.C.P. and D.C.C. of Hampshire	1a Barnes Close, Winchester	1924	1955
17	BROWN	Henry Oswald	C.P. and C.C. of Norfolk	180 Newmarket Road, Norwich	1924	1956
18	KELLY	John Bradshaw	C.P. and C.C. of Huntingdonshire	2 Westwood Close, St. Ives, Hunts	1927	1954
19	STRINGER	Philip Austin Selborne, D.L.	C.P. and C.C. of Wiltshire	Fields, East Rytherton, Chippenham, Wilts	1929	1960
20	MARTIN	Hubert Sinclair, C.B.E., D.L.	C.P. and C.C. of East Sussex	Field Cottage, Belgrave Road, Seaford, Sussex	1930	1959
21	NEW	Leslie Penry	C.P. and C.C. of Cornwall	" Whitegates ", Crowborough	1930	1946
22	JONES	Sir William, C.B.E.	C.P. and C.C. of Denbighshire	Hafod, Ruthin	1930	1949
23	FREER	Lt.-Col. Charles Edward Jesse, D.L.	D.C.P. of Leicestershire	Greenheys, Stoughton Drive South, Leicester	1932	1946
24	WILLWAY	Brigadier Alfred Cedric Cowan, C.B., C.B.E., T.D., D.L.	D.C.P. of Surrey	Kiln Field, Puttenham, Guildford	1932	1946

THE CLERKS OF THE COUNTIES, 1360—1960

	Surname	Forenames	Office formerly held	Address	Date of joining the Society	Date of election as Hon. Member
25	ROGERS	George Foster, O.B.E.	D.C.C. of Surrey	Oaktree Cottage, Rusper Road, Ifield, Crawley, Sussex	1932	1948
26	DAVIES	John Harvey, C.B.E.	C.P. and C.C. of Flintshire	Trevordale, Elwy Avenue, Dyserth, Rhyl, Flintshire	1932	1944
27	LIGHTBURN	John Edward	C.C. of Essex	116 Thurlow Road, West Dulwich, London, S.E.21.	1932	1954
28	HOLCROFT	Edward Stanley	C.P. and C.C. of Essex	Dene Cottage, Abbotswood, Guildford, Surrey	1933	1941
29	COPLAND	Herbert, O.B.E.	C.P. and C.C. of Lincolnshire, Parts of Lindsey	82 Yarborough Crescent, Lincoln	1934	1957
30	GATER	Sir George (Henry), G.C.M.G., K.C.B., D.S.O.	C.C. of London	Barn House, Church Handborough, Oxford	1934	1939
31	PETERS	John Brown Meharry	D.C.C. of Yorkshire, North Riding	" Dilston," Romanby, Northallerton	1934	1954
32	PARRY	David James, C.B.E.	C.P. and C.C. of Glamorgan	23 Llyswen Road, Cardiff	1935	1953
33	CARSWELL	Hugh	C.P. and C.C. of Cheshire	The Lodge, Guilden Sutton, near Chester	1935	1959
34	DAVIS	Herbert Amphlett	C.P. and C.C. of Devon	c/o The Castle, Exeter	1937	1952
35	JOLLIFFE	Archibald Henry, O.B.E., M.C.	D.C.P. and D.C.C. of Lancashire	The Old Kennels, Lache Lane, Chester	1937	1951
36	HEY	William Leonard	D.C.C. of Wiltshire	" Rosemary," Torton Hill, Arundel	1941	1949
37	BISHOP	Gerald	C.P. and C.C. of Kent	Westways, Tower Lane, Bearsted, Kent	1941	1960
38	MILLS-OWEN	Richard Hugh	D.C.P. and D.C.C. of Carmarthenshire	c/o County Offices, Carmarthen	1942	1949
39	ADCOCK	Sir Robert (Henry), C.B.E., D.L.	C.P. and C.C. of Lancashire	West Beach, Lytham, Lancs	1945	1960
40	UPTON	Harry	D.C.P. and D.C.C. of Durham	Rannoch, Farnley Mount, Durham	1945	1960
41	PARKER	Philip, D.L.	C.P. and C.C. of Radnorshire	The Close, Cefnllys Lane, Llandrindod Wells	1945	1958
42	GRAHAM	Ernest, D.L.	C.P. of Surrey	Strathearn, Greville Park Avenue, Ashtead, Surrey	1946	1956
43	ROBERTS	Sir (James Reginald) Howard, C.B.E., D.L.	C.C. of London	Burford, Egham Hill, Egham, Surrey	1947	1956
44	GOODERIDGE	Thomas William Wade	C.C. of Surrey	The White Cottage, Hertford Heath, near Hertford	1948	1952
45	SCOTT	Jack David	D.C.P. of Kent	1408 Premier Way, Calgary, Alberta, Canada	1948	1957
46	LINES	David Hugo	D.C.P. and D.C.C. of Bedfordshire	86 Putnoe Lane, Bedford	1951	1960

APPENDIX V

Rules of the Society, 1960

Name of the Society

1. The name of the Society is " The Society of Clerks of the Peace of Counties and of Clerks of County Councils."

Qualifications for Membership:

Ordinary Members

Honorary Members

2. Membership of the Society shall be confined to those who hold or have held office in England or Wales as Clerks of the Peace of Counties or as Clerks of County Councils and their Deputies.

(*a*) Members of the Society shall be those who hold any one or two of the four offices in question and who are elected to be members.

(*b*) Honorary members of the Society shall be those who have ceased to hold qualifying office, who have been members of the Society *for not less than five years,** and who are elected to be honorary members.

Honorary members shall not be entitled to receive notices or agenda of meetings or minutes of proceedings of the Society, or to attend any meetings thereof, other than meetings of the Clerks of the Peace Golfing Society.

Candidates for Membership:

Ordinary Members

3. (*a*) Membership of the Society as an ordinary member shall be initiated by a candidate being proposed therefor in writing by a member and such proposal being sent to the Honorary Secretary not less than two weeks before the meeting of the Society at which it is to be considered.

The full name and qualification of a proposed member and the name of his proposer shall be set out in the agenda of the meeting at which the election is intended to take place. The names and qualifications of proposed members shall appear on the agenda and be voted for in the order in which their nominations for membership are received by the Honorary Secretary and seniority in the Society shall be so determined.

Honorary Members

(*b*) Membership of the Society as an honorary member shall be initiated by the Honorary Secretary entering the name of the member for such purpose on the agenda of the meeting at which the election is intended to take place.

Method of Election

(*c*) The method of electing members shall be by show of hands except that in lieu thereof any two members may demand a secret ballot. If two or more votes are given against a candidate to be an ordinary member he shall be declared not elected. If a majority of votes is given against a candidate to be an honorary member he shall be declared not elected.

Subscriptions

4. The rate of subscription to the funds of the Society for ordinary members shall be as follows:—

	£	s.	d.
Clerk of the Peace and/or County Council	6	6	0
Deputy Clerk of the Peace and/or County Council	3	3	0

Subscriptions shall become payable on the 1st January each year.

The rate of subscription payable shall be that attributable to the office or offices held by the member on the first day of the year, provided that the rate of any subscription payable in the case of a new member joining the Society during the year shall be that attributable to the office or offices held by him at the date of his election. An ordinary member retiring from membership of the Society on or before the 30th June in any year shall pay, or shall be entitled to a rebate of, one-half of the appropriate subscription for that year.

Every new member joining the Society on or after the 1st July in any year shall pay one-half of the appropriate subscription for that year, but no subscription shall be paid in the year of election if a member is elected too late to be summoned to attend a meeting in the year.

The rate of subscription payable in any unusual circumstances shall be at the discretion of the Chairman.

Honorary members shall not be called upon to subscribe to the funds of the Society.

* The words in italics were deleted from Rule 2(*b*) in March, 1961.

Annual and Ordinary Meetings

5.   The Society shall, in addition to the holding of ordinary meetings, hold its annual meeting in London in March, at which it shall elect for the year next ensuing:

(*a*)   a Chairman and a Vice-Chairman;

(*b*)   an Honorary Secretary and an Honorary Treasurer;

(*c*)   a Parliamentary and General Purposes Committee consisting of all members of the Society who are for the time being members of the Standing Committees of the County Councils Association, for the purpose of considering, either at the request of the Association or at the initiation of the Society any matter affecting Local Government with power in case of urgency to take such action on behalf of the Society as they think fit;

(*d*)   a Law Committee consisting of eighteen members of the Society (including the Chairman, Vice-Chairman and Honorary Secretary ex-officio) of which not more than one-third shall be Deputy Clerks of the Peace and/or Deputy Clerks of County Councils, for the purpose of considering and submitting reports to the Society from time to time on such legal and technical questions as may arise affecting members of the Society;

(*e*)   such further committees or officers as may be desired, provided that nothing in this rule contained shall limit the powers of the Society to elect such further committees or officers at any meeting, as occasion may require.

Limitation of the duration of certain Offices

6.   The Chairman and Vice-Chairman of the Society and the Chairmen of its Committees shall not hold office as such for a continuous period exceeding three years.

Special Meetings

7.   A special meeting of the Society may be called at any time on the authority of the Chairman, or upon requisition to the Honorary Secretary under the hand of not fewer than ten ordinary members setting forth the object of the meeting.

Notice of Meetings

8.   At least one week's clear notice shall be given by the Honorary Secretary to the members of all meetings, specifying the agenda.

The Society's Year

9.   The financial year of the Society shall be the calendar year. For other purposes the Society's year shall be that which commences on the day following the annual meeting in March and concludes at the close of the day of the annual meeting in the year next following.

Motions

10.   A member may supply to the Honorary Secretary the terms of any motion which he may desire to move at a meeting of the Society or any Committee thereof of which the mover is a member. Motions so communicated shall be included in the appropriate agenda.

Dividing the Agenda

11.   If at any time it shall appear to the Chairman to be desirable, there shall be issued two agenda, the one in connection with matters relating to business of Clerks of the Peace and the other as to business of Clerks of County Councils.

Clerks and Deputy Clerks of the Peace as such shall solely be entitled to receive notices of and agenda for meetings at which a separate agenda relating to business of Clerks of the Peace is to be considered, to attend such meetings and to receive separate minutes thereof; and Clerks and Deputy Clerks of County Councils shall similarly be entitled to receive papers relating to business of Clerks of County Councils, attend such meetings and receive separate minutes thereof.

Annual Calendar of Meetings

12.   The Parliamentary and General Purposes Committee shall submit for approval to the annual meeting of the Society in each year a draft programme of meetings of the Society for the ensuing year.

Dinners

13.   Arrangements shall be made by the Society for the members and the honorary members to dine together from time to time at such place and on such day as the Society may determine. The cost of the dinner shall be met by those members attending it, except that the cost of the Society's guests shall be met from the funds of the Society.

Alteration of Rules

14.   These rules may be rescinded, added to, or altered by notice of the proposal being set forth on the agenda of a meeting of the Society and at least two-thirds of those present voting for the proposal.

INDEX OF NAMES
OF CLERKS OF THE COUNTIES

INDEX OF NAMES

The names listed in this Index are those of the Clerks and Deputy Clerks of the Peace and of the County Council appearing in Part I, and also in the Introduction. Where identical surnames and forenames occur, they are distinguished by the addition of the first year of service *as Clerk* of the individual, or, in the case of a Deputy Clerk not subsequently appointed Clerk, the first year of his service as Deputy.

A

Name	Page
Abbot, John	52
Abbott, Samuel	117
Abbott, Thomas	117, 119
Abell, Humfrey	166
Acres, John	161
Adam, Benjamin	150
Adam, Benjamin Addington	150
Adams, Llewelyn	74
Adams, William (1551)	52
Adams, William (1691)	152
Adcock, Sir Robert (Henry)	113
Adderley, Charles	75, 76
Adderley, John	75
Adderley, William	127
Ades, William	150
Admers (Admas), William	91
Akehurst, Alexander	168
Alcock, William	169
Alexander, Philip	80
Aleyn, Thomas	101
Aleyn, William	63
Allen, Charles	131, 132
Allen, Charles Pettitt	12, 14, 130, 132
Allen, Emanuel	130, 132
Allen, Robert	58
Allen, William Edward Romilly	90
Allestry, Roger	75
Alleyn, Thomas	137
Alman, John	161
Alport, Richard	75
Alport, William	159
Alston, Thomas	91
Anderton, James	113
Andrew, William	183
Andrews, George	162
Andrews, Richard	54, 145
Anguish, Edmund	137
Anwyl, David	125
Anwyl, Edward	125, 126
Anwyl, William	126
Appleford, Daniel	178
Appleton, Robert (1736)	183, 184
Appleton, Robert (1746)	183, 184
Archebold, John	158

Name	Page
Armstrong, William Mathew	103
Arnold, Robert	105
Arrowsmith, George	176
Arundel, Thomas	157
Ascough, John	185
Ashe, Thomas	75
Asheton, Samuel	67
Ashfeld, Edmund	161
Ashpoole, Thomas	85, 86
Asketyll, Thomas	137
Askham, Dingley	106
Aslak, John	137
Assheby, John	158
Astley (Ashley), John	182
Aston, Edward	160
Atkinson, Jack	147, 170
Atkinson, John	154
Atkinson, Thomas	154
Atkyns, John	137
Atkyns, Stephen	137
Atter, Frederick	118
Atter, James	118
Atwell, Edward	80
Aubrey, Samuel	107
Audley, Thomas	52
Aukland, Dudley	167
Austen, Francis	110
Austen, Francis Motley	110
Austen, George	165
Austin, Anthony	92
Austin, Walter George	129, 131
Aylmer, Brabazon	85
Aylward, Anthony Case	106, 120
Aylwyn, John	96
Aynscombe, Thomas	169
Ayrey (Ayre), John	176

B

Name	Page
B———, H.	90
Babbington, Zacchary	160
Babington, Edward	122
Backhouse, Horace John	53
Bagard, John	161
Bagehott, William	134
Bagnall, Thomas	159

Name	Page
Bagnold, John	75
Bagott, Anthony	158, 160
Bailey, Frank	78, 79
Baines, Leslie Henry	73, 98, 108
Bains, Malcolm Arnold	98, 111
Baker, John	99
Baker, Thomas	169
Baldwin, George Dimsdale	131
Baldwyn, Ralph	64
Baldwyn, Richard	152
Banester, John	67
Bankes, Robert	120
Bankes, Robert Langton	119, 120
Banks, Joseph	143
Banks, Richard	149
Banks, Robert	143
Banwell, George Harold	120
Barber, Frederic Viccars	96, 98
Barber, Henry (1878)	61
Barber, Henry (1895)	96
Barber, John	76
Barbor, Robert	159
Barbour, Henry	31, 158
Baret, John	80
Barley (Burley), Richard	93
Barlow, George Frederick	87
Barnaby, Gabriel	178
Barnaby, John	84
Barnby, John	150
Barneby (Burnaby), Richard	11, 182
Barnes, John (1609)	105
Barnes, John (1610)	82
Barnes, John (1782)	73
Barnes, Philip	73
Baron, Matthew	137
Barroll, William	158, 160
Barrowe, John	109
Baskervyle, Robert	153
Bastard, Edmund	78
Bateman, Hugh	76
Battisford, John	63
Baty, Thomas	176
Baughan, Roger	99
Baxter, John	75
Bayley, Isaac	150

Baynes, Edward Robert 59	Blackwell, Nicholas 158	Brevens, Baldwin 63
Baynes (later Garforth), John ... 72	Blake, John 95	Brewis, George Oldfield ... 53, 92, 144
Baynes, Richard 35, 176	Blakiston, Matthew Folliott ... 159, 160	Breynton, George 99
Beal, Edward William 103, 131	Blanshard, Richard 183	Briggs, John 150
Beardsley, John 174	Blaxland, William Athelston ... 124	Brinkley, William 163
Beauchamp,—— 71	Blayney, Thomas 10, 181	Bristowe, Thomas 143
Beauchamp, William 71	Blow, Joseph Edward 120	Bristowe, William 143
Beaumont, Richard Melville ... 184	Bloxsome, Edward D. ... 92	Britiffe, Robert 162
Beck, George 63	Bluet, John 119	Brockbank, James Tyrrell ... 144, 193
Beck, Roger 63	Bochell, William 155	Brockett, William 101
Beckett, Ronald Arthur 193	Bodvel-Roberts, Arthur John ... 61, 62	Bromley, Richard 88
Bedford, Thomas 31, 52, 58	Bodvel-Roberts, John Hugh ... 61	Brooke, Arthur 140
Bedulff, John 158	Bodyng, John 91	Brooke, George 85, 87
Beek, William 145	Bolayne, Sir James 137, 161	Brookes, William 160
Bele, John 101	Bolton, John 177	Brookland, George 56
Bell, John 177	Bond, Alan 150	Brookland, William 55
Bell, William Lawrence ... 154	Bond, T. 157	Brough, Job 143
Bellamy, James 107	Bond, William 54	Brough, Job Charlton ... 143
Bendy, William 159	Booth, Philip 71	Broughton, Andrew 41, 109
Bennett, Francis 180	Borton, James 162	Broughton, Arthur Stanesby ... 141
Bennett, Harry Macaulay 156	Borton, John Henry 162, 163	Broun, Richard 75
Bennett, John 155	Boswell, Edward 81	Broune, John 91
Bennett, Philip (1672) 155, 157	Bosworth, Thomas Holmes ... 102, 104	Brown, Henry Oswald 138
Bennett, Philip (1706) ... 155, 156, 157	Boteler, John 172	Brown, Stephen 190
Bennett, Thomas 180	Boteler, William 54	Brown, William 116
Bennett, William 122	Bothe, Christopher 54	Browne, Christopher 155
Benson, Robert 190	Bothe, William 158	Browne, Henry 190
Benson, William 72	Bough, Launcelot 132	Browne, Matthew 97
Bent, William 115, 116	Boughton, Henry 119	Browne, Richard (1577) ... 84
Bentley, John 82	Boulton, Richard 51	Browne, Richard (1589) ... 183
Benyon, John 65	Boune, Abraham 173	Browne, Richard (1603) ... 84
Berdoe, John 94	Boune, Edward 75, 143	Brugge, Thomas 91
Berington, Walter 178	Bourne, John 159	Brutton, Charles Phipps ... 68, 81, 193
Berkeley, Henry Augustus	Bourne, John Hugh Neville ... 68	Bruys, Robert 30, 183
Fitzhardinge 92	Bowdler, Samuel 151	Bruyse, William 91
Bernard, John 161	Bowen, Richard 135	Bryant, Robert 156
Berners, Hatton 137	Bowker, William 154	Bryant, Robert Jeane ... 156
Berney, John 137	Bowman, Seymour 179	Bryckett, Robert 101
Berridge, Christian Gerard	Bown, William Langsdale ... 179, 180	Brydde, John 143
Timperley 86, 87	Bowyer, William (1497) ... 169	Buck, Henry London 131
Berry, Bartholomew 77	Bowyer, William (1564) ... 169	Buckley, John 51
Besson, Anthony 186	Boyce, Frederick Peter ... 104, 138	Budd, William 55, 56
Best, James 182	Boynton, John Keyworth ... 56	Bufton, William Evan ... 74, 148
Bethel, Hugh 183	Boyvill, George 139	Bulkley, Charles 178
Bevercotes, Richard 143	Brabazon, William 115	Bulkley, George 51
Beyvyn, John 155	Brackenbury, Joseph (1787) ... 121	Bulley, Thomas 147
Bickers, Herbert Edwin 106	Brackenbury, Joseph (1809) ... 121	Bullock, William 7, 85
Bickersteth, John Joseph ... 183	Brackenbury, Thomas ... 121	Burges, Thomas 102
Birch, Joseph 189	Bradbury, William 84	Burgess, Clarkson Leo ... 123
Birchall, Thomas (1825) 114	Bradford, Walter 190	Burgeyner, Thomas 63
Birchall, Thomas (1838) ... 114	Bradford, William 183	Burgoyne, John 63
Bird, Clifford Henry 182	Bradley, William 186	Burkitt, Gerald Gale ... 147
Bird, Sir James 123, 124	Bramley, —— 67	Burleigh, William 137
Bird, Thomas 100	Brand, Wilfrid 186	Burnaby, Thomas Fowke Andrew ... 12, 144
Bishop, Charles 66	Breese, David 126	Burnand (Byrnand), George ... 186
Bishop, Gerald 110, 111	Breese, Edward 125	Burnet, William 80
Blackaller, Robert 183	Brenner (Bremer), Thomas ... 158	Burton, John 117
Blackbeard, Richard 183	Brent, Roger 109	Burton, John Francis 121, 122
Blackwell, Joshua 119	Breten, Christopher 139	Burton, Thomas 117

Bury, James 145
Busby, Charles Stanhope Burke ... 76
Butler, Dennis William Langford 180
Butler, Richard 181
Butler, Robert 143
Butler, Thomas 128
Butterworth, Alexander Kaye ... 53
Buxton, John 64
Bykerstaff, John 181
Byne, Henry 165
Byngham, Thomas 143
Byrd, Edward 160
Bysshop, John 169
Bysshop, Thomas 169
Bysshop, William 31, 37, 151

C

Cambe, Arthur 91
Campion, Edward 84
Campion, John (1425) 172
Campion, John (1618) 165
Canne, Robert 63, 105
Cant, Francis Denis Victor ... 100
Carleton, Charles Cuthbert ... 132
Carleton, John 165
Carleton, Thomas 176
Carleton, William 176
Carne, Roger 89
Carrowe, John 84
Carson, James Eric Rutherford ... 65
Carswell, Hugh 68
Carter, Charles Harold 87, 142
Carter, John (1707) 163
Carter, John (1810) 5
Carter, John Richard 118
Carter, Thomas 115
Cartwright, Richard 127
Cartwright, William 190
Case, Philip 137, 138
Casson, Randal 126
Castell, Edmund 54
Castell, William 105
Catesby, Michael 150
Catevan, John 93
Caunton, Nicholas 109
Cavendisshe, William 101
Cawkwell, Thomas 87
Cay, John 69
Cayly, Geoffrey 137
Chaffin, John 178
Chaffin, Leonard 178
Chaffin, Thomas 178
Challenor, John 74
Challoner, William (1668) ... 173
Challoner, William (1701) ... 173
Chamber, Allan 187
Chambers, Charles Graham ... 56
Champantie, John 115
Champion, George 56

Champion, John (1646) 180
Champion, John (1655) 94
Chaplin, Acton 59
Chapman, John 63
Chapman, Robert 121, 122
Charge, John 76
Charnells, Thomas 75
Charnok, William 115
Chatterton, John 158
Chatterton, John Arthur 116, 147
Chauncey, John 102
Chauncy, John 139
Cheales, Benjamin 119, 120
Cheeke, Edward 156
Cheke, John 161
Cheker, John 105
Cherry, James 162, 163, 164
Chettle, William 147
Chetwood, John 166
Chevercourt, John 119
Cheyney, Robert 109
Child, William 181
Chilson, William 71
Christie, Thomas 52
Chute, Robert 157
Chybnale (Chibnell), Godfrey ... 140
Clapham, Richard 190
Clare, Sir Harcourt (Everard) ... 113
Clarendon, 3rd Earl of, John Charles
    Villiers 112
Claridge, John Fellows ... 11, 110, 111
Clark, William Fox 184
Clarke, Henry 97
Clarke, John (1711) 105
Clarke, John (1831) 5
Clarke, Richard 151, 153
Clarke, Robert (1660) 162
Clarke, Robert (1662) 105
Clavelshey, Cuthbert 155
Clay, Frederick William 87
Clay, Robert 69
Clayton, William 99
Cleave, John 100
Cleaver, Harold Willoughby ... 114
Clerc, William 57, 135, 149
Clerk, Henry 127
Clerk, John 99
Clerk, Richard 93
Clerk, Roger 158
Clerk(e), Thomas 99
Clerke, Henry 58
Clerke, Richard 146
Cliffe, Anthony 132
Clifton, William 112
Close, John 189
Clyfford, Thomas 133
Coast, William Stacey 111
Cobb, Paul 2, 52
Cobb, Thomas 94

Cobbe, William 67
Cobbold, Alfred Townshend ... 163, 164
Cockeram, Isaac 107
Cockes, John 58
Cocksedge, Henry 162
Coggere, John 165, 169
Cok, Richard 117
Coke, Henry Simmonds 90
Coke, Thomas 93
Cokke, Thomas 69
Cole, John 86
Coles, Edward 156, 157
Coles, James 156
Coles, William 178, 180
Colles, William 58
Collett, Henry 12, 162, 163
Collett, William 163
Collingbourne, Richard 178
Collins, Francis 175
Collins, John 160
Collins (Collyne), Richard ... 162
Collinson, John 122
Combe, Bryan 80, 81
Comyn, William 77
Conde, John 143
Constable, Robert 180
Conuser (Councer), William ... 145
Conyers, William 189
Coode, Edward (1822) 70, 71
Coode, Edward (1840) 70
Coode, William 70
Cooke, James 116
Cooke, John 120
Cooke, Ralph 73
Cooke (Coke), Richard 75
Cookes, Edward 181
Coombes, E. 150
Coombes, John 150
Cooper, Frank Lyndon 134
Copeman, Charles Edward Fraser 107
Copeman, Robert 11, 138
Copland, Herbert 122
Copnall, Henry Hampton 144
Corbett, Edward 166
Corbett, Robert 166, 167
Corbin, Robert Reeks 97
Corry, Thomas 117, 119
Cosyn, William 63
Cottell, Mark 77, 79
Cotton, Thomas 115
Couphull, John 105
Covell, John 163
Covell, Thomas 162
Coventry, Thomas 181
Coventry, William 181
Coward, Thomas 80, 95
Cowlard, Christopher Lethbridge 70
Cowper, Gabriel 183
Cowper, John 104

Cowper, Richard	191
Cox, Sir Montagu (Hounsel) ...	123, 124
Crachley, Thomas	88
Crafford (Crayford), Guy	84
Crawford, Lionel	84
Crips (Crispe), Richard	145
Crompton, William	159
Crosby, Thomas	82
Crosse, George	58
Crossley, Harry	76
Crouch, Guy Robert	59
Crouch, Lionel William	59
Crouch, William	59
Crow, Patrick	142
Crowe, Thomas (1390)	165
Crowe, Thomas (1395)	109
Crowle, William	190
Crowte, Frederick	153
Cuddon, Thomas	95
Cudworth, Ralph	112
Cuffe, John	155
Cuffold, William	93
Culliford, Edward	155
Curteys, Thomas	165, 169
Curwen (Curwyn), Anthony ...	72
Cust, Edwin	193
Cuthbertson, George	142
Cutler, Henry	115

D

Dacey, William Leslie	88
Dade, John	137, 161
Dalton, Robert Cecil	150
Dalton, Thomas	89, 90
Dalton, Thomas Masters ...	90
Danby, John	185
Danby, Thomas	185
Darell, Philip John	110
Darke, Hugh Cuff	170, 171
Darwin, Francis Alvey Rhodes ...	191
Davenport, George	121
Davenport, Hugh Nares	147
Davenport, John Marriott	2, 3, 12, 20, 146, Plate VI
Davenport, Thomas Marriott	3, 14, 146, 147
Davidson, John	142
Davidson, Thomas (1775) ...	142
Davidson, Thomas (1818) ...	142
Davies, Edward	136
Davies, Ellis Roger... ...	55, 56
Davies, Evan	66
Davies, George Christopher ...	138
Davies, Hugh Christopher ...	138
Davies, Idris	51, 193
Davies, John	135
Davies, John Harvey	88
Davies, Morgan	66
Davies, Richard	66
Davies, William	84

Davis, Alan Robert	144
Davis, Guy Heath	92, 164
Davis, Herbert Amphlett	78, 79
Davyes, William	86
Davylle, Christopher	186
Davyson, Robert (1428)	32, 183
Davyson, Robert (1506)	84, 101
Dawson, G. F.	90
Dawson, Thomas	58
Day, Bartholomew	157
Day, James	64
Day, Neville	106
Daye, William	151
Deacon, Leonard John	154
Deacon, Walter John (1903) ...	154
Deacon, Walter John (1918) ...	154
Deane, William	75
Death, Welcome	117, 119
de la Hooke, Harry	123
de la Mare, Brian	119
de la Pole, Henry	75
de Montmorency, Frank Raymond	170, 171
Dene, John	93
Dene, Robert	161
Dennis, John Newman	131
Denshire, George (1727)	119
Denshire, George (1741)	118, 119
Denshire, Langton	117
Denton, Christopher	142
de Preston, Henry	183
Derby, William	80
Dering, Christopher	109
de Stanton, Thomas	75
de Veel, Robert	80
Develyn, John	80
Dickenson, John	160
Dickson, William	142
Dighton (Deighton), Thomas ...	173
Diston, William	146
Dix, John	123
Dixon, Benjamin	190, 191
Dixon, John Henry	191
Dixon, William Vibart	191
Dolphin, Henry	159
Dolphin, John	159, 160
Domville, Henry Barry	181
Donne, John	156
Dorant, James Annesley ...	103, 104
Doré, Clifford William dos Santos	71
Dorney, Philip	92
Douthwaite, W.	102
Dowe, Richard	85
Dowe (Dowve), Thomas	161
Doweswell, George	91
Down, Thomas	70
Dowse, Thomas	121
Drake, Ralph	167
Drake, Thomas Edward	79
Drakeford, Richard	160

Drakes, Thomas	84
Duckett, Joseph	140
Duffield, Richard	121
Dufton, John	108
Dumville, Peter Williamson ...	103, 104
Duncum, William	82
Dunn, John	83
Dunn, William	156
Dunriche, Edmund	69
Durant (Deraunt), Edward ...	172
Durnford, George	95
Duthy, John	95
Dutten, Thomas	88
Dyer, John	155
Dyer, William	165
Dymoke, Michael	52n, 53
Dyneley, Henry	190
Dysmers, Christopher	178
Dyson, Ralph	115
Dytton, John	139

E

Eales, Richard	11, 12, 78, 79
Earle, Thomas Hughes	95, 96
Eastchurch, Samuel	111
Ede, John	58
Edgcombe, Peter	69
Edge, Richard	114
Edge, William Leonard	153
Edgell, James	179, 180
Edgworth, Robert	172
Edison, Nathaniel	121, 122
Edmondes, Henry	131
Edmunds, George	154
Edmunds, William	54, 145
Edon, ——	115
Edwards, Charles	157
Edwards, George	105
Edwards, John	135
Edwards, Pasco	69
Edwards, Robert	125
Edwards, Thomas	89
Edwards, William Richard ...	171
Egerton, John William	82
Eldred, Edward	85, 86
Eldridge, James	98
Elers, Paul	146
Eliot, Richard	165
Eliot (Elyot), Thomas	165
Ellis, Charles Arthur Hill Heaton	128
Ellis, David	125
Ellis, Henry	60
Ellis, William (1775)	169
Ellis, William (1780)	184
Ellis, William (1806)	170
Ellis, William Joyner	92
Elmys (Elmes), John	58
Elsley, Charles Heneage	190
Elwood, John	117, 119

Elyott, Thomas 165
Emory, Thomas 93
Ennew, Samuel 85, 87
Ensor, Alick Charles Davidson ... 123, 131
Enyver, Thomas 86
Est, Richard 105
Estcourt, Arthur Sotheron ... 108
Etherton, Sir George (Hammond) 23, 113
Evans, David 125
Evans, Ernest Godfrey 134
Evans, Evan 65
Evans, Hugh Robert 64
Evans, Ivor 65
Evans, J. 74
Evans, John 66
Evans, Thomas Henry 160
Evans, Thomas Roberts 51
Evans, William 126
Evans, William Robert 74
Everard, Anthony 165
Everard, Henry 137, 161
Ewbank, Thomas 189
Ewen, Michael 156, 179
Eyles, Charles 130
Eynsworth, Henry 75
Eyres, Thomas 180

F

Fagger, William 169
Fairfax, Thomas 82
Fallowes, Benjamin (1752) ... 100
Fallowes, Benjamin (1804) ... 100
Fardell, John Wilson 108
Farnes, Thomas 170
Farr, William Dale 12, 95
Farrer, John 82
Farrer, Thomas 52
Faryngdon, John 145
Faulkes, John 115
Fawkener, Anthony 96
Fawlkener, Anthony 150
Featherstonhalgh, Ralph ... 142
Felmersham, John 145
Felmersham, William 145
Fenton, Richard 190
Fenton, Thomas 159
Fermor, Henry 127
Fernihough, Thomas 159, 160
Ffooks, Edward Archdall 80, 81
Ffooks, Thomas 80, 81
Ffooks, William 80
Ffoulkes, Richard 135
Field, Algernon Sydney 174
Field, Edward 174, 175
Field, Henry 175
Field, Sydney Riach 174, 175
Finch, Peter 138
Firby, John 52

Fisher, John 173
Fitzwilliam, Henry 77, 79
Fitzwilliam, Thomas 84
Fleetwood, John 97
Fleming, Nicholas 71
Fletcher, Thomas 158
Fletewode, John 67
Foley, Henry Arthur 59
Foljambe, Thomas 191
Folkes, Simon 63, 105
Fooks, John 80
Fooks, Thomas 80
Forbes, Peter 132
Forbes, William 119
Ford, Henry 78
Forest, John 161
Forthey, John 181
Forster, Charles Davison ... 142
Forster, Collingwood 142
Forster, John 159
Fortescue, John 79
Fortescue, Joseph 77
Fortune, John 133
Fortune, Walter 133
Fortune, William 134
Foster, Charles 138
Foster, Jonathan (1784) 115
Foster, Jonathan (1785) 115
Foster, Michael 179
Foster, William John Slade ... 157
Fothergill, George 176
Fouler, John 115
Foulhill, Thomas 77
Fovargue, Reginald West 171
Fowler, Edward George Bennett ... 116
Fowler, John 109
Fox, Charles Burton 134
Fox, John 128
Fox, Thomas 81
Frampton, George 178
Francis, William 131
Frankland, Henry 187
Franklen, Sir Thomas (Mansel) ... 12, 89
Franklyn, John 111
Freeman, Henry 139
Freeman, Thomas (1583) 139
Freeman, Thomas (1628) 86
Freer, Charles Edward Jesse ... 116
Freer, Thomas 115, 116
Freer, William 115
Freer, William Jesse 12, 116
Freman, John 161
Frenche, George 161
Fryer, Henry Charles 65
Fuller, David 110
Fuller, William 173
Fyldyng, Peter 115
Fynchyngfeld, John ... 31, 84, 101, 161
Fyneux, William 109

G

Gage, John 140
Gage, Robert 140
Gane, William Henry 118
Gape, Thomas 155
Gardiner, John 112
Gardom, Edward Theodore ... 92
Garforth (né Baynes), John ... 72
Garnance, John 148
Garnons, Griffith 125
Garnons, John 125
Gartside, Danvers 74
Gater, Sir George (Henry) ... 123
Gauntlett, Peter 95
Gayer, John 69
Gayer, Reynold 69
Gayre, Robert 54
Gent, William 139
George, Christopher 91
George, Thomas Henry Marshall 148, 180
George, William Davies 148
Gerard, Thomas 115
Gernoun, Adam 101
Gibbens, John 155
Gibbon(s), William 173
Gibson, Henry 85, 86, 87
Gibson, Herbert William 86, 87
Gibson, William 85, 87
Giles, John 178
Gill, Alfred 103
Gillings, Charles Edwin 154
Gilman, Denis George 76
Gilmore, William 58
Gilpin, James 82
Ginn, Samuel Reuben 64
Girdlestone, Steed 107
Glynne, Thomas 60
Godber, Geoffrey Chapman ... 141, 153, 193
Goddard, William 157
Goddin, John 111
Godfrey, Edward Smith 144
Godolphin (Godolghan), John ... 69
Godolphin (Godolpan), William ... 69
Godsall, Harold Graham 78, 79
Godynge, William 127
Goldsmith, William 52
Gomme, Sir (George) Laurence ... 123
Good, Arthur 97
Good, Richard 97
Goodacre, Kenneth 129
Goodall, James 64
Goodchild, Frank Ernest 92
Gooderidge, Thomas William Wade 167, 168
Goodman, John 99
Goodwin, John 175
Goodwin, Laurence Eric 83
Goold, John 98
Goold, John Heyden 86
Goreway, Thomas 127

Gorst, Edward 114
Gorst, Edward Chaddock 114
Gorst, John (1800) 114
Gorst, John (1838) 114
Gorstelow, Thomas 140
Gosse, George 173
Gough, John 180
Gouldesburgh, Thomas 85
Goulton, Christopher 189
Gower, Robert 186
Gowland, Samuel 142
Grafton, John 181
Graham, Ernest 167, 168
Graham, Joseph Bramwell ... 53
Graham, Robert Lawrence ... 73
Grape, James 54
Grape, Richard 54
Gravenor, Rowland 151
Graves, Arthur Glendower ... 129, 131
Graves, Richard ... 19, 127, Plate III
Gray, Francis 140
Green, John 190
Green, Theophilus 115
Greene, Benjamin Aislabie ... 106
Greenwood, Harry Bordley ... 177
Greig, Woronzow 166
Grenefeld, John 185
Grenewode, James 115
Gresley, Ferrars 157
Gretheued, Thomas 30, 185
Grevyle, John 127
Griffith, Griffith 125, 126
Griffith, John Lloyd 51
Griffith, Owen 135
Griffiths, David Wynmor Lewis ... 65
Grindley, Samuel 51
Grone, Robert 80
Gross, Charles James 164
Grove, William 54, 56
Gruffydd (Vaughan), John ... 60
Grundy, Francis Estlin Christopher 87
Gryffith, William 51
Guise, Francis Edward 92
Gullett, Christopher 79
Gurneys, John 150
Gustard, Henry Stafford ... 134
Guy, Robert 140
Gwynne, David 148
Gwynne, John 148
Gylby, John Parker 11, 132

H

Hackyluett, John 99
Haggatt, John 155
Hales, John 127
Hall, John 104
Hall, Richard 99
Halle, William 115
Hals, William 77

Hamilton, Richard Neville Dalton 59
Hammerton, John 191
Hamond, Francis 54
Hamond, William 101
Hampson, Henry 91
Hampton, John 178
Hanchett, Thomas 101
Hanchich, Thomas 91
Hand, Robert William ... 159, 160
Hann, William Liddell 64
Hansen, Richard Claussen ... 100
Harcourt, Godfrey 57
Harcourt, Simon 127, 128
Harden, Richard 178
Hardisty, John 132
Hardisty, Robert 130
Hardy, Richard 96
Hardy, Robert 96
Harland, Richard 183
Harmood, Harry 146
Harper, Robert John 113
Harper, William 99
Harries, Henry Frederick William 57
Harries, Richard 151
Harries, Robert Paschal ... 179, 180
Harris, George Montagu ... 171
Harris, Joseph 106
Harris, Richard 94
Harrison, George Devereux ... 136
Harrison, George Rowland
  Devereux 136
Harrison, John Pryce 136
Harrison, Robert Devereux ... 136
Harryson, William 190
Hart, Sir Ernest (Sidney Walter) 129
Hart, Sir William (Ogden) ... 124
Harvey, Ernest Philip 142
Harvey, Herbert Cranmer ... 142
Harvey, William 122
Haselton, John 91
Hasilwode, Edward 139
Hassall, Richard 158
Hatche, John 58
Hatfeild, William 74
Hatley, Richard 58
Hatton, Francis 151
Hautmont, John 145
Haverd, Thomas 99
Haward (Hayward), Philip ... 162
Hawe, James 137, 161
Hawes, Richard 172
Hawkes, William 179, 180
Hawkins, Peter 183
Hawt, James 99
Hayne, Joseph 75
Hayton, William 59
Hayward, Tom Christopher 18, 160, 171, 193
Hayworth, John 101
Head, Henry 109

Heald, George 122
Heathcote, Godfrey 75
Hecham, Henry 121
Heckels, Geoffrey Thomas ... 110, 111
Hedley, Richard 172
Hegon, John 32, 158
Heigham, John 137, 161
Helliar, John 78
Helm, Charles Augustus ... 182
Helps, Arthur 168
Hely, John 130
Henslowe, Ralph 94
Herbert, William 133
Hercy, John 54
Herebene (Hardbene), John ... 117
Herle, Nicholas 70
Heron, James 54
Herris, William 86
Hert, John 77
Hesketh, Bartholomew 112
Hetherington, Arthur Carleton ... 68, 73
Hewitt, Joseph 174
Hext, Samuel 70
Hext, Thomas 70
Hey, William Leonard 180
Hicks, Fabian 54
Hickson, Cuthbert Gollan ... 98
Hide, Edward 102
Higgons, —— 57
Higgs, John 132
Hildersham, Thomas 63
Hill, George 182
Hill, Joseph 55
Hill, Richard 165
Hill, Stephen 186
Hill, William 172
Himsworth, Kenneth Stephenson 177
Hinckley, Arthur 12, 159
Hinckley, Thomas 159
Hind, Jesse 144
Hipperon, John 165
Hobbs, Robert 175
Hodgson, Charles Bernard ... 72, 73
Hodgson, Charles Courtenay ... 72, 73
Hodgson, Charles William Allen ... 73
Hodgson, Edward 189
Hodgson, Joseph 73
Hodgson, Thomas Houghton ... 12, 72
Hodgson, William 72
Hogeson, Robert 127
Holborne, Robert 187
Holcroft, Edward Stanley ... 86, 87, 147
Holden, Thomas Geoffrey ... 147
Holdich, Thomas Hinman ... 120
Holland, Edward 51
Holland, George 151
Holled, Thomas 140
Hollier, Henry 89
Hollis, George 97

Holloway, Richard	97
Hollway, John Hardwick	12, 121
Holme, John	52
Holt, Nicholas	151
Hooker, John	127
Hooper, Edmund Giles	52
Hooper, John	109
Hope, James Kenneth	83, 193
Hopkins, Garth	62
Hopkins, Matthew	155
Hopkinson, John	191
Hopper, William	83
Horde (Horte), Alan	151
Horde (Whorde), Robert	158
Hordere, John	80
Hore, John	109
Horn, ——	30, 178
Horne, John	101
Horne, Thomas	52
Hornyngglowe, Henry	75
Hornyold, Anthony	58
Horton, Henry	52
Horton, John	140
Horwell, Thomas	70
Hosier, John	74
Hoskyns (Hoiskins), Richard ...	133
Houghton, John	137
Houghton, William	67
Howan, Thomas	53
Howard, Richard	60
Howard, Hon. William	183
Howe, Bertram Charles	73
Hudson, ——	176
Hugh ap Meredith Wyn	125
Hughes, Ellis	60
Hughes, John	61
Hughes, Richard	135
Hughes, Thomas	134
Hughes, William	51
Hughes-Hallett, Norton Joseph ...	76
Hughson, Nicholas	63
Hughson, William	63
Hulton, Frederick Campbell ...	113, 114
Humphreys, John	74
Hunsdon, Peter	54
Hunt, Charles Henry	174
Hunt, Henry Oliver	174, 175
Hunt, John	75
Hunt, Joseph (1720)	173
Hunt, Joseph (1730)	175
Hunt, Thomas (1464)	75
Hunt, Thomas (1604)	173
Hunt, Thomas (1802) ...	10, 174, 175
Hunt, William Oakes ...	12, 174, 175
Huntley, Hugh	133
Hurley, Clement Woods	142
Hurst, John	143
Hurst, William	144
Huscarle, Brian	54

Hutchison, Sir Peter	164
Hyde, Ralph	109
Hyde, Roger	96
Hyett, Benjamin	91, 92
Hyllyard, John	80
Hynstoke, Thomas	127

I

Imber, Matthew	97
Imber, Thomas	97
Incledon, Robert	78
Inglett, Giles	79
Ingram, Thomas	101
Inman, Peter Donald	114
Irby, Anthony	119
Irby, Leonard	117, 119
Ireland, William (1612)	113
Ireland, William (1667)	140
Ironmonger, William	158

J

Jackman, Trevor Bromley ...	191
Jackson, Edward Hugh	107
Jackson, Hugh	107
Jackson, James	189
Jackson, John	132
Jackson, Robert	189
Jackson, Samuel	118
Jackson, Thomas	75
Jackson, William	67, 68
Jacques, Warner	115
James, Charles Bartleet	56
James, William	91
James, William Vaughan	148
Jeffereys, John	173
Jefferson, Charles	164
Jefferson, James	130
Jekes, John	52
Jenkin, Abraham	162
Jenkins, ——	134
Jenkins, Edward	89
Jenkins, Richard	152
Jenkins, William Gough	90
Jenkinson, John	105
Jevons, Harold	83
John ap Owen	149
John, Richard	90
Johns, Daniel	66
Johnson, Adrian	105
Johnson, Alan	191
Johnson, Arthur Ainslie ...	56, 153
Johnson, Edward	85
Johnson, George	67
Johnson, Henry Chaderton ...	118
Johnson, Richard William ...	183
Johnson, Samuel	105
Jolliffe, Archibald Henry ...	114
Jolly, Albert	57, 193
Jones, Alexander	133, 134

Jones, Charles	136
Jones, David Alun Rhagfyr ...	65
Jones, David Evan Alun	193
Jones, David Griffith	61, 62
Jones, Edward (1565)	125
Jones, Edward (1676)	60
Jones, Edward (1833)	66
Jones, Griffith	149
Jones, Gwilym Thomas	61, 62
Jones, Herbert	133
Jones, Humphrey	136
Jones, John	74
Jones, John Humphreys	126
Jones, Joseph	136
Jones, Morris	60, 62
Jones, Oliver	88
Jones, Owen Meurig	141
Jones, Reginald Cecil	191
Jones, Richard (1606)	60
Jones, Richard (1660)	66
Jones, Robert	125, 126
Jones, Ronald Laughton	157
Jones, Rowland Guthrie	126
Jones, Samuel	133
Jones, Thomas	66
Jones, Walter Owen	51
Jones, William	51, 62, 193
Jones, Sir William	74, 193
Jones, William Hugh	88
Jones, William Neville Pritchard ...	193
Jones-Williams, Dafydd Wyn ...	126
Joskyn, James	115, 139
Joy, Richard Eustace	159
Judd, James Edward	180
Jukes, George	135

K

Keatlewell, Timothy	143
Keen, George	160
Keen, William	160
Keene, Morgan	95
Keith, Giles	85
Kele, Robert	121
Kelly, John Bradshaw ...	56, 81, 106
Kelly, Redmund	78
Kelly, Thomas Thelwall	88
Kelynge, John	86
Kemeys, George	133
Kempson, Anthony	85
Kennaway, Mark	78
Kennett, John	110
Kent, Godfrey Lawrence Dunsterville	182
Kent, John	178
Kent, Robert	121
Kenyon, Bernard ...	42n, 191, 193
Kenyon, George (1698)	112
Kenyon, George (1728) ...	12, 112
Kenyon, Roger ...	2, 19, 112, Plate IV

Kenyon, Thomas	114
Kenyon, William	113
Kerby, Peter	97
Kilvington, John	184
King, Harold	83, 156
King, Samuel	63
Kinnersley, James	100
Kipling, William	163
Kirkpatrick, James	156
Kirton, John	77
Knevett (Knyvett), Edmund	137
Knevett, Henry	137
Knight, Clifford	116
Knight, Henry	69
Knott, Charles	97
Knottesford, James	181
Kyffin, Watkin	74
Kyme, John	121
Kympe, John	69
Kyrkeby, John	150

L

Lacock, George	143
Lacock, James	143
Lacon, John	152
Lacy, Henry	150
Lacy, Thomas	190
Lake, John	77
Lambard, John	178
Lambe, William	127
Lambert, A.	81
Lancaster, Roy Cavander	111
Lane, Douglas Charles Swancott	149
Lane, Walter Ernest	98, 122
Lang, Gordon Robert	116
Langridge, William Balcombe	7, 169
Langridge, William Kirby Johnson	170
Langridge, William Vidler	170
Lanning, Robert	148
Large, John	68
Latham, Ralph	112
Launder, John	165
Laverack, John Anthony Smith	106
Lawley, George	109
Lawrence, Thomas	96
Lawrence, Vernon	134
Lawrence, William (1573)	96
Lawrence, William (1840)	154
Lawson, Charles John	7, 12, 166, 168
Lawson, D.	168
Lawson, Francis	166, 168
Lawson, Frederick William	166
Lawson, J.	168
Lawson, John	166
Layton, Thomas	82
Leach, Edward	148
Lecche, Henry	91
Lee, John	93
Leeke, Gifford	84

Leeman, George	41, 183
Leeman, Joseph Johnson	184
Legh, John	155
Lepla, James	150
Levett, Theophilus	159
Levinge, Thomas	75
Lewen, Robert	80
Lewis, ——	130
Lewis, Ambrose	51
Lewis, Benjamin	66
Lewis, David	65
Lewis, Henry	88
Lewis, John	60
Lewis, Lawrence George Lisle	87
Lewis, Peregrine	133
Lewis, Richard	51
Lewis, Thomas	132
Lightburn, John Edward	86, 111
Lightfoot, George Cecil	23, 163, 164
Linacre, John	176
Lines, David Hugo	53
Littleton, George	181
Lloyd, Herbert	65
Lloyd, James	65
Lloyd, Jeremiah	65
Lloyd, John (1660)	66
Lloyd, John (1662)	57
Lloyd, Richard	74
Lloyd, Robert (1597)	135
Lloyd, Robert (1699)	125
Lloyd, Thomas (1623)	125
Lloyd, Thomas (1719)	74
Lloyd, Thomas (1734)	35, 65
Lloyd, William	88
Lloyd-Jones, Evan John	126
Llwyd, Richard Jones	66
Lockett, William Jeffrey	75, 76
Lockwood, John	184
Lok, Eliazer	105
Lomas, James	83
Long, Charles	122
Long, George	94
Longe, George	127
Longmore, Sir Charles (Elton)	103
Longmore, Philip Elton	103, 104
Longmore, Philip Raynsford	104
Loughton (Langton), John	58
Love, ——	150
Lovekyn, Arthur	109
Lovell, Edward	157
Lovell, Edwin	156
Lovell, George	143
Lowe, George	68
Loxdale, John	152, 153
Loxdale, Joseph (1802)	7, 152, 153
Loxdale, Joseph (1820)	153
Loxdale, Thomas	153
Lucas, Charles Vivian	79
Lucas, John	109

Luck, Thomas	64
Lugg, Adam	143, 144
Lund, John	184
Luty, Thomas	52
Luyt, Thomas	127
Lygon, Roger	99
Lynacre, John	158
Lyndres, Robert	181
Lyndsell (Lyndeseye), Richard	84
Lyne, John	70
Lyne, Philip	70
Lynford, John	137
Lyon, John	58

M

Mace, Thomas	183
Macdonald of the Isles, Sir Godfrey (Middleton Bosville)	184
Machyn, Robert	86
Madok, Robert	74
Maidman (Maydman), Edward	167
Major, John	115
Malet, John	155
Mallett, Gabriel	52
Manchester, John	143
Mann, John (1624)	86
Mann, John (1735)	83
Manning, Richard	169
Mansfield, William	190
Manson, John Neville	104
Maples, Edward William	100
Marcy, William Nichols	12, 181, 182
Margetts, William	106
Mariott, John	104
Markham, Charles	141
Markham, Christopher Alexander	141
Markham, Henry Philip	12, 141
Marks, William Woodfine	53
Marris, Harold Colquhoun	118
Marsh, John	52
Marshall, Henry	166
Marshall, Ralph	132
Marshall, William	183, 186
Marston, Richard	99
Marten, John	160
Martin, Adam	155
Martin, George	82
Martin, Hubert Sinclair	23, 141, 170, 171
Martin, John Hawksley	98
Martin, William	79
Martyn, John	58
Martyn, William	77
Mascall, Thomas	109
Mason, Bartlett	173
Mason, William	11, 87
Mathew, Thomas Limbrey Sclater	95
Mattock, Charles	85, 87
Maude, Arthur Grey	131, 132
Maule, Edward	106

Maule, John Percy 106
Maule, Montague George ... 106
Maurice, John 60
Mawdesley, Robert 113
Maynard, Anthony Lax 75
Maynard, Thomas ... 181
Mayne, Robert 117
Maynwaringe, Peter ... 67, 68
McCall, Charles Patrick Home ... 113, 114
McComb, James Ellis 114
McGrath, Sir (Joseph) Charles ... 191
McIlveen, Hugh John Turnly ... 170
McVicar, Sidney James ... 191
Meaby, Kenneth George
 Tweedale 79, 83, 144
Medland, William 103
Meek, Thomas William ... 157
Mence, Nathaniel 182
Mence, Richard Mugg ... 182
Mennell, Robert 82
Mercer, William 145
Meredyth, Hugh 126
Merrifield, Frederic ... 3, 170, 171
Merriman, Robert William ... 179, 180
Merriman, William Clark 179
Merston, Richard 143
Merton, Thomas 31, 139
Metcalfe, Charles 107
Metcalfe, Frederick Morehouse ... 107
Meyrcke, Rice 89
Michaell, Richard 51
Michell, James 169
Michell, John 169
Michelmore, Henry 78
Michelmore, Henry William ... 79
Middelton, John 176
Middleton, Christopher ... 72
Middleton, David 132
Midleton, John 72
Millard, Richard Edward ... 59
Miller, Brian Stothert ... 78, 79
Miller, Thomas 166
Milles, Francis 41, 94
Millicent (Milleson), Edmund ... 42, 162
Millicent, Thomas 63
Millington, Herbert Ashlin ... 141
Millington, John 62
Millington, John Boyfield ... 118
Mills, John Spencer ... 87
Mills-Owen, Richard Hugh ... 66
Milne, Alexander 177
Milton, Humphrey 68
Minshull, William 59
Mitton, Adam 151
Moffet, Robert ... 33, 65, 66, 148
Moland, John 67
Moleyns, Thomas 80
Moon, Arthur Neville ... 103, 104
Moon, Richard Lovering ... 92, 175

Moore, James 187
Moore, Maurice Peter 120
Moore, Richard 169
Moore, Thomas (1615) 58
Moore, Thomas (1756) 64
Moore, William 187
Mordant, John 52
Mordon, Robert 101
More, Marmaduke 85
More, William 181
Morgan, Charles (1769) ... 140
Morgan, Charles (1799) ... 66
Morgan, David 52
Morgan, Henry 133
Morgan, Isaac 90
Morgan, John 65
Morgan, Rice 135
Morgan, Richard 133
Morgan, Thomas 90
Morgan, Watkin 90
Morgan, William 89
Morland, Francis John ... 56
Morland, George Bowes ... 55
Morland, John Thornhill ... 55, 56
Morrell, James 147
Morris, John Jones ... 61, 62
Morris, Richard 135
Morse, Robert 91
Morte, Thomas 114
Mortimer, Samuel 79
Moseley, Gilbert Watson ... 149
Motham, Isaac 137
Motton, Thomas 109
Mullisworth, William 105
Munsey, Laurence George Hensman 164
Muspratt, John Petty 114
Mychell, —— 138
Mylsent, John 63

N

Nanfan, William 69
Nares, Ramsey 168
Neale, Francis 58
Needham, Edward 115
Negus, Raymond Ewings ... 86, 87
Nelson, Richard Albany ... 100
Neobard, Harold John Cooke ... 55, 56
New, Leslie Penry 53, 71
Newbury, Henry 54
Newton, John 115
Newton, Joseph (1629) ... 115
Newton, Joseph (1681) ... 142
Nicholas, John William ... 66
Nicholls, Thomas 102
Nicholson, John 176
Nicholson, Joshua 176
Nicholson, Sir Richard 1, 2, 3, 12, 20, 102,
 103, 104, 123, 128,
 129, 132, Plate VII

Nicholson, Thomas 111
Noble, Michael 159
Noel, Walter 160
Noke, Thomas 54
Nops, Geoffrey Austin ... 167, 168
Northcote, John 77
Norton, George 144
Norton, John (1595) ... 173
Norton, John (1625) ... 173
Norton, Robert 186
Notcutt, Thomas 163
Nyn, John 109

O

Oakeley, John 132
Oakeley, Richard 132
Oakes, Sir Cecil 163
Oakes, Richard 138
Ogle, Richard 117
Oldfield, Norman 157
Oldham, John Hugh 111
Oliver, Laurence Herbert ... 124
Oliver, Richard 115
Ollard, John William Arthur ... 107, 193
Ollive, Thomas Holt 88
Onslow, Richard 168
Ord, John 142
Ord, Thomas 142
Orston, Thomas 143
Osborne, John 75
Oseney, Richard 181
Oteley, Richard 151
Overall, Francis 105
Overton, Benjamin 132
Owen, —— 88
Owen, Charles 148
Owen, Edward 125
Owen, Hugh John 126, 193
Owen, John 148
Owen, Owen 51
Owen, Philip 110
Owen, Richard 51
Owen, Robert Penrhyn ... 114
Owen-Jones, John Eryl ... 62

P

Paddy, Samuel 109
Palmer, Edward 115
Palmer, Jeremy Fish ... 52
Palmer, John (1446) ... 115
Palmer, John (1805) ... 104
Palmer, Thomas 117
Parkar, Thomas 91
Parke, Reuben 115
Parke, Samuel 150
Parker, Charles George ... 85
Parker, John 84
Parker, Philip 149
Parker, Robert (1482) ... 84

Parker, Robert (1776)	111	Phillips, John (1730)	89	Pygot, Richard	58
Parmeter, Robert William ...	138	Phillips, Joseph	120	Pykorn, Stephen	137
Parr, Thomas Henning	160	Philpott, Nicholas	99	Pyne, John	63
Parry, David James	90	Phipps, Walter Thomas	120	
Parry, Edward	74	Phythian, Charles	64	**Q**
Parry, George	148	Pickering, Thomas	176	Quadring, Robert	121
Parry, John	60	Pickmer, Francis	140	
Parry, Thomas	91	Pigeon, Charles	162	**R**
Parry, Vincent	60	Piggott, Francis	55	Radcliffe, Charles	190
Parys, Richard	63	Piper, Arthur Drury	120	Radcliffe, Sir Clifford (Walter) ...	129, 131
Paul, Thomas	189	Piper, Walter John	86, 87	Raddon, Edward	77
Payn, James	56	Place, Thomas	190	Railton, Anthony	72
Payn, Robert	80	Platts, Walter Leslie	71, 110	Rakett, John	82
Payn, Thomas	137	Plomer, John	91	Rakett, Richard	82
Payne, Thomas	91	Plummer, Robert	84	Ramme (Rame), Francis	84
Payne, Toby	99	Polreden, Paschoe	69	Randall, Edward	64
Payne, William (1578)	52	Pomeroy, John	54	Randall, John	80
Payne, William (1689)	137	Pomeroy, William	54	Randall, Terence George	124
Paynter, William Evans	148	Poole, John Rea	53	Randolph, Bernard (1543)	34, 112
Peables, John	190	Poole, Owen Anthony	61	Randolph, Bernard (1549)	127
Peachell, Thomas	121	Poole, Richard	51, 125	Raven, James	97
Peake, Henry	120	Poole, Richard Anthony	61	Ravenscrofte, John	169
Pearmain, Edmund Alfred ...	149	Poole, William Price	51	Raymond, George	91
Pearse, Robert	70	Poole, William Thearsby	61	Raymond, Thomas	77
Pearse, Theed (1798)	52	Popham, Thomas	155	Rayson, George	115
Pearse, Theed (1847)	52	Pordage, Samuel	178	Read, John	135
Pearse, Theed William	52, 53	Pottes, Thomas	183	Reddall, Ambrose	52
Pearson, George	82, 83	Potts, Charles	10, 68	Rees, David	130
Pearson, Reginald Arthur	120	Potts, Charles William	67, 68	Rees, Henry	148
Peck, Robert	63, 64	Potts, Henry	67	Rees, Thomas Morgan Haydn ...	88
Peck, Thomas	115	Potts, Hubert	68	Reeve, William Napier	116
Peele, Edmund Cresswell	152, 153	Potts, Reginald	67	Repynghale, Robert 31, 40, 117, 119, 121	
Peele, George de Courcy	152	Powell, Edward Griffith ...	62	Reyner, John	58
Peele, Joshua John	153	Powell, Hugh	151	Reynold, Richard	115
Peers, Joseph	12, 74	Powell, John (1550)	66	Reynold, William	115
Peirson (Pearson), Richard ...	72	Powell, John (1812)	57	Reynolds, Charles	85
Pemberton, Christopher	12, 64	Powell, Richard	90	Reynolds, John (1542)	51, 125
Penington, James	52	Powell, William (1553)	151	Reynolds, John (1691)	130, 167
Pennaunt, Edward	158	Powell, William (1681)	57	Reynolds, Lewis	135
Pepiatt, John	52	Preston, James (1736)	41, 187	Reynolds, Samuel	85
Pepler, George Richard		Preston, James (1762)	41, 187	Reynolds, Solomon	135
Summerland	122	Preston, Thomas	75, 143	Reynolds, Timothy	58
Peppyr, Thomas	121	Price, Barrington	82	Richards, Alexander	190
Percival, William	105	Price, James	66	Richards, Michael	89
Peregrine, Gwilym Rhys	66	Price, John	62	Richards, Thomas	102, 104
Perkins, Christopher	58	Prince, Edward	146	Richardson, John (1634)	82
Perry, James	63	Pring, Thomas	78	Richardson, John (1660)	82
Perry, Thomas	92	Prior, William	97	Richardson, John (1799)	176, 177
Pestor, William	155	Pritchard, Thomas	74	Richardson, Robert 117, 119, 121	
Peters, John Brown Meharry ...	189	Procter, John Robert	183, 184	Rickards, Ernest Stanley	156, 157
Pettefar, George	107	Prosser, Walter Byron	110	Riddiford, George	92
Peyto, Thomas	167	Prothero, Charles	134	Ridlington, ——	150
Peyton, Higgons	97	Prouse, Nicholas	77	Rigby, Alexander (1573)	113
Phelips, James Henry Caswall ...	182	Pryce, Edmund	135	Rigby, Alexander (1612)	112, 113
Philipson, Miles	176	Pulley, Richard	85	Rigby, Alexander (1621)	112
Philipson, Ralph Park	82	Pulleyn, Thomas	190	Rigby, George	112
Phillips, George Godfrey	160	Pury, Thomas	91	Rigby, Joseph	112
Phillips, James	148	Pychard, Edward	63	Rigby, Roger	112
Phillips, John (1705)	71	Pye, John	142	Ring, Richard	157

Ring, William (1724) ... 42, 156, 157
Ring, William (1740) 42, 156
Roberts, Arthur Troughton ... 88
Roberts, Eric John 118
Roberts, Evan Wynne 148
Roberts, Frederick Richard ... 65
Roberts, Frederick Rowland ... 65
Roberts, Hugh 88
Roberts, Sir (James Reginald)
   Howard 124
Roberts, John 74
Roberts, John Rice 51
Roberts, Sir John (Thomas) ... 61, 62
Roberts, Mathew 127
Roberts, Nicholas 91
Roberts, Owen 51
Roberts, Thomas (1505) 127
Roberts, Thomas (1861) 68
Roberts, William (1676) ... 125
Roberts, William (1930) 74
Robertson, William 143
Robinson, Arthur Desmond ... 171
Robinson, Daniel 177
Robinson, John ... 19, 176, Plate V
Robinson, Joseph 176, 177
Robinson, Matthew 117, 119
Robyns, Thomas 137
Rodenhurst, John 151
Rodgers, Frederick Harrod ... 177
Roe, Bertram Charles 81
Roger, John 109
Rogers, Donald George 92
Rogers, George Foster 168
Rogers, Timothy 140
Rokeby, Thomas 183
Rolfe, John (1681) 138
Rolfe, John (1704) 167
Rolfe, William 138
Rolleston, John 75, 76
Romney, John 109
Rook, David James 107
Rooke, Benjamin (1780) ... 102, 103
Rooke, Benjamin (1813) 102
Roscarrock (Restorrak), John ... 69
Rose, James 146, 147
Rosseter, Christopher ... 117, 119, 121
Rowden, Francis 85
Rowe, Henry 114
Rowe, Nicholas 77
Rowe, Samuel 132
Rowland, Henry David 89
Rowlands, William John ... 74, 126, 193
Rowlandson, Richard 176
Rowlatt, George 116
Rowley, John 102
Rudhale, John 181
Ruff, William Willis 167, 168
Rumsey, Lucas Eustace 116
Rumsey, Walter 133

Rushworth, —— 118
Rushworth, Charles 117, 119
Rushworth, Victor Henry ... 168
Russell, Francis 110
Russell, Henry 181
Rutter, William 84
Ryall, Frederick 107
Ryllington, William 183
Ryves, Edward 146

S

Sadler, Samuel Campbell Hulton ... 114
Salmon, Sir Eric (Cecil Heygate) ... 124
Salter, John (1462) 151
Salter, John (1490) 151
Salter, Thomas (1562) 151
Salter, Thomas (1590) 151
Salway, Richard 181
Sambourne, Thomas 191
Sambrooke, Francis 180
Samwell, John 145
Sanby, —— 127
Sanderson, Stephen 142
Sapsford, Henry 121
Saul, George 176
Saunders, Robert 109, 110
Saward, John 157
Sayers, Warwick Waghorn ... 123
Scawen, Edward 127
Sclater, John 75, 150
Scorer, Charles 122
Scorer, Eric West 122
Scot, Richard 82
Scot, William 190
Scott, Francis Gerald ... 147, 171
Scott, Jack David 111
Scott, John 183
Scovile, Richard 80
Scrimgeour, Geoffrey Cameron ... 67, 68
Scruton, Walter 83
Scudamore, Frederick 111
Scudamore, William (1615) ... 99
Scudamore, William (1822) ... 111
Scurfield, William Russell ... 83, 182
Scutt, William 170
Seacome, Robert Owen 182
Seagars, Francis 109
Seager, John Edward 171
Searle, Gilbert 94
Searle, Robert 169, 170
Seitborne, Richard 99
Selby, Henry Collingwood ... 12, 128
Seyliard, Thomas 64
Seymour, John 58
Shapcott, Thomas 77
Sheers, Thomas Angrave Homer ... 71
Sheldon, Richard 181
Sheldwych (Sheldwyth), Nicholas ... 109
Shelley, Timothy (1661) 169

Shelley, Timothy (1669) 170
Shelton, Edward 127
Shelton, Theophilus 190
Shephard, Henry John 184
Sherard, Caryer 106
Sherard, Robert 105
Sherley, William 80
Shoolbred, Claude Frederick ... 131
Shottessore, William 91
Shute, Richard (1586) 139
Shute, Richard (1690) 167
Simey, George Iliffe 83, 156
Simey, Ralph 82, 83
Simmons, John 193
Simpson, Hugh 72
Simpson, Lancelot 72
Simpson, Thomas 72
Simpson, William 190
Skelton, John 191
Skelton, William 121
Skepper, George 189
Skinner, Alan Frank 141, 164
Skinner, Horace Wilfrid 76
Skrymsher, John 152
Skrymsher, Thomas 151
Skrymshyre, Thomas 151
Skynner, John (1488) 165
Skynner, John (1507) 165
Slade, Richard 105
Sleddall, Thomas 72
Slegge, Roger 162
Smallpeice, William Haydon ... 168
Smith, Eric Pope 154
Smith, John 127, 132
Smith, Nathaniel 117, 119, 121
Smith, Robert (1616) 121
Smith, Robert (1749) 81
Smith, Thomas (1676) 173
Smith, Thomas (1689) 58
Smith, Thomas (1738) 140
Smith, William (1629) 80
Smith, William (1788) 154
Smyth, Arthur Hugh Manistre ... 98
Smyth, Christopher 141
Smyth, Henry 143
Smythe, John 62
Smythe, William 166
Snellinge, John 101
Snow, Charles 165
Sockett, Richard 182
Soley, John 181
Somerscales, Robert 121
Soper, Thomas 101
Southcote, George 77
Southcote, John 77
Spencer, Alfred 124
Spencer, John 52, 105
Spencer, Leonard 137, 161
Spencer, Richard Evans 90

Spencer, Robert	...	...	...	52
Spencer, Thomas	...	...	...	52, 105
Spenser, William	...	...	...	105
Spicer, William (1580)	...	...	60
Spicer, William (1660)	...	...	60
Sprigge, William	...	...	...	145
Spry, William	...	...	...	78
Sprye, George	...	...	...	69
Sprye, John	...	...	...	69
Squire, Francis	...	...	...	168
Stable, Lorenzo	...	...	...	132
Stacy, Walter	...	...	...	143
Stampe, Edward	...	...	...	145
Stampe, Thomas	...	...	...	84
Stanesby, Richard	...	...	...	94
Staniland, M.	...	...	...	118
Staple, John	...	...	...	156
Staples, William	...	...	...	178
Stapleton, William	...	...	...	169
Staverton, Richard	...	...	...	127
Stede, John	...	...	...	181
Stephen, Harry Lushington	...	...	90
Stephens, Edward	...	...	...	112
Stephens, Humphrey	...	...	...	112
Stephens, John	...	...	...	67
Stephens, Sir (Leon) Edgar			18, 21, 175, Plate XVIII
Stephens, Thomas	...	...	...	91
Stephens, William	...	...	...	149
Stephenson, Richard Shepherd	...	176
Stephenson, Thomas	...	...	...	184
Stephenson, William	...	...	...	105
Stevens, Edward	...	...	...	122
Stevens, Frederick Brewerton	...	53
Stevens, Henry	...	...	...	54
Stevens (Stephens), Richard (1591)		145
Stevens (Stephens), Richard (1662)		145
Stevens, Thomas	...	...	...	54
Stevenson, William	...	...	...	117
Stewart, Charles John	...	...	...	123
Stickland, Nathaniel	...	...	...	81
Stirling, Thomas	...	...	...	130
Stockdale, Robert	...	...	...	188
Stoke, Thomas	...	...	...	77
Stokes, Adrian	...	...	...	126
Stokes, Henry Sewell	...	...	...	70
Stokes, William	...	...	...	138
Stoneham, Robert	...	...	...	93
Stonehewer, Richard	...	...	...	82
Stonehewer, Thomas	...	...	...	82
Stonywell, Nicholas	...	...	...	119
Story, John Samuel	...	...	102, 104
Stoughton, Anthony	...	...	...	165
Stoughton, Gilbert	...	...	...	145
Stoughton, John	...	...	...	165
Stowre, Adam	...	...	...	84
Stratford, William	...	...	...	91
Stratton, Thomas	...	...	...	52
Straunge, Antony	...	...	...	91

Straunge, John	...	...	...	91
Strensham, Robert	...	...	...	178
Strethay, John	...	...	...	158
Strethay, Philip	...	...	...	172
Stringer, Philip Austin Selborne	...	64, 179
Strong, Isaac	...	...	...	154
Strong, William	...	...	...	154
Stuteville, Thomas	...	...	...	64
Style, John	...	...	...	58
Swayne, James	...	...	...	179
Swayne, John	...	...	179, 180
Swift, Alfred	...	...	...	123
Swift, George Norman Cyrus	...	73, 104
Sworder, Thomas Joseph	...	...	104
Sybley, William	...	...	...	105
Sydall, James	...	...	...	99
Sykelpruys, Reginald	...	...	...	117
Symes, John	...	...	...	80
Symonds, James Frederick	...	...	100
Symonds, John Reginald	...	...	100
Symonds, Thomas (1599)	...	...	181
Symonds, Thomas (1656)	...	...	181
Symonds-Tayler, Richard Herbert	...	100
Symons, William	...	...	...	122

T

Tabrum, Ashley	...	...	...	64
Tagg, Thomas	...	...	...	67, 68
Tailboys, Robert	...	...	...	82
Taillard, Walter (1414)	...	...	63
Taillard, Walter (1415)	...	...	143
Tallents, William Edward	...	...	144
Talton, Thomas	...	...	...	93
Tarrant, Thomas	...	...	...	166
Tasker, Nicholas	...	...	...	121
Tatham, Henry	...	...	...	176
Taunton, Thomas Henry	...	...	146
Taunton, Sir William (Elias)	...	146, 147
Taylfar, John	...	...	...	82
Taylor, James	...	...	...	114
Taylor, William	...	...	...	132
Templeman, Arthur Cowley	...	81, 193
Templeman, William	...	...	...	80
Tharrold, William	...	...	...	119
Thelwall, ——	...	...	...	74
Thelwall, Edward	...	...	...	88
Thewe, John	...	...	...	121
Thirkill, Francis (1783)	...	...	118
Thirkill, Francis (1812)	...	...	118
Thomas ap Harrie	...	...	...	65
Thomas, David	...	...	...	57
Thomas, Edmund	...	...	...	89
Thomas, Henry Edgar	...	...	...	57
Thomas, John Henwood	...	...	154
Thomas, Thomas	...	...	...	90
Thomas, William (1542)	...	57, 135, 149
Thomas, William (1615)	...	...	169
Thomas, William (1621)	...	...	89
Thomas, William (1684)	...	...	89

Thomas, Wynne Simpson	...	...	66
Thomson, Thomas	...	...	...	190
Thong, Thomas	...	...	...	105
Thorley, George	...	...	...	160
Thornburgh, William	...	...	...	82
Thorne, Harold Underhill Hatton	...	56
Thorneloe, J.	...	...	...	182
Thornely, Samuel	...	9, 13, 43, 171, 182
Thorneton, Richard	...	...	...	186
Thornley, Sir Hubert (Gordon)	12, 21, 182, 188, Plate XIII
Thornton, Christopher (John?)	117, 119, 121
Thorowgood, Henry	...	...	...	102
Thorp, Robert	...	...	...	142
Threlfall, Charles	...	...	...	131
Thurlow, Richard Francis Gardom	...	107
Thyckenes, Robert	...	...	...	158
Tilby, Henry Albert	...	...	...	88
Tildesley, Arthur	...	...	...	160
Tindal, Acton	...	...	...	3, 59
Tindal, Thomas	...	...	...	3, 59
Tindall, George	...	...	...	190
Tiplady, John	...	...	...	83
Toller, Bostock (1689)	...	...	102
Toller, Bostock (1720)	...	...	102
Tombes, John	...	...	...	104
Tomkins, James	...	...	...	134
Tompson, Alexander	...	...	...	114
Topham, Edward Charles	...	...	189
Topham, John	...	...	...	189
Topham, Lupton	...	...	...	188
Toppyng, Henry	...	...	...	52
Torr, John Leslie	...	...	...	81
Tounlay, Robert	...	...	...	181
Townerawe, Henry	...	...	...	143
Traunter (Tranter), Simon	...	...	99
Tregasle (Tregattle), John	...	...	69
Tregold, Robert	...	...	...	121
Treise, John	...	...	...	69
Treu, William	...	...	...	158
Trevor, Thomas Tudor	...	...	189
Trevor, William Charles	...	...	188, 189
Trewyk, John	...	...	...	69
Tryce, Richard	...	...	...	154
Trygarn, Morris	...	...	...	60
Tudor, William	...	...	...	12, 92
Turner, Chatfield	...	...	...	170
Turner, John (1571)	...	...	...	169
Turner, John (1700)	...	...	...	181
Turner, John (1782)	...	...	...	179
Turner, John Alan	...	141, 147, 175
Turner, Richard	...	...	...	78
Turton, Zouch	...	...	...	133
Tutté, Randolph	...	...	...	170
Twisden, Francis	...	...	...	109
Twitty, George	...	...	...	181
Twitty, Thomas	...	...	...	181
Twyford, Edward	...	...	...	145
Tylly, John	...	...	...	109

Tylney, John 190
Tyrrell, Avery 54
Tyrrell, William 55, 130

U

Uffenham, John 178
Underhill, William 172
Underwood, Henry Laurence ... 159, 160
Underwood, Henry Louis ... 83, 148
Unwin, Joseph 131
Upton, Elias 69
Upton, Harry 83

V

Vaghan, Charles (1612) 77
Vaghan, Charles (1646) 77
Vaghan, Hugh 77
Vallys, Richard 80
Vaughan, Hugh 77
Vaughan, Hugh Vaughan 149
Vaughan, John 62
Vaughan (alias Gruffydd), John ... 60
Vaughan, Richard 133
Vaughan, Thomas 132
Vaughan, Thomas Wright ... 132
Vaughan, Tudor 125
Vaughan, William 90
Veell, Robert 155
Verger, Edward Thomas 71
Viell, Richard 77
Villiers, Hon. George 113
Villiers, John Charles, 3rd Earl of
  Clarendon 112
Vincent, Thomas 54
Vyncent, John 165

W

Waddington, Alexander 134
Waddington, Walter Hargreaves ... 124
Wadland, Thomas 116
Wailes, William (1787) 188
Wailes, William (1796) 189
Wailes, William (1819) 189
Waite, Alan Charles Victor ... 168
Walbanck, John 58
Walcott, Humfrey 117, 119, 121
Walden, Harry George 106
Waldram, Thomas 115, 150
Waldyene, Thomas 145
Walker, Christopher 127
Walker, Francis 181, 182
Walker, Kenneth Hamblett ... 134
Walker, Thomas 146, 147
Walker, Timothy 159
Wall, William 121
Wallen, Leonard Paul 157
Waller, James 128
Waller, John 130
Waller, Samuel 170

Wallinger, John 84
Wallis, John 80
Wallop, Richard 93
Walsh (Welsh), Philip 71
Walter, Arthur Clifford 90
Walter, Hugh Albert Harold ... 118
Walter, Peter 128
Walters, Tom Vivian 90
Walton, Hugh Merscy 147
Wannock, Simon 169
Warcupp, Robert 54
Ward, Anthony (1684) 163
Ward, Anthony (1689) 130
Ward, George 177
Warde, Anthony 87
Waren, John 75
Warmington, Sampson 71
Warncombe, John 99
Warncombe, Richard 99
Warner, Edward 139
Warren (Waren), William 143
Warry, George 157
Warter, Robert 189
Waryner, Henry 101
Washeborne, Richard 145
Waskham, Robert 93
Waterfall, Christopher William ... 138
Waterman, Nicholas 137
Waters, John 133
Watkins, John 182
Watkins, Roger 133
Watkins, William 133
Watson, John (1550) 75
Watson, John (1553) 127
Watson, John (1873) 83
Watts, John 115
Way, John 81
Wayte(s), William 137
Weale, William 53
Weare, John 99n, 100n
Webb, George Arthur 96, 98
Webbe, John 109
Weeding, Thomas Weeding ... 167, 168
Weedon, Cavendish 58
Weedon, Thomas 58
Weekly, John 111
Welbeck, John 127
Welbek, Richard 165
Welbore, Michael 84
Welbye, Humfrey 117, 119
Weldon, John 139
Weldon, Thomas 139
Weldon, William 139
Welenhale, Roger 158
Welles, Samuel 59
Wellington, George 54
Wells, Charles Martin Sidney ... 57, 120
Wells, Edward 181
Wells, Henry 58

Wells, John 191
Wellys, Henry 169
Wellys, Thomas 158
Weltden, Richard 185
Weltden, Robert 185
Weltden, Thomas 185
Welyngton, John (1426) 99
Welyngton, John (1470) 99
Welyngton, Thomas 99
Wentworth, Matthew 105
Werden, Richard 67
Werell, Henry 91
West, James 117
West, John 31, 172
Weste, William 104
Westhorp, Sterling 163, 164
Weston, Edward 137
Weston, Stephen 137
Wharton, Gerald Blisson 82
Wharton, William 190
Wheatley, George 176
Wheatley, George Andrew ... 73, 96, 193
Wheatley, Robert Albert ... 83, 148
Wheeler, Malcolm Hele ... 189, 193
Wheeler, William (1671) 177
Wheeler, William (1678) ... 169, 170
Whinyates, Charles 154
Whitby, Robert 67
White, Andrew 64
White, Edward 155
White, Francis Thirkill 118
White, George 84
White, Percival Edward ... 108, 136, 153
Whitehead, Peter 147
Whithorne, Conway 92
Whitley, John Manners 153
Whitley, Raymond Archer ... 126, 184
Whittingham, William 136
Wickham, William 190
Widdens, William 67
Wilcok, Henry 63
Wildes, Henry Atkinson ... 110, 111
Wiles, George 120
Wilkes, William (1598) 151
Wilkes, William (1607) 135
Wilkin, William 176
Wilkins, John 57
Wilkinson, Edward 184
Wilkinson, Joseph 184
Wilkinson, Thomas 130
Willard, Thomas 111
Williams, David 125
Williams, Edward 57
Williams, Gruffydd 60
Williams, Harold Beck 168
Williams, Herbert 133
Williams, Humphrey (1573) ... 135
Williams, Humphrey (1817) ... 125
Williams, Idwal 88

Williams, John	60	Witham, Nathaniel	87	Wyche, Richard 154
Williams, John Jones	125	Withycombe, Arthur John ...	78, 79	Wyghall, John 185
Williams, Paul	99	Wode, Robert	161	Wykes, Edward 155
Williams, Richard	166	Wodehill, John	54	Wykes, Nicholas 155
Williams, Robert Thomas David	193	Wolley, Richard	181, 182	Wylde, Francis 143
Williams, Thomas (1573)	66	Wolryche, James	158	Wymondeswold, John 115
Williams, Thomas (1590)	89	Wolseley, Robert	158	Wyndham, Wadham 82
Williams, Thomas (1710)	99	Wolvedon, Robert	69	Wynn, John ... ... 19, 60, Plate II
Williams, Thomas (1720)	88	Wood, Edward	149	Wynn, Owen 60
Williams, William (1640)	133	Wood, John (1798)	89	Wynne, Robert 166
Williams, William (1690)	57	Wood, John (1815)	89	Wynne, William (1765) 88
Williams, William (1815)	62	Wood, Wilfred Knoyle	180	Wynne, William (1792) 88
Williams, W. M.	57	Woodcock, Roger	85, 87	Wythe, Edmund 138
Willinghale, Thomas	84	Woodd, William	188	
Willis, Robert Metherell ...	175	Woodham, Thomas	97	**Y**
Willway, Alfred Cedric Cowan ...	168	Woodham, Thomas Burnett ...	98	Yeamans, Thomas 157
Willymott, James	102	Wooldridge, William Henry ...	108	Yeoman, Thomas Lawrence ... 188
Wilson, John	135	Wordsworth, Richard	176	Yeoward, William 177
Wilson, Rowland Holt	164	Wortham, Hale	64	York, Thomas 64
Wilson, Thomas	114	Wotherspoon, Robert Andrew ...	76, 188	York, William 31, 158
Wilton, Edmund	82	Wright, John (1609)	84	Yorke, Ralph 188
Wingfield, George	153	Wright, John (1718)	76	Young, Richard 169
Wingfield, Robert	85	Wrighte, Lawrence	143	Young, Robert 91
Wingfield, Thomas	152	Wyatt, Osmond Arthur	134	Young, William 82
Winter, John	57	Wyatt, Sir Richard (Henry)	123, 166, 167	Yoward, Ralph 187
Withall (Whithalgh), William ...	158	Wybergh, Thomas	190	